# North American Game Animals

# North American Game Animals

by BYRON W. DALRYMPLE

*Illustrated by*
DOUGLAS ALLEN

OUTDOOR LIFE

CROWN
New York

Library of Congress Catalog Card Number: 77-6556
ISBN: 0-517-53486X

Manufactured in the United States of America

For

E. F. D.

# Contents

# Introduction

This book is about the lives of the mammals of North America that over the centuries have commonly been called "game" animals —about where and how they live, their daily and seasonal routines of feeding and movement, their sex lives, the birth and development of their young, how they use their keen senses, what signs they leave indicative of their presence, and about their unique relationships with man, past and present.

This group of animals, which includes all of the larger land-based mammals of the continent, plus numerous smaller ones, was selected not because they have long been called *game*, but because they are in general the most interesting, most abundant, most visible, their lives the most dramatic, and closely entwined for centuries with man's. They are the animals about which wildlife enthusiasts of all inclinations invariably seek to become better informed. Although no creature is unimportant to the large scheme, and every life form is linked to every other, it is this group of animals that is envisioned by most people when the phrase "our wildlife heritage" is used.

These creatures are indeed the important nucleus of that heritage. The word "game" which links them together obviously derives from the fact that from earliest times these animals were taken by man for food, furs and hides, and in modern times particularly by the sport hunter. That link is an important one in our age, what with the new spirit of concern for the environment and for wildlife.

No one can possibly know all there is to know about the animals even of one county of a single state, let alone all those of the entire continent. Even narrowing it down to the so-called game animals, the scope of endlessly accrued knowledge is vast and all but unmanageable — and still there are empty spots. For over half a century I have been an observer of the animals selected here, and for more than half that time a writer about them. Their lives, and our human relations with them, are endlessly intriguing studies. I have attempted to gather here knowledge gained from my own observation plus much more from research of the studies of others.

Today we are all slowly learning that the preservation of these animals is important not just to hunters, but to all of us. Their continued existence in healthy numbers illimitably benefits both practically and aesthetically the total environment, of which we too are simply a part, although an overwhelmingly disproportionate part so far as our influence upon the lives of other creatures is concerned.

There is no question that in the past, from the days of the white man's first settlement, man the hunter has committed many excesses. Before him, the Indian, invariably shown nowadays erroneously as a thoughtful conservationist, also in numerous instances pressured these animals to excess, by no means always taking just what were needed. However, Indian population was not large enough — as ours is — to create many problems. Hide hunters, meat hunters during days of early exploration and settlement did awesome damage. There was no regard for what we now know as "game management."

Fortunately, most of the excesses were recognized in time. It was these — the disregard for conservation — that finally focused attention on the need for restraint and order in our relationships with these animals. The hunter came to understand that rules had to be made, and obeyed. And from these first stirrings the intricate and fascinating science of the management of wild animals was born. Today this is often called "game" management, but the fact is that science is being applied steadily more and more to all animals.

The benefits of concentrated management are many, and important to all of us. Deer, down to a half million animals years ago, and entirely exterminated in state after state, now number in the many millions. Elk and antelope, brought to the brink of extinction by hide and meat hunting, have been astutely managed into stable abundance in every expanse of habitat suitable to each on the continent.

Very slowly we are beginning to realize—the hunter who coined the term "game" for these creatures, the non-hunter who enjoys observing and perhaps photographing them, and the anti-hunter—that all have a common goal: to keep these animals as abundant as available habitat will permit. Particularly concentrated attention is being given to those few of the larger predators which appear threatened or endangered.

We are learning, even though perhaps too slowly, that *living room* is the key to the abundance—the very existence—of these animals. Some, to be sure, like the whitetail deer and the cottontail, adapt rather readily to man's pressures and learn to live on the very fringes of dense human settlement. Others cannot make do without true wilderness. An end to the incessant destruction and degradation of habitats suitable for these animals must be the chief concern of all those, regardless of their views for or against hunting, who wish to keep these creatures among us in abundance. The crucial matter is preservation and improvement of remaining habitat. No longer is the so-called "balance of nature" possible, if indeed it ever was. Man long ago irrevocably upset the balance, but in his current attention to scientific management as a substitute, he has been and continues to be tremendously successful, and indeed can be even more so in the future.

Perhaps in the long view it will turn out to be true, curiously, that past excesses sparked our learning. A few excesses do indeed continue, but the effort among hunters themselves and law enforcement personnel to stop or control these is truly prodigious, and will, it is hoped, succeed. Perhaps in the future wildlife enthusiasts, regardless of diverse views, will join forces, realizing that in truth all have the same goals. If this book can lead readers to a better understanding of the lives of the so-called game animals, their ways, their needs, their present-day relationships with man and his activities, it may offer at least a small service in bringing together in concentrated common effort all those, of whatever bent, who wish them well.

# North American Game Animals

# Whitetail Deer

*Odocoileus virginianus*

The whitetail deer might well be designated the official antlered animal of North America. It is a true native; there are few theories that like some of our other animals it may have crossed a land bridge from Asia millions of years ago. It is of all large animals on this continent the most popular with both hunter and non-hunter. For all practical purposes, the word "deer" means whitetail deer to almost everyone. Paintings and drawings by tens of thousands of this trim creature, possibly the most handsome of all our larger mammals, have graced calendars, greeting cards, magazines, and books decade after decade. The whitetail is an inseparable part of the continent's culture and heritage.

Presently it is the most numerous of our larger animals. No one can be certain precisely how many whitetails there are, but estimates place their numbers at probably somewhere from 8 to 15 million. The range is enormous, covering much of southern Canada and most of the entire lower-48 states except two or three in the west, and reaching south throughout Central America.

Paradoxically, this shyest, most nervous, and wariest of all our deer is the one that was able somehow to adapt to and cope with

Whitetail Deer

DOUGLAS ALLEN

man's progress and to thrive with the thrust of civilization and progress all around it. In fact, the whitetail has proved to be one of the most successful animal colonizers of all time. It abounds in the big woods of northern Maine, and in the deep saw grass and hammock swamps of Florida. It thrives in the farmlands of southern Saskatchewan and grows so fat it can barely waddle in immense corn fields of the Dakotas. It is thoroughly at home in the cactus and thornbrush of southern Texas and on into Mexico, as well as in the forested areas of eastern Oregon and Washington.

Certainly the whitetail was abundant when the colonists first settled at Jamestown. But it may not have been as plentiful throughout the continent as it is today. Cutting of the climax forest and the forming of "edges" as agriculture and logging spread across the country enhanced whitetail habitat immensely. Yet this deer was to come close to extermination before it learned to live with its new neighbor, the white man, and finally to respond to his expert management. The story of the whitetail in this century is one of the great game-management stories of all time.

Early settlers utilized the whitetail for meat and hides, just as the Indians had, but increasingly in far great quantity. Need turned to greed when it was realized that both meat and hides were a valuable commodity. Hundreds of thousands of whitetail hides were shipped to England and Europe yearly, and matching numbers of barrels of venison went by ship or were utilized in budding American cities. Market hunting through the nineteenth century brought the whitetail population down to only a scant 250,000 to 500,000 animals. Commercial hunting stopped because there was no longer profit in it; deer were too scarce.

More important, however, the sport hunter now entered the scene. In some states — even Virginia, from which the whitetail had been named as the "type" species (the type from which all other whitetails would be judged in naming subspecies) — the whitetail was either totally or almost extinct. Setting of hunting regulations, and finally the science of deer management, which in the beginning employed trapping and transplanting of wild deer to ancestral ranges from which they had disappeared, has brought the whitetail to abundance or at least to stability on practically all suitable ranges on the continent. And in the meantime the animals themselves have become so adept at sharing man's habitat that in numerous instances deer live within city limits, although keeping their lives for the most part wholly private.

## THE WHITETAIL DEER

COLOR: Differs in shading locally, among subspecies, and seasonally; in general brown to gray-brown winter, reddish-brown summer; darker along back, shading lighter down sides to white beneath; nose black with white band behind at either side; white circles around eyes, white inside ears, over chin; white throat patch; upper inside of legs white, outside brown; tail brown above, some subspecies reddish, with black center swath, snowy-white long hair beneath and over rump area covered when tail is down.

MEASUREMENTS, MATURE BUCKS: National average overall length 5 to 6 feet; height at withers, 3 to 3½ feet, variable among subspecies.

WEIGHT, MATURE BUCKS: National average 125 to 160 pounds; highly variable locally and among subspecies, from 75 to 300-plus pounds.

ANTLERS: Main beams curving up, back, then well forward; unbranched points rise from main beams; a brow tine near the front base of each antler; total number of points differs (six, eight, ten, twelve) with age and vigor.

DOES: Smaller by an average one-fourth; less blocky build.

GENERAL ATTRIBUTES: Graceful appearance; superb agility; nervous, extremely wary personality; unbranched antler tines except in nontypical or "freak" instances; white tail (beneath) raised upright and waving side to side when animal is startled and fleeing; animal actually smaller in height and length than most observers envision it, thus able to conceal itself in cover lower than might seem possible.

It is an odd commentary on whitetail abundance that Pennsylvania, one of the top whitetail states for numbers of deer, and for hunting, early in this century had almost none. Today Pennsylvania hunters annually harvest well over 100,000 on the average—and an astonishing and deplorable total of an additional 25,000 or more are killed annually on Pennsylvania highways by automobiles! In Texas, where the whitetail was considered on the way to extirpation at the turn of this century, it is possible to observe in the south-central area as many as a hundred grazing during late afternoon on a small green-sprouting winter oat patch in early fall. The Texas herd, largest in the nation, is estimated at well over 3 million!

Generally speaking, whitetails of northern latitudes are larger, and darker, than their southern relatives. Maine checks in numerous 300-pounders (field-dressed) each season. Exceptional —possibly freakish—specimens have been taken much larger: a

440-pound buck in Iowa; two of 481 and 491 from Wisconsin; an astonishing 511-pound buck from Minnesota. Of the thirty subspecies recognized from the continent, seventeen of them are above the Mexican border. The majority of the subspecies especially within U.S. and Canadian borders, however, mean little today because most have been so diluted by transplants and interbreeding with others that few of the strains are pure. Further, a number have, or had, exceedingly limited ranges. Several, for example, are limited to individual islands off the Atlantic and Gulf coasts, and have developed specialized physical characteristics only because of their isolation.

The big northern woodland whitetail of New England and the Great Lakes region, *Odocoileus virginianus borealis,* is undoubtedly a pure race over much of its northernmost range. The same is true of the often larger Dakota whitetail, *O. v. dacotensis,* of Canada's Prairie Provinces, the Dakotas, eastern Montana, and Wyoming. It may surprise many whitetail enthusiasts to know that in the official (Boone & Crockett Club) record book there are more whitetails from west of the Mississippi River by far than from east of it in what most hunters generally consider the prime whitetail country. Another surprise is that Saskatchewan has put far and away the most heads into the book.

Another large subspecies, the Kansas whitetail, *O. v. macrourus,* has been intergraded it is believed to extinction. However, the big northwest whitetail, *O. v. ochrourus,* of eastern Washington, Oregon, and into Idaho and bordering Rockies states, is probably pure in areas where it cannot intergrade. The handsome Columbian whitetail, *O. v. leucurus,* of small parts of coastal Washington and Oregon, is now a severely endangered subspecies, not hunted. Changes in land use have all but done it in. The tiny Florida Key whitetail, fully protected and with its own refuge, a deer which seldom weighs more than 75 pounds, is interesting because of its dimunitive size and the fact that a special refuge saved it from extinction.

The one most important subspecies so far as hunters and most observers are concerned is the Coues or Arizona whitetail, *O. v. couesi.* This is a small, gray deer—mature bucks seldom weigh over 100 pounds—of the grass and oak and juniper of southeastern Arizona and southwestern New Mexico, most abundant at around 6000 feet altitude. Because of its isolation from others, this one is recognized separately in the record book, and is the only subspe-

## Range of the Whitetail Deer

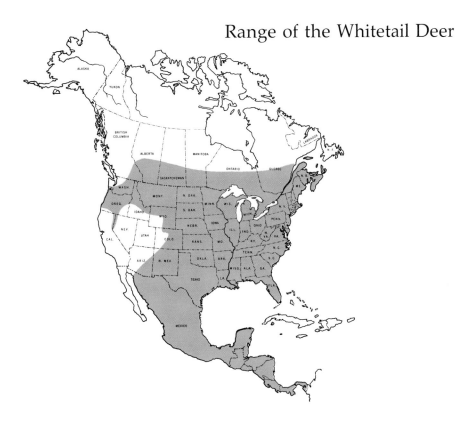

cies so recognized. A second subspecies of diminutive stature living high up in small, individual mountain ranges of the Big Bend Country of western Texas and on across into Mexico is the Carmen Mountains whitetail, *O. v. carminis*. It is an unusual and handsome trophy indeed, but intergrades at lower altitudes on its home range with the large Texas whitetail, *O. v. texanus*, which is also present in the general area.

Except in the case of a few subspecies such as the Columbian, the whitetail deer is presently in no danger whatever. Its natural enemies have been so severely controlled that predation is a negligible influence except in local noncontinuing instances. Although man — the hunter — may be classed as a predator, he is actually a key to proper management, not a danger as relates to hunting. The worst enemies of the whitetail deer are the expansion of industry and human population, which incessantly snip away at available habitat. Some estimates claim that an average of 3000 acres per day of possible whitetail living room are usurped — by roads, mining, lumbering, oil exploration, urban sprawl, and changing agricultural land use. That's over a million acres a year!

Starvation and diseases related to malnutrition cause the greatest number of whitetail deaths. Occasionally these dieoffs are massive. And usually they are caused by overpopulation on certain ranges. The whitetail is a prolific creature, capable of doubling its numbers each year. Drought and severe winters when food supplies give out often cause these local debacles. The science of whitetail management, however, has been brought to a high art. Hunter quotas for antlerless deer are a tool used to keep herds tailored to their available food supply. Because of meticulous management, the handsome whitetail with its broad white flag waving as it bounds away will unquestionably be present in abundance over a vast area throughout the foreseeable future, for hunter and non-hunter alike to enjoy.

### HABITAT

Trying to describe the habitat preferred by whitetail deer is like trying to be understood by several nationalities while speaking a single language. What an experienced New England deer hunter recognizes as perfect deer country is totally unrelated to what a hunter from near the Mexican border or from the land's-end swamps of southern Louisiana sees. As noted previously, the whitetail has been able to adapt to very different habitats, and to thrive in them. Yet the astute observer will soon perceive that the basics of habitat are easily related no matter how dissimilar the terrain may appear.

This deer is by personality an animal that must have numerous hiding places. Yet it never reaches high population levels in climax forest—that is, forests that are mature and thus have very little understory. It is commonly spoken of as an "edge" animal. Let's say there is an expanse of mixed forest, some conifers, some hardwoods, cut by creeks, perhaps with a small lake or two thrown in, and here and there throughout a given expanse small to large openings. The openings may have scattered brush or shrubs, but they are ringed by denser mixed forest. The stream courses, the lake shores, the openings all encourage growth of forage, shrubs, and grasses. All these are edges of the forest, and it is these that are essential to the success of any whitetail deer herd.

In numerous locations where small farms checkerboard the countryside there are scores of privately owned woodlots, with perhaps larger tracts of state or national forest interspersed. Usually such part-farm-part-woods mixtures form optimum deer habitat. It is the brushy or wooded edges that furnish the most food for the deer; water is seldom a problem; and the thickets and denser forest serve as hiding and bedding places. A mule deer, an elk, or a caribou may bed down spang in the open where it can see far and catch a good breeze. Or the mule deer in particular may bed down high on a slope beside a single small bush or rock. The whitetail is totally different. It is secretive. When the terrain and growth allow it to both rest and feed without coming into the open, it will do so. Seldom will a mature whitetail cross an opening of any size. It will follow the edge, keeping to cover. In heavily settled states many a huge buck has lived undetected and unsuspected for some years in a near-town farm woodlot, feeding only at night.

In swamps of the south, deer find the all-important edges along the rim of the swamp itself, where large tree growth begins and where brushy thickets intergrade between forest and swamp. Lumbering operations along southern stream courses enhance whitetail opportunity. In the heavily agricultural areas of, for example, the Dakotas and Nebraska, there are willow-grown creek bottoms and gullies, plus windbreaks and even in season high stands of corn that serve as foraging and hiding places.

In the desert that the whitetail has been able to colonize, such as the so-called Brush Country of southern Texas, a rolling expanse of seemingly endless cactus and thornbrush, there are densely grown creek bottoms. These "creeks" deserve the name only during infrequent rains. But the water encourages thick vegetation. These are favorite hiding places for whitetails, which incidentally grow to trophy size in this rather unusual deer habitat. The grid of bulldozed ranch roads and seismograph trails from oil exploration throughout this large-ranch cattle country forms needed edges. So do openings where cattle ranchers clear the thornbrush so grass will grow.

Thus, you see, the habitat of the whitetail deer cannot be precisely detailed, as it can for moose, or elk, or pronghorn. It is highly and most interestingly diverse, in looks, altitude, latitude, vegetation growth, climate, and aridity or lack of it. Yet the fundamentals — dense thickets in which to hide and move about, edges to furnish much of the food — are in each case abundantly present.

## FEEDING

Just as the nature of the habitat differs so broadly over the vast domain of the whitetail, so too must the varieties of plants, shrubs, and trees available in a given region. It is amusing, for instance, for a southwestern whitetail hunter to hear a New England deer hunter extol the value of an old apple orchard as a magnet for drawing deer, and telling how apple scent should be used by all deer hunters to overpower the human smell. To a whitetail on the Mexican border, which has never seen or tasted an apple, the smell might be frightening. There are in fact instances of men holding a deer-hunting lease in that country putting out bushels of corn in feeders to help keep the deer fat and in residence—only to discover that the animals wouldn't touch it. They had never tasted corn, didn't know it was fit to eat, yet they avidly gobbled up huajillo brush, a standard item of desert diet, which no doubt no Vermont whitetail would touch, given the opportunity.

Thus the hunter or wildlife enthusiast interested in whitetails should make a point of knowing which are favorite and abundantly available foods in his general region. These are only a few out of several hundred that deer are known to eat. Wherever oaks grow, for example, acorns are an extremely important item of diet. Buds and twigs of maple, sassafras, poplar, aspen, and birch are all staples. Sumac, beech leaves and mast, witch hazel, blueberry, blackberry, in the west mountain mahogany, varied ferns all over the continent, and wintergreen are all palatable to whitetails. Wherever they are found, wild grape vines, mulberry, basswood, serviceberry, wild rose, holly, and honeysuckle have a place in the diet. Wild clover, green grasses in spring, aquatic plants of lake and stream shores, and a broad variety of waste grain and vegetable crops as well as those upon which deer cause depredations are on the important list. So are chokecherry bushes, persimmon, greenbrier, and in specialized situations as in the southwest, yucca, huajillo, prickly pear cactus and its fruits, comal, ratama, and various tough shrubs often lumped under the name "buckbrush."

Wherever conifers grow, these are utilized, but chiefly in winter when other foods are scarce: jackpine in the Great Lakes region, juniper in the southwest, hemlock, white cedar, fir, and others wherever they are available. These are not the most nutritious foods. Whitetails do not migrate to winter ranges, thus in snow country are inclined to "yard up" during severe winter in so-called cedar swamps and jack pine stands. Here they gain protection from

*Whitetails in winter often have to rear on their hind legs to reach conifer browse.*

weather, and feed on the browse. Many a northern "deer yard" has seen the browse line creep up and up until only the largest animals, rearing on hind legs, can reach any food at all. Then finally none is left and if deep snow continues, starvation wipes out scores of deer.

There have been many experiments in winter feeding. Hay has been used, but is not a proper diet. Occasionally volunteers working with game-department personnel go into a forest and cut poplar close to the yarded-up deer, so they can get to the twigs. But such measures are makeshift at best. Many whitetails starve or die of dis-

*Deer chew bushes almost to the snow line, until the branches are too thick to bite.*

eases caused by malnutrition during winter. This occurs in the south, too, when food runs low, and especially in snowless places like central Texas, where deer are extremely abundant and not all years offer substantial acorn crops to help pull the animals through to a newly green spring. Like all members of the family, whitetails have no upper front teeth. The size twigs they can handle are thus, compared to their size, modest.

Deer do much feeding at night, especially on moonlit nights. Some observers believe whitetails prefer daytime feeding but are driven to night foraging when disturbed by the hunting season. This is a pat theory but probably only that. Conceivably under heavy pressure of the hunting season in a few areas deer may stay hidden all day. But the fact is, their eyes, which contain millions more light-gathering rod cells than the human eye, are tailored perfectly for night vision. Shine a light on a deer at night and its eyes glow; those of a human do not. It is a fact that regardless of hunting pressure deer move less as a rule in daytime during the bright moon phases than during the dark of the moon. Also, during hot weather the cool hours of dusk, night, and dawn are simply the most comfortable.

By and large, their chief feeding periods are from before dawn until several hours after, and again from late afternoon until dusk. The availability of food dictates how long it requires during each session to fill the paunch with 5 or 6 pounds of forage. In winter deer may be forced to nibble away much longer. They are also amazingly fussy and selective when enough food is present, passing up numerous edibles for those they most relish. Also, when there is a bonanza crop of an especially desirable food, whitetails, just like any other animal, including man, take the easy way, moving as little as possible. During years when acorns literally by bushels are on the ground, whitetails may feed and bed down without ever showing themselves and without traveling more than a few yards a day. Life is then easy, and lazing away the day chewing cuds in safety and seclusion is far better than nervously searching the edges for scattered tidbits.

### MOVEMENTS

An examination of the slender and almost dainty lower legs of the average whitetail deer would make it seem patently unsuited for swift travel through brush, over rocks and obstacle courses of downed timber in a forest. Yet this is the most agile of all our deer. It bounds at 30 miles per hour when really frightened, zigzagging through the most tangled terrain, hurdling obstacles and even high bushes in graceful flying leaps. A whitetail can stand feeding beside an ordinary farm fence, raise its head to see something that startles it, and clear the fence from a standstill with an unbelievable flow of barely perceptible muscle motion. To successfully pen whitetails, an 8-foot fence is needed, and even then many go over the top.

Hunters have long said that a whitetail buck commonly runs away, flag flying, without even knowing for certain what startled it. And unlike its relative the mule deer, which may slow to a walk and start feeding again just over the ridge, or even pause on top to look back, the whitetail may clear several ridges before pausing. When running — bounding — this deer comes down first on its forefeet and the hind feet strike next, but past the fores. This typical running gait, plus the broad, raised, waving tail, plus the nonbranching points of the typical whitetail antlers are its chief easily recognized identification tags. The mule deer bounds so that the hind feet strike close to but behind the forefeet, its small-diameter stringlike tail (except in the Columbian blacktail) is seldom raised at all, and its antler points branch.

As an aside here it should be pointed out that both whitetails and mule deer bear nontypical or freakish antlers in many instances. The record book allows for this, having classes for both typical and nontypical. Certain areas of range invariably produce more, or less, of each class; mule deer are inclined to show nontypical antlers more often than whitetails. Genetic characteristics may be the reason for such antlers; mineral content of soil also may be a factor.

A whitetail deer walks most of the time when in motion, strolling slowly and with grace. It has a trotting gait also, raising a foot on opposite sides—perhaps left fore, right hind, then repeat oppositely—as it moves. The trot may be used when an animal is mildly concerned, or even when it is hurrying to join a companion, or to go to food or water. The bounding all-out gait is for escape, and it utilizes all the power of the animal, with the tremendous push from all fours that unwinds its bunched body into a sailing leap that may cover 15 to 25 feet. Whitetails are also adept swimmers, often entering large streams and drifting along as if for pure enjoyment. They also swim into lakes to escape predators such as feral dogs, or to visit islands. Does occasionally give birth to their fawns in such places, to add to seclusion and safety.

Whitetail deer utilize more "body language" movements than any other of the family. A feeding doe puts her head down, jerks it up five seconds later to look nervously around. She cocks her ears forward, staring at some imagined or real danger. She moves her head stiffly from side to side, the better to focus on the object or to make certain it isn't moving. She may stamp a front foot impatiently, possibly hoping to make the danger give itself away. This process, and the steady staring, may continue for a full minute or more. Then she gives a little switch of her tail. To a trained observer of whitetails, this is the "all clear." Immediately her attention will shift and her head lowers to feed again.

However, if the foot stamping continues she may begin to snort or "blow." This may be to prod the danger into making a show, or it may merely indicate growing nervousness. Now her tail begins to rise. At straight out—half mast—she may still eventually settle down. If it raises past that point and is cocked over to one side, she is about to run. Then it comes up straight, she whirls, snorting, and bounds away, flag moving from side to side.

If you are observing a feeding deer and it raises its head, cocks its ears, but not tensely, and is not looking at you, it may have heard or seen or sensed another deer. Many a deer gives away another's presence by this movement. Or during the rut a doe seems to glide out of a thicket into an opening. She pauses, looks back over her shoulder, ears moving. Then on she glides. Watch closely the thicket behind her! A buck will almost certainly soon appear. Such are examples of the body movements of the shy, wary whitetail that can impart to an observer the deer's intent or state of mind.

So far as travel as such is concerned, the whitetail is the least inclined. Of all our deer its home bailiwick is the smallest, and it will not leave the environs into which it was born, even to avoid starvation. On a range where food is genuinely abundant around the year, many whitetails do not utilize more than half a square mile of territory. On the average, a square mile contains nearly all, except that bucks in rut may break out of the home-territory barriers to trespass on the domains of neighboring bucks.

Some extremely interesting scientific studies have been done to monitor deer range. In one recent instance in Texas, a monitor station was set up and manned twenty-four hours a day at least two days each week. Deer of the vicinity were trapped, fitted with electronic collars, and released. Wherever they were, the monitoring station could pick up their individual signals at any time, know where each deer was and which one it was. During the test none was ever outside a plotted square mile, and several never got more than a half-mile away.

Whitetails, living in such small home bailiwicks, come to know every stick, stone, tree, stump, and land contour intimately. That is why they are so uncannily able to escape pursuit, or to detect danger. This may be likened to a man driving a mile to work each day along the same route. Even the smallest new sign that goes up or the most minor chuckhole in the pavement is immediately noticed. In deer domain, anything that looks, sounds, or smells unfamiliar is suspect.

Biologists love to tell of the Michigan hunting experiment in the Upper Peninsula some years ago. A square mile of forest was fenced deerproof, and over a period of many weeks a tally on the deer population meticulously made, a task none too easy even for experts. Six top-notch deer hunters were then turned loose in the study plot. Nine bucks were present, plus thirty does. During four days of hunting this single square mile of what was home ground to the deer, no antlers were sighted. It took over fifty hunting hours before the first kill was made.

Whitetails make no migrations to winter range, as some mule deer do. As has been noted, they do yard up within their own territory during heavy snow. A mass migration to better feeding grounds might save them, but they seem unaware, and totally reluctant to leave home. Movements at any time to water or food or to bed down are all very brief. And routines are quite predictable. The resident deer follow certain trails, although these may shift seasonally as foraging or water supply dictates, or upon disturbance. A saddle in a ridge, a stream crossing, a path deer-made around the head of a steep canyon are all used day after day unless human intrusion forces the animals into new patterns.

These habits are advantageous to hunters, of course, but not if the animals are pressured. Whitetails driven off a ridge where they are resting in cedars, let's say, may bound down and across an opening once or twice and thus offer a waiting hunter or photographer a shot. But after that they will quit the resting area to seek a new one. It should be stated that a bedding ground is never any permanent location. Whitetails do not return to use beds that served previously. They lie down wherever they happen to be and feel safe, although certain locations in the domain obviously serve best for the purpose and thus are used more than others.

All of the foregoing is by no means intended to indicate that the whitetail deer is a sedentary creature. Far from it. It is the most acutely tuned to its environment of all the deer. But it is also simply and strictly an incurable homebody.

### BREEDING

The whitetail has scent glands between the two parts of the hoof on all four feet. It also has a musk gland called the metatarsal gland on the outside of each lower hind leg, and the larger tarsal gland on the inside of each hind leg at the hock. Scent from these glands is probably used by deer for keeping in touch with each other, and to leave a scent that may be followed by another deer. When fall and the rut arrive the tarsal gland becomes wet with its secretion and smells very strong.

By September the antlers of bucks have been rubbed clean and polished; they begin mock battles with small saplings and bushes.

Whitetail bucks are not especially gregarious with each other at any season, as mule deer may be. But now as fall wears on they become more than ever loners. By mid-September in some latitudes and later on into November in others, the rut begins.

Each buck now stakes out his territory. He has made "rubs" on numerous saplings in his bailiwick while polishing his antlers. Now at several locations he makes what hunters call a "scrape." He paws out a spot in soft earth, generally beneath an overhanging branch. He urinates in the scrape and reaches up to nuzzle, nibble, and touch his antlers against the overhanging branch. Just why he does this last is not well understood but it is commonly part of the breeding-season ritual.

These scrapes denote his territory. He also ranges outside his own area, and other bucks raid his. Thus battles ensue. Whitetails at times become vicious fighters. Injuries, and locked antlers, are fairly common. Whitetail bucks do not make any attempt to gather a harem. Does come in heat for a brief period, twenty-four to thirty hours, each twenty-eight days. A doe in heat may find the scrape of a buck, urinate in it, and leave her musky trail as she moves away.

Does in heat are coquettish. When a buck pursues, the doe may run, usually circling. She pauses. The buck rushes up to her. She runs again. A buck whitetail during the peak of the rut is totally concentrated upon breeding. This is the only time of year when it loses all caution. Bucks often pass within a few feet of a hunter, mouth open, eyes glassy. They also become quite fearless and occasionally dangerous. When following a doe, the buck sometimes runs with its tail held rigidly straight out behind. This is a kind of body language which hunters or observers can use to advantage.

Whitetail deer are not vocal creatures. But now and then during the rut a buck may be heard to utter a low, rasping grunt, not loud but repeated several times, as it follows a doe. Often a second buck, eager for a doe, will trespass and try either to fight another for the doe with it, or else to run her off. Many years ago the art of rattling antlers for whitetails was conceived for use during the rut. It supposedly originated along the Mexican border of Texas and spread somewhat from there. But it may have been used by various Indian tribes elsewhere.

A hunter saws a pair of antlers from a skull, takes a stand, and clashes the antlers together. He rakes brush and gravel, all of it simulating the sound of two bucks fighting over a doe. The trick is effective, of course, only during breeding season. Some bucks rush in with eyes wild, ready to fight. Some sneak in as if intent on lur-

ing the presumed doe away while the simulated fight goes on.
Young bucks are especially silly. One may run up to the antler-
rattling hunter's hiding place, dart off, race back, always watching
to make sure no mature buck is in sight. If one appears, it immediately retreats.

The neck of the whitetail buck, like that of most deer, is swollen
during the rut. The rut period for each individual buck generally
lasts about a month. Each services a doe during her brief period,
then leaves her to find another. The tarsal musk and the urine leave
readily followed trails. Occasionally two or more bucks may chase
after a single doe. Then a fight is almost certain. Although the buck
may service a number of does during the rut, the whitetail seldom
becomes quite as bedraggled as bull elk do with their large harems.

If a doe fails to be bred during a first fall period, she will probably be bred the next month, or even the third. Thus some fawns appear later than others, and a few are seen each year with their spots
still evident well along in fall. The overall period of the rut on the
average is from October through December. It differs from place to
place and especially season to season. Some breeding action may be
evident some years as early as September and as late as late January.

During this period when the heavily haired tarsal glands are wet
with musk, hunters sometimes cut them off the legs of a freshly
killed animal and use them on a stand as an attractant, or to mask
human scent. Just how effective this may be is questionable. However, many hunters slice away these skin glands from the inside of
the hind leg before dressing out the animals, to avoid getting any
musk on the meat.

Once the rut is over the personality of the buck reverts to normal
once again. The wide ranging that has occurred during this period
ceases. Each now stays within its own range and is shy and secretive once more. Through December and January as breeding ceases
for each individual buck, the antlers begin to loosen and are shed.
From that time on through the winter the bucks usually consort
with other deer of either sex. Not until the new antlers form do they
begin to get the urge to stay apart.

For many years it was thought that only fully adult whitetails
were capable of breeding. It is now known, however, that on optimum range a substantial number of doe fawns are bred during
their first fall, and have their first fawns when they are only a year
old. Some bucks breed when they are long yearlings—into their
second fall; the vigorous activity, however, begins for most in the
third fall.

## BIRTH AND DEVELOPMENT

When spring is well along in the woodlands and ground cover green and high, the reddish-colored fawns, dappled with white spots, begin to appear. Each doe gives birth a bit over 6½ months from the time she was bred. Twin fawns are common among adult does, and triplets not rare. Yearling does seldom drop more than a single fawn.

There is no group fawning area. Each doe finds her own haven. Whitetail fawns are unable to stand when first born, and are very wobbly on their legs for a few days. At birth they weigh only 4 to 5 pounds. For at least the first couple of weeks of their lives, and sometimes longer, the fawns stay at or within a few steps of the spot where the mother has led them as soon as they can walk. This hiding place or nursery is shady, possibly in deep grass beneath bushes, where the youngsters will be comfortable and safe. They do not follow their mother around.

This often leads to a "lost" fawn being caught and taken home by some well-meaning tourist. The fawn is not lost. It stays put while the mother forages. She does not go far, and she comes back to the hideaway several times daily to allow the fawn to nurse.

*A fawn in the protective posture it assumes at the first sign of danger.*

When a fawn is first able to move about over a small area around the hiding place, it will drop to the ground with head outstretched at any indication of danger. An immobile fawn in dappled light and shadow of cover is difficult to spot, and apparently has little odor. When it is around a month old it begins to follow its mother.

Now and then it mimics her, nibbling at a plant here and there. Presently it is taking forage, and progressively becomes less dependent upon milk. By fall the spots and fawn color are replaced by the first grayish coat of winter. Fawns of either sex may stay with the mother on through the first winter, or they may not. Buck fawns are more likely to wander off on their own.

Throughout their lives, as mentioned earlier, whitetails are not especially vocal. Very young fawns bleat on occasion. Grown fawns in their first fall may utter this sound if they have strayed from their mother. An injured adult deer is capable of uttering a startlingly loud "blatt" or bawl. This is not a common sound. Rarely an injured mature buck utters a low, harsh, rasping cry. The whistle or snort of a disturbed whitetail is the sound most often heard.

While the fawns are weaning and losing their spots, the bucks are off by themselves, their new antlers bulging in velvet. There are many misconceptions about whitetail antlers. Many wildlife observers, especially hunters, still believe the deer adds a point on either side annually, and thus can be aged by counting points. This is untrue. Antler growth depends upon the quality of the basic habitat — that is, the soil. If it contains proper minerals, these are passed along in food and water, and antler growth will far exceed that on poorer soils.

Further, the type of season is all important. If winter forage is abundant, weather is not too severe, and there is a "good" spring, the bucks will be in excellent physical condition as the antlers are forming and this will be evident in heavy, dark, well-formed antlers in fall. In poor seasons antlers are invariably slender, smaller, pale, and sometimes ill-formed.

Ordinarily a spring fawn will be in fall what hunters term a "button buck." The antlers are mere nubs that barely break through the skin, if at all. As a long yearling the buck will probably be a spike — each antler a single spike from 3 to 5 inches long. However, under the best conditions it may be a forkhorn, or even more. On the average over most whitetail range, the males progress from button bucks to spikes to forkhorns — each antler simply forked and with no brow tine. The following fall it may have six points or eight points. But there is no rigid rule. An "eight-pointer" is a buck with brow tines, two points rising from the main beam of each antler, plus the point formed by each main beam.

Some whitetails at maturity never show more than eight points. Others, vigorous, well-fed animals, are ten-pointers, or more. By and large, typical antlers of ten points total are the standard for mature bucks in their fourth or fifth year and onward. A few develop twelve points or more. Most antlers with numerous points fall because of their unsymmetrical conformation into the nontypical class.

The soil quality of the range, which is responsible for abundant or poor forage, is partly responsible for antler development. Recent experiments show that a high-protein diet assists antler growth. Deer fed all they will eat of such a diet often skip the spike stage and become six-pointers or better their first year. However, parallel studies at the Kerr Management Area in Texas, continued over a period of six years, indicate that genetics is an even more powerful influence. Massive-antlered bucks beget the same. When high-protein diet and plenty of it, plus genetically superior deer are combined, a kind of "superdeer" is produced. Somewhat similar studies in Tennessee with hybridizing of whitetails and blacktails show that there are sex links in the genetic carry-over: a blacktail buck bred to a whitetail doe gets progeny with bifurcate antlers like the male parent, and vice versa.

Bucks in their fourth and fifth years usually are at peak, but if one remains exceptionally vigorous over the next couple of years, it is likely to have extremely heavy antlers. Old bucks past their prime may not even have antlers, or may grow gnarled, ill-formed spikes.

Although not common, the incidence of color variations in the whitetail is far from rare. True albinos seldom occur, but at least one instance is recorded of a doe in New York State that gave birth to several albino fawns, along with fawns of normal color. The curious aspect of these albinos was that the skin was pink, and one, a buck, grew antlers that in the velvet were pure white.

"Paint" whitetails—spotted with blotches of brown and white—show up annually in hunter harvests. Usually a certain area produces these with fair consistency over the years, indicating a genetic aberration in a race of that location. Such individuals are not albinos. On the 7500-acre Seneca Army Depot in New York State a small herd of pure-white mutations has evolved from a single buck seen there in 1957. These also are not albinos. During a

*In April a mature whitetail buck shows two nubs where antlers are going to sprout.*

*By late June the antlers have reached partial growth and are covered in a velvet-like substance that supplies nourishment.*

*In September the bucks rub the velvet from their full-grown antlers in readiness for the rut. This is an eight-pointer.*

*The whitetail's antlers are typi-fied by a single main beam on each side with a number of tines, or points, growing off each beam.*

recent count the strain had proved so dominant that about a fifth of the deer on the depot were white. These deer are carefully pro-tected. A few token hunts, meticulously supervised, have been allowed to keep the animals tailored to their range.

Melanism — a black phase, the opposite of albinism — apparently is much more uncommon among whitetails. No wholly melanistic specimens are known, but occasionally partial melanism appears. It has been recorded occasionally in the Adirondacks, and a portion of one county in the Texas Hill Country has turned up a number of very dark-coated bluish-black animals over recent years.

### SENSES

The keenness of the sense of smell in the whitetail is legendary. The slightest whimsical air movement will waft scent of danger that is picked up at long distances even in the most meager amounts. Hunters report taking a stand in a tree and having whitetails walk right under them without recognizing their presence, yet deer 300 yards away snorted and fled as they came across the scent-drifting flow of a breeze so gentle the hunter was unaware of it.

Most animals that live in heavy cover are well equipped with highly developed scenting ability. They need it more here than, for example, does the antelope on wide-open plains. On days of high wind that gusts from varying directions, whitetails are especially nervous and easily spooked. They cannot keep a steady "scenting beam," and in addition their hearing is impaired by the noise around them.

By and large the whitetail depends first upon its nose, and then begins to focus the other senses to the degree the situation allows. Anything a whitetail hears or sees it immediately tries to smell. Scent is the real clincher of danger. A deer coming in to rattled antlers, for example, will circle if there is the slightest breeze. It may not be the least suspicious, but instinctively it tries to sniff out what's going on in order to authenticate what it has heard. Anyone who wishes to observe whitetails unaware must remember to keep even the slightest air movement in his favor.

Whitetail hearing is also acute. But it is secondary to scenting ability, because often the deer hears something and does not properly identify it without help of the nose. This is one reason why a whitetail will often race away at some slight sound and keep right on running over the next two ridges. It has heard something it could not check out with its nose. Conversely, experimenters have reported sitting well camouflaged in a blind above the ground and mumbling in low voice at deer down below. The deer might become nervous, but would soon also become accustomed.

One interesting aspect of whitetail hearing is that they seem to recognize the sounds made by another deer walking along, for example over rocks that clink. They've been observed merely cocking ears toward this sound, unconcerned. Yet a man making the same sound is instantly recognized as a disturbing element.

Whitetail eyesight is sharp for any movement. But it is not acute unless there is movement. A deer will recognize something amiss in its domain—a hunter hunched in camouflage, for example—but simply looking at it may be no more than mildly disturbed. The slightest movement, however, will put the animal to flight. Whitetails are colorblind, and thus colored clothing does not disturb them, unless in high contrast to the surroundings in the shade of gray they see. The eye placement and physical build of deer make it difficult for them to see above, and also at acute angles out to the side. The eyes are set chiefly for looking ahead and at right angles outward to the sides.

SIGN *(Tracks are illustrated on page 250.)*

Earlier the scrapes made by bucks during the rut were described. Rubs were also mentioned. The rub of a whitetail buck is usually made on a rough shrub, such as a small balsam in the north, a sapling pine or cedar in the south. It is simply a place where antlers have scraped bark from the sapling, and broken branches. Seldom are large trees used. Those an inch or less in diameter are most common. Where cattle and horses are pastured these domestic animals commonly rub their necks on larger trees, quite low to the ground. Occasionally a hunter mistakes these for deer sign. The size of the tree utilized is the clue.

The rub of a deer also is at head height of the animal or slightly lower. This means lower than a man's belt line, as a rule. In any given area bucks seem to select certain sapling or shrub varieties as favorites for rubbing. If one learns these, it helps locate animals. As an example, the green-barked, thorny retama of the southwest seems to attract whitetails in that region where small conifers are not present.

Over almost all of their range, deer tracks cannot possibly be confused with other tracks. They are totally unlike tracks of any domestic animals. Over the eastern half of the continent within whitetail range there are no other hoofed big-game animals. In some places of the west, whitetail and mule deer tracks may be confused. That makes little difference. Further, the terrain types favored by each help keep them fairly well separated. Galloping whitetails leave tracks with hind feet ahead of the forefeet, as noted earlier. Mule deer bound with hind-feet prints behind those of the forefeet. It is not really possible to distinguish between whitetail and mule deer tracks except when the animals are running.

Fawn tracks and javelina tracks might cause confusion in the javelina's range. Fawn tracks, however, have sharply pointed toe imprints. Those of the javelina are blunt and rounded.

There has long been argument among hunters about how to tell buck tracks from doe tracks. The fact is, there is no sure way. A buck may or may not sink in soft earth more deeply. It depends upon his age and size. A buck, it is sometimes said, drags his feet more, showing drag marks in snow. All deer show drags in snow an inch or more in depth. Drags in a light skiff of snow may well indicate the track of a buck—or of a big old doe!

Deer droppings are another sign. Depending on the size of the deer, and the type of forage, these may be anywhere from a half-inch to over an inch in length. When the deer are eating soft summer food the droppings do not separate into individual pellets. Except in mule deer range droppings of whitetails cannot be readily confused with others. Occasionally rabbit droppings may cause a puzzle, but they should not because those of rabbits are round, not elongated.

Deer beds give some indication of the presence of animals on the range, but they are not purposely reused, so they are of interest only in passing. The only close-focus information the flattened grass or leaves or melted snow of deer beds will offer is a guess at what sexes made them. A group of three is almost certain to be left by a doe and two fawns. A single, large impression may be a big buck—or a big doe. Although whitetail bucks very occasionally wallow in mud of a scrape in which they have urinated, deer wallows are rare and this sign likewise.

### HUNTING

Hunting whitetails is a tricky endeavor indeed because of their wariness. However, from 10 to 20 percent of hunters collect deer on the average range, and 50 to 75 percent are successful on ranges where the deer are extremely plentiful, which proves that the hunter can still outwit his quarry, if he uses craft.

Many volumes have been written on the how-to of whitetail hunting. It is an involved subject, with many facets. Basically, however, there are four main methods in use today: stand hunting, still hunting, driving, and calling. One has already been partially explained—the calling technique which involves rattling antlers during the rut. An adjunct to that kind of calling is the use of deer calls now marketed and quite popular. Full instructions come with these. Don't expect miracles, however. Deer calls are interesting to experiment with, but hardly solve all hunting problems. Many hunters also nowadays add scents. Some supposedly attract deer, others serve to mask human scent. Scents are used by still hunters and stand hunters as well as when calling.

Stand hunting is undoubtedly the most popular over all white-tail range, possibly because it entails the least exertion for the hunter and avoids disturbing the deer. It is most successful early and late in the day, when deer move most. The hunter selects a stand, preferably one which places him above where deer may move, as on a ridgeside or a knoll. Because whitetails utilize cover and skirt the edges of openings, clinging to cover as much as possible, small openings scattered over the viewing area are preferred to large ones. Stands taken near a scrape during the rut or positioned to allow watching a well-used trail, a saddle between knolls, or a stream crossing all are possibilities. Any area where deer have been steadily utilizing any landscape feature will bear watching. In farm country deer habitually jump a particular low spot on a fence to and from woodlot and field. This makes a perfect spot to watch.

The stand is selected so that any breeze is either toward or angling from the front across. The hunter conceals himself, either sitting with back against a tree, or in a thicket from which he can see out plainly. Never should he be skylighted. Camouflage clothing and even camo grease paint for the face, or a headnet, help the stand hunter "disappear." He should remain immobile and silent. Binoculars are all but mandatory. In fact, for any kind of deer hunting they are invaluable. Where it is legal nowadays many hunters use a tree stand. In some areas they also use metal seats high on a tall tripod of steel poles. These are currently marketed. Such placements allow the hunter to see into and over dense cover, and place him where deer are not likely to see him.

The still hunter slowly prowls the terrain, watching for deer. Again, the breeze must be kept in one's favor. Camouflage clothing is an assist. But most of all, slow movement counts. This means much slower than most hunters move. The hunter who spends an hour moving 300 yards sees more, makes less noise, and is far more likely to be successful than one walking along at normal speed. The still hunter utilizes every bit of cover, and is ever alert and with rifle ready. Many a bedded buck has been collected by the expert prowler. And many a deer feeding along and unaware has been taken by the still hunter who keeps a sharp lookout ahead, then makes a perfect stalk.

In both stand and still hunting, an intimate knowledge of the terrain and the habits of the local deer plus utilization of this knowledge to one's best advantage are what bring success. The same is true, of course, when making a drive. The whitetail drive is more popular in the east than elsewhere. It can be dangerous unless hunters are well disciplined. And it is seldom successful for the tyro because he does not know enough about the habits of the deer.

A drive is made by placing several hunters at strategic locations near which deer pushed out of a resting place are most likely to move. A wooded ridge, let's say, with under cover suitable for a bedding spot, may overlook a small field at its end, with cover around the field rim. Drivers moving through the cover along the ridge push the deer off it before them. The deer may race across the small opening, or run along its edges, offering opportunity to hidden hunters.

There are many variations, but in all the terrain is used to force the deer to go where the shooters wait. Whitetails, however, are masters at doubling back. Expert drivers always try to check out where the deer have been moving naturally. They have normal travel routes. A drive that gently pushes them without undue disturbance along a normal travel route has the best chance of success. In a few states and provinces driving deer with dogs is still legal. This rather specialized technique, used chiefly in the south over many years, is presently declining.

Many different rifle calibers are adequate for whitetails. One should certainly not go undergunned, but the heavy magnums are hardly necessary. Shotguns using rifled slugs are mandatory in numerous heavily populated areas, and of course the bow and arrow is nowadays the favorite of many deer hunters.

Even with the rather astonishing annual harvest of whitetail deer, this much revered and stately creature has a bright future, given proper continuing management, for many years ahead. As stated earlier, hunting is in fact the prime tool of management to keep this animal, which has so brilliantly adapted to utilizing the fringes of civilization as well as wilder places, matched in abundance to available range. The whitetail has few serious enemies in the wild, none of any real consequence among wild predators. Some are killed by coyotes, and a few by bears, bobcats, and the occasional lion. The worst predator over much of the range is the domestic dog. And the worst killer of all in every well-settled area is the automobile.

Starvation and disease do take a heavy toll at times. But the whitetail is capable of an astonishing replacement whenever its numbers are depleted. The continuing and ever increasing loss of habitat because of man's so-called progress is the worst danger the whitetail faces. Yet even that, for the foreseeable future at least, seems incapable of diminishing whitetail numbers to a danger point.

# Mule Deer

*Odocoileus hemionus*

The mule deer is a true westerner with a personality radically different from its more numerous and wider-ranging relative, the whitetail. On occasion it has been called low in intelligence, but that is a gross misinterpretation. It may be more naive and less wary than the whitetail simply because it is a true creature of the wilderness. Although mule deer are forced in some instances to live on the fringes of civilization, they seldom do well under such circumstances, and seem unable to adjust as well as the whitetail to man's progress and presence.

Throughout the west the mule deer is as much revered by sportsmen and wildlife observers as the whitetail is eastward. It gives the appearance of a big, rough, burly character, and indeed it is. But it is also a placid personality, not given to jittering and racing off without knowing what frightened it. Its curiosity about strange sights in its domain often gets it into trouble as it stands to stare, bounces stifflegged with a pogo-stick gait a few steps, stares again, finally runs, then perhaps stops atop the first ridge to look back. Nonetheless, mature bucks know every inch of their mountainous bailiwicks and can be canny indeed, perhaps not wary in

Mule Deer

the super-alert manner of the whitetail but simple, direct, and crafty at staying out of sight, slipping away unnoticed, or simply moving away from disturbance to more remote regions.

It has been estimated that there are possibly half as many mule deer as whitetails, perhaps more. Figures are set variously with a top guess of around 7,500,000. Although the range of the mule deer is not as great as that of the whitetail, it nonetheless stretches over a vast area, from southeastern Alaska where the Sitka blacktail sub-species lives to far down into Mexico. It is especially interesting to note that the type species, the Rocky Mountain mule deer, has the broadest distribution of any antlered or horned game animal on the continent, from slightly above the 60-degree parallel in the far north to about the 35th in the middle of Arizona and New Mexico.

Although the mule deer has been a remarkable colonizer over an immense north-south expanse, curiously it has never been able to extend its range eastward in the same proportion as the westward thrust of the whitetail. It has been found sparsely in western Minnesota, abundantly in the western Dakotas and Nebraska, in token groups in far-western Kansas and Oklahoma, abundantly in the Trans-Pecos region of Texas. Yet within the vast expanse of range from north to south it has pushed into several drastically differing areas, from the aspen and conifers of the Rockies to the rain forests of the Pacific slope to the arid deserts of the southwestern United States and central Mexico.

Although the big push of settlement and industry was from the east toward the west in early days, and the buildup of human population greater east of the Mississippi, the mule deer herds nonetheless were decimated in their time by market and hide hunters, just as the whitetails were. They were tremendously abundant, were not very wary, and lived in more open country than the whitetail, and thus were somewhat easier for market hunters to collect.

There are old records, for example, telling of a single shooter killing more than a hundred mule deer from a single stand in a mountain pass in the middle Rockies in the late 1800s. At a dollar a hide, some 1500 deer were taken in a few weeks from one area of Montana by three hide hunters, the carcasses left to rot. Tens of thousands were killed by professional hunters as food for army camps, mining settlements, and railroad crew camps, and by settlers who lived year-round on venison.

However, there were generous reservoirs of mule deer herds in remote wilderness areas of the mountains, and in the dense rain forests of the Pacific coast. By the time general settlement had been

## THE MULE DEER

COLOR: Gray-brown, winter, reddish-brown, summer; differs widely among subspecies; desert mule deer pale, Rocky Mountain mule deer darker, others variable in shading; nearly black atop head; nose and muzzle band black; face and eye area gray-white; gray-white throat patch; brisket blackish; ears dark-rimmed with whitish interior; belly and inside of legs whitish; very distinctive large white rump patch encircles base of tail; tail narrow, small, white with black tip, in some subspecies broader with grizzled to blackish upper surface in varying amounts and shadings.

MEASUREMENTS, MATURE BUCKS: To 3½ feet at shoulder; overall length 6 to 6½ feet, variable among subspecies, with Columbian blacktails and Sitka deer of Pacific coast averaging substantially smaller; ears averaging 11 inches long as compared to 7 for whitetail; tail 7 inches long as compared to 11 for whitetail; metatarsal gland on outside of hind leg as much as 5 inches long, differing among subspecies, as compared to less than 2 inches for whitetail; Pacific coast subspecies noted above smaller in ear, tail, and metatarsal measurements.

WEIGHT, MATURE BUCKS: Type species (Rocky Mountain) average, 150 to 220 pounds, with occasional specimens 300 to well over 400 pounds; desert subspecies and some others smaller; Pacific coast subspecies seldom at maximum above 150 to 175.

ANTLERS: Typically with antler tines branching, as opposed to the unbranched tines of the whitetail; seldom curving around and forward over brow as in whitetail; younger bucks commonly without brow tines, and with nonbranching tines rather similar to whitetail; nontypical antlers with many points not uncommon.

DOES: Seldom more than 150 pounds; less blocky build.

GENERAL ATTRIBUTES: Exceedingly blocky, powerful appearance; far more placid personality than the whitetail; congenially gregarious among its own kind; branched antler tines; stringlike white tail with black tip (except Columbian blacktail and Sitka deer of Pacific coast, which have broader tail, dark above); tail held tightly down when running (except Pacific coast subspecies noted above, which sometimes raise tail to hoirzontal or even perpendicular, but without side-to-side waving as in whitetail); distantly evident white rump patch (except Pacific coast subspecies); bounding gait when running that strikes all four feet on ground at once, hind feeting striking behind forefeet.

effected, hunting regulations also had been brought to bear, and during this century deer management moved to a high plane of accomplishment. The handsome mule deer was transformed from a frontier commodity to a true game species, and from a low of possibly less than 250,000 animals it was brought back to an abundance that must in numerous locations be cropped severely nowadays to keep the herd tailored to its possible range.

Although mule deer certainly are in no danger, problems do beset them that do not pertain in such severity to the whitetail. Predation is undoubtedly a serious problem in some places. Coyotes, abundant throughout most mule deer range, unquestionably account for many fawns. In the north, where deep snow with a crust may occur in winter, and where coyotes are much larger than their southern counterparts, they are at times responsible for severe predation on adult deer, which break through and founder while the coyotes do not. The mountain lion, under substantial protection, presently accounts for a good many mule deer. Wolves, bears, bobcats, and other predators collect their share. The mule deer range blankets the most populous modern ranges of all the larger North American predators.

Starvation, and diseases often related to it, account for many mule deer. Their winter forage problem — not without exception but often — is quite different from that facing whitetails. Vast numbers of mule deer must utilize different summer and winter ranges. The quality of the winter range dictates entirely the size of any given herd. Lush summer forage may serve scores more animals than a meager or overbrowsed winter range can. Thus, starvation and diseases aggravated by low nutrition unduly thin out many a mule deer herd in winter.

Perhaps, however, the most serious present difficulty facing the mule deer, the one with most influence upon the future, is the ever increasing settlement of wild portions of the west. Unlike the whitetail, the mule deer seems unable to cope with human disturbance. No one knows precisely why. Possibly because it is truly a naive product of the wilderness, it elects to retire rather than scheme toward survival on the fringes of civilization. In some instances a ski or winter resort has usurped ancestral winter range, or cut off passage to it. An entire herd that summers over a huge expanse of high country is thus doomed.

Nevertheless, at this time and for the foreseeable future the mule deer, though facing problems, is certainly not in serious trouble. Biologists dedicated to deer management in every western state diligently seek answers to some of the management questions presented by this burly and exceedingly popular citizen of the slopes and the foothills. Unquestionably they will eventually find most of them.

The Rocky Mountain mule deer receives the most attention because it is most numerous and occupies the greatest range. This "type" species is found over about 75 percent of the entire range, but southward, and along the Pacific where climate and terrain drastically differ, the mule deer has evolved into a number of other subspecies. There are ten of these. The preponderance of them fill rather small or restricted ranges and are not really very important for hunters or others to be able to recognize.

There are, for instance, the California mule deer, *Odocoileus hemionus californicus*, of some middle and southern California counties; the Inyo mule deer, *O. h. inyoensis*, of a small range along the east slope of the southern Sierra; the southern mule deer, *O. h. fulginatus*, which ranges in extreme southern California and on down into Lower California; the Peninsula mule deer, *O. h. peninsulae*, still farther south; and two subspecies named for and isolated on Tiburon and Cedros Islands. There is also the so-called burro deer, *O. h. eremicus*, found along the lower Colorado River in both California and Arizona and on down the east side of the Gulf of California into Mexico.

Much more important than these is the desert mule deer, *O. h. crooki*, a handsome, pale-gray animal of the desert mountains of southeastern Arizona, southern New Mexico, and the Trans-Pecos region of western Texas, plus a range deep into central Mexico. Although this deer is smaller than the Rocky Mountain deer, in both maximum body and antler size, it is very popular with hunters, and offers a unique experience because of the unusual desert terrain.

The mule deer subspecies that is the most important, however, in addition to the Rocky Mountain deer, is one that has caused all kinds of puzzles and arguments not only among hunters but also among scientists. This is the deer of the west slope along the Pacific from portions of British Columbia to central California. It is commonly called the blacktail deer, even though some references call all mule deer blacktails. But anyone in its ranges knows what is meant by blacktail as opposed to mule deer. Originally believed to be a distinct species, and named *O. columbianus*, it was later determined to be a race of mule deer differing markedly, at least superficially, in size, color, tail, and antler development.

Some writers attempt to make no distinction between this race and the type species, a patently ridiculous stance. Properly it is the Columbian blacktail, a mule deer subspecies, *O. h. columbianus*. The Boone & Crockett records list it this way, but do not distinguish record-wise between it and the Sitka deer or Sitka blacktail, *O. h.*

## Range of the Mule and Blacktail Deer

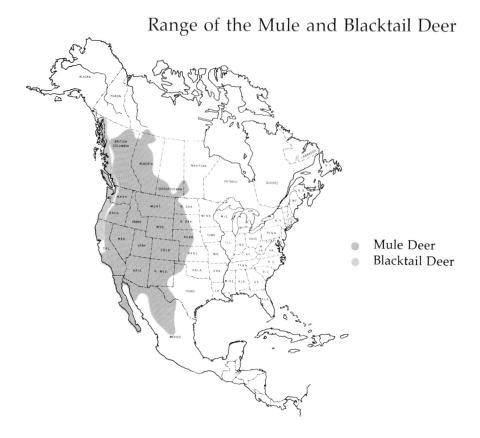

Mule Deer
Blacktail Deer

*sitkensis,* a race that is much like *columbianus,* but which extends the range northward along northern coastal British Columbia and southeastern coastal Alaska.

Interestingly enough, locations where records of these two deer have been taken indicate that no true Sitka deer yet has made the book. But the Columbian blacktail is an exceedingly abundant and important animal along the Pacific from the crest of the Cascades in Washington and Oregon to the coast and on the various islands, and on into California down to Monterey County. It is, in fact, the only deer on this slope over much of its range, although where contact is made with Rocky Mountain and California mule deer there are intergrades.

One of the most interesting theories concerning the Columbian blacktail put forth by several scientists renowned for their deer studies is that here is a perfect example of evolution at work, of a geographic race of deer drawing perhaps closer and closer to becoming a full-fledged species. It is such a different deer—the most "different" of all mule deer races—that though covered here with the mule deer it requires at least some individual attention.

Many hunters might at a cursory glance confuse the blacktail with the whitetail. It is more generally comparable in size, and its ears are shorter than the Rocky Mountain deer and are not tipped and edged with dark hair. There is no large, distinctive white rump patch. The base of the tail is brown, but the tail is always black toward the tip, and usually black on top throughout its length. It is quite brushy, reminiscent in that respect of the whitetail, but shorter. It is white beneath. Its summer coat is much redder than that of other mule deer. The antlers are seldom as broad and heavy as those of the Rocky Mountain deer, are inclined toward less spreading, more upright growth, and usually in adults they have fewer points.

### HABITAT

The Columbian blacktail's world is one of dense, humid forest, or in its southern ranges thickets of heavy brush and trees often in arid settings, such as in California. It is a deer invariably of thick cover. Because of the dense cover this deer has developed basic habits more like the whitetail's than like those of the other mule deer. When it hears suspicious sounds or scents danger, it is inclined to sneak away along trails it knows well in the thick habitat, or to stay utterly still hiding in a thicket until danger has passed. It is known to flush wildly, run a short distance, and hide again, even lying down to escape detection.

Both the Columbian blacktail and its relative in southeastern Alaska, the Sitka deer, live in heavy cover; the Sitka deer is confined to all but impenetrable spruce in a narrow strip near the coast over much of its range. Oddly, perhaps because native hunters and visitors both prefer larger game, the Sitka deer receives very little hunting pressure. It overpopulates in good years, and suffers drastic die-offs during severe winters. Sometimes it is forced to scrounge for food such as kelp right on the beaches.

This habitat is highly specialized, as are the deer. The Rocky Mountain mule deer lives in an entirely different world. Basically it is not by preference an animal of dense mountain forests. It may bed down in heavy conifer thickets, but most of its life is spent along the fringes of mountain meadows, in the mixed forest of aspen and evergreens. It is primarily a deer of open forests and of brushlands broken by openings. Typical of mule deer terrain are the mountain foothills where sage and scattered juniper merge higher up with piñon or other pines and spruces, and aspen.

In Wyoming, for example, mule deer are abundant in all such foothills lands of the Rockies. In addition they are found during summer way up at timberline, among the highest aspen growth and the fringes where trees begin to give way to low growth such as willow. Yet to the east where tree growth becomes less and the country changes to a rough and somewhat barren interspersion of grasslands and sharply eroded gullies rimmed by brush, and with steep shale hills thrusting up here and there, the deer are right at home, utilizing the meandering, deep gullies and hiding in them and in brush, far from the nearest tall trees.

The desert mule deer has colonized a still different habitat. It may be jumped from a bed right down on the desert floor in Arizona, where cactus and thornbrush spread across a narrow valley with steep, rocky slopes nearby. In western Texas, in the desert mountains of the Big Bend Country, desert mule deer feed and even bed down on wholly open slopes. Though they also are found up higher here, where tree growth begins, they are always more abundant among the rimrocks and the sotol and scattered brush and shrubs of the steep lower country.

Without question the most interesting aspect of mule deer habitat is that regardless of subspecies, these deer apparently are unable to colonize level country. Why this is so no one is certain. But the history of the species shows that mule deer shun level woodlands and forests, and avoid flat or even gently rolling open grasslands. In any fringe prairie habitat where they are found, there is always a skein of rough creek or river bottoms with brush and eroded places. In western Texas, for example, deer may be observed crossing broad flats, but they are invariably moving from one slope to another. Much of the time that movement is along steep washes rather than up on the flats. And almost without fail, groups of deer observed feeding are on or at the base of a slope.

Undoubtedly this overwhelming affinity for steeply angled terrain has been an ancestral barrier to the eastward incursion of mule deer into the plains and across the Mississippi. In addition, the northward distribution is stopped by dense boreal forests of spruce. And in the south, areas of barren desert also have been a barrier, yet almost anywhere southward that ample forage on steep slopes is available, the deer have pushed in and lived successfully. Conversely, the whitetail, which easily tolerates both mountains and flat country as long as there is ample cover, was able to extend its range almost completely from coast to coast.

### FEEDING

Just as habitats of mule deer differ widely over their vast range, so too do the items of their diet. A blacktail hunter in California might watch for a buck beneath a big oak laden with and dropping acorns. In the Rocky Mountain states, however, where oaks are by no means abundant, aspen shoots or mountain mahogany might serve as the staple of diet. In the range of the desert mule deer, a slope covered with the low-growing, sharp-spiked lechuguilla leaves may be a favorite foraging ground. The deer paw out the roots and eat them.

Especially in the mountains, grasses are an important part of mule deer diet, particularly in spring. Some scientists believe that mule deer graze more persistently than whitetails. Grasses over the broad range are of infinite variety. Grama grass, fescue, bluegrass, and needle grass are among those commonly abundant. Others are brome or "cheat" grass and wheat grass. Groups of mule deer are seen all summer and throughout early fall grazing at the edges of mountain meadows. But it is in spring that grasses are the most important.

Of course during summer, the easy time of year, there are endless varieties of twigs, berries, flowers, and mushrooms to be eaten. Even in desert terrain, fruits such as those of prickly pear cactus are eagerly eaten, and also the juicy pear pads, regardless of spines, form part of the diet. Wherever oaks grow, the leaves, the acorns, and the twigs are all staples of diet. Several varieties of small oaks live in canyons and near water sources over much mule deer range. Not all oaks bear acorns every year. During good acorn years, these of course are of prime importance.

The same is true of piñon nuts. These small pines, of which there are four species, grow only in the semi-arid regions of the west. They are abundant, for example, in portions of New Mexico and southern Utah and even in high, isolated locations of western Texas. The seeds are literally small nuts, very rich and nutritious. In years when the pine nuts are a bonanza crop, mule deer gorge on them and often become unbelievably fat. Juniper berries also add at times to the diet. Mountain mahogany, a shrub with a feathery bloom, is a favorite mule deer food for browse. So is manzanita.

Sage forms a considerable part of the diet. On some winter ranges, it and bitter-brush are staples simply because the deer are forced to eat them. These are not especially nutritious or palatable. All of the fruit plants, vines, and shrubs such as grape, elderberry, raspberry, and chokecherry add variety to the diet, both with leaves and fruit in season. Summer and winter, if it is available, aspen makes up a substantial portion of the daily intake.

On winter ranges, mule deer are not inclined to dig for grasses, as do elk. Now most of their food is browse. Willow, sagebrush, and cliffrose are among the shrubs available. They also turn now to juniper and cedar, to jack pine, and on the far-northern ranges to fir. These are not especially desirable, but the deer are able, with whatever additions they can scrounge, to get through the winter on them.

It must be pointed out that while deep snow and severe cold are difficult for mule deer to endure, and cause many deaths from low nutrition and exposure, even in the warmer parts of their range the winter or nongrowing season is a lean time, too. Grasses dry down, there are no fruits, no green leaves. Browse can become quite scarce, and of course the fatty crops such as piñon nuts have by late winter been consumed.

Like the whitetail deer, mule deer feed much at night, and may be especially active during moonlit nights. The routine is to feed until fairly full, then bed down for an interval, then feed again. Dawn and the first hour or so after are a period usually of heavy feeding activity. Hunters take advantage of this habit. In summer, of course, the deer feed little after the sun is well up because they dislike heat. In fall and winter, especially on cool mornings, mule deer will be out all over the slopes until possibly 9:00 a.m. Then most of them disappear, bedding down until late afternoon. By about 4:00 p.m. they begin to reappear, and feed heavily until and after dusk.

A big mule deer buck requires as much as 10 pounds of food to fill its paunch. With the variety and abundance available during the growing season this seldom takes more than an hour or two. But in winter deer are sometimes seen wandering and picking away at browse over many hours. When full they then bed down and, like all deer, spend several hours chewing small cuds which are then passed on into the second part of the stomach.

All young deer, and especially those of the mule deer ranging the Rockies where winters are severe, live a precarious existence in relation to food. Winter starvation is an ever-present threat, especially because though a summer range may be large, deer from it may be forced into a much smaller winter range. Young deer, perhaps less vigorous or unable to forge through deep snow or to reach limbs of browse trees and shrubs, suffer most. One Oregon study showed that in a four-year period some 1800 mule deer starved on a single winter range. Of these, in different years from 60 to 90 percent were fawns of the year or yearlings.

Hardships and deaths related to food do not necessarily end with the lush explosion of spring. Once green grasses blanket the range, the deer, many of them thin from malnutrition, gorge on the succulent crop. The new grass is rich in nutritive value, but it is also extremely high in water content. The quick change of diet may trigger another survival problem. Many deer contract severe diarrhea, called "the scours." On certain ranges deaths from the scours run high.

## MOVEMENTS

Mule deer are just as powerful as they look. They seem to be physically fashioned for the terrain in which they live. A startled buck goes bounding effortlessly up a slope so rough and steep that a following hunter could negotiate it only with plodding gait, pausing to rest and catch his breath every few steps. When running all out, although the mule deer is graceful, it gives the impression not of deft agility, like the whitetail, but rather of sheer power.

As has been explained, mule deer bound and land on all fours, hind feet properly behind the forefeet. Whitetails land on the forefeet and the hind feet pass them and strike next. The mule deer lands and pushes with all fours to bound again. A big buck can cover as much as 20 feet to the bound, even going up a modest grade. On the level it has been measured at 26 feet per bound. At top speed it matches the whitetail, at about 35 miles per hour. But it cannot sustain that speed for very long without panting heavily.

Sometimes the vertical height reached as a mule deer bounds is as much as 4 feet. Trapped mule deer have cleared an 8-foot fence with only a short run. The blocky, muscular build of this deer and its bounding run with the push of all fours sending it into the next leap are both unquestionably specialized adaptations to the terrain in which it lives. Even though capable of speed and long leaps, the placid mule deer when undisturbed seldom runs at all. It walks

*When a mule deer is alerted, it often breaks into a peculiar stiff-legged bounce.*

casually, big ears flopping, and is not inclined to the incessant nervous, quick motions of the whitetail. In much of its domain it can see over a large expanse, and it is calm and unconcerned.

Often when alerted but not unduly disturbed, mule deer go through an antic routine that is comical to observe. The deer stares, let's say, at a photographer who has stalked close. It looks literally amazed, yet puzzled. Almost as if embarrassed, it begins to walk away, stiffly, lifting each forefoot high, meanwhile moving its head out and back in a line parallel to the body with each step. After a few such steps, it may trot a few feet, then it begins a bounce—not a bound. It jumps up and only slightly ahead, using all four legs as springs, and coming down stifflegged only to bounce up again.

These bounces are in rather quick rhythm, but take the deer only a short distance, possibly 3 or 4 feet to each one. After this it may stop and stare back. If it finally decides things look serious, it really runs. But it may run only to a nearby ridgetop and pause again for another backward look. From there on it may simply trot over the ridge out of sight, and start right in grazing again. Out of sight, out of mind.

The majority of mule deer have little need to swim, and on some ranges probably none ever have. Nonetheless, they are powerful swimmers when need be. The Sitka blacktail of the southeastern Alaskan coast seems to have no hesitation about striking out for some distant island. They have been observed as much as 5 miles offshore, unconcernedly headed for an island at least that much farther away.

Daily movements of mule deer may extend over a somewhat wider range than in the case of the whitetail. Perhaps this is simply because their mountain habitat is so vast that it seems to beckon the animals into exploration. However, when forage is adequate and water nearby, the bailiwick in which any individual deer lives is not large. Notoriously, a trophy buck that has been reared around a certain mountain meadow will be seen there week after week. However, daily movements to food, water, and cool bedding sites may require more travel than the snug cover of the whitetail. A deer feeding before and through dawn may have to walk a mile to water, then climb another mile up to a rimrock where it will bed down in the shade of overhanging rocks.

It should be noted that mule deer are exceedingly gregarious. Where the country is fairly open, observers may see a group of does, fawns, and a scattering of young bucks totaling as many as forty head. They may be scattered out on a slope, feeding, or even traveling in single file across a flat or up a mountain. Even mature bucks like to hang out together, something few whitetails do. On large ranches in the west where mule deer are abundant, landowners have often reported a half-dozen to a dozen mature bucks staying together during summer and fall right up until the rut begins.

The movements for which mule deer—some of them—are famous are their seasonal migrations. These are rather similar to the migrations of elk, and are caused by a need to leave the deep snows of the high country and drop down to lower elevations to a winter range. By no means do all mule deer follow this routine. The Columbian blacktails of the Pacific slope seldom need to. Some do move lower, and there are instances where mule deer move at least a short distance when they really have no need to. This is thought to be an influence from the past, perhaps based genetically.

In desert ranges there is seldom any seasonal migration. There is not enough vertical difference in altitude—often only a couple of thousand feet—to make any difference. The deer utilize the same

range around the year. However, in the true high country of the
Rockies most mule deer follow the seasonal migration pattern.
Many of these movements are famous. In Colorado, for example, for
many years hunters in several areas—Meeker is a renowned one—
awaited the downward drift of the deer in order to collect a trophy.
The ancestral routes are in such cases well established, and every
fall as soon as snow obliterates forage up high, the deer move down
to their traditional winter range.

Often a winter range may be crowded, with herds from several
sectors of nearby mountains utilizing it. In some instances late-
season hunters have looked over as many as fifty trophy-size bucks
on a wintering ground in a couple of days, in an area of only a few
square miles. Some of the classic migrations in the west cover long
distances. Instead of simply moving down to lower altitude on the
same mountain, an entire herd may travel as far as 100 miles.

The fall migration may be slow, if the weather is not too severe,
or it may be a forced march under pressure of high-country blizzards. The return in spring, however, is usually much slower. Now
new growth moves up the slopes as snow melts and the temperature rises progressively, week by week, creeping higher and higher
up the mountains. There is good forage appearing now step by step
in altitude, and the deer move with its explosive growth to their
final summer range. Many of the bucks arrive first. Does heavy
with fawns lag somewhat behind.

**BREEDING**

Summer in the high country is never long. By September bucks
are rubbing the dried velvet from their antlers and polishing them.
The deer are now fat and sleek. A change slowly comes to them.
Bucks may lie chewing a cud and watching intently a group of does
and fawns nearby. The actual beginning time of the rut depends
upon latitude, and to some extent upon weather. In northern latitudes breeding season is in progress about middle to late October.
It may last in some instances into December. In southern portions
of mule deer range the rut may not begin until November, and run
on into January.

Scientists have found that the period of first severe winter
storms in the mountains assists in triggering mating. Cool weather
and a low barometer seem to presage mating activities. Deer that
make migrations to winter range may be breeding along the way.
Just as the does come into heat for only a brief period—twenty-four

to thirty hours — every twenty-eight days, not all bucks are in rut at once. This is why the breeding season may extend over a fairly long period. It also virtually assures that all does will eventually be bred.

Although mule deer bucks are determined, their personality even at this important time of year is less frenzied and volatile than that of the whitetail. Their necks swell, they cease to be as gregarious among their own sex as previously, yet not as many serious battles ensue. On occasion several bucks may pursue a doe and yet not enter into any violent fighting. Usually fighting mule deer push each other around some, but after a few charges break off.

The does also are diligent, during their brief periods, in pursuit of bucks that may be haggard and therefore not especially interested. Commonly, in fact, a doe ready to be serviced tantalizes a lackadaisical buck until he acquiesces. Although mule deer do not gather harems and fight to keep them or to drive off trespassing bucks, they do sometimes consort with two or three does at the same time.

The bucks may travel long distances during this period, not adhering to the comparatively modest domain patrolled by the whitetail. A big buck may turn up far from country it has been living in, and even out in areas not of suitable range. It crosses such places in search of new conquests, perhaps on a distant mountain. This is not routine, but is fairly common. Some scientists believe such treks are responsible for the far-flung dispersal of mule deer and at times for the expansion of their range. Conversely, in individual instances where deer are plentiful, a big range bull or a buck may live on and around the base of a small rock outcrop covering little more than a half-section. It will be there all summer and will not leave it during the rut. Thus is a blood line passed along to progeny at that site. Just as cattle bred to an exceptional bull drop calves to match, an especially big, vigorous, heavy-antlered mule deer buck passes along his own extraordinary qualifications. In several years another exceptional buck will replace him.

The tarsal gland on the inside of the hind legs at the hock secretes a strong, distinctive musk during the rut. Hunters often remove these with a patch of surrounding skin to avoid getting any of the wet secretion or its odor on the meat. Incidentally, a mark of distinction between mule deer and whitetail is the color difference in the hair surrounding the metatarsal gland, on the outside of the lower hind leg. In whitetails the hair is ordinarily white or at least mixed with white. In mule deer it is brown.

In the chapter on whitetails the hunting technique of rattling antlers to simulate a buck fight and lure bucks to it was described. The rather gentler—or at least calmer—nature of the mule deer precludes such ready response. Experiments in rattling up mule deer have never been very successful. Some hunters believe this is because the rut falls at a different period, often outside hunting season. The fact is, most bucks just aren't that interested in getting into a fight. Does are seldom scarce and the rut is simply not that competitive. Curiously, however, mule deer will sometimes rush wildly to the wail of a hunter blowing a predator call. Possibly they mistake it for the anguished bleat of a young deer in trouble.

After breeding season is finished the bucks lose whatever belligerence they have nurtured during it and revert to their old habits. They are now thin and without great spirit. By about the middle of January in the southern part of the range, and a month earlier in the north, the antlers loosen and drop off. There is now little sex distinction or grouping. The serious business of eking out a living on the winter range or on a depleted year-round range now requires full attention. Bucks, does, and fawns now intermingle freely and with only mild bickering.

### BIRTH AND DEVELOPMENT

By the time spring has arrived and the movement back to the summer range has been completed, the fawns are born. Whether or not a migration is made, the fawning period is roughly the same, from late June on into July. The fawns are born about seven months from the time the does were bred. Interestingly, this gestation period is on the average some two weeks longer than that of the whitetail deer.

Mule deer fawns are reddish, with white-spotted coats which presumably serve as camouflage as they rest in the grass or in the dappled shade of a thicket. Does giving birth for the first time normally bear a single fawn. From then on twins are the rule and triplets not rare. The youngsters weight 6 or 7 pounds at birth, have difficulty standing up at first, and are wobbly for a brief period. The mother coaxes the fawns to follow her as soon as they can walk, leading them to some spot she deems safe where vegetation will hide them. She leaves them, coming back every few hours to allow them to nurse.

It is an interesting commentary on planning or evolution in nature that in a few exceedingly arid locations at the far-southern end of mule deer range, the rut is much later in winter. This guarantees that the fawns will be born much later, during the one period of the year when most rains, and therefore the best opportunities for foraging, occur. It is also interesting that the milk of deer, whose young lead a most precarious and rugged existence during the nursing period and need extra sustenance, is from two to three times richer than that of domestic cattle.

The fawns stay in or very near the spot where their mother has taken them for ten days to two weeks. Then they are strong enough to follow her, and soon they are sampling the vegetation they see their mother eating. However, they continue nursing on into early fall. At that time they begin to shed their spotted coats. The new hair which comes in is their first gray winter coat. There seems to be good planning here, too. This coat is somewhat shaggy, whereas winter coats of adult mule deer, though thick, are beautifully smooth and glossy. The youngsters are not as well prepared for winter as the adults, and thus need this little extra protection from weather.

As stated in other chapters, deer are not especially vocal creatures. However, mule deer fawns bleat like lambs when strayed from their mother. The does also "talk" occasionally, uttering a deep-pitched, coarse blatt. Mule deer also snort by blowing out air through the nose, similar to whitetails. However, although it is believed that young mule deer may bleat more than young whitetails, both adult sexes seldom are as inclined as whitetails to snort when disturbed.

By the time the winter coats of the fawns have come in, the young deer are usually weaned. They continue to follow their mother, however, and it is now that quite often large groups of does, fawns, and a scattering of young or forkhorn bucks consort. Meanwhile, the adult bucks have been off by themselves, not always seeming to avoid the others but simply spending their time as loners—particularly old bucks—or with a few of their own sex and general age group. During the rut the fawns of the year get in the way and a buck may run at them, grunting, or even give them a prod with his antlers. He is no real danger to them. The young are simply a distraction.

The fawns stay with the mother throughout the winter, and large mixed groups are common. When she is ready to give birth again, if the yearlings have not begun to wander off, she drives them away. Later, after the new fawns are tagging along, whether or not the same yearlings rejoin the same doe or not is questionable. Some probably do. Others simply tag along with the group.

During the summer the antlers of the bucks are in the thick, soft velvet stage. Young bucks are growing their first ones. Forkhorns are very common among young mule deer bucks. This means antlers with no brow tines and with a simple fork on each one. Most of these bucks run with groups of does and fawns and make up a high percentage of the annual harvest in many states. They are easier to find, with the groups of does, and quite naive.

The next year a buck may have several more points, but the antlers probably will be thin. Counting points on mule deer, incidentally, is a confusing matter to many hunters and observers of wildlife because of the traditional western method. Most hunters native to mule deer range use a term referring to only one antler, and the brow tines are not included. Thus a mule deer with brow tines and with two simply branching beams on each antler, a typical mature buck, would be called a four-pointer—four on a side.

Where this can get even more confusing is with heads that have uneven numbers of points, perhaps four on one side and five on the other. Practically, therefore, it is far easier and plainer to refer to heads by counting brow tines and the total of points of both antlers, just as whitetail heads are counted. One reason brow tines are discounted in the west is that for some reason mule deer often do not have any. Further, the brow tines of mule deer are usually smaller than those of whitetails of comparable age and antler size.

In general, mule deer antlers show more variety and deviation than whitetail antlers. Some of it may be regional. For example, the first antlers of young bucks in the southern part of mule deer range show a higher percentage of spikes than farther north, where few spikes develop and most are forkhorns. Some mule deer racks just happen to form almost exactly like a set of whitetail antlers. A common formation of this sort is a head with brow tines and with main beams from which two long, unbranched points rise from either side, for a total of eight points. Such antlers when cut from the skull cannot be distinguished from similar whitetail racks.

There are also more nontypical heads among mule deer—that is, antlers with a conglomeration of points large, small, palmated, sticking out every which way. Certain geographical areas produce more of these than others, although genetic influences may be responsible. As this is written, the Boone & Crockett records list almost as many nontypical as typical mule deer heads, while there are nearly a hundred more typical than nontypical whitetails.

The best mule deer antlers are grown when the bucks are six, seven, or even eight years old. Trophy mule deer antlers are always

*The antlers of mule deer usually have a greater spread than those of whitetails. Typically, the main beam of each antler forks part way up, and each fork has two tines.*

much heavier and usually rougher than those of whitetails. As mentioned earlier, they spread wide as a rule rather than curving around toward or over the brow. Some of the spreads are astonishing. Years ago one was collected from the Kaibab Plateau in northern Arizona that was 45 inches! Spreads of 30 to 35 inches are not rare. A whitetail head with a spread of 22 inches inside measurement would be an excellent one, but a similar mule deer rack would be only average. Racks of 26 to 28 inches would be far more outstanding. Although numerous points are common among mule deer, among typical heads those of ten points (eastern count—five on a side counting brow tine) are considered a kind of standard for mature bucks. The antlers of Columbian blacktails all in general into measurement classes closer to those of the whitetail.

The quality of the winter range and of the spring growing season are directly related to antler formation. If food is scarce during the time when the antlers are forming, and the spring and summer are dry and forage is thus at a minimum, mule deer antlers will almost certainly be thin and pale in color. This is especially true in the desert ranges where severe drought is more common than in the mountains. With ample winter forage, and a lush spring, antlers will be heavy, dark, and rough at the bases, an indication of the vigor of the animals.

Color variations among mule deer are rare. Among whitetails, albinism and partial albinism are not at all rare; pure-white non-albino whitetail sports sometimes occur, and dark or melanistic specimens turn up here and there. There are shading differences from dark to light among the geographic races of mule deer, but these are natural adaptations, probably to the general shading of the habitat each occupies.

### SENSES

Like all deer, mule deer have an extremely acute sense of smell. They use it to great advantage. But their rugged, steep-sloped habitat causes them to adjust use of all senses to it. For example, in all mountain terrain the flow of air is upward during the warmer hours of the day, and downward as the valleys cool. Obviously severe storms may inhibit these thermal currents, but on most days they occur. Mule deer almost without fail thus move upward to bed after the sun is over the ridges. Like many mountain game animals, they seem not to expect danger from above. Meanwhile, as the warmed air from below rises, any disturbing scents are wafted up to them.

However, high bedding places are invariably selected where the deer can also see over a large expanse. Typical are the shady sides of rimrocks, rocky points overlooking a valley, or a wooded point where the deer can see out and down yet has two escape routes along either side of the point. Good observation placement therefore undoubtedly is a part of the bed selection. Like other deer, mule deer have keen eyesight, but they are not always certain of what they are seeing. Because they are colorblind, a patch of a highly contrasting shade—like the orange jacket of a hunter set against dark conifers—will instantly get their attention. The deer knows its domain intimately and may instantly realize that this blob is out of place. But if the object doesn't move, the deer is not at all certain what it is. The animal is simply alerted, and now zeroes in its nose, and its ears, to attempt identification.

Any movement is immediately detected by the eyes of mule deer. Because of their mountain habitat, they can watch distant as well as close movement. It may not disturb them unless a scent reaches them. It is indeed common to glass an open slope and spot a big buck lying in the shadow of a single small bush. A passing vehicle on a trail down in the valley below, or a walking hunter, will not necessarily flush this deer. It assumes it has not been seen. But it watches intently, seeing every movement and straining for scent.

Thus in the fairly open habitat where most mule deer live, nose and eyes are used together constantly. In the dense habitat of the black-tail along the Pacific slope, of course, the senses are used somewhat differently. Scent obviously is as important as ever, but hearing may be more important than sight on numerous occasions. The deer hears a disturbing sound and slips quietly away, circling to pick up scent.

As an aside, mule deer fleeing at a disturbance, particularly a serious one, even such as being shot at at close range by a hunter, sometimes exhibit a most curious trait. Let's say a hunter jumps a buck at 50 yards on a slope that is dotted only with scattered shrubs and a few small thickets maybe 10 yards across surrounded by yellow grass. He shoots and misses the deer. It bounds out of sight behind one of the small thickets. He assumes in excitement that it has gone on, and is at a loss when it fails to come into view again. What it actually does is whirl and plunge into the thicket. There it stands, absolutely immobile, watching the hunter. Its combined senses seem to tell it there is no escape across the open. Some bucks get away with the ruse. Many don't.

Without question scenting ability is the most acute of mule deer senses. Hearing is keen. Some observers like to believe the big ears are a development toward uncanny hearing ability. That is doubtful. Mule deer give no evidence that they hear more acutely than the smaller-eared whitetails. It may be that they pick up more distant sounds, but this is simply because sounds normally carry farther in mountain terrain.

### SIGN *(Tracks are illustrated on page 250.)*

Earlier in this chapter the track configuration of running mule deer was explained. The hind feet strike behind the front feet. In some soils it might be possible to distinguish mule deer tracks from whitetail deer tracks by noting this. Running whitetails strike first on the front feet, then bring the hind feet past. But in most materials, track identification by this method would be difficult.

Of course, over much of mule deer range there are no whitetails. Yet many states have both on certain ranges, even though the whitetails may stick closer to dense cover. Within blacktail range on the Pacific slope there cannot be confusion because there are no whitetails, except a very few of the endangered Columbian whitetails in two or three locations.

Most hunters firmly believe that mule deer tracks are much

larger than whitetail tracks. This is an illusion. It is true that most of the largest mule deer leave tracks slightly larger than most of the largest whitetails. The size runs roughly 3¼ inches in length for the mule deer to 2⅞ inches for the whitetail. However, mule deer slightly smaller match the whitetails. Columbian blacktails, although usually smaller than Rocky Mountain mule deer, leave imprints roughly the same. Again, geographical location would identify the blacktails, except on the crest of the Cascades or at other places where the two mule deer intermingle.

The plain fact is, however, that no reputable student of animal tracks claims to be able to positively differentiate among tracks of any of the three deer. The same is true of trying to infallibly tell a buck track from a doe track. Identification is not very important anyway. Within mule deer range the tracks of no other big-game animals would very likely be confused with deer tracks. Conceivably pronghorn tracks might cause difficulty, where both animals use the same range. Antelope, however, have no dewclaws—which show on deer tracks in a deep, soft material—and the rear of the antelope track is broader. Mule deer tracks do differ distinctively according to the type of range. On rocky and hard ground the toes are usually worn off to some extent, and therefore leave a blunt imprint. On soft soils they are more pointed.

Mule deer droppings, like tracks, are not easily distinguished from those of other deer. But again, this is not important. On summer foods that are soft and succulent, the droppings are a mass. In fall and winter when the deer eat browse and dry forage, pellets are formed, of varying shapes depending on forage type. They are from ¾ to ⅞ inch in length.

Like other deer, mule deer when rubbing velvet from the antlers break branches on shrubs and scar the bark or peel it off from a space of sapling trunk. Because of the rather open habitat of much of the range, and the broader individual domain of many bucks, these rubs are neither so abundant in any one area nor show up so prominently as those of the whitetail. The same is true of scrapes.

In some places mule deer leave browse lines on trees or shrubs. These occur as a rule only where they are hard put for forage, or where they have overpopulated. Because of careful modern management, this sign is seldom as prevalent as it once was. Other feeding signs may be spotted, however, that tell of a prosperous deer population. In western Texas, for example, slopes covered with lechuguilla, a plant that grows densely with broad, spike-ended leaves about a foot high, are a favorite feeding ground. The deer paw out or chew out the base of the plants. Javelina also do this, but they rip out the leaves and scatter them.

A caution about mule deer sign concerns the discovery of numerous shed antlers. By the time they are seen — chiefly in fall by hunters — they will be whitened by weathering. These are antlers dropped the previous winter. And, in any area where mule deer make vertical seasonal migrations, most of the antlers will be on the winter range. Thus an abundance of them would indicate a place on which hunting time should not be wasted, unless it is very late in the season. Oddly, droppings may lie on winter range for the winter, summer, and into the fall, and if they happen to be wet from rain or dew, at a cursory glance they can be confused with fresh ones. Thus, careful appraisal on winter ranges is necessary.

### HUNTING

Mule deer hunting has evolved numerous practices adapted to the specialized habitat and habits of the animals. The technique of locating a migration route and taking a stand in a narrow pass or other likely spot at proper season has already been mentioned. Knowing the location of a winter range and hunting it — given open season — after the deer have arrived for the winter is at times almost too easy. Deer are concentrated on relatively small acreages. A few states offer early-season high-country trophy hunting. This, of course, is on the summer range. Sometimes the deer are still in velvet. The hunt is challenging, because it is certain to be rugged, at high altitude, and with the deer scattered.

In general, because of mountain habitat, glassing is far more important when hunting mule deer than when hunting whitetails. On large ranches or in National Forest lands where vehicle trails cover much territory, many hunters cruise slowly along them, not so much intent on jumping deer — which quickly move back from such trails once the season opens — but pausing to carefully glass distant slopes every few minutes. A great many deer are located thus, and stalks made. The gregarious habits of mule deer are advantageous to a hunter. A whole herd of does and fawns may be spotted together. If one has an antlerless permit, taking one of the group is seldom very difficult. Young bucks may be with the does too. It is true that very old bucks are often loners, super-wise and retiring. But groups of four- and five-year-olds consort commonly. This makes spotting them easier.

Glassing open slopes with scattered cover at dawn and for an hour or so after locates feeding bucks. Experienced hunters never are eager to shoot the first deer thus spotted. Often a slow glassing of the entire slope will show four or five or even a dozen bucks scattered along it. This habit is an assist in selecting a trophy. Glassing during the day is just as important. Mule deer will commonly bed down in places that would terrify a whitetail—right out in open sage on a slope, or under a single juniper, or in the shade of a single bush or rock. If the region is arid and the weather hot, mule deer thus bedded will lick their noses to keep them moist. These shine in reflected light inside the spot of shade like a discarded bottle or light bulb. Looking for such unnatural shiny spots has pinpointed many a deer, sometimes a whole group.

Over much of mule deer range, hunting is done on horseback simply because of the vastness of the territory. It should be done slowly and quietly, however. Horses will frighten deer, in an area much hunted, and they will run ahead or duck back around. Prowling on foot after tying a horse is a better method, or else the hunter can have a vehicle drop him off and arrange for a pickup later in the day at a specified meeting place. Although glassing from valleys finds deer, whenever possible it is best to get above the deer or their presumed locations to make stalks. They are not much inclined to watch above.

For the hunter who is a crack shot on running game, prowling the shady side of the rimrocks during midday is a productive method. Fat mule deer do not like heat. A day that may seem cool to a hunter may still be too hot for a deer to be in sun. Sometimes they even get up as the sun moves and change sides of a ridge to regain shade again. When hunting the rims or in certain terrain the headers of eroded gullies, bucks may be jumped from beds. They'll duck and run swiftly, but an expert who plans his approaches can often collect.

The giveaway sign on standing deer in open country is the white rump patch. Distantly these may appear to be pale rocks on a slope. Glassing turns them into deer. The blacktail, of course, has no readily discernible rump patch. It could not be seen very far in the cover common to blacktail habitat anyway. When mule deer are startled and run off, most of the time they go up. A hunter not adept at running shots should hold fire. Even mature bucks will usually pause at ridgetop for a backward look. If the deer goes over the ridge or disappears into timber, a short wait and then a stalk with the breeze in one's face or across may put a hunter in range. Many a mule deer settles down quickly once danger is out of sight.

When hard pressed, however, mule deer will move back into remote country. Whitetails might stay on the same range simply because they are masters at keeping out of sight. Mule deer do not like disturbance and as a rule have plenty of vast territory into which to fade.

Some hunters attempt to make drives on mule deer. This is common with coastal blacktails. Hunters are stationed on a canyon rim, and drivers move along the canyon floor. This works fairly well if one knows the terrain intimately. But the deer are still quick to spot an opening and skirt the drivers or lie down and coolly let them pass. Drives in big-mountain country can sometimes be successfully arranged by placing a hunter or two atop a forested mountain where several draws run up from the bottom of the slope and top out fairly close together. A couple of hunters on horseback riding the brush and timber down low will push deer out. The deer will drift up the draws. If the wind is carefully considered, they may come right to properly stationed hunters up on top. By and large, however, the drive is not a popular method in Rocky Mountain and desert mule deer country.

Although hunting from a stand during a migration is productive, stand hunting is not nearly as popular with mule deer as in whitetail hunting. The mountain country is simply too vast and there are too many places deer may wander. Rarely a trail can be located going, perhaps, from a watering place up to a rimrock bedding ground. If it shows much use, this may be a good stand. Or there may be well-used trails leading from slope to slope. Nonetheless, cruising via horseback or vehicle and glassing incessantly, or combining quiet still hunting with pauses for distant glassing where the cover is open enough, are the basic methods of mule deer hunting.

Most hunters favor a flat-shooting but powerful rifle for mule deer hunting, and a scope either of variable power or at least of 4-power. Shots may be long in the mountains. Big bucks can be tough to put down. Although in qualified hands the .243 does well, any of the calibers comparable to the .30/06 and .270 are standard.

There will probably always be arguments between eastern and western hunters as to which venison is best. On the average a fat mule deer is invariably fatter than a fat whitetail. It is a calm animal, far less nervous. Undoubtedly this is partly responsible. As with any of the horned and antlered animals, bucks killed at the peak of the rut or immediately after are not very desirable table fare. On the whole, although both whitetail and mule deer are excellent meat, the mule deer probably has a slight edge.

As stated earlier in this chapter, the mule deer does have some problems nowadays, mostly because of the heavy thrust of human population into the wilder country of the west. But it is still abundant and certainly will be for the foreseeable future. Although the whitetail is graceful and revered, the rugged, muscular true trophy buck mule deer is without any question the most strikingly handsome of North American deer.

# Elk

*Cervus canadensis*

The American elk has often been referred to as the monarch of the forest. No title could be more apt. The bull elk unquestionably has the most regal bearing of all North American deer, seemingly haughty, arrogant, and totally untamed. The animal is almost perfectly proportioned, with not the slightest suggestion of ill design by nature. Although elk in modern days succumb to man's blandishments occasionally in winter — the offer of food when times are difficult — in personality this is the wildest of the continent's deer, a true creature of the purest wilderness terrain still extant within its range. Among North American antlered animals it is second only to the moose in size, and not by very much at that. Of the large members of this continent's deer family it is by all odds the most handsome.

Indians called the elk *wapiti,* a name which numerous staid references even to this day insist is the only correct one. Hunters and observers of wildlife have never accepted the term. Some of the early insistence on the Indian name stemmed from the fact that originally the animal we call "moose" was called "elk" in Europe.

57

Elk

This was a confusion to early settlers on this continent, at a time when elk were present and well known to them over much of the eastern part of the continent. To further compound the confusion, the red stag or red deer of Europe is close kin to the American elk, and rather similar in general appearance.

The elk of the present are almost entirely animals of the high mountains of the west, with only a few scattered herds, small, isolated, and only moderately successful, elsewhere that have developed from transplants within this century. Interestingly enough, large numbers of elk in the early west were creatures not of forests and mountains but of the plains along the river courses, for example in eastern Montana, Wyoming, and the Dakotas.

Because elk meat is delectable and has a flavor not at all controversial, the elk had difficult times during this continent's early settlement and onward even into this century. Elk were virtually wiped out in the east by meat hunting and human settlement. Westward, elk meat fed explorers, settlements, and whole army camps. Soon, too, elk leather was appraised as a valuable product, and hide hunters slaughtered tens of thousands. One record from Ft. Benton, Montana, notes a Missouri riverboat loading of 33,000 elk hides in a single shipment to St. Louis.

In combination with and following slaughter of elk for meat and hides was the fad for elk teeth, the two unique rudimentary canines or "tusks" of the upper jaw that match with none in the lower and thus have no known use. These, polished and worked by jewelers and others, gained amazing popularity not only with the Elks organization but with the general populace. No one knows how may elk were killed for this single pair of teeth alone.

Thus, because of all these influences, elk were brought by the turn of this century to the brink of extinction. There is no question whatever that the modern sport hunter and the game-management experts his money hired saved this continent's elk. From a range of much of the northern half of the continental United States and small portions of lower Canada, remnant elk herds were left in the early 1900s only in the general Yellowstone region, on the Olympic Peninsula, and in the Prairie Provinces.

Today, thanks to astute and farsighted management over several decades—paid for entirely by sportsmen's money—elk are currently present in abundance, which is to say they inhabit all terrain reasonably suitable to them, in numbers carefully tailored to the range and the forage available. No one knows the exact number of elk presently existent, but estimates that are probably quite accu-

## THE ELK

COLOR: Distantly, brown fall and winter, but in summer reddish-brown; fall coat, close-range, body much lighter brown than head, neck, legs, and with sides and flanks of bulls often still more so; brisket, belly, back line, neck mane nearly black; rump and short tail pale yellow-tan.

MEASUREMENTS, MATURE BULLS: Differs among subspecies; overall length 7½ to 10 feet; height at withers 4½ to 5 feet.

WEIGHT, MATURE BULLS: 700 to 1000 pounds; Alaska introductions occasionally somewhat larger. Rocky Mountain elk, *C. canadensis canadensis*, is the standard; Roosevelt or Olympic subspecies, *C. c. roosevelti*, slightly larger (and darker-colored); Tule elk, *C. nannodes*, much smaller.

ANTLERS: High, heavy, branching, sweeping up, out and backward; typically in mature bulls six points to the side, occasionally more or uneven by sides, seldom nontypical or freakish; up to 5 feet or more beam length, spread 4 to 5 feet; weight 40-50 pounds.

COWS: Much smaller than bulls, averaging 30 percent less in weight; generally paler in color.

GENERAL ATTRIBUTES: Exceedingly blocky; powerful build; leg-length-to-body proportions well matched; regal bearing; mane on underside of neck distinctive, very pale rump area likewise; stub tail.

rate set the total running average at upward of 500,000. Today, amazingly, hunters are allowed to take, after meticulous surveys, as many elk *annually* as were in existence early in this century—from 70,000 to 80,000 average—and herds everywhere remain surprisingly stable and vigorous. The elk story is indeed one of the several truly great wildlife conservation achievements of this century.

The races and subspecies of elk originally on the continent are conjectural, and not wholly agreed upon by taxonomists. The eastern elk, the first race seen by colonists, was named *Cervus canadensis canadensis,* and eventually the elk of the intermountain region became *C. c. nelsoni.* Generally today the elk of the Rockies and the prototype eastern elk are considered to have been the same. The original elk of the southwest—western Texas, New Mexico, Arizona —were *C. merriami,* Merriam's elk, now extinct but replaced by transplants of the Rocky Mountain type. The small Tule elk is left only as a protected remnant in the Owens Valley in California. In the southern Prairie Provinces of Canada an elk darker and with antlers smaller on the average than the Rocky Mountain variety is

# Range of the Elk

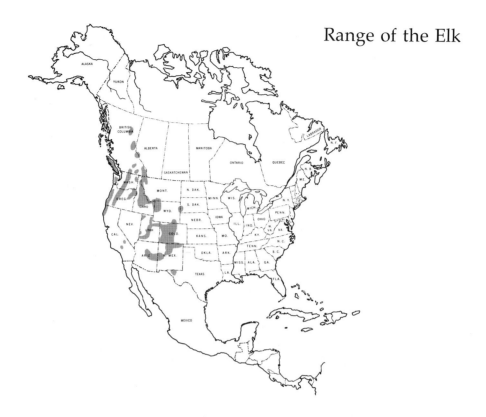

found, *C. c. manitobensis.* The dark, heavy Roosevelt or Olympic elk inhabits the Pacific coastal forests.

Thus the important elk today, by numbers and expanse of range, are the Rocky Mountain and the Roosevelt. The first is reestablished over most of the mountain states, and present in small transplant and token herds in such places as the northern Lower Peninsula of Michigan, the Black Hills of South Dakota, and a few counties of Oklahoma. The second ranges coastal mountains from British Columbia to northern California. Elk therefore are by no means endangered. It is doubtful that their range can be expanded substantially, but unless human interference destroys high country and coastal forests, elk under careful management will continue to be present in abundance.

Animal enemies are few. Some calves are killed by bears, lions, and coyotes, but predation is not an important influence. Nor is disease especially important. Several states trap sample animals from individual herds annually to test them for diseases. Overpopulation is locally the worst problem, where low-altitude winter ranges cannot sustain the number of animals that thrive on high-country summer range. Some starve, or commit depredations upon ranch haystacks, or must be fed, as at the refuge at Jackson, Wyoming, each winter. Tailoring herd size by hunting quotas is to date the best tool found to keep the elk bands healthy and vigorous.

### HABITAT

Elk in the present day are, as noted, almost entirely mountain animals. Both in the Rockies and along the coast ranges of the Pacific they live out their lives on the steep slopes all the way from above timberline in summer down to winter range in the valleys and foothills. Many of the Wilderness and Primitive Areas of the National Forests are among the most productive habitats for elk.

Although transplants of Rocky Mountain elk to such places as eastern Oklahoma, where the forest is heavy and the terrain hilly, have done fairly well, the animals are fundamentally attuned to a colder clime. A few large ranches in Texas have of late experimented with elk. To be sure, they sustain themselves and produce offspring, but they are never as lusty and robust as on their natural range, where summers are crisp and the seasons definite and often severe. Most typical of elk habitat is the mixed forest of the western high country. Here spruce, fir, and various pines intermingle with stands of aspen and other deciduous trees. Some of the conifer areas are awesomely dense, with jackstraw debris of blowdowns covering its floor. These offer resting places, and it is amazing how easily the huge bulls, in full antler, move through the thick timber.

All of the best elk range is, like most of the mountain country, interspersed liberally with mountain meadows, or, as some westerners say, parks. Fringing the meadows are the quaking aspen stands. This tree, which grows over most of the elk range, is in fact associated in the mind of every elk hunter or observer with the animal. But it is the meadows and the open grassy slopes that are the real clue to elk presence, for the big animals are primarily grazers. They are browsers only as seasonal forage conditions force them to be.

Far up atop the high mountains, where trees run out, low willows and grassy expanses, many of them surprisingly boggy, replace the aspen and conifer configurations. Summer finds many elk up here, too. All of the prime elk country is cut by swift, clear rivulets and larger mountain streams. Glacial lakes are scattered in blue droplets across the high mesas and the timberline region. Actually the elk of this modern day are confined almost entirely by the barriers of crowding civilization to the wild and more remote forests of the Rockies and the coastal ranges.

## FEEDING

In the mountains latent spring seems in the final moment to come with a sudden rush. Snow still lies heavily on the highest peaks and slopes, but lush grasses swiftly carpet the meadows, pushing right to the edges of the snow. Dandelions and other early flowers paint the slopes, the pale chartreuse of new aspen leaves frames the meadows, and every rivulet is bordered by varied succulent plant life such as marsh marigold and watercress. This is a time when elk herds, having moved from their lean wintering grounds at lower altitudes to pursue the upward-exploding spring line, have the easiest time of the year.

Ribs show plainly from the sparse feeding of the winter, and the animals, now shedding winter coats, look bedraggled and far from regal. But making a living is now a simple matter of gorging anywhere they happen to be. Elk are basically grazers. Throughout their range the slopes furnish a wide variety of grasses. Wheat grass, June grass, various sedges, bluegrass, needle grass, and many others grow in profusion on the spring-moist slopes and continue on through summer and into the mild early fall. Dandelions, cinquefoil, even the piquant plants of the stream courses are all eagerly eaten.

During all of the growing season elk browse hardly at all. They have no need to. In some instances they must share their summer range with domestic stock — cattle, sheep, horses — but seldom is there a shortage of food. Even for animals as large as elk, filling up at this season is not very time-consuming. The general pattern is to begin feeding well before dawn and to continue until the paunch is filled. Then they seek a comfortable, shady spot and lie down. Like domestic cattle, elk are ruminants. Much of the day in summer is spent resting and chewing a cud.

Late in the afternoon a second feeding period occurs, lasting until dusk. By and large elk are daytime feeders. If disturbed, as in hunting season, they may stay in heavy cover during the day and come out to feed only at night. They also feed occasionally on bright moonlit nights. In late summer, when grasses have matured and turned dry and yellowed, filling up is more time-consuming. Now some light browse is also taken, such as young aspen and willow, wild blackberry, and serviceberry. When wild fruit is ripe some is eaten, and also both spring and fall mushrooms, such as the morels so common in spring in western mountains, form incidentals of diet.

When the first snows begin, the animals paw and sweep away the covering with front feet to get at dead grasses. On some elk ranges they are able at moderate altitudes to stay in the same area all winter. But in most instances the bands must move, when deep snow comes, to lower altitude, to a winter range. Elk are extremely gregarious animals most of the year. Thus bands that live together on a specific range in summer move practically en masse to winter quarters. Both ranges are commonly ancestral. Generation after generation uses them, unless human settlement or some other degrading influence forces the animals to seek new feeding grounds.

The winter is a most precarious time. Winter ranges are never as large as those of summer. In summer a whole mountain range offers abundant food. In winter deep snow to some extent impedes travel, food is of course scarce, and confinement to valleys or other suitable wintering areas limits the acreage over which the bands may roam. Now they begin taking almost anything within reach—mountain maple and mahogany, berry bushes, sagebrush, the heavier twigs of reachable aspen. And at last they turn to the conifers. Fir needles, juniper, and other evergreens furnish a substantial part of the winter diet. Browse lines up as high as the animals can reach begin to show in the timber stands.

Bark also is eaten. Elk commonly strip bark from maples when available, and from large serviceberry shrubs. They also systematically gouge out hunks of aspen bark. Most elk ranges thus show a blackened scar line, from old gouging, along a stand of aspens fringing a meadow, and on close examination new scars beside the old. Willows along winter-range creek bottoms also are eaten almost to the ground.

None of this desperation diet is very nutritious, and all of it is difficult to digest. In severe winters the animals become very thin. Now disease takes its toll. Weakened animals die from pneumonia, and from infections caused by eating too much roughage. Starvation is common. It is a rigid rule of nature that the condition and size of the winter range dictates the size of any elk herd. If overpopulation degrades the forage potential of the winter range past the point where it can recoup in summer, then regardless of how

*Aspens in elk wintering areas often show gouge marks where the animals have eaten the bark.*

many calves are born on the lush summer range or how many animals the summer forage can fatten, the herd will be tailored automatically the next winter, by disease and starvation. This is why wildlife biologists make careful population surveys and set hunting quotas for both sexes. Good management dictates that herds must be kept at a size level that can be sustained on the winter ranges without unduly harming them.

Winter elk ranges in many states are in valleys where farms and ranches are numerous. Thus the elk get into difficulty by tearing stacks of baled hay to pieces, hay meant to tide cattle over the hard winter. They smash fences and become an intolerable nuisance to the landowners. Some states attempt to feed or disperse bands that cause complaints. And in some, state laws demand that the game department reimburse landowners for damage.

## MOVEMENTS

Elk are tremendously powerful, well-coordinated animals. A big bull can walk at a pace, when hurrying, that will lose a man trying to keep up. It can run with a bounding gallop at 35 miles an hour, trot for miles on end at 20-plus, hurdle a ranch fence with grace and ease, or even, when unduly disturbed and running, barge right through it. Supposedly "gameproof" fences at 8 feet high cannot hold elk determined to escape. They go over the top. One large ranch game preserve in northern New Mexico has to build an 11-foot fence in order to keep elk on its lands.

Although on a good summer range an elk band may stay in an area of modest size for days or weeks, distances in their vast mountain domain mean little to them. A group may drift along a slope or traverse a series of ridges, covering several miles for no apparent reason. When severely disturbed, as elk often are during hunting season in areas heavily pressured, a spooked band may take off at a run and keep right on going clear out of that part of the country, moving at a swift trot as much as 10 miles. There is an inherent wildness in elk more pronounced than in other deer.

In summer, of course, there is not often much disturbance in the high and remote wilderness country. A feeding and travel bailiwick of a few square miles will contain a resident elk population. The daily routine is to feed through the cool dawn and shortly after, then retire to timber or to a knoll from which vision is possible over a wide expanse, and rising thermals bring scents that might indicate danger. Here they bed down, and chew the cud. In the alpine meadows where most elk summer, insects are not present in irritating numbers, and breezes always blow.

Trips are made to water, but these seldom entail any long travel. Elk country is laced by streams large and small, and small lakes are often numerous. Elk are strong swimmers, and seem to enjoy splashing and rolling in cold high-country waters in summer, even occasionally swimming across a lake apparently just to get to the other side. Salt licks, commonly found in moist places or beside lakes and streams, are visited often. Ordinarily these do not show visual evidence of salt, but the earth contains it and the animals chew it, or gulp soupy muck.

When the bulls are in full antler, they are capable of slipping through dense timber with uncanny ease, often seeming not to touch a branch as they move. The nose is held high and the antlers laid along the back. In fact, heavy-antlered bulls can run all-out through timber the same way, without catching a tine on a branch. When running, all elk, even the cows, hold the nose characteristically high and outstretched, as if alert to every sound and scent carried down the breeze.

Although there is some separation of the sexes during summer months, there are no special movements to keep apart. Several bulls may hang around together, cows and calves consort, but the herd instinct, the gregarious nature, is still strong. Elk in this respect are much like cattle.

It is when first snows come to the highest summer range that the truly distinctive movement of the elk bands begins. The animals start to drift downward, sensing that food in the alpine meadows will soon be covered by deep snow. The rut still takes place in the high country, but usually well below timberline, down in the aspens, conifers, and meadows at middle elevations. But finally the exodus to the winter range is launched in earnest. This is a phenomenon like none other in nature. Some animals, such as mule deer in high mountains, make seasonal migrations. But seldom are the movements as long as those of the longest elk treks.

As noted earlier, not all elk herds find it necessary to make the downward migration. In a few specialized instances summer and winter ranges are one. Nor do all that travel move the same average distance. For some groups the trek is only a few downhill miles. But for others the ancestral routes, followed in some instances almost exactly year after year, may be anywhere from 25 to 100 miles. These long vertical migrations are of course more common among Rocky Mountain elk than those of the Roosevelt race, which dwell in a much milder climate.

In general, when the downward drift first starts, small groups of bulls move together. Straggling along behind come the cows and calves. There may be anywhere from a dozen to fifty of those moving together. As the rut begins the bulls scatter and take over their harems, then after the rut is finished the urgency to reach the winter range sends all the animals down toward the lower valleys. Because of human instrusion, numerous established migration routes have been cut off or changed, or the elk have been forced to winter on ranch lands or in some cases — as in Jackson, Wyoming — on refuges.

On some migration routes, individual groups from several series of summer-range and breeding-range slopes and ridges join as they move. The movement is chiefly during the hours of darkness. Then, if a slope or upper valley has been reached by dawn that offers ample forage, the herd may pause to feed and rest a day or so before moving on again toward the lower valleys. On some winter ranges a number of herds are forced to join. During the peak of the movement as many as a hundred or more elk may be traveling together. Weather conditions during any particular fall dictate the speed or casualness of the movement, and how bunched or strung out the elk may be.

When spring finally touches the valleys, the reverse trip begins. This one may not be as hurried. Forage growth moves progressively up the slopes, and the animals can move with it, feeding as they go. Now, too, most of the cows are heavy with their calves. Here and there a number will drop out of the band at moderate elevations to give birth and then later on move upward to the higher altitudes the bulls and the yearlings have long since reached.

## BREEDING

During August there is already a promise of coming fall in the mountain air. Bulls that have grown fat together and placidly consorted over the summer begin to be edgy as the velvet shrivels and dries on their now-hardened antlers. They rub off the velvet and polish and clean their antlers, using spruce or other conifer saplings about 2 inches in trunk diameter as favorite rubbing trees. Then after the antlers are cleaned they begin to rip at brush and trees in mock fights.

It seems fitting that the breeding season for elk is the most beautiful time of year over most of its range. Aspens draw stunning swaths of gold across the slopes by middle to late September, first snows may lightly cloak the highest peaks, and the dark conifers form a backdrop to set off the beauty of the frost-touched landscape. Necks of the bulls, now engorged with blood, are swollen. They begin gathering harems, and bugling.

The bull elk is a true sultan. No other American deer gathers at maximum so large a number of cows. A dozen, often with calves tagging along, is routine. Twenty to thirty are common, and big bulls have been observed with forty to sixty. Usually a bull simply takes over a herd of cows that has started to migrate toward the winter range. But if he can force others to join up, or take them away from another harem, he is ready and willing. The bull elk is a classic male chauvinist. He brooks no nonsense from the group of cows. Typically the bull does not lead the harem. He drives them along in

*A bull elk during the rut makes a wallow in soft earth.*

front, giving slow individuals the prod of an antler, and in no gentle terms.

The bull now makes a wallow by digging in soft black earth at the edge of a meadow or beside a lake. He urinates in the mud, wallows in it, plastering himself. A mature bull in full rut is a wild-appearing, smelly, raunchy creature indeed. Wild-eyed, nose running, caked sometimes with dripping muck, it urinates and ejaculates on its own hocks and belly, and screams defiance until the mountains ring.

The so-called "bugle" of the bull is a sound like none other in nature. It begins on a low, rasping pitch, rises as the animal stretches out its neck and partly opens its mouth, and ascends across several octaves, breaking then and dropping to a grating, harsh scream, all of this followed by one or more rough coughs or grunts. At a distance there is a bell-like quality, but at close range it is a hair-raising sound.

Bulls have quite individual voices. Spikes have a reedy quality, but old, mature bulls are far louder and awesomely rough. Hunters learn to distinguish the sounds of the big bulls, and upon this bugling during rut is based the technique of calling bulls by using a "whistle" made to imitate the bugle. To a listening bull the sound is both a challenge and a warning. A lone bull may come to it, imagining he is going to be able to steal a part of a harem.

The bulls eat little if at all during the rut, which lasts from four to six weeks. They patrol the harem fringes and incessantly service cows as they come in heat. The highest activity is at dawn and during late afternoon, although bugling may occasionally be heard, usually by a harem-less bull, at any time of day. There are always smaller bulls hanging around the fringes of the harem. The old sultan charges them, but he tries to avoid lengthy battles because this is the perfect opportunity for yet another bull to run off his cows.

Young bulls seldom have the spirit to take on a big one in his prime. On occasion, however, two fairly evenly matched do enter all-out battle. The scene is one of primitive fury and ruthlessness. Now and then a bull is seriously hurt, or a sultan, beginning to grow past his prime, is deposed. On rare occasions antlers become locked and the bulls die, of broken necks or simply because neither can twist free. Antlers are often broken during fights. Numerous quick-trigger hunters have been disappointed to walk up to what they thought was a stunning trophy only to find half an antler snapped off.

Most elk calls used by hunters are tuned to mimic the thin, reedy sound of a spike—that is, a youngster with its first set of nonbranching antlers. Having these pipsqueaks hang around and challenge them infuriates older bulls, which love to make a run at the youths. When a mature but still young bull does gather a harem, it commonly gives up its claim in a hurry if a big fellow moves in.

When the harem-gathering process first starts on a range where there are many elk, it does not take long to establish which bulls are the conquerors. An old bull just short of over the hill may take over a herd of cows and calves but quickly be deposed, without a fight, by some vigorous six-pointer. Or he may be challenged, attempt to fight, and be swiftly whipped. The old one then wanders the ridges, constantly bugling, but usually afraid from there on to tackle another challenger.

Bull elk are unpredictable during the rut, and short-tempered. They have been known to chase saddle horses and riders, to charge hunters, and even to become a nuisance around range cattle. As the rut period wanes, however, the bulls are more than docile. They are totally exhausted and bedraggled. Ribs prominent, a bull itching to fight and service cows a few weeks previously now all but staggers along, often with head low, barely able to carry its heavy antlers. Now the bulls must begin feeding heavily, gaining back fat, for winter is not far off. All told, the breeding period for elk, and the ac-

companying display, is one of the most rigorous in nature, a phenomenon of procreation unmatched among the larger animals.


## BIRTH AND DEVELOPMENT

Late in the winter the bulls lose their antlers, and as spring
moves closer the cows show irritation with the yearling calves that
still follow them. Some calves have already drifted apart from their
mothers. In late May or early June, with the movement back to summer range well started, the first new calves are born. Individual
cows drop off from the moving bands. Some calves are born in
dense thickets, hidden away by their mothers. Many cows, however, seek open meadow or grasslands where there is almost no
cover at all. Yearling calves move along up the slopes with the bulls,
the barren cows, and the few cows not yet ready to give birth.

Twin elk calves are not common. The rule is a single offspring.
The average calf weighs about 35 pounds at birth. It is dark, rich
brown in color, with white spots like those that decorate whitetail
and mule deer at birth. Presumably the spots serve as a kind of
camouflage of light and shadow when the wobbly calf lies hidden
in grass or brush.

Elk are more vocal than other deer. The fawns bleat in a high-
pitched voice, the cows reply in deeper tone. The cows also occasionally bugle, much like the bulls in rut but by no means as loud.
Cows banding together with calves in summer often emit a sharp
bark, a warning sound. And when groups of elk of both sexes and
varied ages feed or water together during summer they rather commonly utter varied bleats, barks, and squeals.

It does not take a newborn calf long to learn to get around. The
mother may seek a better hiding place than the spot where it was
born, nurse it, and then shortly coax it to follow in slow stages as
she seeks the company of other cows with new calves. The urge for
banding together, the herd instinct, is dominant. And there is
greater safety for the calves when a number of cows join. There is
little bickering among them. In fact, if danger looms, such as a
prowling coyote intent upon seizing a calf, the entire band of cows
is likely to rush the intruder. The animals are exceptionally brave
and determined where the young are concerned.

For the first four or five weeks the calves nurse their mothers,
but by then they are beginning to try nibbling at grasses and
leaves. The cows push them away now, allowing only brief nursing
periods. Calves protest vocally, but more and more the cows are irritable with them, and the weaning process continues sometimes

well into fall. A gawky calf now must drop to its knees to nurse, and the cow is not patient for long. The white spots have disappeared at least by middle to late August. The typical pale rump patch now shows plainly, and in a few weeks the long calf hair will be shed and a full new coat will grow in for the coming winter.

During the same weeks of summer the bulls have hung around in small groups, or some of them have remained loners. Their new antlers have been growing swiftly, covered with velvet. The long-yearling males — calves of the previous year — have been sprouting their first antlers. Except for rare freaks, these first antlers are simply spikes, from 8 to 15 inches or more long.

Unlike most other deer, the normal two-year-old bull does not go through a "forkhorn" stage. It moves from spikes to five points on a side, or, rarely, four. These antlers will, however, usually be rather thin and light. In the third year, if the bull is in good health, it ordinarily becomes a "six-pointer" — six on a side. But these antlers also are likely to be fairly slender. From here on each year the antlers are likely to remain six on a side, but grow more and more massive. However, in some instances unusual bulls show seven on each side, or six and eight, seven and eight, or even one antler with nine. The true trophy elk are bulls that have remained exceptionally vigorous at six, seven, or eight years old. In record scoring today the number of points is not as important as the beam length, width of spread, tine length, and massiveness (girth) of the main beams.

### SENSES

There is no question that of the several elk senses the sense of smell is the most acute. In its mountain and forest habitat there is almost always some air movement, either from whimsical breezes that seem to bend around the ridges, or from rising thermals over the warm part of the day and downdraft thermals as the valleys cool. Elk in fact quite commonly take up feeding or bedding positions in accordance with these air movements. Under ideal scenting conditions for the animals, no hunter could get close.

However, two factors related to habitat force elk to use their ears as much as their nose. One is the broken nature of the forest and meadows, and the other in conjunction is the fact that air currents are forever eddying and swirling in steep terrain. As any high-country hunter or wildlife observer knows, a breeze may be straight into one's face for five minutes and then suddenly hit the back of the neck. Thus, although scent is dominant, it cannot always be trusted, and the elk know this. They are therefore forever listening, bringing these two main senses to bear to solve any problems of danger. Their hearing is indeed acute. Further, like the whitetail deer, any disturbing scent or sound is not likely to make an elk curious, or pause to wonder what may be wrong. It runs first and wonders later! But unlike the whitetail, if thoroughly disturbed it may not stop running for several miles.

Eyesight is also keen, even though like all deer elk are color-blind. Far from handicapping them, this undoubtedly makes their visual world all the easier to interpret. Like all deer also, the eyes of an elk are not well suited to properly identifying immobile objects. The slightest movement, however, is instantly noted.

Mountainous terrain broken into timber strips, meadows on the slopes, and open stream valleys are easy to scan over long distances. Any living creature that moves in the open or along the timber edges is certain to be noticed. Any danger moving through dense timber is likely to be heard. And if both those well-developed senses fail, the sense of smell seldom will. The whimsical breeze may cover an interloper briefly, but in seconds it may not. And when it does not, an elk even several hundred yards distant is certain to be informed by its nose. This battery of well-developed senses, added to an inherent wildness to match its domain, keeps the elk well posted as to suspicious happenings within its baili-wick.

### SIGN *(Tracks are illustrated on page 250.)*

One any game range in order to recognize sign without confu-sion one must know what other animals are present that might leave somewhat similar sign. In elk range there are deer, but tracks and droppings of elk are larger and not easily confused. In a few Rocky Mountain states there are also moose. Moose tracks are larger, and not as rounded. Droppings are larger. Further, moose are not herd animals and so there are not likely to be the wealth of signs that elk bands leave.

Cattle present a different problem. Commonly elk and cattle are on the same ranges, and in groups. A careful observer of tracks will quickly discover that those left by large cattle are much more blocky and generally more rounded than elk tracks. Domestic calf tracks, however, are quite similar, but sharp observation shows them a bit larger than elk calf tracks, by possibly an inch in overall length, and smaller by at least an inch than an adult elk track. Tracks of adult elk measure about 4 inches long on the average.

It may well be that both cattle and elk tracks intermingle. To sort them out, look for droppings. Certainly cow droppings are not remotely like those of elk. When eating soft summer foods elk "chips" resemble to some extent those of cattle, but they are much smaller, at maximum perhaps 6 inches in diameter. On firm foods as in fall, droppings are pellets of varied shapes, always larger than those of mule deer and in lesser quantity than those of moose, with which some confusion may be possible. Elk pellets will be from 3/4 inch to about 1 1/2 inches long.

Hunters especially should keep an eye out for dropped antlers. Many weathered antlers usually indicate that this is winter range, for the antlers are dropped along toward March. Nonetheless, if dropped antlers and fresh tracks and droppings are all present, conceivably this is a year-round range.

Bark scars on aspen were noted earlier. These easily indicate how long elk have been using a range, by comparing old and fresh scars. Rubs (where bulls fight saplings) definitely tell of use during the breeding season. These further, when fresh, establish that a bull is in the general vicinity. Several of them around a mountain meadow edge state that this is a certain bull's definite bailiwick. Elk rubs are easily distinguished from deer rubs. They are at greater height, the twigs and branches are ripped over a longer reach of the sapling trunk, and the tree is usually larger than one a deer would select. Spruce saplings 8 feet or so tall and 2 inches in diameter at base are a favorite size and variety.

Salt and mineral licks were also mentioned earlier. These may not always be in mud. In the coastal rain forests of the Pacific, elk commonly tear rotten logs apart, paw at the under portions, and chew the pulpy interior. There are also wallows used by bulls in rut. In general the location of such a wallow is along the edge of a meadow, at a place where the ground is wet, with black dirt the deep topsoil, and with few rocks to interfere. Bulls paw and dig in such wallows until often one is a dozen feet across.

Close searching during the rut will turn up spots where a bull has ripped into tall grass and turf with his antlers, and also scraped angrily with forefeet. Back in the timber it is not unusual at any season to discover a cluster of beds, spots where the grass has been matted down where a group has been lying to rest. Because they are gregarious, and extremely active, roaming animals, elk leave a

*Stripped saplings are signs that a bull has been in the area, scraping the velvet from his antlers.*

welter of signs. The informed observer can make a valid judgment of how many and what the herd makeup is by carefully evaluating all these indications of their presence.

### HUNTING

The classic, most dramatic and thrilling approach to elk hunting is by calling during the rut, the bugling season for the bulls. It may not be the best time to collect an elk for its meat. Right at the beginning of the rut the bulls are extremely fat, and the meat is excellent. But as the rut progresses and they lose weight the meat gets tough and eventually, at peak of the rut or immediately following it, hardly fit to eat, except possibly when made into sausage. If the season for mature bulls opens as the rut begins, however, it's a fine time to be in the mountains, the easiest and most exciting time to bag a trophy.

Elk "whistles" are available from sporting goods stores. Some old hands make their own, often from electrical conduit cut into the shape of an old-fashioned whistle. The hunt begins simply by listening at or before dawn. If no bugling is heard, it's a sure bet a move to another area should be made. If several bulls are heard, the hunter generally works on the closest one. If he gets an answer he can soon deduce if the animal is moving toward him. Some bulls bugle constantly, some come silently. Some rush in wild-eyed, some sneak in. This is what makes the endeavor highly dramatic.

If a bull answers but won't come to the whistle, often it can be stalked. The hunter moves in, keeping any breeze properly in his face or across. He refrains from too much calling. As long as the bull continues to bugle, or answer, he prowls closer. Many a trophy has been taken this way as it stepped out of a timber edge into a meadow to peer across toward where the last whistle originated.

There is nowadays much hunting for "any elk"—that is, for a cow or a young bull or a yearling calf. Most states set antlerless quotas because it is necessary to crop the herds meticulously, keeping them from overpopulation A young elk or a fat cow is by all odds the best meat animal, and elk meat at its best rates with fine beef on the table. It is easy to take a cow during bugling season by getting a bull with a harem to answer, or simply listening for bugling bulls and making a stalk. In most instances a bull will be with cows. It's a matter of selecting the one you want.

Warm weather, or the period of exhaustion following the rut, often sends bulls into dense timber. Trying to hunt one in such cover is virtually a waste of time. A hunter cannot move quietly, and if he does kill a bull, getting it out is a terrible problem. Most elk seasons are set so that hunters have two opportunities: during the bugling season, and later on after the rut, even in December, when there is snow, the animals have moved lower down, and the bulls have gained weight again.

Some hunters carefully check signs and deduce that elk are using a certain valley or meadow. They take a high stand early and late, watching for elk to come out to feed or to pass along a trail. This is often successful, for those who are able to sit still over long periods. The majority of elk hunters operate on horseback. It is difficult to approach elk from below. The technique is to ride the ridges, watching far off below and across. Or the hunters tie the horses and sneak to a ridge top, careful not to skyline themselves, and glass the far valley and the side draws.

Elk can occasionally be driven, but this requires that hunters know the terrain in detail. One or two hunters take a stand overlooking spots where elk pushed by drivers working through timber with the wind must break into the open. Although this sometimes produces success, elk are by no means easy to drive, and are likely to know the terrain better by far than the hunters. By and large, riding the high slopes during the day under cover of rising thermal air currents and taking a stand early and late are the most productive methods.

In a late season, with much snow, tracks help locate bands, and also the elk will require longer feeding periods, sometimes finding it necessary to be out much of the day. A prime rule for success is to make every attempt to hunt where there are few hunters if at all possible. Elk will not abide much disturbance, and once they take to dense timber because of harassment, hunting is exceedingly difficult.

Elk are difficult animals to put down. They are powerful and tenacious. It pays to go well armed with a substantial caliber. Many of the magnums nowadays are favored, especially because most shots at elk, except when calling, are certain to be fairly long, up to 300 yards and occasionally farther. A good scope, and binoculars, and, if you are after a true trophy, a spotting scope are all mandatory equipment. So are an ax, bone saw, and proper knives for dressing. When a big elk hits the ground, the real work begins!

Modern hunters can feel proud of their contribution to the wildlife scene by reestablishing elk over practically all suitable range still available on the continent. It has been solely the interest and the money of the sportsman that have made elk available both for sport and for the nonhunter, the casual observer of wildlife. Happily, elk are by no means endangered in the present day, and they are not likely to be as long as their ranges can be kept from destruction by human intrusion and by industry. Elk management has bloomed into a successful and well-ordered science. The bugling of bull elk is virtually certain to ring through the high forests of the west every fall for as long as those forests exist.

# Moose

*Alces alces*

No one could possibly look at a moose without being impressed, first by its size and then by its generally preposterous appearance. At first glance it seems to be a patchwork of nature in a wry mood, ungainly, ill-proportioned, utterly homely of mien. Its legs seem too long, its feet too large, its shoulders far overbalancing its hams, its enormous floppy upper lip and snout ridiculous.

All of this, however, is deceptive. A more careful observation, especially of a mature bull in fall with huge antlers well polished and gleaming, produces an altogether different impression. Here is a tremendously regal creature, an awesome reservoir of muscular power. Looked at with that view, homeliness fades, and one begins to realize that here is a creature brilliantly tailored to the harsh environment of northern wilderness, bitter cold, bog and forest in which it has for a million or more years been a successful colonizer throughout most of the northern areas almost around the entire world.

The long legs are precisely adapted to wading deep snow or mud. The outsized hoofs splay wide to steady and balance the great

Moose

bulk in a bog. They also assist in swimming, at which moose are masters, as they need to be in their world which in many places is as much water as land. The enormously powerful shoulders and huge barrel with ample lung room adapt the animals for tireless swimming, or running if necessary, and for plunging through deep muck and dense stands of arctic scrub. The more slender hind-quarters easily trail anywhere the fore end can go. Even that ugly snout is a valuable adaptation, in a world where so large a creature must browse much of the time on tough shrubs and branches to stoke its big furnace against winter's below-zero temperatures.

Although this animal lacks the grace of what we ordinarily call a "deer," it actually is a deer, the world's largest. Relatives of North American moose are found in both Asia and Europe. The moose of this continent easily runs away with the title of largest North American game animal. It is in fact the largest antlered animal in the world, and so far as is known the largest ever to have developed on earth.

As an animal personality the moose is a bit on the stodgy side, often rather sedentary and dull-witted, presumably with an intelligence level adequate only for its simple needs. Much of the time the animal is docile, yet a cow tending her calf can be a fury against an interloper, and a bull in rut extremely ill-tempered and fearless, even to taking on a train in battle, which has happened often in the northern bush.

It is a general law of nature that the larger an animal, the greater amount of living room each individual must have, and therefore, the fewer the total number. Thus moose are never abundant in any one locality in the same sense that, for example, deer may be. No one knows precisely how many there are on the continent, but across their vast range the aggregate of estimates from various states and provinces would put their numbers at somewhere between 300,000 and 500,000.

This is by no means an endangered species at the present time. Like all creatures, moose have their ups and downs of population. In Newfoundland, for example, to which they were introduced early in this century, an exceedingly high population evolved, then plummeted, but is recovering. Animal enemies of such a large creature are, of course, few. There are only three of consequence: man, wolves, and bears. Moose have always been a prime food source for natives of the north country, more often than not standing between them and starvation in winter. In modern times they became also an important game animal. Nowadays the total of moose taken both

## THE MOOSE

COLOR: Distantly, black; close-up, dark-brown upper area, paler beneath, lower legs grayish.

MEASUREMENTS, MATURE BULLS: Differs among subspecies; overall length 8 to 10 feet; height at withers 5½ to 7½ feet; height to top of antlers 8 to 10 feet.

WEIGHT, MATURE BULLS: Alaskan, *A. a gigas,* largest of the subspecies, 1400 to 1800 pounds; Canadian or eastern *A. a. americana,* and northwestern, *A. a. andersoni* (close to identical and considered so in trophy records), 1000 to 1400 pounds; Shiras or Wyoming, *A. a. shirasi,* 900 to 1200 pounds.

ANTLERS: Broadly palmated, with numerous points along outer palm edges; spread 4 to 6 feet, occasionally over 6 feet; weight 40 to 90 pounds.

COWS: Considerably smaller in all measurements, weight 600 to 800 pounds; after spring shedding somewhat paler brown than bulls.

GENERAL ATTRIBUTES: Long, broad, flexible down-turned snout; unusually long legs (from ground to belly on mature bull up to 3½ feet); massive forequarters with humped shoulders; comparatively slender rear quarters; pendulous dewlap; mane on shoulders of hair 6 to 10 inches long; extremely abbreviated (3 to 4 inches) tail; large hooves and dewclaws; comparatively small eyes; large ears.

for food only and for food and sport is thought to be about 80,000 annually.

Thus the moose is economically an extremely important wilderness resource. Fortunately, it is carefully managed nowadays in all states and provinces, with hunting quotas set annually after population surveys. Natural attrition by wolves, which is considerable, is not an important limiting factor. Bear predation is usually successful on adults only in snow that is so deep they founder yet hard enough to allow bears, with their large feet, to move on top.

The fact is, moose have lost little range in modern times, and have even greatly expanded it in some areas. This is especially true in portions of Alaska, into which they moved late in the last century and early in this one, finding lush food in massive burns that it is thought may have accounted for the large size of the Alaskan race. They also pushed down the Rockies into ranges—Wyoming, for example—where they had not been found by early explorers and trappers. Even in northern Minnesota, where once a moose was a rare sight indeed, usually a straggler from Canada, they have so successfully established themselves that several hunting seasons have recently been allowed. If the moose ever becomes endangered, it will be because of the shrinking of its wilderness domain by encroaching human settlement and industry.

### HABITAT

A glance at the range map shows that the habitat requirements of the moose are rather specialized, and that all their range has a unique sameness. Whitetail deer, for example, have been able to establish themselves in a great variety of climates and terrains. But moose have never been able to populate areas south of a limit of severe cold, or outside areas clothed in typical forest mixtures of the northern part of the continent—that is, conifers intermingled with deciduous trees such as aspen and birch, and those abundant, hardy browse shrubs of the north, the willows.

On the northern fringes of their range, moose do not live past the tree line. They cannot, because the foods they require are not present. Long ago the species did apparently live as far south in the United States as Pennsylvania, in mountain terrain with suitable tree cover. Over vast expanses of their range there is an immense amount of water. Some of the highest moose populations, in fact, are in the Canadian provinces and Alaska, in regions liberally sprinkled with lakes.

Here the animals are almost as much at home in the water as on land. They wade, swim, slog through swamps. They do, of course, live in mountains, too, in the northern Rockies of the United States and in western Canada and in Alaska. But this is only because they found the climate and forest cover suitable. Typically the home of the moose is in dense conifers, birches, and willows of the north, where in summer the ground is wet and muddy and in winter frozen and heaped with snow.

There are, of course, forest openings in many moose habitats. Mountain meadows and open valleys are utilized for feeding and movement. Huge willow flats of the north and even treeless mountain slopes make moose easy to spot in certain locations, particularly in the northern parts of their range. But seldom will a moose be far from a thicket of fir, spruce, or willow into which it may retire for safety or drowsy comfort. Nor will the water of a stream or lake, or the mud of swamp or bog, be far away.

# Range of the Moose

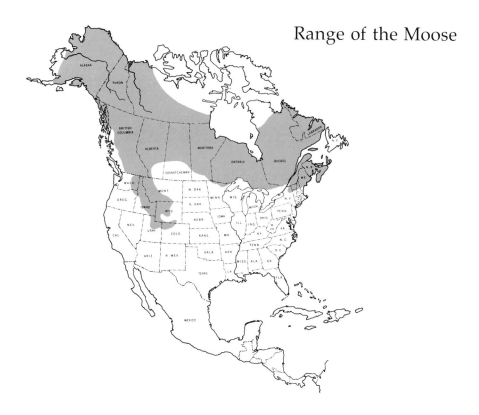

## FEEDING

As with all animals, gathering food is the main day-to-day concern of the moose. In normal years, during spring, summer, and early fall few food-gathering difficulties are encountered, the chore of eating is not especially time-consuming, and variety of menu, even in the sparse habitat of the north country, is ample. In winter, however, diet is likely to be spartan, travel to forage is occasionally limited because of deep snow, and the lakes where succulent greens grow in summer are sheathed with ice.

Fortunately, moose do not require any broad variety. Basically they are browsers, eating leaves and brushy twigs and branches as the season demands. The low-growing willows so abundant across much of moose domain are a kind of staff of life, a preferred food wherever found. These, plus aspen and birch and various conifers, are the staples. In fact, even during the growing season when a variety of soft plants is present, woody browse is the major part of diet.

Aquatics — water lilies, floating duckweed, various reeds — are a favorite side dish in summer. Floating varieties such as the duck-

*The moose plunges its head below the surface of a lake to feed on bottom-growing lily stems and roots.*

weeds are slurped off the surface. To gather stems and even roots of lilies, the animal plunges its head under. Wading, and feeding wet in the breeze across a lake, aids comfort in summer heat and assists in driving away the hordes of biting insect pests that swarm in northern forests in summer.

During the growing season the animals also eat varied grasses and sedges. But their legs are so long they cannot reach these without kneeling. A moose thus engaged presents a laughable picture, down in the fore on its knees, moving slowly along and cutting a swath of greens. To get at high leafy branches it commonly goes in the opposite direction, rearing up on its hind legs and tearing them off 10 or 12 feet above ground. It can easily stand naturally and reach up 8 feet or more. When desirable branches are too high to reach, a moose bends saplings down to convenient level with its snout or teeth, or it rears up and rides them to ground.

Along with the staples a variety of other browse is consumed where it happens to be present. Some of the favorites are alder, raspberry, mountain ash, ground hemlock, maple, and choke-cherry. During the summer not much use is made of fir, cedar, or other conifers. Those are winter browse, not as palatable or nutritious but serving when times are lean.

In winter they also eat bark of aspen when forced to, gouging out chunks with the lower teeth, which must do the job because a moose has no upper incisor teeth. Occasionally in aspen stands where moose are plentiful, bark scars, which turn black as they heal, form a visible horizontal line at moose-head height along the edge of a mountain meadow. Bark, however, is by no means a preferred item of diet.

There is no strict feeding routine. The animals may feed at night as well as by day. Normally, when food is plentiful, as in summer and fall, there are two periods of heaviest daytime activity. These are from before dawn to a couple of hours after, and again late in the afternoon. These are the times when one wishing to observe moose ordinarily has the best opportunity. Commonly at those times the animals are in the open along a lake shore or a forest-edge feeding ground. When filled up, they retire to a thicket to drowse and chew their cud.

Unusually severe winters occasionally have a disastrous effect upon a moose population. This is especially true when a summer has been exceptionally dry or cold and plant growth thus inhibited. As winter wears on, food becomes more and more scarce and snow piles up deeper and deeper. It takes a lot of snow to founder a moose, but it does happen. As the food supply dwindles and getting to it becomes more and more difficult, fat put on earlier is burned up in the continuous battle against below-zero temperatures.

In an ever weakening condition, animals are now susceptible to numerous diseases, such as pneumonia, and to internal parasites. Starvation is a real threat, and does at times literally wipe out a local moose population. As the animals lose strength, predation also becomes a factor. They are much easier kills now for wolves. Even in a normal winter, the quality of the previous growing season is directly related to how well a herd will come through to spring. Winter is the time when cows are pregnant. The spring calf drop is directly related to the health of the cows during those months. A

*A cow moose uses her height to browse on willow saplings.*

bad winter after a poor growing season invariably means a meager addition of calves to the herd. Further, it is in spring when the antlers of the bulls begin to sprout. A bad winter and a slow spring point toward poor antler growth, and trophies are likely to be few the next fall.

### MOVEMENTS

Notwithstanding its size and strength, the moose is not much of a traveler. Under ideal forage conditions certain individuals may live out their entire lives — on the average ten or a dozen years, an extreme of twenty — within a bailiwick of a mere 500 to 1000 acres. An area of 5 square miles contains the casual wanderings of most. In their wilderness there is not much disturbance. A pack of wolves may jump a moose in timber, forcing it to bolt for a lake and start swimming, where the wolves will not follow. During hunting season, man's intrusions disturb a few animals. But theirs is a vast domain and most of the time a fairly peaceful one where the huge beasts can afford the luxury of laziness.

The major part of the daily routine is made up of eating, making short trips to water, and lying or standing sleepily in a comfortable thicket. Sometimes a big bull will stand for hours in cover, its brain presumably in neutral, enjoying the utterly simple and pleasurable animal pastime of doing nothing. In fact, often prior to the rutting season, when all moose realize instinctively that they must feed well to put on fat to be drained away during the frenetic breeding activity, a big bull may adopt an especially lush expanse of savory willow as a temporary home, and gorge there for several weeks, moving out only to take on water, which is usually nearby.

This is not to imply that moose are incapable of fast and strenuous action. Far from it. The walking gait is one of long strides that eat up distance. When urgency of some kind breaks that rhythm, the animal shifts into an easy trot. An observer watching this movement is immediately aware that even in its ungainly configuration a moose does have astonishing grace. When the trot is accelerated by either anger or suspicion of danger, speed and evident power still further dispel any idea of awkwardness. The next shift in speed, when it is needed, is to a gallop. Curiously, these large deer gallop much the same as their small relatives, the whitetail, bounding, so that the rear feet strike slightly ahead of the front ones.

Moose are startling runners when under pressure, going full out for miles without seeming to tire. Amazingly, with their great bulk, they still turn in better time under stress than smaller deer such as the whitetail. They have been clocked with fair accuracy at about 35 miles per hour—trotting. A moose going all out in a gallop and unimpeded by mud or snow can up that, it has been estimated, by another 10 miles per hour! Unlike the smaller deer, however, moose are not jumpers, except under pressure. They are capable of clearing hurdles possibly as high as their shoulders, but they seldom encounter a need to jump. With their long legs it is simply too easy to walk over anything that gets in the way.

Swimming, previously mentioned, is a strong point. Moose commonly wade into a lake and swim straight across, covering several miles. Water, perhaps, is a shortcut, to save walking clear around the shoreline. They make good speed, and appear tireless, although occasionally because of misjudgment one drowns.

Whether from lack of fear and confidence in their enormous strength, or from low intelligence, a moose will plunge into a swift

*Moose often plunge into a swift stream and swim across.*

stream and go with the current while attempting to cross, or enter
without hesitation the deepest bog. Animals have been observed
down to the withers in ooze, bucking away a few feet at a time, resting periodically and finally making it across the sinkhole. In summer daily trips may be made from the forage area to a mudhole
beside lake or stream which serves as both a salt lick and a wallow.
Or the lick and wallow may be at separate spots and visited routinely. Wallowing in mud cakes the hide to make it impervious to
black flies and other biting insects. Muddy places that contain salt
are eagerly sought, and several animals may use the same one. It's
not a "lick" in the strictest sense — they simply eat the muck!

Over the flat to rolling parts of moose range, most of it in the
eastern half, no late-fall migration is necessary. The animals stay on
their home tracts around the year, often "yarding up" in winter in
heavy conifer cover, several together, and making trails through
deep snow that they keep open by daily foraging trips. In mountain
terrain, however, they may find it necessary to make at least short
vertical migrations. As snow piles up on the higher slopes and food
becomes scarce, they drift down to the valleys. Rivers and creeks
with stands of willow or alder along the banks are a winter home
and feeding ground. When spring greens the upper country, the
animals work their way back up to spend the summer.

An intriguing aspect of moose movements is that with all their
size and bulk even the largest heavy-antlered bull can slip through

cover without a sound when he wants to. Natives who live in moose country know this trait well. An animal spotted distantly and stalked to close range may not crash away noisily if aware of the hunter but simply fade into timber without a sound.

Moose are not herd animals, nor even especially gregarious. Bulls may be loners for months at a time, and so may cows with their calves. But certain seasonal movements of the two sexes are rather ritually followed. Cows and calves may cling to streamside thickets while bulls will be found scattered in the hills. Normally the two sexes do not consort purposely except during breeding season. In hard winters when groups band together in a yard it is apparently not a matter of seeking company but of finding the most comfortable, well-protected place.

### BREEDING

It is during the fall rut, or breeding season, that both bull and cow moose are at their most active, traveling more than at any other time of year. A bull now may roam outside his home bailiwick, seeking cows. He forgets all about feeding. When he strays into new territory he may wind up in a fight, or find one waiting in his own domain with a bull also crossing home boundaries. When a fight actually occurs, it is invariably between bulls of similar age and size. A young bull may be able to breed when it is about $1\frac{1}{2}$ years old, but the young ones know they are no match for six- or seven-year-olds in their prime. One may hang around, even when a large bull is with a cow. But most know better than to mix it up with a mature male, and the larger one doesn't have to make too many crashing runs at the youngster until he takes to his heels.

Bull moose do not collect a harem, as do elk. Now and then a bull may consort with two or three cows in a group. Generally, however, the bull is content with one amorous cow at a time. He stays with her a few days, then leaves her to seek a new companion. The rut begins about when leaves turn color in fall, which is roughly middle to late September in the north. Bulls have been rubbing velvet from their antlers from late August on into September, and polishing them, ripping at trees and brush in mock battles.

The rut lasts from a month to six weeks. When it starts the bull's antlers are gleaming, he is stately and arrogant, and his temper is short. Anything from a hunter to another bull to a freight train on a backbush line that gets in his path is fair game. By the end of the rut, having serviced as many willing cows as he can find, his temper is still short but he is spent, thin and bedraggled, often carrying his head low because antler weight is almost more than he can drag around.

The cow is possibly the most aggressive of all deer. Most are in their third year when first bred, although they may be mature enough earlier. The cow runs in excited circles, bawling hoarsely an invitation to any listening male. In fact, the breeding season is the only time of year when moose are especially vocal. Both sexes utter grunts and coughs occasionally at any time. But during the rut the raspy wail of the cow and the deep, coarse grunting of the bull indicate the excitement of this all-important season.

These vocal antics, incidentally, are the basis for calling moose by hunters and photographers. Natives mimic the sounds using a bark horn or cupped hands. Nowadays there are even modern recordings of the sounds, which sometimes bring in a bull on the run crashing through brush. Indian hunters even learned long ago to dip a bark megaphone into water and spill it out, to imitate a cow urinating in a lake. At this season that sound, used with the mimicked wail of the cow, often proves irresistible to a rut-crazed bull.

When one bull hears the coughing grunt of another, he makes no silent sneak attack. He goes crashing through timber, furiously swinging his huge antlers. This sound also is imitated by native hunters by beating brush with a stick to bring a bull into sight. It is interesting to note that during most of the year an altercation between moose is settled by rearing and slashing out with front hooves. This is a typical deer maneuver, especially common with whitetail does. But during the rut the bull wastes no time on such passes. He puts his head down and charges. Although there is probably not any great amount of serious fighting, when two mature bulls do tangle all-out their fury is startling. Now and then one is killed, or antlers become locked. If that occurs, both bulls usually die, one of a broken neck, the other because his victim is his own nemesis.

Wallows, previously described, are of a different kind during the rut. Bulls make them as a kind of sex symbol. On occasion a summer wallow is used. More often, however, fresh ones are made, usually at the edge of cover. Mud is dug up by the front hooves to a depth of a few inches to a foot or more. The bull urinates in it and on his own hocks, and wallows in the reeking mud sometimes until his body is caked and dripping. Probably his odor is a kind of "call" all its own to cows in the vicinity.

*When two mature bulls fight during the rut, their fury is startling.*

The seasonal occurrence of breeding is timed precariously, as with all animals living in severe winter climates. The rut for moose winds up around the beginning of November or a bit earlier. That is when winter begins to close in. Bulls must now spend all their time diligently feeding, to regain weight lost during the rut and to put on fat to be burned as winter progresses, to hold body heat and ward off cold. Cows must fatten swiftly to feed both themselves and their burgeoning offspring.

### BIRTH AND DEVELOPMENT

It is roughly eight months from the time a cow is bred until her calf or calves are born. This puts calving time into May or June when spring is well launched. Young cows may drop a single calf. Twins are common among older ones. The ungainly little creatures do not have white spots, as do whitetail and mule deer, but their color is quite different from their parents. They are red-brown, and weigh up to 25 pounds.

In the several weeks previous to birth the cow becomes quarrelsome and irritable with her offspring of the previous year, if they are still following her around. They commonly do stay with their mother all year, tagging along even during the breeding season, when they are a nuisance but are tolerated by the bulls. But now as birth time for the new crop approaches, the mother makes menacing rushes at the gawky yearling until in fright or perplexity it takes the hint and either drifts away or she sneaks away and leaves it.

At birth moose calves do not have the humped shoulders of the adults, nor the huge overhanging snout. The cow seeks a secluded thicket or an island in a lake to give birth, and she and her calf stay within a small area for several weeks. Calves utter low bleats and are able to run swiftly when only a few days old, and soon they swim with their mother, getting a free ride when they tire by laying their heads across their mother's back and letting her do the legwork. After that first several weeks close to the birthplace, calves go wherever the cow goes, staying near her from then on through summer, fall and winter, until it comes their time to be driven out into the wilderness world on their own.

There is a substantial loss of young moose to various enemies. Bears and wolves, and even the lynx and bobcat, account for some newly born youngsters. All during their first year they are vulnerable because of their modest size. However, the cow is extremely watchful and determined in her attacks on interlopers. Fishermen and others horsebacking into wilderness moose country in summer occasionally have hair-raising adventures when an irate cow takes after them. Unquestionably exposure, varied diseases, and accidents take a greater toll of young moose than do predators.

The yearling chased off by its mother to begin life all on its own is possibly now more vulnerable than at any other time to large predators, and to accidental death. It is at first giddy, confused, naive, bumbling. There are many instances of moose-country travelers finding loner yearlings not even wary enough to show fear.

Soon, however, the yearling begins to catch on. While it is becoming oriented and experienced in its new life, the mature bulls have been doing nothing much during the summer except eating and growing new antlers, which began as tender, velvet-covered knobs and take full shape with summer growth, after which with blood flow ceasing the velvet-rubbing and polishing process begins once more, in preparation for another breeding season. Even the long-yearling bull generally has his first antler-growing experience. These antlers aren't much. Usually they're simply spikes a few inches long.

At two the young bull pursuing a normal antler growth pattern has flattened forks. The next year his antlers begin to show the first

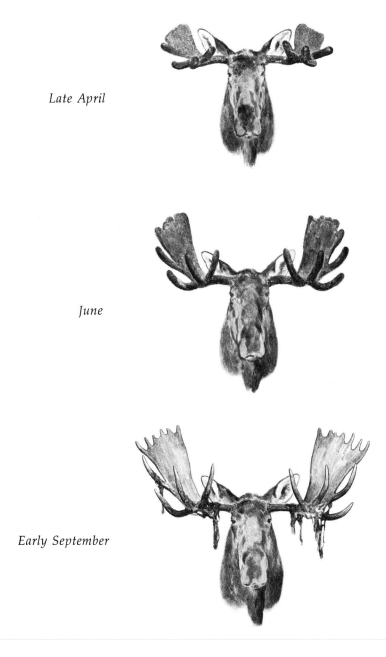

*Late April*

*June*

*Early September*

real palmation, but the palms are narrow, small, and with few points. Each year thereafter, if good health and vigor continue, and seasons are amenable, the antlers are larger and larger. At six or seven a bull is in his prime. He may, however, if especially vigorous, continue to produce still larger, heavier antlers for ten years or more, after which, in declining old age, the antlers retrogress. In sheer weight, the antlers of a mature bull moose are heavier than those of any other of the earth's antlered animals.

## SENSES

As in all deer, the sense most highly developed in moose is that of smell. Most creatures living in an environment that contains large expanses of heavy cover have an exceedingly acute sense of smell. Creatures preyed upon and living in brush and tree cover must use this sense constantly.

The same is true of hearing. Listening for danger is ever important. The ears of a moose are keen indeed. Conversely, moose do not have especially keen eyesight. Like all deer, they see motion very well, but are not equipped for, or adept at, interpreting the meaning of motionless objects. Sometimes they are not even very concerned with distant moving objects.

Part of this may be because such large animals are not especially fearful. Part may also be because of a rather modest intelligence level. The senses of all animals are attuned to what use they need to make of each. In cover a moose cannot see distantly anyway, and in the open it is chiefly concerned with its immediate surroundings. So perhaps it sees all it needs to see. Further, like all deer, moose are colorblind. They live in a world of gray. This is not necessarily a handicap. Conceivably surroundings all in shadings from black to white may make far less confusing the chore of sorting out objects of which to be wary.

Observers, whether simply lovers of wildlife, photographers, or hunters, must always bear in mind, however, that when one animal sense is alerted, the others are brought to bear immediately like a battery of electronic devices, all trained and tuned in to bring messages to the brain. Thus with its moderate seeing abilities, when a moose spots something to be even curious about, it begins listening harder. It may circle to get the wind on the object, a position from which it also can hear better. It is therefore equipped to take good enough care of itself—as its success in staying abundant on earth for hundreds of thousands of years well attests.

**SIGN** *(Tracks are illustrated on page 250.)*

Anyone looking for moose needs to recognize the signs they leave. Because of their size, all their signs are quite obvious. Tracks are, of course, one of the most numerous. Over much of their range no other hoofed animal is resident, so there can be no confusion. However, in some places there are deer, or elk, or caribou. The size of moose tracks easily separates them from those left by whitetail or mule deer. Caribou tracks are exceedingly distinctive, the two hoof portions spread and very rounded, with rather blunt toes. Some confusion is possible between moose and elk tracks. However, moose tracks almost without fail are much more pointed, and more narrow. They are also larger among mature animals.

The medium in which tracks are imprinted—for example, mud —often exaggerates their size and shape. But a clean moose imprint of a bull may measure, the two large hoof portions, 6 to 6½ inches in length. From dewclaw prints to front point of track may be over 10 inches. Cow tracks are smaller, by about an inch.

Tracks are not always a good measure of moose abundance. It doesn't take many moose to leave a lot of tracks in the places that print them most plainly. Droppings are a sign that give both indication of presence, and a hint of abundance. The pellets are most easily identified in fall and winter when the animals are eating little succulent, green or soft food. They are rounded or elongate, occasionally rounded with one concave end, and measure 1 to 1¾ inches in length on the average. This is larger than those of elk. In summer the droppings seldom have pellet form and may appear as a soft shapeless mass. The quantity of moose droppings at any given stopping place, such as around a bed, is invariably larger than that left by elk, simply because of the animal's size.

It is doubtful that moose beds, in either vegetation or snow, can be easily distinguished from those of elk where both are on the same range. Numerous bedding spots do give some indication of abundance. Earlier, the bark signs on aspens were noted. In winter when moose feed heavily at times on fir or other conifers, a "browse line" up as high as they can reach is easily seen in such a timber stand, with all twigs and branches cleaned off. Willow expanses show many broken bushes. On winter ranges some patches are overbrowsed until all but destroyed.

Wallows, used both in summer and during the rut, and salt licks are other easily spotted signs, although not as numerous as the others. On a winter moose range where a number of animals may be forced to spend several months, shed antlers, dropped during midwinter and usually whitened by exposure when found, offer evidence that the animals have been there and probably will be back the next winter.

## HUNTING

How moose are hunted depends on the terrain. Over the eastern half of the range, which is on the average rather flat and with dense cover, hunting from a canoe is a productive and popular method until freeze-up. Sign is checked along a lake shore or a stream, and hunters patrol quietly, the best hours early and late in the day. Glassing carefully and distantly is important. A moose across a lake may look as black as the upturned muck-filled roots of a blowdown, and be casually passed up as one. With wind right, often a moose seen distantly can be approached by canoe to within rifle range. Shots should not be taken when the animal is belly-deep in water, however. Getting it ashore for dressing is an awesome task.

In the west where terrain is more mountainous, hunting is traditionally done on horseback, with long pauses to glass surrounding country from a high point. This type of hunting may continue all day, watching for moose not only when they are out early and late but also when they may be resting in thickets during the day. A hunter on foot, however, if he is wise, checks sign first, then takes a stand early or late in the day where he can watch a likely spot for a bull to emerge into a meadow or other opening.

In either case when a bull is spotted, if he is out of range a stalk is made on foot. Keeping the breeze in one's face or crossing is mandatory. So is moving quietly and utilizing cover whenever possible. If stalking cover is lacking, the hunter moves only when the bull is feeding or has his gaze turned away. The moment the bull looks in the hunter's direction, he must freeze until scrutiny ends.

Throughout moose range, calling works rather well during the rut, as has been mentioned. Few modestly experienced moose hunters are adept at it, and they may arouse suspicion rather than eagerness in a listening bull. The majority of moose hunters are guided, and it is best to leave calling to the guide.

Many hunters like to go after moose when snow is on the ground, if the season is still open. This still hunting—and obviously it can be done at any time of season—is a matter of heading into the breeze, moving very slowly along moose trails, old logging roads, or lakeshores, or even following a track to try to jump a bull from his bed. One should go quietly, prowling, pausing every few yards to carefully scan the area within view. Often only the glimpse of an antler of a bull bedded in a thicket is seen. This is one of the sportier hunting methods, requiring much craft and patience. Still hunting or stand hunting can be combined with horsebacking or canoeing. Locating a good stand by riding, or exploring inlets with a canoe, is productive. Or a moose spotted distantly from a canoe can be stalked by keeping the craft behind a point to get as close as possible, then putting the hunter ashore for a stalk.

Moose hunters should never go undergunned. The great bulk of a bull dictates using a heavy-caliber rifle and large bullet—and not listening to the tales of natives who've been harvesting moose all their lives with a .30/30. They pick their shots and get close. A trophy hunter may not always be able to. In addition, any hunter should be sure that he or his guide is equipped with saws, knives, and ax, as well as rope and compact winch or other equipment that may be needed to get a moose into position for dressing, and then doing the job. It is a prodigious task.

In some places any moose is legal, or there are quotas of cows and yearlings. The meat of a young moose is excellent. So is that of a fat cow. A bull taken during rut is strong and a long way from delicious. Immediately following the rut it is all but inedible. After a few weeks, however, when fat has been put on again and it is "on the mend," it is good fare. The thousands of pounds of moose meat gathered annually, and the outfitting and guiding business based on moose hunting, make this animal an important resource of the north country. Management methods—lengthy flying surveys to check moose populations and the meticulous setting of quotas and seasons to crop surpluses and keep the population in balance with available food supply—give this magnificent animal every chance of a bright future, perhaps in some quarters even more abundant than ever.

# Caribou

*Rangifer tarandus*

The caribou is an authentic enigma, the most specialized and puzzling in personality of all North American deer. It looks and acts at different times both magnificent and ridiculous, intelligent and stupid. On this continent attempts to domesticate it have never been successful, yet its European counterpart, the reindeer, for all practical purposes identical to the New World animal, has been a domesticated, harness-broken beast of burden since early times.

Caribou are animals of the far north, where they live across the tundra far past the tree line. They also range southward into some portions of Canadian forest. In days of early settlement in the United States they were known to range in remnant bands into New England, the northern fringes of the Great Lakes states, and into Montana, Idaho, and Washington. The great herds originally found on this continent undoubtedly numbered in millions, and stretched from the Alaska Peninsula to Newfoundland, spreading northward across the Arctic islands to land's end.

Because caribou are extremely gregarious, and some of them make long cross-country seasonal migrations, all northern peoples since ancient times have utilized caribou as a staple of diet and the hides for clothing and shelter. Many still do. The herds are by no means as large today, and in certain areas they have had drastic fluctuations. They are not, however, presently endangered. In Alaska caribou are the most plentiful big-game animals, with total population estimates of 500,000 to 600,000. They are fairly plentiful in the Yukon, the Northwest Territories, and parts of British Columbia. There are herds of moderate size stretching across the northern portions of the Prairie Provinces. Eastern Canada — Quebec, New Brunswick, Labrador, Newfoundland — contains substantial numbers. Thus there are undoubtedly well over a million still left on the continent, and almost everywhere they seem to remain fairly stable.

The personality of this animal is anything but stable. It is a whimsical character. A big bull may be feeding along as the rut approaches, suddenly rear up with forefeet pawing the air, whirl and run off some distance, then suddenly begin to graze again. Sometimes hunters find caribou as shy and wild as whitetail deer. Sometimes also the animals seem totally addled, standing to watch a hunter make his stalk. At times, apparently out of curiosity, a group or a lone bull will walk right up to examine a hunter, or even a pack or saddle horse.

When shedding their winter coats, caribou look like a bunch of ragged tramps. Yet a mature bull in its full winter raiment and with a great curved rack of antlers is a magnificent sight, as, alerted, it trots at a swift pace across the tundra. But it can as quickly change, when resting, to a clumsy-looking, dumpy, ill-proportioned creature that seems to have no sense at all. Every time it takes a step, the tendons and bones of the ankle make a clicking sound. The feet are so big they're preposterous. No two sets of antlers on the bulls are similar, and a good many are not at all symmetrical. The poorly developed antlers of the cows look like an afterthought of the Creator.

The long migrations caribou make are as whimsical as their other traits. Year after year for some seasons thousands may move together along an identical route. Then suddenly some season they fail to appear, having for reasons of their own switched travel lanes. That idiosyncrasy is a serious matter to native peoples of the far north who wait for the herds that some winter fail to appear. People of many an outpost settlement have starved because of it.

Notwithstanding its odd traits, the caribou is a highly specialized creature almost perfectly adapted to its severe environment. In a land where it is one of the most important forage animals for the

Caribou

## THE CARIBOU

COLOR: Winter coat, body dark brown to gray-brown; sides of neck pale gray to white; mane on underside of neck gray to white; rump patch, underside of tail, ring around each eye and above each hoof pale gray to white; varying amounts of pale gray to white running from neck and chest mane back across shoulders and along flanks; color differs, lighter or darker, among subspecies; white ruff and neck grows more distinctive as bulls age; races in northernmost Arctic nearly white.

MEASUREMENTS, MATURE BULLS: Differs among subspecies; overall length 6½ to 7½ feet; height at withers 3½ to 5 feet.

WEIGHT, MATURE BULLS: 300 to 400 pounds average; exceptional specimens, certain races, to 600-plus.

ANTLERS: Main beams sweeping back, up, then forward; ends of main beams, and one or more branches from each main beam, usually palmated, and with several points; unique brow tines palmated and with several offshoot points, and set vertically; these brow tines extend over the face and are called "shovels"; commonly there is only one palmated brow tine, the other a simple spike. Curve of beams may measure 4 to more than 5 feet, with greatest width nearly comparable. Antlers seldom symmetrical, and highly varied.

COWS: Smaller; antlered (the only American deer with this characteristic); antlers much smaller than those of male.

GENERAL ATTRIBUTES: Clumsy-appearing build; chest and neck mane of bulls in fall striking; stubby tail; blunt muzzle, haired; horselike face; extremely large feet with hooves almost round.

large predators—man, wolves, bears—and where most of the year is winter and weather and general climate are seemingly unbearable, it has managed for thousands of years to thrive. Not only have caribou evidenced an amazing tenacity for survival in large numbers, they have meanwhile diversified over their vast range until they've become for scientists a taxonomic nightmare.

Seldom do two zoologists agree as to how many species and subspecies there are. Some years ago one authority listed three species and fifteen subspecies. It is easy to understand how variations in animals from location to location came about. Because of their strong herding instinct, and seasonal movements, over many years numerous individual herds built up in their own specific areas. These in some cases eventually began to show different physiological characteristics—differences in size, antler develop-

# Range of the Caribou

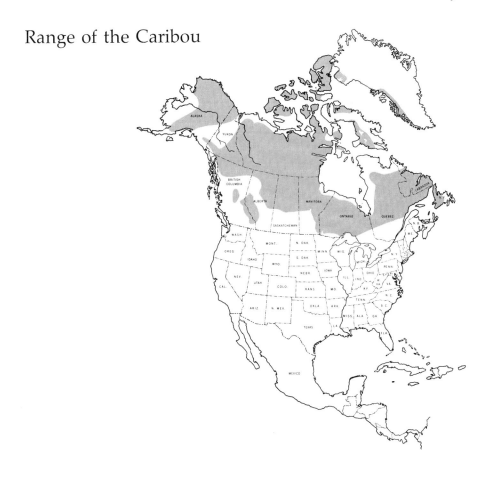

ment, and color. In Alaska, for example, there are presently eleven fairly distinct herds, ranging in numbers from a few thousand to over a hundred thousand.

As the herds anciently developed clear across the top of the continent, differences in habitat and geography produced animals differing enough that scientists who studied them first set up several distinct species, and then subspecies within those ranges. In Alaska there is the Barren Ground caribou, usually given the scientific name *Rangifer tarandus*. There is a subspecies on the Alaska Peninsula known as the Grant's caribou, and so it is tagged *R. t. granti*. Another nearly white race, the northernmost form, on Ellsmere Island and named for Admiral Peary, is *R. t. pearyi*.

Some taxonomists carried the subspecies system to hair-splitting lengths, and some still do. Some claim that today there are twelve subspecies on the continent, others that there are but seven. Further, the present most accepted opinion is not that there are three distinct species — the Barren Ground, woodland, and mountain — but that all caribou are of a single species, *Rangifer tarandus*, and that the three main varieties are all subspecies, and that there are crosses on the fringes of various ranges among the subspecies.

The Boone & Crockett Club, keeper of official big-game records, has undoubtedly worked out the most sensible system in trying to set up classes for animals from varied locations. Obviously they all could not be lumped together because of widely differing sizes of animals, and antlers, from different ranges. One category is for the Barren Ground caribou, with scientific subspecies names listed as follows: *R. t. granti* and *R. t. groenlandicus.* These heads are all from Alaska, the Yukon, and the Northwest Territories. Next comes the mountain caribou, listed as *R. t. caribou* "from British Columbia." Third is the Quebec-Labrador caribou, with scientific subspecies names the same as for the Barren Ground. Fourth is the Woodland caribou "from eastern Nova Scotia, New Brunswick, Newfoundland." The scientific name for this one is the same as for the mountain caribou of British Columbia. In general Barren Ground caribou have the finest antlers and the mountain strain are the largest animals.

Probably the classification puzzle is far from finished. Hunters still speak of the outsize Osborn caribou of northern British Columbia as a separate subspecies *osborni* (sometimes *R. arcticus osborni*), and consider it a strain of the mountain caribou, which some books list as *R. montanus.* The record-book listing of the Quebec-Labrador caribou is believed by some experts to be a cross between races of both the Barren Ground and the woodland. Thus, you see, naming of these eccentric, whimsical deer is as much of a puzzle as their oddball personality.

Nor is that quite all. In the late 1800s and early 1900s some brilliant government planners decided to import European caribou — reindeer — for allegedly starving Eskimos and Indians in Alaska. A few hundred were brought in, stocked chiefly in southern Alaska. There were even Lapland herders brought along to show natives how to manage the animals. Several decades later these reindeer had exploded to a total population of several hundred thousand.

During this period residents were encouraged, ridiculously, to kill off wild native caribou, because they attracted groups of valuable domestic reindeer and drew them away. It is said that thousands of reindeer were thus lost, and that the native caribou blood was to some extent diluted by that of the smaller and less vigorous reindeer. There are many tales about mismanagement by both government and native tribes to account for the eventual debacle of the imports by the 1940s. Whatever the authentic story, happily the reindeer drastically declined and the experiment ended. Conceivably, however, there may be remnant European reindeer blood in some North American carbiou still today.

## HABITAT

Across its vast range there is much diversity in caribou habitat. The names given the three types describe these quite well. The Barren Ground caribou lives on the tundra where all vegetation is low to the ground. Many ranges have no trees at all. Wherever there are trees they are dwarfs only a few inches high. However, these animals move down to the tree line at times, and some of them live where there are scattered trees but seldom true forest.

Some of the northernmost herds, living on Arctic islands not far from the North Pole, spend several months each year in continuous night, and of course several more in continuous light. Here vegetation is indeed sparse, and the land a desolate, unmarked, and seemingly endless expanse.

The mountain caribou has adapted over much of its range to terrain identical to that utilized by moose in the same region. It is in fact hunted along with sheep, bears, and moose. It lives on the steep, high slopes, often ranging as high as mountain goats. As high as soil goes, the caribou is found. In this mountain terrain, of course, there are more trees than on the barrens farther north. Clumps of conifers break up the lower landscape, and there are large thickets of willow and other low growth.

The woodland caribou has adapted to forested regions, just as its name implies. Some of this variety live in mountainous areas, too, but in general where there are trees. This is the caribou that originally was found in the mixed forests of the northern states, particularly in New England, where, especially in Maine, it was fairly common late in the last century.

## FEEDING

It might seem that in their northern habitat food would become a major problem for an animal as large as a caribou. However, there

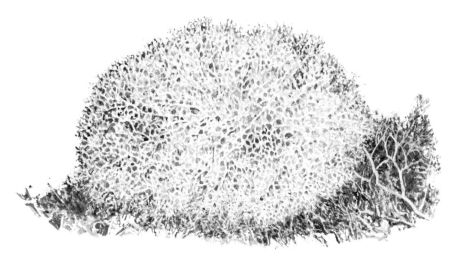

*Lichens from the main part of the caribou's diet over much of its range.*

are greater riches of forage than one might envision. The staple of diet for many caribou herds, and the item commonly associated with them and Old World reindeer, is the lichen usually called caribou moss or reindeer moss. It is a pale, spongy, mosslike growth of the Barren Grounds and also of much of the southward caribou range that grows anywhere from an inch or so to a couple of feet or more thick. Vast areas are literally paved with it.

This lichen tides the herds over hard winters, yet the animals relish it so much that they seldom pass it up even during the brief growing season, when other fare is available. Caribou moss, so some researchers have long believed, is one of the chief reasons for the nomadic wanderings and migrations of caribou bands. When a group is feeding it does so with concentration, each individual moving in a circle and cleaning up most of the lichens in reach, then moving ahead of its feeding neighbors to repeat the process. Thus any area where lichens are plentiful may be quickly overgrazed.

At these latitudes renewed growth is exceedingly slow. A heavily grazed expanse may take several decades to renew. Conceivably this is why caribou herds are constantly roaming, ever seeking new and lush forage, and why after several seasonal passes along a certain migration route they give it up. Their huge feet trample possibly more than they eat, and this is actually more destructive than the grazing.

Of course lichens are by no means the only fare in the far north. Summer growth over most of the caribou range is swift and abundant, and surprisingly varied. There are grasses and sedges, both staples of diet. The flats and the stream courses abound in low willows, which are eagerly stripped. Dwarf birch receives the same treatment. From midsummer on there are abundant mushrooms and varied fungi. Caribou are fond of these, although the nourishment potential is low. Blueberry bushes cover the slopes, along with crowberry, mountain cranberry, and bearberry. Labrador tea is also avidly eaten.

Basically caribou are grazers. However, the woodland variety has more opportunity than the others to accept browse, such as birch and willow. In some areas aspen also is important to them. Nonetheless, for all the races of caribou the grasses and mosses are the meat and potatoes of their menu. In winter, of course, they must take whatever they can get. The lichens now are more important than ever, and so are dead grasses covered with snow. The animals dig deep holes through the snow to get at them, pawing with flying forefeet down 20 inches or more to uncover them.

It is in winter that the long treks are made seeking food. This takes some herds from tundra to the tree line, where browse of varied kinds is available, and now of course they are forced to utilize it. In some ways caribou are wasteful foragers. Commonly they have been observed moving along at a fast walk, or even a trot, mashing moss with their ungainly feet and lowering their heads to seize a mouthful every few steps, chewing and swallowing as they travel. When they dig in the snow and trample it, the compressed areas become hard and icy, making further effort there difficult, so the group simply goes its nomadic way.

Except when forced to feed in darkness because of sun position in the Arctic, caribou feed during daylight hours. When the period of the "long sun" comes they may be out at any time. But when full, like other ruminant deer, they bed down and chew their cud. Invariably the bedding spot during the summer months is on a high bench or an open spot with a breeze, and on a patch of snow if any are present. In such places the animals stay cool, and swarming insects, a terrible irritant throughout the Arctic summers, are inhibited.

For many years the lore has been passed along that caribou use their flattened, vertically set brow tines actually as shovels to dig away snow that covers forage. Since the palmated tines never extend, even in the largest bulls, past the muzzle, and are in a plane

*Caribou use their sharp hoofs to kick through the snow and find lichens.*

parallel to the face, that would be a neat trick indeed. To accomplish it with any efficiency the bull would need to stand on his head. The "shovels" of cows and young bulls are much smaller, and calves have none. Double shovels are rare. The forefeet, not the antlers, do the shoveling.

### MOVEMENTS

Although well-antlered bulls in winter coat are certainly impressive, the caribou in its specialization to its environment is not as graceful on the whole as are elk and the smaller deer. It appears blocky and clumsy, chiefly because of its outsize feet. But there is a reason for these. The animals constantly travel on spongy moss, over boggy tundra and muskeg, or on ice and snow. They need both stability and utmost support in soft or slippery going. Thus nature has supplied them with feet far larger in ratio to their weight than those of any other deer, even the much larger moose.

The hoof is very nearly round. When weight is put upon it so that the two portions, or toes, splay apart, the track, quite unlike any other deer track, is sometimes wider than long. The front feet are larger than the hind ones, individual tracks as much as 5 inches long. The hind foot, when the animal walks, slightly overlaps the track made by the corresponding front foot. The dewclaws are very large and prominent and low to the ground, and in a soft medium give added stability; their use is more pronounced than among the other deer species.

There is a seasonal specialization in the feet. During the warm months the center of the hoof grows a prominent spongy pad in its center. This apparently buoys the weight in deep lichens or bogs. When winter comes, however, the sponge shrivels and hair grows over it for protection. The edges of the hooves become very sharp and hard now along the outer rim, and the shrinking of the center pad makes them more concave. The grip on ice or frozen tundra is thus improved.

When a caribou walks it appears somewhat awkward and shambling. The head may droop and the animal appears like some wildlife bum. It often stands, at rest, with head down. But when it trots it is literally regal, especially a big bull in full winter regalia. Now the head is up, the nose outthrust so that the antlers lie rigidly and unswaying along the back. Possibly because of its big feet, and the spongy tundra growth, the trotting animal raises its legs higher than other deer at this gait, like trotting horses in sulky races. The trot is swift, with long strides, and it is tireless. But when the caribou breaks into a gallop, it again appears rather awkward. Yet it is fast, going full-out probably close to 35 miles an hour. However, at this gait it soon tires, often to the point of opening its mouth to gasp in more air. Shortly it must drop back to the trotting gait once more.

As already mentioned, the ankles of the caribou are built so that as they walk or run the bones and tendons make an audible snapping or clicking sound. Hunters listening intently have located a herd of animals on the far side of a low ridge by picking up the sound. During migrations of large numbers the sound can be detected at a substantial distance.

The migrations are perhaps the most notable characteristic of the caribou. Although scientists have from time to time voiced uncertainty about what causes the mass movements, it is rather well substantiated that the need for forage sparks them. In summer most caribou are seen in small bands. The woodland variety especially is more solitary than the others. It is in fall that the animals begin banding together. As food supplies for large numbers of them dwindle they begin their nomadic treks seeking fresh supplies.

While the actual reason for the mass movements may be simple enough, native imaginations have been gripped since ancient times by their sudden appearance. A tundra can be covered with moving caribou one day and perhaps empty of them the next, with the observer having no idea whence they came and where they went. Eskimo and Indian legends note well these ancestral movements. Thousands of people of the far north have lived well over many winters on the "beef of the Arctic," which is among the best of all wild game. Thousands have also starved when, lying in wait along the usual migration route when it was time for the caribou to appear, none have.

It is said that during the largest of these mass movements bands have been seen with a dozen or more on the average abreast and thousands of followers trailing out for several miles behind. Hunters have ridden mounts over 100 square miles of territory looking for a trophy bull and seen not one, only to awake one morning in camp and discover the tundra covered with caribou. The opposite commonly happens, too. A hunter after a mixed bag pays no heed to the swarming caribou, because a good one will be easy to tag after sheep, moose, and grizzly have been taken. By then, however, every caribou is gone!

Not all herds find long migrations necessary. Certain herds trade about over their local domain. A few move north rather than south. Most move southward toward the tree line if they are on open tundra. The Barren Ground caribou is ordinarily the longest migrator. A 100-mile move is nothing. Some are said to migrate seasonally 600 to 700 miles, or even farther. Woodland and mountain caribou in general make much shorter shifts. Migrations begin as early as August, there is a pause during the rut a few weeks later, and then the movement continues.

Caribou are excellent swimmers, especially when in winter coat. The underfur is dense wool, with an outer coat of long, hollow, air-filled guard hairs blanketing it. This coat is not only freezeproof but also exceedingly buoyant. When caribou come to a river, they plunge in, swimming dexterously and swiftly. They cross lakes the same way.

### BREEDING

Caribou bulls put on an enormous amount of fat during late summer, to tide them over the rigorous rut. It lies in a thick sheath over the back all the way from the withers down across the rump, where it is several inches thick. Over the period of late August and on through September the animals grow their winter coats and strip the velvet from their hardened antlers. Although bands may have been composed of all sizes and both sexes, the bulls have been staying to themselves and together. But as the time for the rut arrives about late September, bulls that had been buddies a few weeks earlier are now edgy and unfriendly with each other.

Their necks are now swollen. Individual bulls begin acting a little bit silly, leaping about, racing off for no apparent reason, then pausing as if they've forgotten what they had in mind. By this time of year herds that migrate are well on their way. But the rut, which lasts overall about six weeks and in most latitudes has its peak from late September to the middle of October, interrupts everything. Whatever the intent may have been previously, bulls now have only a single concern, to gather a harem and keep it for themselves.

They cease feeding. Sparring among the bulls begins. It is the four- and five-year-old bulls that generally have the finest, largest antlers. Fighting grows swiftly until severe battles are entered. Each bull is now intermittently a wryly comic sight. Between bracing other bulls, fighting, running hither and yon disciplining his cows or trying to inveigle more, he is busy to the point of total frustration. Harems are generally not as large as those gathered by elk. A dozen cows form a large one. But the master is extremely attentive and ready to battle to retain his dominance. Some battles end in serious injury—loss of eyes, broken antlers—and occasionally in locked antlers. Many young bulls are discouraged by the older ones, however, simply by rushing charges.

Caribou are not vocal, like elk, during the rut. In fact, caribou of both sexes utter few sounds, except for occasional coughing grunts used apparently to keep in touch with each other. By the end of the rut the herd begins moving again, but the once magnificent bulls are now gaunt and bedraggled.

### BIRTH AND DEVELOPMENT

The bulls must now feed avidly, to lay on fat for winter once again. Within a couple of months after the rut, they drop their antlers. This is earlier than most other deer. The cows keep their spindly antlers longer, on into the spring. As winter wears on after the rut the bulls gradually get together again. Their groups, especially of older individuals, wander off from the cows and yearlings. Commonly as a migration continues the cows go farther than the bulls.

Most of the cows become irritable with their tag-along yearlings at least by April. Many simply drive them away. The youngsters then band together in herd-fringe groups, apparently able to console each other by their own numbers. By April, too, most herds are on the move again, slowly heading back to the summering grounds. As noted earlier, this is chiefly true of the Barren Ground variety. The others seldom have as far to go, the mountain caribou moving only higher up and the woodland caribou possibly out of the forested areas to more open country.

Late in May and on into June is the calving season. There is a most interesting adaptation among the caribou species regarding number of offspring. Twins are common among woodland caribou. This variety is always likely to have a less fragile and more assured food supply. Seldom, however, do Barren Ground caribou give birth to twins. Scientists believe this may be because too many fawns would build up herds faster than the tundra forage could support. Many twins, with fair survival, could double the herd size every several years. Few Barren Ground cows bear more than a half-dozen fawns in a lifetime.

Caribou are the only North American deer that seem to have little regard for where the fawns are born. Cows make little if any attempt to select a hiding place or a protected site. Wherever they are when the time arrives, they simply stop and give birth. This habit also is a specialized adaptation of nature. Unlike other fawns, baby caribou, though somewhat wobbly at first, are able to stand and run, and thus follow their nomadic parents, as soon as they are dry.

The fawns are not spotted. They are a uniform brown, with dark lower legs and nose. They are not very large, averaging 9 or 10 to possibly 12 pounds. But they are tough little creatures, able to cover many miles alongside their mothers. Some, of course, are caught and eaten by various predators. However, it is interesting that the wolf, with which caribou have lived since ancient times, seems to have little effect overall on ups and downs of the caribou population. In certain areas where wolves have become overly plentiful they are believed to have wiped out herds. But it is especially interesting that wolves are said to be unable except in rare instances to run down and kill healthy adult caribou.

Certainly calves do fall prey to the lynx, and to bears, wolverines, and wolves. But usually there are enough sick or injured or simply aged animals tagging along behind the main herd to keep predators filled. In general the calves as well as all adults are surprisingly healthy. As summer moves along, hordes of mosquitoes and black flies bedevil them. Nose flies enter the nostrils and produce larvae that go through a year-long cycle, living in the nasal passages, but these are not usually fatal. The Barren Ground caribou lives out the insect period where stiff breezes blow and snow patches may offer relief. The caribou of the forests to the south are not so fortunate and suffer more.

During summer the calves grow swiftly, quadrupling their weight at least by late August. Over spring and early summer the little calves look sleek, but from an aesthetic viewpoint adult caribou are at their worst period of the year. Great patches of the winter coat loosen and shed, or hang down, exposing the bare black skin. Soon, however, the summer coat comes in. It is much thinner than the winter one, in a shade of brown or gray. It does not stay long. Very soon the long, hollow winter guard hairs begin to appear.

With the adult sexes more or less separated during summer, all are beginning to grow their new antlers. Long-yearling calves do not form branching antlers. They produce only spikes, with no brow tines. Now once again, by August, the short summer is already gone. Individual groups that have wandered for some weeks begin the turnaround for another nomadic trek, or the mountain animals begin drifting to lower elevations. Once more preparation for the rut is underway, the prime bulls bulging with fat and beginning to stand off and gaze suspiciously at other bulls who have been their summer companions.

### SENSES

It is probably not quite fair to say that caribou are not very intelligent. Nonetheless, they rather often do give that impression. Perhaps the fairer view is that they live out their lives in a sparse environment where disturbances are few and where dangers of the area are well known and have been tolerated anciently, and that therefore the animals are actually a naive product of a simple environment.

The sense of hearing is adequate, but not especially well developed, as compared to that of a whitetail deer. The ears of the caribou, which are comparatively small, seem to indicate that the animal hears only what it needs to hear, and that is not much. Unusual sounds are not often present in its domain. Hunters have stalked sleeping caribou on occasion so close they practically had to prod them awake. Bush pilots report having flown low over dozing groups that either didn't hear or weren't interested enough to get on their feet.

Characteristics such as curiosity, naivety, and perplexity are difficult to separate and evaluate when dealing with animals. Because

caribou—most of them—live in an open environment, unquestionably it is their sight they depend on most to apprise them of
danger or unusual presences. Yet their distance vision is only fair.
And, like all deer, they respond only if there is movement. A caribou is quick to spot an unusual object—perhaps a hunter, standing
in sight glassing it from some hundreds of yards. But it has no way
to know what the object is, and oddly caribou in general seldom
seem to react with much good sense.

One may bolt wildly at the slightest distant movement. But it
may then come back over a ridge to have a look at what it fled from.
Groups have been observed in the presence of danger when the
animals scattered every which way, ran in circles, bunched up,
stood, snorted, pranced, and some even started toward the danger
to get a better look. This is obviously a sign of indecision. It may
also be an indication that the simple routines of caribou existence
do not require any high degree of intelligence, and that the animals
don't have much.

The sense of smell is acute. Because the animal is likely to see an
unfamiliar object before it can smell it, the eyes are generally used
first, and the very average sight, for an open-country creature, alerts
the animal to the necessity to bring its nose into focus. Yet even
here the animals can be perplexing. They may spot a hunter, for example, then circle, even at a run, all the while in plain sight and
perhaps in rifle range, to get around to where they can catch the
scent on a crossing breeze, and even then they seem confused.

Many guides with long experience in caribou country consider
them plain dumb. Perhaps so. Still, on occasion they can be most
elusive, and wild as hawks. Newfoundland hunters have often had
exasperating experiences with them. Hunt pressure in the sector
where the hunting is done may account for some wildness. It may
be also that solitary animals are likely to act more wild because they
are uneasy without a crowd of their own kind around. Certainly
their senses must be acute enough, since they have survived in
numbers over thousands of years in a harsh environment. Perhaps
a student of wildlife should consider their seemingly low intelligence and lack of sophistication as an appealing quality perfectly matching the simplicity of their lives.

SIGN *(Tracks are illustrated on page 250.)*

To the hunter, wildlife observer, or photographer, sign is not as
important with caribou as with other big game animals. This is
because sign does not necessarily mean the animals themselves are

in the vicinity. Their roaming habits preclude this. Except for migrations of some elk and mule deer bands to winter ranges, most big-game animals live out their entire lives on a reasonably compact acreage. Caribou can be anywhere.

For example, you might find several rubs of whitetail or mule deer, where they have polished antlers, and assume that the buck that made the sign was within a square mile or less. Caribou rubs may be profuse in the timber where the woodland variety lives, or in low brush on tundra locations. But the animals may be miles away. Caribou trails, in any area they inhabit abundantly, can be seen in profusion. Some ancestral trails are cut like ruts from stagecoach days left on the western prairie. Yet again, even though a trail may have fresh sign, all it means is that bands of animals passed this way. They are not necessarily in the vicinity.

In the section on movements, the feet and hooves, and the tracks, of caribou are described. Certainly in territory where other big game ranges—moose, sheep—there is no chance for even a tyro observer to mistake caribou tracks. They are so nearly round that they are unmistakable. Droppings are another matter. They might be confused even with the smaller deer, or with sheep or moose. The hard pellets formed from the more solid foods average about ½ inch long but appear in varied shapes. At their largest they are seldom an inch in length. When soft green forage is being taken, it is difficult to decide, on a range where several game species live, which is which.

Again, it is not very important. Caribou are seldom traced by signs left during their passing. The animals themselves are either there, or they are not. Abundant sign may help evaluate a good range and a general route of movement. Even the presence of abundant food, especially lichens, may help. But an old rule of the north is that whoever looks for caribou looks for caribou period. An interesting minor sign that any nature student should be aware of is the possible sighting of caribou breath. In extremely cold weather, breath vapor arising on still air from a moving band is occasionally visible before the animals are.

### HUNTING

Caribou season for sport hunting traditionally opens early. The Barren Ground bulls, in August and early September, are likely to be at the tundra edge or into the trees, stripping velvet from their antlers. Mountain caribou are most often collected high above the timber, and the woodland variety in areas of open forest.

There is nothing very specialized about hunting technique. Early and late in the day the animals will be out feeding, if the rut is not in progress. It is best, by far, for meat, to hunt before the rut. Only a few days after breeding begins the meat becomes strong and fat is swiftly lost.

The most difficult part of hunting is locating animals. This may require a lot of riding. Or the country may be full of them. During the day the bulls lie up along slopes and gravel ridges and on snow patches. Walking does not cover enough territory, and anyway, hunters in these lands — except in most cases in Newfoundland, for example — are invariably mounted. "Walking up" a trophy is a tough proposition. At least one should be prepared for a long hike.

Distance, all told, is the logistics problem for the hunter. Just getting into caribou country means a long trip. Most outfitters fly hunters into base camps, from which they ride to spike camps out of which they hunt. They can change from one spike camp to another if necessary. Most hunters are after a mixed bag, although a few, in remote locations, go strictly for a trophy caribou. Walking is awesomely difficult in muskeg country, but horses used by outfitters are used to it, and on horseback one can cover 10 to 20 miles a day if necessary.

Sometimes hunters simply ride the high slopes, pausing intermittently to glass. Or they ride or climb high, then carefully glass, with binoculars and spotting scope, vast expanses of surrounding country. Much of the caribou domain is open, and the animals are easily spotted. Stalking entails one major difficulty. Most big-game animals when moving and feeding stay on a course that can be plotted or guessed at with reasonable accuracy by a hunter or guide who watches for a few minutes. Caribou may, or may not, stay on course. A band may whimsically shift direction at any moment.

The trick is to make a stalk to avoid being scented or seen, if possible. However, a spooked bull may run right back to see what frightened it, or even stalk the hunter. They are quite unpredictable. Some hunters who spot a desirable trophy in the morning keep watching until it beds down. Then the stalk is made. When caribou are moving, trying to catch them on foot is virtually useless. They go too fast. Nor is following on horseback much better. Guides invariably appraise the terrain, then ride under concealment of knolls or ridges to circle and cut the course, or even to get within range of bedded animals.

At the last place of possible concealment the remainder of the stalk is made on foot. Cover may be only low growth. It may be necessary to crawl. Caribou feeding with heads down or pointed away can be stalked a few quick moves at a time. When their heads rise or they turn, the hunter freezes. Now and then ruses work, such as hunching over and walking steadily, slowly right at the quarry. They may run around and stare but be overcome with curiosity. If one must hunt during the rut, the bulls are likely to act so totally addled and stupid that getting one is not even much sport. Although the early season prior to or at the very beginning of the rut may see some bulls with tattered velvet clinging to their antlers, the rack is nonetheless hard and can be cleaned, and the meat will be superb.

Hunters should be wise enough not to go undergunned. It's not that a caribou is especially difficult to put down, but in much of the range, at least across Alaska and western Canada, grizzlies are present. The average hunter will be out for a mixed bag, perhaps including moose and sheep. Thus heavy rifles adequate for larger game are the rule. This means, in today's world of highly specialized arms, one of the big and popular magnums. Below that, the .270 or .30/06 and comparable calibers will be next in line.

Just what the future of the caribou may be is difficult to judge. Certainly the species is not presently endangered. Some time ago it declined drastically in Newfoundland, where hunting had long been some of the best. But over recent years the animals have made a strong comeback. However, there is suspicion among some conservationists that the determined probe across the Arctic for oil and the settlements devoted to various mining and other activities indicate problems for the caribou.

As more people push into their domain, with ever easier methods of travel such as the snowmobile, more and more animals will be required simply as food. In several locations even today there is no limit on how many native peoples may take, or when. If migratory herds are blocked from their ancestral movements, or the incessant nibbling away of habitat by industry and the settlement it brings continues on an ever-growing scale, the beautiful but dumb caribou could be a casualty.

# Pronghorn Antelope

*Antilocapra americana*

The American antelope is part and parcel of western tradition and heritage. It is one of the most handsome and elegant of North American big-game animals, a highly specialized creature fitting a niche of habitat that other large animals, except the once-abundant buffalo, were not able to utilize in numbers. It is a true native, having been on this continent for millions of years. Indeed, it evolved here in several varieties long ago, has no close relatives anywhere in the world, and is the sole remaining member of its family.

Thus it is especially curious that the animal is the victim of a misnaming which has caused confusion and argument among hunters and observers of wildlife since the country was settled. Presumably early explorers and pioneers in the west called it "antelope" because it is in some physical attributes reminiscent of the antelopes of Africa, Asia, and elsewhere. But there are no antelopes outside the Old World.

The popular name stuck, until scientists discovered that the animal was not one of that tribe. To set the record straight it was given the official name "pronghorn" because of its unique horn configuration.

Although attempts were made to teach the general public to use the name "pronghorn," they were to no avail. Many scientists nowadays bow slightly to common usage and try to avoid misunderstanding by using the term "pronghorn antelope." To the hunter, the westerner, and the tourist interested in looking at wildlife, however, these dashing speedsters of the plains will always be simply antelope — American antelope.

Although the antelope ranged in prehistoric times over some suitable country east of the Mississippi River, as proved by fossils discovered in Illinois and Wisconsin, pioneer Americans found none there. The range west of the Mississippi was broad, from the Baja Peninsula and much of northern and interior Mexico north throughout all habitable areas from California and southern and central Texas to Washington, the Dakotas, and the Prairie Provinces.

It is said that there were millions of antelope in immense bands almost everywhere throughout this vast range, with the concentration in its general center. Some estimates place the number at 50 to 100 million. These obviously are just guesses. Whether accurate or not, certainly the animals were supremely abundant. The incursion of pioneer settlement soon and drastically cut the population. Tens of thousands were killed for meat, to feed settlements, army camps, railroad crews, and so on. The coming of fences decimated the herds. Although perfectly capable of jumping a fence, they had never encountered such barriers and had never learned to jump. Running at high speed, entire bands were killed when they struck fences.

Vast numbers were rounded up and slaughtered when domestic cattle and sheep came to the western ranges. They were considered competing nuisances that consumed valuable forage. Numerous attempts were made to utilize antelope hides. These proved failures. The hair is brittle and loosely attached. Hides could not be tanned with hair on. The skin itself makes a thin, stretchy, porous, and inferior leather. Nonetheless, with all such influences chipping away at what had seemed a sea of endless antelope waves across the plains, the species was brought precariously close to extinction. By early in this century, careful surveys showed them gone from most of their ancestral range. Only a meager 12,000 to 20,000 antelope remained.

A last-minute all-out cooperative effort among landowners with

Pronghorn Antelope

## THE PRONGHORN

COLOR: Rich tan over upper body and outside of legs, shading reddish-tan in north to pale on southwestern desert ranges; white beneath, inside legs, and large patch on rump; throat white interrupted by a pair of wide dark tan bands; lower jaw and cheeks below eyes white; face of buck covered by black or very dark brown mask up to horns; doe with only suggestion of darker color on face; nose, both sexes, black; buck with black neck patch on upper throat and rear of lower jaw, also with a few long, black-tipped hairs on mane; short tail tan above.

MEASUREMENTS, MATURE BUCKS: 3 feet or a bit more at shoulder; overall length 4 to 5 feet.

WEIGHT, MATURE BUCKS: 100 to 120 pounds, exceptional specimens a few pounds heavier.

HORNS: Black; 10 to 15 inches outside measurement, rarely to 18 or more; tips generally rather cylindrical, curving backward and a bit inward, but this is highly variable, some tips curving forward or directly inward; a single usually concave short, flattened prong on front of each horn about midway, thrusting forward and up; horns from skull to prong flattened laterally; normally horns appear to slant slightly forward.

DOES: 10 to 20 percent smaller; with horns, but inconsequential, seldom more than 4 inches high and normally without prongs.

GENERAL ATTRIBUTES: Graceful, handsome, beautifully proportioned; unique ability to flare white rump patch broadly when disturbed or angry; astonishing speed when running; possibly world's fastest animal over substantial distance; phenomenal eyesight in treeless plains habitat.

new understanding, lawmakers, and the new crop of game managers coming onto the scene saved the antelope. Transplants reestablished them in suitable portions of their original domain. Today under careful management and cropping to keep their numbers tailored to available habitat, a rather stable herd estimated at about 500,000 is present. Today's range, of course, is considerably smaller than the ancestral range, but remaining animals are in no danger.

Because of their specialized habitat, and man's intensive use of most of it, there is no possibility of enlarging the present antelope range. However, on the plus side, antelope have learned to live with fences, still very seldom jumping, but crawling under or through. Landowners generally tolerate them. And they are unique in having few predaceous enemies actually capable of disturbing population balance. Bobcats, coyotes, and eagles do prey incessantly and successfully on fawns. In some areas, half of the fawn crop is gone by fall. Coyotes and bobcats also kill a substantial number of adults. Pressure from those predators depends much upon the supply of staple rodents and rabbits. Except in deep snow, a coyote or group of them cannot easily run down and kill an adult antelope. The pronghorn is too fast. Antelope also fight viciously, striking with sharp hoofs to defend fawns or themselves. They have often been observed, several does together, running a marauding coyote clear out of the country.

A severe blizzard with deep snow is one of the worst enemies of the pronghorn. They may be forced to drift before it, and they may pile against fences, smother by lying down too close together in concentrations, or starve because they cannot paw down to forage. However, the animals are remarkably adapted to withstand severe cold. The pithy, hollow hair contains large cells of air. Although the fine undercoat is rather inconsequential, a highly specialized set of muscles in tissue under the skin allows the antelope to raise or lower the main coat hairs, adjusting the angle to the weather. At zero or below it is held close and flat, forming perfect insulation. In hot weather it can be raised and slanted to take advantage of cooling breezes.

Considering the speed at which antelope are able to run, and the rough, often rocky terrain they encompass, one might suspect that accidents would take a high toll. This is not the case. The animals are astonishingly adept at maneuvering at full speed over hard and uneven terrain. They have an uncanny sense for avoiding deep mud or quicksand. Although the legs appear fragile, the bones are highly specialized for adaptation to rough usage. They are unbelievably strong. Arthur S. Einarsen, in his book *The Pronghorn Antelope and Its Management,* tells of an experiment he conceived and had carried out to determine the maximum load weight each leg bone could bear without breaking, as compared to the leg bones of cattle. The results showed that the foreleg bone of a domestic cow, which is seven times greater in weight than an antelope, was crushed at 4000 pounds less pressure. The antelope bone withstood over 45,000 pounds per square inch!

There are some records of accidental deaths, of bands racing over a cliff in a snowstorm, for example. By and large, however, aside from predation upon fawns, disease and parasites which weaken the animals are undoubtedly the chief causes of mortality on the range. Antelope are not, however, particularly long-lived.

An animal five or six years old, or at most eight, is on the downhill side.

The two most emphatic facets of antelope personality are extreme nervousness and curiosity. The nervousness does not seem to stem from constant fear, but from a super-acute alertness to everything that occurs around them. Their eyes are ever scanning. Some imaginary danger may put them briefly to flight. Or a sudden impulse will send a band or a lone pronghorn racing off, circling, standing to pose atop a ridge. An almost constant movement is the way of their lives, inherent in the very nature of the terrain. Even sleep is fitful, a few moments of dozing, then the head comes alert and the big eyes scan the surroundings.

Any unusual sight arouses overwhelming curiosity. A scrap of paper blowing across a plain may have several antelope stalking it with prancing walk or trot. This strong curiosity has got many a pronghorn into trouble. Hunters since the early pioneers have used ruses such as tying a cloth to a bush so that it flutters in the wind. Hiding nearby, they wait for a curious antelope to investigate. Lying down and waving a hat gets the same kind of attention. Some individuals may come a mile to find out what is going on.

The type species, *Antilocapra americana americana,* makes up the bulk of the antelope population. Four subspecies are recognized, but they are not very important to the casual observer or hunter, and not numerous. One is the Oregon antelope, which presently resides in extremely modest numbers in the sagebrush country of eastern Oregon. The Mexican pronghorn is a southwestern subspecies found on plains and deserts in parts of west Texas, New Mexico, and Arizona. The Sonora pronghorn is an endangered desert subspecies of the Mexican state for which it is named and of a small area of southern Arizona. The Peninsula pronghorn is found in Lower California. The four subspecies make up certainly no more than 50,000 in aggregate, if that, of the estimated 500,000 animals.

The center of antelope abundance within the entire range is in Wyoming. This state contains perhaps a fifth of the total continental herd. Montana is second to Wyoming. Sustained antelope abundance in this general two-state region indicates that here is located the optimum type of range. Other states and provinces with antelope offer proper natural habitat, or proper habitat not denied to the animals by human changes in land use, only in modest amounts.

## HABITAT

The pronghorn is a product of the wide-open, treeless country of the west, a creature of the rolling plains and grasslands, and of the sagebrush flats and lower foothills. The preponderance of the very best range, and most of that in regions outlying from the optimum center, is not, as it has sometimes been described in romantic western literature, any endless sea of waving yellow grass. Indeed, much antelope habitat is quite rugged. Barren buttes and plateaus thrust up from the undulations of the lower country. Rocky outcrops show through the low vegetation.

In northeastern New Mexico, for example, where some of that state's prime antelope range is located, the land is "malpai" country, where grass and weeds and low brush grow from among jumbles of "bad rock," the black hummocks and ridges spewed eons ago from extinct volcanoes. In the Big Bend Country of western Texas, antelope habitat is in the slanted, rocky desert valleys and low ridges between desert mountains.

Sage and antelope are a duo over much of the animal's territory. There may be flat dry lake beds on which bands wheel and play, or flat expanses, but the arid ridges with hard, stony soil and sage generally will not be far away. Just as the mule deer seems unable to colonize flat lands, the antelope cannot abide the confinement of forest. It must be able to see for long distances in order to feel secure.

The distribution of antelope has always been limited by two types of barriers. One is stands of heavy timber. Antelope refuse to enter them. As an aside, it is interesting to observe that when antelope are coming to a waterhole, for example, and tall sage thickets of 6 feet or so are present nearby, the animals invariably skirt them. Enemies might lie in wait there, particularly at a waterhole, the gathering place in an arid country for all wildlife. Besides, while passing through the tall sage, the antelope cannot see far enough.

The second barrier of terrain is what are generally called badlands. These are severely eroded areas. In numerous instances where excellent range was present on one side of such an expanse, antelope have failed to find and utilize it, yet they have drifted along the edges of the region distantly to populate a range of inferior quality.

Even though heavy timber acts as a barrier to distribution, in certain parts of their range antelope have been forced into quasi-

# Range of the Pronghorn

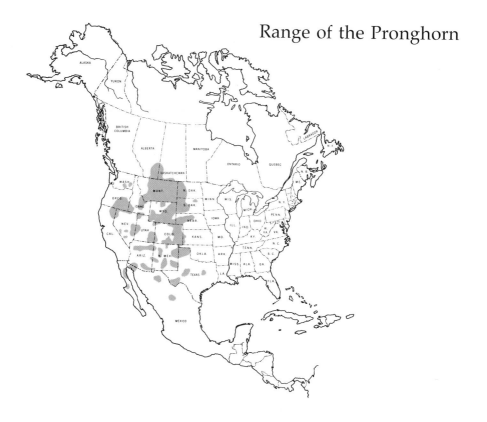

timber areas by the encroachment of man and his land uses upon their preferred domain. These habitats are not forest or woodland in the literal sense. But they are the fringes of it. In Arizona, for instance, antelope presently utilize country of scattered juniper quite unlike the prime habitat of eastern and central Wyoming. The same is true in Texas and New Mexico. In part of the Oregon range they were also forced by human pressure into stands of juniper. It may well be that originally antelope utilized authentic pure grasslands far more than they do today, even on the better ranges. Piñon, juniper, and varied brush and weed associations now are utilized here and there, not always by choice but because that is all that remains or because of man's influences upon the original grasslands.

The span of elevation within antelope habitat is broad. But it appears to have its most definite limitation on the lower side. Only in the prairie provinces of Canada do pronghorns find congenial altitudes of only 2000 to 2500 feet. Elsewhere over virtually every state where they are found the favored altitude is from 4000 to 6000 feet, except in locations such as the Dakotas and Baja California, where they occupy an average altitude between 3000 and 4000 feet. Whether or not altitude is a fact or influence related to abundance is not known, but the level at which pronghorns are most abundant in range center is from 5000 to 6000 feet. Pronghorns move higher than that, however, to 8000 feet or more on certain open mountains.

All of their habitat is arid in varying degrees. But it is never waterless. There have been suggestions in some writing that antelope can live without water, utilizing that from their forage. This is untrue. The animals can get along for several days without water if necessary. But the waterhole is a hub of any pronghorn habitat, even though it may not be visited without several miles of travel, or every day. Wholly waterless country cannot sustain pronghorns, although some astonishingly barren-appearing places with seemingly scarce forage can.

### FEEDING

The antelope is a very nervous animal. Its feeding habits reflect this. An animal may walk along taking a nip here and another there, suddenly race off at a run for half a mile, stop abruptly, pick out a certain weed that seems appealing, eat several bites, then perhaps wheel and race back to where it was to start. Possibly because antelope quite literally have perfected the art and science of running, thus expending much energy whether disturbed or simply racing around in play, they feed over longer periods than do deer. And they may feed at any time, day or night.

Researchers doing stomach analyses on antelope have noted the unusual fact that with few exceptions the stomachs are totally full. This would seem to indicate numerous feeding periods around the clock, with only short rests in between. At one time landowners believed that antelope were a scourge on the range, competing with cattle or sheep for grass. Scientific studies long ago proved differently. Browse plants are the mainstay of antelope diet.

Wherever sage is available—which takes in much of antelope territory—it is one of the most important items of diet. In winter especially, when other plants are not available in abundance, sage of one variety or another is a staple. Although the palatability of sage may not be high, studies have shown it to be an important protein source, and to contain more carbohydrates and much more fat than such rich cattle feeds as alfalfa. Common additional browse plants are rabbit brush, saltbush,, juniper, and bitter brush. There are numerous others.

Next in importance after the browse plants, which are eaten all year, are various weeds, or forbs. These grow in antelope habitat in infinite variety. Sour dock, chicory, dandelion, Russian thistle, mustard, wild peas, lupine, mullein, larkspur, various clovers, and even wild onion and locoweed are examples. Grasses are taken in the least quantity, and chiefly in spring when green shoots appear. The ratio overall is roughly two-thirds browse, as high as one-fourth weeds, the remainder grasses. This ratio, of course, differs from area to area, depending on what is available. In some instances browse may make up as much as 85 percent of the forage.

It is apparent that pronghorns are perfectly fitted to their environment even in their digestive system. Compared to bulk of food eaten, there is very little body waste. They also are what might be called conservation-minded feeders. Most large animals bite and pull at the same time, thus tearing out the roots of low-growing forage plants. Antelope are almost dainty in the way they snip each stem with a clean bite. This allows a reissue of the plant and very little plant destruction by the animals on any range. This is important in public relations, since they must in our modern day share range with cattle, which quite oppositely are accomplished root pullers.

Although antelope range widely while feeding, and may be active at any time, their loose routine is to move about early in the morning, then take a rest for cud chewing for an hour or more. But there is usually a second feeding period following this. If the day then becomes hot, the animals lie down during the worst of it. A late feeding period then begins as afternoon wanes. However, whimsical and nervous as they are, bands may be up feeding and moving at any time.

Because present-day antelope range is almost all in multiple use, either privately owned ranchland or else federally owned land used for grazing, the welfare of the animals depends almost entirely on their acceptance by cattlemen and sheepmen. Occasionally where crop fields such as alfalfa border antelope range, the crop makes up part of the diet and the animals become exasperating pests—not, however, from their feeding on it, which does little real damage, but from their constant jittering, running hither and yon through it, lying down to flatten one patch and then nervously jumping up and moving off to try another spot.

As far as open rangelands are concerned, however, it is a curious fact that even large numbers of antelope seem to have little if any adverse effect upon it. Where cattle are excluded from a range used by numerous antelope, native grasses instantly begin to thrive. On seriously overgrazed lands, antelope get along well while cattle must be removed. As soon as the cattle are taken off, the range begins to restore itself. It is this modern understanding of the feeding habits of the pronghorn gleaned by science, that has gained the cooperation of landowners in helping to keep the population at a stable level. Interestingly enough, certain areas in the southwest capable of producing only the sparsest plant life cannot sustain cattle, yet are utilized by antelope.

MOVEMENTS

The antelope, one observer has said, is motion at its best. The wide-open habitat with its endless distances seem to invite wild, free, and swift movement. The antelope is so specifically attuned to it that it evolved as possibly the world's swiftest runner. And it runs with unbelievable grace and flowing motion. A band running together is reminiscent of a flock of wheeling birds, swirling with evenly flowing motion as if it were one individual.

At 20 miles per hour antelope are barely at a good full trot. They can run for miles at this speed. At 35 miles per hour they hit what might be called a fast cruising speed. They have been clocked at this pace over a course of several miles without showing the least sign of tiring. A bedded antelope can catapult into the air when disturbed and land running. The gait is not a series of bounds such as deer make. It begins as a kind of trot, left front, right hind, and vice versa, but each foreleg reaches far out and the animal is almost instantly revved up to 30, then progressively to 35, 40, 45, 50.

It moves at the higher speeds only when chased or encouraged, but it still has lots left for serious occasions. Whole bands have been clocked running together at 50 and above. Probably 55 miles an hour is average maximum. However, there are observer records touching 60, and some believe individual animals under proper conditions may be capable of 70 for a short spurt.

The pronghorn has several special adaptations to make possible such speeds. The front feet are larger than the hind feet, in mature bucks close to 3 inches long, as compared to about 2½ inches for the rear feet. It is the larger forefeet that hit the ground hardest when the animals are running, and that support most of the weight. The lungs are extra-large, and the heart is double the size of that of animals of comparable weight.

There is a nerveless cartilaginous padding on the hoofs, particularly thick on the forefeet. This serves to cushion the strike of the feet at high speeds. Because of it, antelope seldom show any lameness or tenderfootedness regardless of the rough character of the terrain. There are no dewclaws, which conceivably might be a hindrance to swift movement on rough or rocky ground. Further, the design and fitting together of ligaments, tendons, and bones of the lower leg are so perfect that it is virtually impossible for the animals to suffer sprains or other related leg injuries. This is one reason pronghorns are such miracles of swift flight over broken terrain.

One of the most unusual specializations for speed over substantial distances is found in the windpipe. When a pronghorn runs at high speed it always does so with mouth open. This has fooled some observers into believing the animal was tiring or out of breath and gasping. It is gasping all right—pulling in great drafts of air that its nose could not accommodate. The windpipe, however, easily accommodates this large intake. It is oversize, indeed twice as large as that of several animals of double the weight.

Antelope are notorious for their irresistible desire to race any moving object in their domain. This trait was noticed by early pioneers on the plains. Spotting a galloping horseman, a moving vehicle, a train, they commonly run on a long slant toward it, eventually come alongside, then appear to take great joy in speeding up not only to outdistance the competitor but also to bound across in front. At 50 miles an hour an antelope may suddenly spurt ahead and make a leap of 20 to 25 feet barely ahead of a moving vehicle.

No one is quite sure what the motive is for this. Perhaps it is really a form of race, of enjoyment. It may also be a quirky escape idea, a feeling that safety lies not only in outdistancing an "enemy" but in getting on the other side of where it was first sighted.

Although the antelope can make long, low, vaulting leaps, such as across a ranch road, as noted earlier it has never learned to jump vertically. It is easily capable of clearing any ordinary ranch fence. But in its bailiwick it has never had to leap *over* anything, and so simply never learned. A band often runs right at a fence of several barbed-wire strands and hardly slows. Each animal ducks through between strands or else underneath the lowest one. The loosely attached hair is raked out in an explosion drifting on the breeze and on the animals go. On some ranches there are locations where a woven-wire fence corners with or meets a stretch of barbed-wire fence. Antelope often wear a trail along the woven wire, straight to the spot where the barbed wire begins. There they duck through.

Yet indeed they can jump. One observer in Wyoming, trying to get a buck antelope out of an alfalfa field surrounded by woven wire, chased it with a vehicle until it became so tired it lay down. All the time there was an open gate for it to go out through—the way it came in. But curiously, when pressed and running, bands commonly pass an open gate time after time as they circle a field, somehow dubious of moving through it, or else too intent on running to notice. At any rate, when jumped from its resting place again, the buck bolted straight at the fence, sailed over it easily and beautifully, then ran up to a ridgetop and posed almost arrogantly, looking back.

How far antelope move in a day, or a season, depends on several factors: the amount of forage readily available; the proximity to water; disturbance; and how closely they may be confined by fences. It must be remembered that in modern times on ranches here and there bands of antelope are inhibited from movement because they were "fenced in." A new fence is built splitting a big pasture. Antelope in one section may have water and food, but will live out their entire lives happily enough, with only modest movement possible. They are trapped.

Generally speaking, however, the individual range of antelope bands where there are no barriers over large expanses is much broader than that of other horned and antlered animals. This is simply because movement to them is not labored. They are the most easily mobile of all hoofed creatures on the continent, and are mentally adjusted to wide movement. Nonetheless, a band or a big lone buck may live for weeks or months covering no more than a square mile or so. It will water at the same location, feed on a favored flat, bed down on a favored ridge, pass time after time through the same saddle of a narrow valley between ridges.

Even sometimes undue disturbance, as during hunting season, won't drive a band out of the country. It will become awesomely wild, running at sight of a man or vehicle a mile off, but next morning the group may be in the same area. If there is an especially rough piece of country, with snug valleys and high, rocky ridges, bands will commonly move into those when harassed out in the rolling country, coming out only to water.

The trek to water is usually made only once a day. Occasionally it may not be made every day. Much depends on the temperature. However, the daily trip is the rule. Individual bands or animals may differ in timing of the water trip, and it may differ in varying latitudes. A group of archers who hunted several consecutive seasons in Wyoming and set up sage blinds near a waterhole on a small creek observed that without fail bands there came to water in the middle of the day.

Although antelope groups like to hang around old dry lake or pond beds, sometimes because they serve as salt licks, seldom do they stay long at a watering place. In an arid expanse it is a magnet for all creatures, prey as well as predator, and thus dangerous. Coming to water, the animals often stand on a ridge and look things over carefully, then move skittishly down toward the water. They jitter about, finally move to water's edge, lower their heads, maybe flush suddenly like a flock of quail, then move gingerly back. Once they decide all is safe, they drink. With little dilly-dallying, they then prudently leave.

The uniquely specialized white rump patch of the pronghorn is related to movement from danger. As mentioned earlier, all of the pelage can be erected or laid flat by an intricate web of muscles in tissue below the skin. The rump patch is so well endowed with these muscles that every hair can be individually flared. The white rump hair is almost twice as long as the body hair. When wholly flared and looked at from the rear, the patch protrudes past the basic body contours at least 3 inches. The patch thus appears at least twice as large as when the hair is laid flat. Presumably this flaring is a signal to others in the band, or to any other antelope within sight range—which may be a couple of miles—that something is amiss. It's time to run.

This signal is known to everyone who has seen or read about antelope, but most casual observers are unaware of what occurs previous to this final and obvious danger signal. When puzzled and suspicious, first the animals raise the tan hair along the back. The bucks also erect the 3-inch black hairs of the mane. Pronghorns may begin to walk or trot slowly away with a stifflegged gait as the back hair comes up, meanwhile flaring the rump patch. Then usually they explode into a headlong run. Once the band comes to a stop, out of danger and probably several miles away, it may pose on a high place to look back, and all the animals make a quick shaking motion, smoothing all the flared and erect hairs back into place. After this antic they are by no means as highly visible.

Scientists studying antelope have long been convinced that among their important movements is authentic play, not just among fawns but among adults as well. A lone pronghorn may make a sudden dash at a group, even some that are lying down. It races around or past. They instantly are on their feet, giving chase, circling, racing. The group may fan out, then some individuals will

PRONGHORN ANTELOPE 135

cut through the running pattern of the others. Such displays are
common, are not related to sexual motivation, and appear to be
thoroughly enjoyed by the group.

The so-called migratory movements of antelope are commonly
misunderstood. There really are no true migrations in the strict
sense. In winter antelope gather as a rule in large bands. They may
drift some distance to a wintering area. But the movement is not
necessarily routine, season after season. And it bears no relationship to latitude. That is, one band may move a few miles north, another south. Drifts from one feeding ground or waterhole to another
occur at any time. So do switches of altitude. Weather and seasons
may influence all such movements.

In a very few instances, in the northern fringe of range in the
prairie provinces, for example, a wintering ground may be distant.
This trek occurs because of deep snow which forces a long move to
forage. One of the most interesting winter movements in the north
is to high altitudes. The animals do not seem bothered by low temperature and bitter winter winds. When a valley fills with snow,
they move right up atop the highest windswept peaks or plateaus
in the area. Here forage is swept partially clean of snow by the
winds. Antelope do dig through light snow occasionally to uncover
food, but it is not a routine habit.

There is seldom need for antelope to swim. They are known,
however, to cross large rivers now and then with no hesitancy. The
coat with its air-filled hair is buoyant, and they are strong, calm
swimmers. They do avoid wet bogs and sinkholes, seeming to
know that they may get caught in such places.

BREEDING

Some other antelope movements are related to the fall rut, to
breeding. On most ranges late summer is a dry time; water is scarce
and numerous bands may be forced to gather at the same watering
places. These concentrations may be congenial enough until mid-
August or early September. Then mature bucks which have been
hanging with groups of does and fawns, as well as old loner bache-
lors and small groups of bucks hanging out together, begin to get
restless. Soon scattered individual bucks pass into what some observers have called their "crazy" period.

A big buck in perfect physical condition may stand apart from a
group, listless and with head hanging. He flares his rump patch
now and then and looks more alert, and an incessant tremor of the
rump hairs is noticeable, caused by twitching of the muscles that

erect the hair. He may suddenly make a wild sideways leap, or race in a quick circle. To some extent this is reminiscent of the ludicrous antics of bull caribou as the rut begins. These weird antics of the buck draw the curious attention of the group.

Soon, however, other bucks are going through the same personality change. Curiosity wanes in the others, and now the forerunner activity of the mating season begins to speed up. Mature bucks that have been hanging around with does become jealous of them. Other adult bucks race frantically around urging does to join them. This is the period of harem forming. Bucks dash madly about vying for does. They get together a small band—three or four to a dozen—and are violently possessive.

It is wryly comical to observe the dilemma of a buck with a fair-sized harem that is being challenged. Another buck without does comes tearing in toward the flock. The herd buck gives chase. Eyes popping viciously almost out of their sockets, rump and black mane hair upended, he closes on the interloper. About then he thinks twice. What's happening behind him? Will still another buck sneak in and steal his harem? He charges back, only to be followed by the other buck. Off he goes again, determined this time to appear as formidable as possible and run the other clear out of the country. There are again second thoughts. Back he races to his does.

During this period of forming and attempting to control small harems, movement is frenzied. The dry flats are constantly inscribed by myriad floating dust plumes as buck after buck flurries around his group of females or chases other bucks. Now and then there are battles. Most of these amount only to bluffing, some shoving, an occasional severe charge during which heads come together and, usually, horn prongs catch as guards to fend off any serious damage. Sometimes horns are broken or knocked off. The horn tips, being curved back or inward or forward, cannot cause any notable wounds, but the often-sharp prongs might. Very occasionally a buck is badly hurt and bleeding, or put down and slashed with front hoofs until he is mortally wounded. It should be emphasized that this is uncommon.

Timing of the mating season differs somewhat from latitude to latitude. In general it occurs during September and October. The peak activity is rather brief. Antelope does, it is believed, have only a single short mating period, unlike deer. Thus if one is not bred when ready, or does not become pregnant from a mating, she will be fawnless that year. This belief seems to be substantiated by studies which show that in spring all but a very few fawns are born within a period of a couple of weeks, whereas late fawns are common among deer, and the fawning period of deer stretches over a month or more.

The frenzied breeding period wears all the animals down. But it is soon completed and the fierce competition and incessant running cease. This volatile several weeks has long been a problem to game managers trying to set a proper hunting season. Most are set in late September or occur in October or even into November. A few states wisely launch their season in late August. This gives hunters a chance to collect animals in the primest condition and with meat the best. And it probably does little harm to the breeding population because of the harem-gathering habits of the animals. The problem in a late season is that the horn sheaths (discussed below) loosen soon after the rut. Many a late-season antelope hunter has dropped a trophy only to have the horns fly off when it hit the ground.

### BIRTH AND DEVELOPMENT

Virtually all of the does are bred the first time when they are long yearlings—that is, only two to four months past one year of age. This well may be a specialization to keep population level high, for antelope, as we have said, are not long-lived. Few live past seven or eight. Although mating is earlier in general than for deer, the fawns are born at about the same period of spring, in May and June, depending upon latitude. This means that the gestation period is long, approximately eight months.

The fawns are very pale, grayish rather than tan, and weigh only 4 or 5 pounds. They seem to be all legs, and stand only 16 inches or so at shoulder height. They develop with astonishing swiftness and are able to run within a few days, if necessary, up to 20 or more miles an hour. However, for at least the first week they lie flat most of the time, hiding in cover. The young does give birth to a single fawn as a rule, but twins are common thereafter, and triplets are not rare.

Fences nowadays prohibit the does in some places from selecting a kidding ground that they might move to if the range were open. Thus many observers have been led to believe that the young are simply dropped anywhere the doe happens to be. Given a free choice and proper variation in habitat, however, this is hardly the case, and the selection of a fawning place is uniquely interesting. Invariably they will select a small basin or valley with ridges nearby, and with vegetation about a foot high.

The fawns—or kids—are born down in the lower area. If there

*A newborn pronghorn fawn.*

are twins, the doe gives birth to one and then moves away, sometimes several hundred yards, to bear the other. This instinctive plan is an aid to protection of the young, or saving one if some predator finds the other. After the births she drives off the youngsters and then leaves, commonly moving as much as a half-mile away, but invariably up on the ridge. Again no doubt instinctively, she has selected the low vegetation for giving birth so that now from her higher vantage point she can watch closely over her offspring, whereas if they were deposited in high cover she would be at a disadvantage.

The young are believed to be practically odorless, and they lie tight to the ground. The doe comes often to let them nurse, but immediately leaves to take up her watch from above. By the end of the first week the fawns are able to follow their mother, and by two weeks their white rump patches have developed and they flash them in flight just like the adults.

Like deer, antelope are only modestly vocal. The fawns bleat on occasion, their voices high-pitched and quavering. Does may respond with a low blatt, but this is unusual. A wounded buck has been heard to utter a deep, short blatt, again an unusual utterance. The only common sound antelope make is a kind of snort through the nose when they are either disturbed or aroused.

While the fawns are growing during the summer, yearling bucks and does are beginning to form their first horns. Pronghorn horns are not similar to either the antlers of deer or to the true horns of cattle and the true antelopes and other horned animals. The handsome pronged horn that is seen as a trophy by hunter or observer in summer and early fall is actually only the outer sheath. Inside it is a core fed by a circulatory system. The sheath is rather lightly attached to the core. After the rut—and sometimes accidentally during it—the outer sheath is shed.

Thus the antelope horn is a kind of in-between type of growth. Antlers, for example, begin growth with an outer covering of velvet, which is really a blood-vessel system on the outside. At full growth the blood system dies, shrivels, and is rubbed off; the antler has hardened and is eventually totally shed, and a new growth begins the following spring. A true horn has a core supplied with blood vessels that nourishes growth throughout life of the outer bony portion, which is never shed. The outer sheath of the pronghorn horn is composed of a hairlike substance fused into a solid, but not truly bony, mass.

Before the outer sheath is shed in fall, a new sheath is already beginning to sprout inside, at the tip of the core. The core is smooth and short and without any prong. Early in the year—by January or February—the new sheath sprouting at the tip of the core is 3 inches or so in length. The manner of growth is now unique. The tip is hard and shiny, like a regular horn tip. The continued growth, however, is downward toward the skull. In addition to the bony tip, the outside of the core is covered with a membranous material which covers it down into the hair at the base. The hair surrounding the core at its base also is growing swiftly as the sheath grows. As the new sheath reaches downward, it eventually covers and fuses with this hair. The complicated process is generally finished by midsummer. The new horns at that time and on through August are unmarred and in their most handsome state.

To give an idea of how large antelope horns may grow, the longest in the record book are 20⅛ inches right, 20 left. The animal was killed in 1899. The preponderance of records—which of course do not depend just on length—run in length from 15-plus to 19-plus. The older a buck, with some exceptions, the larger the horns. But because the animals are relatively short-lived, there is a built-in limit. Further, cropping by hunting to keep herds in line with available range tends to skim off the larger bucks each season. In most areas nowadays a 12-to-14-inch horn is considered a good trophy. Nonetheless, for hunters who believe that chances at a

*A pronghorn skull showing the bony cores, one covered by its outer sheath, the horn, which is shed every year.*

trophy that might make the book are presently meager, a check of records will be encouraging. Over a recent six-year period slightly more than one-third of the entire 230-plus record-book heads were taken, some of them placing up toward the top.

### SENSES

Sight is the all-important sense of the pronghorn. The size of the eye has often been compared to that of the horse's eye. It is larger, even though the antelope weighs only a fraction as much. The eyes are so placed out at the sides of the head that the animal has extremely wide-angle vision. It is even capable of picking up movements behind. Even though the eyes bulge, they are extremely well protected by the skull design. Researchers have even found it necessary to chip away the bone above the eye in order to remove one.

Some scientists believe the antelope eye has magnifying power. It is often likened, whether provable or not, to an 8-power telescope. It is a fact that antelope detect movement of very small objects several miles away. The high specialization of the eyes is of course an adaptation to the open habitat. This super-keen sense, coupled with the just as highly developed running ability, forms the combination upon which the well-being of the animals almost wholly depends. Add to this the fact that pronghorns—except for occasional individuals—consort in bands and are incessantly and nervously scanning their domain. With so many eyes watching at once, the odds are high against close approach and surprise by any predator, including man.

Scenting ability is well developed, but by no means to the degree that it is, for example, in whitetail deer. At modest range, antelope pick up scents of danger on a breeze. But they have no real need for distance scenting ability. Hearing is certainly acute, but again, the source of any sound an antelope hears has invariably already been detected by the eye.

**SIGN** *(Tracks are illustrated on page 251.)*

Signs left by antelope are not very important, so far as using them to locate the animals is concerned. Certainly tracks around a waterhole or on a dry lake bed give some indication of animals present. But the point is, simply scanning an area either with unaided eye or binoculars soon locates the animals themselves, if they are using a given range. A band lying down on a hillside is difficult to spot at times. It blends well, but the white portions, which may appear to be pale rocks at a distance, catch the observer's eye and are quickly turned into antelope by use of binoculars.

As noted earlier, antelope have no dewclaws and thus their track prints simply show the two halves of the hoof. The forefoot track measures from about $2^7/_8$ to $3^1/_4$ inches in adults, the smaller hind-foot track about $2^3/_4$. The rear of the track is a bit broader than that made by deer. However, on some antelope ranges mule deer utilize the same feeding areas and waterholes and distinguishing positively between the two tracks is difficult if not impossible. Much depends on the experience of the tracker, and of the medium in which the prints were made.

Droppings also are rather similar to those of deer. Some of them may be smaller, about $3/_4$ inch, but many mule deer pellets are of the same dimension. When utilizing soft forage, droppings are a soft, irregular mass. This type is much like the same left by deer. During the summer when a combination of foods is being eaten, a more distinctive type of dropping is left. It is a rounded, elongate mass with pellet formation apparent.

The most distinctive sign left by antelope are scrapes made by the forefeet, in which the animals urinate and leave droppings. A small scraped-out place is dug with the sharp hoofs and body wastes are deposited in it. This is such an ingrained trait that individual animals leave numerous such scrapes daily. The problem in making use of such sign is that pronghorns move around so much. An undisturbed group may stay within 600 or 700 acres for days at a time, but it may visit practically every part of that area during an hour or so.

### HUNTING

In modern days the sport of pronghorn hunting has often been badly abused by the use of vehicles to chase the animals and to put a hunter within "flock shooting" range. In almost all instances this is illegal, and many game-department people really crack down on hunters who stoop to it. Although antelope hunting would seem to be a simple process, since the animals are easily spotted, it is actually one of the most challenging of endeavors when approached in a sporting manner.

Shots at antelope tend to be long, but there is a pronounced tendency among numerous hunters to try them much too long, out to 500 yards or more, and even at running animals. It is far more sporting, and more productive for that matter, to employ craft and stealth.

One common method is to cruise ranch or public-land trails in a vehicle, watching and glassing for distant bands. If a hunter is willing to be patient, this method will often locate a real trophy buck. And a couple of days of scouting may pin down the fact that the buck is using a certain basin or general area as a home base. This method is possible only where hunters are not numerous and chousing the bands around. The less disturbance the better.

Once a desirable specimen is located, an approach must be planned. There is little cover in antelope territory. But a small draw or a low ridge or series of ridges may form an avenue for a careful hunter to close in to rifle range of 200 to 300 yards. The exasperating part of this is that a stalk that requires much time may find the animals long gone before its climax.

Sometimes it is possible to use a vehicle or even another hunter as a ruse to hold antelope attention. A driver cruises slowly along and the hunter drops out on the off side in some small depression. The vehicle goes on and while the band watches it, the hunter, taking advantage of every small bush and depression, crawls along making his stalk. On occasion ranch or other vehicle trails may curve around so that a vehicle will start a band racing off in the direction of the stalker. In this case the driver—in most states it is illegal to drive off-road while hunting—tries to get on over a ridge out of sight, hoping the animals will stop running by the time they get into range of the hunter.

Although scores of hunters shoot at running antelope, sometimes firing thirty or forty rounds without collecting a trophy, running shots should be avoided. It is easy to wound animals this way, or to shoot the wrong one in a band. Standing shots should by all means be the goal.

Experienced antelope hunters check out a given expanse of hunting country, seeking the roughest portion. It is here, in the tight basins and narrow valleys between steep and often high ridges, that many an old loner trophy buck will hang out. It is here also that every antelope from flatter country in the region will head when a swarm of hunters begins combing the flats. Many mill-run hunters used to vehicle hunting don't want to tangle with the rough places, so the hunting isn't crowded. Further, these roughs lend themselves best to a careful stalker. Moving toward a ridge crest, then lying down and creeping up to peer over may put a trophy in the sights below within easy range.

It may or may not be legal in the state where you hunt to take a stand within range of a waterhole. If it is legal, a small blind of sage set up on a ridge perhaps 100 yards distant from a waterhole known to be used is a productive plan. Stands may also be taken beside a fence near an open gate where bands habitually pass, or near a much-used fence crossing. A small depression beneath a fence may be used daily by a band moving from one pasture to another. Their sign—scraped-off hair, and tracks—will indicate usage.

A stand between a watering place and a series of ridges and roughs, if properly planned, can also be effective. Perhaps there is a deep saddle in an otherwise steep, high, long ridge. The waterhole, let us say, is half a mile or so west of this north-south-running ridge. Animals from the roughs behind the ridge will stream through the deep saddle as the easiest path to water. This movement will probably be sometime during the middle of the day. Given a breeze from the east, a stand taken along one spur of the west side of the saddle will put antelope, probably passing in single file at a walk, within range before they know the hunter is there.

In undisturbed country, a band with a good buck may use a very small basin with a dry pond bed as a resting place. If hills around it are high and rough, the only approach is from one of these, and from the top the range may be too long for a shot. But the band can be purposely spooked out of the basin. Then the hunter moves down within range of the dry bed, and, well camouflaged if possible, lies down in a small depression behind a low bush. There is an excellent chance that the band will drift gingerly back into the snug hideaway within a couple of hours.

A trophy buck may stay right out in the middle of a large flat where a sneak approach is absolutely impossible. A ruse that sometimes works in this case is to walk in plain sight on a shallow angle toward and past its position. While giving the illusion of simply moving on by across the plain, the hunter is actually, although slowly, closing the range, never once looking toward the buck. Very occasionally curiosity will hold the animal immobile, watching intently until, at maybe 250 yards, the hunter can drop down and get off a shot.

Earlier in the chapter, tolling antelope in by appealing to their curiosity was mentioned. This is a great sport. They also will come now and then on the run, or walking stifflegged, to the sound of a high-pitched predator call, perhaps believing it is the bleat of a youngster.

Rifles for this sport should be flat-shooting because of the long ranges. They do not need to be anything heavier than standard deer calibers. The .243 is an example of an excellent antelope rifle. It should, of course, be fitted with a scope, preferably of the variable-power type. Good binoculars are also a must item. The challenge of antelope hunting in a sporting manner is the stark simplicity of the terrain. There are few hiding places for either hunter or game. The eyesight and speed of the quarry offset any decided advantage of the reach of the rifle.

Whether one hunts the pronghorn, stalks it with a telephoto lens, or simply watches bands swirl across the rolling plains, the thrill is supreme. This is one of the most handsome of North American big-game animals; it is well managed and far from endangered. It was snatched from the brink of extinction quite literally because of the interest and determination of sportsmen. They furnished the money for the management that built back and still nurtures the national herd for everyone to enjoy. It is a conservation story of which they may well be proud.

# WILD SHEEP

# Bighorn Sheep
*Ovis canadensis*
# Dall Sheep
*Ovis dalli*

The wild sheep of North America are among the most beautiful and appealing of our larger animals. Their intelligence and wariness and the remoteness of their domains are legendary. They have played dramatic parts in the journals of early explorers, have been romanticized in many modern wildlife films, and are among the most desirable, difficult, and taxing of all trophies to acquire. Yet curiously, notwithstanding all the attention and publicity they have received, only a comparatively few Americans, chiefly hunters and their guides, and game-management people, have ever seen one alive and on its home grounds.

This is because wild sheep are not only highly intolerant of human disturbance, but also in today's world (and indeed much of history) live out their lives for the most part in high, awesomely rugged wilderness situations that are visited by only a few determined hunters, backpackers, wildlife researchers, and photographers. The wild sheep of this continent were never abundant in the way that deer, elk, and antelope were and are. Their specialized remote worlds, from the snowy ranges of northern Alaska to the steep above-timberline meadows of the Rockies and to the arid,

Bighorn Sheep

burning desert ranges of northern and peninsular Mexico, preclude authentic abundance.

Nonetheless, when the white man first knew this continent sheep were at least numerous within habitat suitable to them. The white sheep of the far north and their darker phases ranging down into northern British Columbia were never disturbed to any serious extent by man until trophy hunting for them increased substantially during this century. The bighorns of the Rockies in the contiguous states, the southern portions of western Canada, and northern Mexico, however, were hard pressed during days of early settlement and onward by meat hunters. In many places, especially throughout the southern half of their range, they were totally extirpated. The meat is delicious. Sheep helped feed many a settlement and mining camp, or went to market as a wild delicacy. Particularly in the arid southwest, where sheep were dependent upon meager water supplies, they were waylaid at waterholes and entire bands or populations were wiped out.

Competition with domestic livestock also brought the wild sheep to extinction or the verge of it in numerous locations. It is believed that the desert bighorns of western Texas' Big Bend Country, for example, received the final coup, after severe poaching, by the influx of domestic sheep from which they contracted diseases. For many years under more enlightened approaches, from the 1930s onward, there was very little legal hunting within the lower-48 states. Sheep were fully protected. Unlike deer, which have extended their ranges in many places over the past century, the history of the bighorn in particular, because it has been in such common contact with man's intrusions, is one of constant retreat.

However, reestablishment by transplants and management have been wonderfully successful. Although far from abundant, sheep are certainly not generally endangered today, thanks to the intense interest and the money of sportsmen who have pushed to make certain game managers keep whatever populations are possible on every suitable range. In fact, an idea of "where the most sheep are" can most easily be gained presently by a check of where hunting is allowed. Some of the hunts are indeed merely token, the annual cropping of a very few mature or old surplus rams. Probably Alaska has the most wild sheep. These are the white Dalls. The Yukon and the Northwest Territories also have substantial numbers, and so does British Columbia, which also has bighorns in huntable numbers, and does Alberta. Within the contiguous states, ten have bighorns in modestly huntable numbers—Washington,

## THE WILD SHEEP

COLOR: **Bighorn,** in the north dark gray-brown, usually but not always paler in southern desert subspecies; large, conspicuous yellowish-white rump patch; muzzle, around eyes, and rear of all legs pale to whitish; short tail dark to black. **Dall sheep,** sparkling white; numerous color phases generally progressively darker from northern to southern part of range, beginning with a scattering of black hairs in tail, to a black tail, to partial black or gray saddle, to general gray with pale head and neck, to overall blue-gray to blue-black; all these darker phases with light rump patch, belly, and rear border of legs.

MEASUREMENTS, ADULT RAMS: **Bighorn,** 3 to 3½ feet at shoulder, depending on latitude, the larger specimens in north; overall length 5 feet to 5 feet 10 inches. **Dall,** generally comparable in measurements to the smaller bighorns.

WEIGHT, ADULT RAMS: **Bighorn,** from 150 to 200 pounds for desert subspecies to 300 for northern races. **Dall and subspecies,** 180 to 225 pounds.

HORNS: **Bighorn,** heavy, dark brown in north to gray-brown in south; round at base, massive, tightly curled above and around ears in circle close to face; weighing as much as 20 pounds. **Dall and subspecies,** pale yellowish color; thinner, curling but also flaring rather widely outward from face; sometimes somewhat flattened toward ends; all wild sheep horns with conspicuous annual growth rings.

EWES: At least one-fourth smaller; in the dark sheep much paler-colored than rams; with horns, but inconsequential, flat, slender, and not forming more than the beginning of a circle.

GENERAL ATTRIBUTES: Rounded, compact, powerful, rather short, chunky body, but exceedingly well proportioned and graceful; intelligent mien; amber to yellow black-centered eyes with phenomenal vision; unbelievably sure-footed and agile in rugged, steep terrain.

Oregon, Montana, Idaho, Wyoming, Nevada, Colorado, South Dakota, New Mexico, and Arizona. There are also some sheep in North Dakota, California, and Utah, with occasional token hunts currently in Utah. Some of these animals are reestablished or newly established.

Even given the comparative scarcity and the intense protection and management of wild sheep, there is still an exasperating amount of illegal killing. During the late 1960s in California, it was discovered that wealthy trophy hunters were paying high fees to a group of "guides" who took them into a refuge! Dozens of rams had been collected. In Mexico, where the desert bighorn is present here and there in remote areas in fair numbers, poaching is common.

Dall Sheep

Douglas Allen

Illegal trophy shenanigans, at a price, presumably involving officials, have been going on for years.

It is doubtful that the present ranges of any of the sheep can ever be appreciably extended. Transplants do add new pockets—a mountain here, another there. But within the vast perimeters of total sheep range, local populations have always been spotty. A certain individual mountain range may contain a fair number, another none. As a good example, in the Big Bend Country of western Texas a project has been underway for years now to reestablish the desert bighorn, once fairly abundant there. If it ever succeeds, the final population is certain to be modest, wholly dependent upon the protection of owners of large ranches, and with only a few sheep on scattered small individual mountain ranges.

To a large extent, sheep populations around the world were even ancestrally thus grouped. Abundance was scattered. Wild sheep of wide variety and quite closely related are found clear around the northern hemisphere. It is believed that the sheep of North America anciently reached this continent from Asia. No wild sheep of the northern hemisphere is closely related to domestic varieties. But several Asian species are undoubtedly close relatives of the Alaskan Dall and its phases.

The pure-white Dall of the type species, *Ovis dalli dalli,* and its white subspecies of the Kenai Peninsula, *O. d. kenaiensis,* blanket much of Alaska except the western portion and reach into the Yukon and the Northwest Territories and southward into northern British Columbia. The two are considered as one in Boone & Crockett records. However, there are subtle and progressive changes in color of the type Dall toward the southern portion of the range. It is true that there may be "sports" showing darker color differences among bands of Dall sheep anywhere in their range. This is a matter of current progressive evolution. Also progressively, the number grows as one moves south.

In the northern Yukon, for example, the sheep may appear pure white but close examination may show a scattering of black hairs on the tail. Farther north the entire tail may be black. These sheep are at the very northern fringe of the range of another subspecies, and are examples of infusions of it, the Stone sheep, *O. d. stonei,* which is typically charcoal or bluish-gray in color. But this subspecies of the white Dall varies highly in color. Some specimens appear to be perfect intergrades between white and very dark. These are gray, with neck and head gray-white. Most taxonomists list these as a distinct subspecies, the Fannin's sheep. Others, however, including the Boone & Crockett records, undoubtedly with good sense, give only one classification for color phases, the Stone. Many of the darkest Stones live in northwestern British Columbia, where the best trophy heads have been taken.

Classification of subspecies is confusing not only to the layman; scientists have long differed among themselves. One recent generally accepted authority, however, gives a listing of three phases of the Dall, including the type species, and seven for the bighorn. The Rocky Mountain bighorn, *Ovis canadensis canadensis*, is by far the most important among the bighorns. This burly brownish sheep blankets the greater share of the bighorn range, from southern British Columbia and Alberta southward through the Rockies states. Southward and spottily into the southwest United States and parts of Mexico a somewhat smaller-bodied subspecies, the desert bighorn, *O. c. nelsoni*, replaces it. The desert bighorn evolved from its spare habitat. It is by no means abundant nowadays; its existence is at least somewhat precarious, and it is managed everywhere with exceeding care.

The California bighorn is another subspecies, *O. c. californiana*. This sheep, native to California but in meager supply, is even present nowadays in southern British Columbia. There is also a subspecies called the Peninsula bighorn, of Lower California, and presumably a hybrid between it and the desert bighorn which is claimed as another subspecies. Only the Rocky Mountain type species and the desert subspecies are of importance to hunters or casual observers. The record book, always a good guide, gives a special listing to the desert sheep, but for record purposes lumps all other bighorn races together.

Wild sheep are hardy creatures, as evidenced by the curious fact that they are not found in areas where living is lush and easy, but were able to colonize not only much of the most remote and rugged country on the continent, but in extremes of climate, from the bitter winters of the far north and the high country of the Rockies to the seared and arid reaches of northern Mexico and Baja. It is logical that in such difficult living areas natural attrition is severe. Deep snows may keep bands from feeding, or cover what food is available. In the desert ranges, lack of water takes its toll.

Indeed it is believed by most researchers that the severity of the terrain and climate rather than predation are the dominant population controls. Coyotes undoubtedly kill many lambs. Mountain lions, not now abundant themselves, account for some adults as well as young. In the north, wolves do decimate the bands, drive

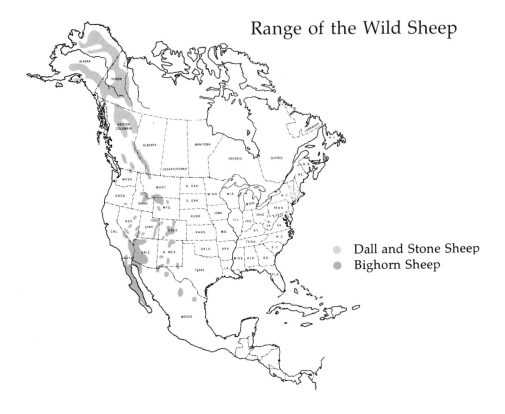

# Range of the Wild Sheep

Dall and Stone Sheep
Bighorn Sheep

them from lower altitudes to less congenial ranges, and probably are a definite limiting influence. Eagles are believed to kill many lambs. Throughout the enormous range of wild sheep, however, disease, parasites, and starvation, often in continuation, are the chief enemies, ever waiting in the highly specialized and remote habitats outside which these awesomely shy animals are apparently unable to cope.

## HABITAT

Experienced sheep hunters exploring new territory commonly judge a certain mountain as almost sure to be "a good sheep mountain." It is difficult to describe precisely what they mean. But it is true that sheep show a preference for certain peaks, and that each has its own character, and that sheep hunters and their guides probably know more about the wild sheep of North America than anyone else. Terrain varies widely from the home of the Dall to that of the desert bighorn, but certain characteristics fit rather generally for all.

The domain of the wild sheep is invariably high. To a man climbing into it, most of it is indeed rough and precipitous. Yet the specific places most sheep like best and in which they consort most are likely to be only gently angled, with broad basins and ridges with comfortable saddles scooping out undulations in them. Usually they select ridges with broad offshoots thrusting out in triangles overlooking valleys below, or overlooking an entire mountainside.

There are two nearly invariable characteristics of sheep country. A grassy alpine basin or point on a ridge must offer a broad view, for the animals depend almost wholly upon their superb vision to keep tabs on their surroundings. And there must be rough, usually steep and far more forbidding higher terrain nearby. If startled they utilize this jumbled backstop as escape territory. Almost without fail, their escape is upward. Here again the impulse is to be able to see what's going on below. They choose rough, rocky areas for escape because none of the sheep varieties seems sure of itself or feels secure running on level ground, but all are master maneuverers in difficult, rocky going.

It is true that under certain conditions of weather and season sheep use lower elevations. Desert sheep are known to cross broad, low valleys, and sheep in the north may come down to river valleys and even into timber-fringed meadows. But much of the habitat of all wild sheep is situated in the mountains chiefly above the heavy timber, and commonly where there is none. Altitudes of 8000, 9000, 10,000 even 11,000 feet or more are home at least in summer to most sheep in the far north and in the Rockies within the contiguous states.

The life of the white Dall sheep is lived out almost entirely above timberline. This is a land of ground-hugging vegetation, and of endless rock slides and steep shale slopes. At times these sheep move from peak to peak, which necessitates crossing lower valleys where higher vegetation grows. But fundamentally the highest, most remote treeless regions are their home.

It is curious that these sheep, though difficult to spot against snow, stand out conspicuously to anyone scanning snowless distant slopes from below. They seem to beckon as easy targets, but any hunter or predator who has gone after them soon knows the fallacy. Much of the best range is too rugged for use of horses. There's no way to reach the sheep country except to climb. The

Stone sheep, and the intermediate Fannin's, populate a rather restricted range, and within it appear to utilize somewhat lower elevations at times than the Dall.

It should be mentioned that many wildlife hobbyists think of mountain sheep and mountain goats as inhabitants of the same terrain. While they may be found, within goat range, even on the same mountain, the goats are animals of the most awesome crags and ledges. A sheep is a surefooted animal, but it could not live where a goat can without being in constant danger of fatal accident. Goats often are found temporarily on sheep range, but sheep seldom enter the ultimate in rugged knife-edged terrain in which the mountain goat is perfectly at home.

The Rocky Mountain bighorn has a more diverse habitat than the Dall and Stone. It spends much of its time above timberline, too. But it also comes down into fringes and patches of timber. In fact, this sheep is an exceedingly adaptable animal. It must be remembered that the present range of wild sheep, and emphatically of the bighorn, is not more than a twentieth of the area covered before settlement. The bighorn does not require high mountains as an absolute, except nowadays. The first explorers and settlers in the west found them even along the Missouri River brakes, and in the badlands of the Dakotas. Scores of buttes and outlying series of rough hills surrounded by plains far from authentic mountains were inhabited by sheep in Indian times. The reason almost all bighorns are in high, remote places now is that these are all the habitable undisturbed places left for them.

The desert bighorn habitat is for the most part not very high, because the mountains where they live are not as high as in the north. Much of their ancestral range was only from 3000 to 5000 feet. Many desert bighorns still live at such elevations. They are presently found along the Colorado River in southern Arizona, for example, and they often feed in Mexico way down on the flats between ranges of mountains. However, the terrain the desert bighorn selects as its favorite is possibly the roughest and most barren inhabited by North American sheep. In Mexico, for example, it seldom if ever has inhabited well-vegetated mountains easily accessible to it, but stays by choice in the most arid situations, where ragged upthrusts of rock, bleak cinder cones, and the jumbled rocky rims of northern Mexico's deserts form some of the most forbidding places on the continent.

**FEEDING**

On these typical desert ranges there is a wider variety of forage than one might expect, but the desert sheep must utilize more heavily than their northern cousins various types of browse plants. Wild sheep are predominantly grazers. Under proper range conditions they live on a soft diet of grasses, which account for as much as 95 percent of their intake. In the desert terrain, however, that much grass is difficult or impossible to find.

The desert sheep do eat any tough grasses available, but browse makes up a substantial part of the diet. The flowering centers of sotol are grubbed out, and buckbrush, yucca, and the green twigs and bark of the paloverde are gouged. Amazing as it seems, the bark of the viciously thorny, slender-stemmed bunches of ocotillo is eaten. Agave or century plant is in some locations a staple. Mesquite and catclaw add to variety. Mountain mahogany and sage, when available, are eagerly eaten.

Grasses such as grama grass and needle grass are scattered on the desert slopes, and are avidly sought. One feeding habit of the desert bighorn that is notable is the large intake of varied cacti. Part of this foraging is for liquid as well as food. Rams smash the barrel cactus and gorge on the pulp. They eat the fruit and pads of prickly pear. In the relatively modest range where the huge and viciously wire-spined saguaro cactus grows, somehow the sheep are able to gouge deep holes in the trunks. No one seems quite sure how they do this without serious harm.

Farther north the Rocky Mountain bighorn has an easier time of it. Grasses are numerous and usually abundant. Vetch, needle grass, wheat grass, and fescue are common. In places sedges abound, and in others there are rushes. There is also clover, and a wide variety of forbs or weeds, most of which the sheep find palatable. In some instances where a certain plant is abundant and palatable, the bighorn is a most selective forager. It may simply snip off the budding flowers, for example, on a patch of smartweed, and leave the plants alone.

When snow arrives the diet must change. Dry grasses are still eaten if not buried too deeply beneath the snow. But now substantial amounts of browse are taken. Sagebrush and greasewood as well as rabbit brush, scrub wild cherry, willows, and alders all are eaten. If forced, the animals also snip off twigs of juniper, spruce, and fir. In spring when the aspens and birches launch buds, these furnish a large part of daily diet.

Up in the Dall sheep's domain there are varied grasses in the alpine basins, and there are also lichens and mosses to complement them. Several low-growing shrubs also furnish browse. The dwarf willow is one of these. Blueberry and raspberry bushes are also present in some areas. Invariably there are ridges swept clean of snow by winds in winter that offer good foraging locations, and of course both the white sheep and the Rocky Mountain sheep must now and then move lower to find food enough to sustain them.

Unlike the antlered animals, which routinely feed both night and day, sheep are almost wholly diurnal. It is thought that two influences have molded them thus. One is that they depend so heavily upon their exceedingly keen distance vision that they are at a great disadvantage at night. Thus they retire early and follow a routine of staying in a bed throughout the entire night. The other is that in their world they are not used to undue disturbance, and thus have little reason to be up and down around the clock.

They are, however, early risers. They are up at or before dawn, sometimes in summer as early as 4:00 a.m. to begin feeding. By the middle of the morning they are ready to rest. The younger animals are inclined to drop down just wherever they happen to be. Adults may go through a cursory pawing of the ground, pawing a few times with each front hoof on a level spot to remove stones, and then lie down. These daytime beds are invariably in a basin or in a ridge saddle or on a slope where the sheep cannot be surprised from any direction. Because most sheep are quite gregarious, and a band lies with individuals facing differently, approach of any danger is certain to be distantly spotted.

During the morning rest period the animals chew their cud. Depending upon the food supply, and the restlessness or lazy comfort of the animals, they may stay bedded until midafternoon, or they may be up having a snack at noon or early afternoon. Then a casual bed is again the rule, and more cud chewing until the serious afternoon feeding begins. These daytime beds are quite different from the night bedding places, discussed below. The late-afternoon feeding sessions in long shadows must produce bulging stomachs to last through the night. Thus they may be long, and rather intense.

While feeding the animals are not erratic, but are thorough foragers, walking along slowly, making a business of filling up, yet always on the watch distantly for any disturbance. By the time the sun hangs low, draping the valleys in shadow and flooding a weak light across the peaks, the sheep are ready to call it a day and move toward their nighttime beds.

*Dall sheep resting in their daytime beds. Each animal faces in a different direction to watch for danger.*

## MOVEMENTS

This movement, which is usually brief, is sparked by an instinct and habit that is unique among antlered and horned animals of this continent. When a sheep strikes out for its nighttime bedding area, it knows exactly where it is going. The bed it will use is one that it has used many times before. If the sheep moves to a new mountain, it will make a fresh nighttime bed, but should it leave and then return to the same mountain, chances are it will use the same old bed.

The sites for these permanent beds are chosen with infinite care. As a rule the lee side of a ridge or the base of a shale slope or rocky outcrop is selected. Many are below the crest of a ridge in a protected spot. Occasionally a small cave is used. These may also be used to give protection in the desert in daytime from the hot sun in the southern range, or from rain elsewhere. The location is invariably where the approach of danger from all directions can be heard in time for an escape up into a rough area.

These night beds are pawed-out spots several feet across. From much use they are smoothed out 6 inches to a foot or more in depth.

They are smelly places. Droppings are piled around the edges. When a sheep arises in the morning it generally urinates immediately, without moving outside the bed. Conceivably this is a kind of mark that stakes out the bed as belonging to a certain individual. Because sheep country is high or arid, with little moisture in the air, the beds seldom become soggy but remain dry. Some of these beds show evidence of use for several years.

The hooves of sheep are fashioned with sharp, hard edges and with a concave interior filled with spongy tissue. Although sheep seldom walk the knife-edged pinnacles and crags that goats casually traverse, they are fantastically sure-footed and agile. Rams when disturbed often plunge nonchalantly down a 50-degree slope. They are able to walk down nearly vertical cliffs if there are even the slightest small toeholds en route. When it is necessary to jump, the animals have no trouble covering 15 feet or more across a chasm, and easily fly as high up as 4 feet in the air on the way.

Jimmy McLucas, who for many years trapped big game for transplant for the Montana game department, once keep losing rams from out of an enclosure where they were being temporarily held. It was surrounded by a plank fence 8 feet high, the planks 2 inches thick. He caught a ram in the act of leaping, touching the 2-inch top of the fence with all four feet and bounding down to the other side.

Most of the movements of sheep are a casual walk. If disturbed they may trot for some distance, and when severely frightened they gallop up a slope at high speed. On level ground they may be capable of 25 to 35 miles an hour, but only briefly. Even when undisturbed they are masters at leaping across broad fissures. Or they casually jump off a ledge to land 20 to 30 feet below. Their sturdy legs flex like springs to bear the body weight as they land on all fours.

A few sheep hunters and naturalists have observed a most interesting and amazing ability of sheep in ascending extremely broken country. A vertical cleft in a cliff may rise from its base to a mesa above. It may be several feet wide, with minor horizontal ledges a few inches wide here and there on either face. Such formations, often used, sometimes have been called "sheep ladders." They are like chimneys open on one side, in the face of a cliff. Fred Bear, the renowned archer and wildlife photographer, once saw a group of sheep go up such a ladder. Lining up single file, the first one leaps upward, strikes its hooves against one side, aiming for the slightest hold and sometimes none, then flips aside in midair to bound again, higher, and strike the other side. With a few quick left-side, right-side leaps, pushing each time outward and up, it tops out, and the others follow in their turn.

Although wild sheep cannot be termed truly migratory, many of them do move seasonally. These movements are entirely dependent upon weather and availability of food. Cold does not bother them. Wild sheep do not bear wool like domestic sheep. Their coats are of hollow hair, which provides superb insulation. But no matter how well shielded they may be against bitter weather, if snow gets too deep for them to move about, or covers forage deeply, they must move down to a lower altitude.

It is common for some sheep bands to winter at only 2000 to 4000 feet, far below their summer range, and sometimes requiring a trek of 25 miles or more. Some, however, are able to stay all year on the same range. The northern sheep seldom have any difficulty finding water, but the desert bighorn sometimes must travel far to a remote spring. In summer a movement to an area of reliable water may be necessary. Desert sheep do not necessarily go to water daily. Sometimes they manage several days without drinking, utilizing cactus pulp to satisfy their thirst.

All sheep are to some extent wanderers. They may move whimsically from slope to slope or mountain to mountain within their domain. Conversely, some of them stay for weeks within a very small range. The white sheep, most observers believe, are less inclined to wander than the bighorns. All sheep avidly seek salt licks. These may be at a salty spring, or formed of clay inlaid in a bluff. Occasionally the animals find brittle rock deposits that contain salt, and chew these. Mineral licks are constantly visited. Some show signs of use for many years and even are responsible, researchers believe, for keeping sheep in the area. Studies have shown that trips to a particular lick sometimes may cover 10 or 15 miles.

### BREEDING

There is a definite caste system among sheep during most of the year. The rams form small groups, and these are usually composed of males of similar age. Here and there an old ram is a loner, perhaps crotchety and unsociable, or else off by himself because other more vigorous rams bedevil him. The rams usually spend the summer higher up than the ewes and lambs. But by late fall they cease being quite so friendly with one another and begin to seek out the ewes.

As early as October in the north, rams begin to play at fighting,

*The crash of two rams colliding in battle can be heard a half-mile way.*

locking horns and wrestling, or shoving. But presently the play becomes rougher, and finally there are awesome battles. Curiously, rams do not fight for the favors of one or several ewes. They do not attempt to form harems, although one may try to dominate several ewes briefly. Actually the rams are wholly promiscuous. Two may battle fiercely, then one backs off and the other breeds a nearby ewe. He may then leave her, seeking another, while the ram he was battling with breeds the same ewe. The ewes are in heat very briefly. And the rams have the unique physical ability to breed several within only a few minutes.

When a battle builds up between two rams, they may approach each other as if unaware. The routine is a highly stylized ritual. Suddenly when a short distance apart, and not even necessarily looking at each other, both animals rear up on their hind legs and rush together. They may drop down again and then rush headlong, but usually as they strike head-on both have the forefeet off the ground, slamming with full body force and momentum. The massive horns come together evenly; the left of one is matched with the right of the other. Observers have heard the crashing sound as much as a half-mile away.

Immediately after each impact, the rams rear their heads back and back away, often shaking their heads. Then as if on signal, they smash together again. They appear to gauge very carefully the head-on strike, to avoid severe physical damage. Occasionally severe injuries do occur—horn or eye or brain damage. The length of the battle depends on how evenly matched the rams are. Eventually one will break off. The winner may quickly breed a nearby ewe several times, then wander off seeking other conquests. No ram "owns" a ewe.

The peak of the rut in the north is in late November and into December. This assures that the lambs will not be born until early spring has come to the wintering grounds. Among desert bighorns, however, breeding is much earlier, and the rutting period lasts much longer. This is a device of nature to assure that the lambs will be born at a time when winter rains have brought green and abundant forage briefly to the desert. And the long season, which may start as early as August or even late July and run on through into fall, helps to assure that the desert sheep, spread thinner in population than their northern relatives, all will find each other and mate.

### BIRTH AND DEVELOPMENT

Once the rut is finished, the rams revert to their male-chauvinistic ways, disregarding the ewes entirely and joining in groups of their own once more. The sexes may be forced together on a winter range. How closely depends on the quality of the range. Six months from the time the ewes were bred, the lambs are dropped. This places lambing time, except for the desert sheep, in May and June. A single lamb is the rule, although there may be twins.

When it is time for her lamb to be born, each ewe leaves her group and seeks a high ledge or the foot of a cliff high up, where there is protection from weather and from where she may keep watch over a broad area for danger. Lambs of the bighorn are a fuzzy dark gray with a darker streak along the back. Those of the Dall are white. Both stand less than a foot high at the shoulder and weigh about 8 pounds. Rocky Mountain bighorn lambs may be a bit larger.

The ewe is a nervous, constant guardian. The lamb is able to stand on wobbly legs and nurse within a few hours, and it grows swiftly. But as a rule the ewe keeps it at the birth site for about a week, leaving only to grab a quick bite of forage now and then. Often while the youngster sleeps, the mother stands alert guard. After seven or eight days the lamb is allowed to follow closely with its mother. Presently she rejoins the band of other ewes and their lambs. This band also contains young of the previous year, still hanging with the ewes. Lambs of both ages play vigorously.

*A three-month-old Dall lamb.*

Soon the young are nibbling at grasses, and within a month most of them are at least partially weaned. During this training period the mother lets them start to nurse, but then abruptly leaves. Here and there a less firm mother allows a lamb to continue nursing on into the fall. Although wild sheep are silent most of the time, the young lambs do bleat, and the ewes now and then answer with a blatt. Even an adult ram may blatt explosively in challenging another. But by and large sheep are not vocal creatures.

By the time the lambs are weaned their horns are sprouting. Yearlings and even two-year-olds still stay with the flock, and particularly the lambs of the year and the yearlings play together, but ewes become annoyed if the large ones get too rough, and will run them off. Occasionally a single ewe baby-sits with a group of lambs while the others feed nearby. The mixed flock contains no mature rams, and indeed adult rams are utterly disdainful of the lambs. Curiously, however, when forced into contact with young and ewes, adult rams are often stoic and solicitous. Big-game trappers transplanting bighorns have discovered that when moving sheep by truck, for example, the animals are quite calm, intelligent, and sensible. A big ram will allow a lamb to crowd under its belly and will not harm it. Conversely, goats under similar circumstances sometimes will kill each other.

The long two-year-old rams are not allowed with the bachelor gangs of mature rams. Some wander away from the flock in their own groups and some do not. It is believed that the first successful breeding of the rams occurs when they are long three-year-olds. Ewes are able to breed when a year younger.

At breeding age the horns of the rams have grown to roughly a half-circle. Hunting regulations in most places require that a legal ram have at least a three-quarter curl. Such animals are in the four-to-five-year age class. Seldom is a full curl attained until a ram is at least seven. At twelve to fourteen a ram is very old, and some of the best trophy horns—age can be deduced from horn growth rings—are from rams in this age group. A few animals may live longer. A young desert ram of known age brought to the Black Gap Wildlife Management Area in the lower Big Bend Country of west Texas in an attempt to reestablish desert sheep there lived to be seventeen.

Because of the massiveness and beauty of wild sheep horns, they have been a fetish of sportsmen throughout the history of hunting all around the world. Horns of the bighorn sheep generally curl in a wide C around behind the ear and in a circle forward back around toward the massive base. Most, but not all, grow rather close to the face. Because full-curl bighorn horns are so heavy, they often interfere with an animal's vision. The ram then rubs and scrapes the ends against rocks and "brooms" them off. Many of the finest trophies have broomed horns. Some, of course, may have the tips broken during battles, but among the bighorns brooming is common.

The white sheep and their relatives have a somewhat different horn configuration. They are not so massive, are yellowish instead of brown in color, and almost always flare widely out away from the face. They are thus broomed less, because they are not so likely to interfere with vision. Numerous specimens of Dalls and Stones have more than a full curl with perfect tips for that reason, and also a wider tip-to-tip spread because of the flare. The Stone sheep generally bears horns slightly more massive than the Dall.

To illustrate with measurements the basic characteristics of sheep horns, the longest bighorn horns in the record book are presently: right, $49\frac{1}{2}$; left, $48\frac{1}{4}$. The tip-to-tip spread is $23\frac{7}{8}$. The first-place (and longest) Stone sheep horns, the longest sheep horns taken to date on the continent are: right, $50\frac{1}{8}$; left, $51\frac{5}{8}$; tip-to-tip spread, 31 inches. The top-ranked Dall: right, $48\frac{5}{8}$; left, $47\frac{7}{8}$; tip-to-tip spread: $34\frac{3}{8}$. Horns of the desert rams, even though the animals are often smaller in body, rank in length, spread, and base circumference just about as large on the average as those of the Rocky Mountain sheep. Comparative base circumferences of first-place records give a good idea also of horn types among the several varie-

4 DEEPEST RINGS

3rd YEAR
GROWTH RINGS

2nd YEAR
GROWTH RINGS

*A ten-year old bighorn ram with a superb set of horns. The growth rings, starting from the tips, clearly show the animal's age. The tips have been "broomed" by the ram, else they would have obstructed his vision as the horns continued to grow.*

ties. Rocky mountain bighorn: both horns, 16⅝. Desert bighorn: right, 16¾; left 17. Stone: both horns, 14¾. Dall: right, 14⅝; left, 14¾.

### SENSES

Like that of the pronghorn on the plains, the visual ability of wild sheep has often been likened to that of man assisted by an 8-power binocular. Sight is far and away the most important sense. The immense vistas among which the sheep live allow them to scan incessantly and over great distances. In somewhat the same way as the antelope of the plains, they also keep danger at a distance by recognizing it from afar. Unlike antelope, however, sheep cannot escape predators by outrunning them on flat expanses. But any predator has a difficult time apprehending an adult sheep, first because it sees the danger long before it is near, and second because when it takes to its heels in the broken high terrain always nearby, leaping off ledges and bounding across gashes in the rocks, it is practically uncatchable.

Sheep do not always recognize immobile objects. A prone hunter glassing from a distant slope may be passed over with a cursory scanning. But the slightest movement brings the sheep alert and curious. In fact, curiosity now and then gets a ram into trouble. A pair of hunters, knowing they have been sighted because a bedded band has arisen and stared at them, sometimes successfully use the ruse of having one stay put while another drops off a ridge behind and circles for a stalk.

Interestingly, when sheep spot an intruder, it seldom works to try to get out of sight quickly. A hunter, knowing he has been seen distantly, has an urge to duck back over a nearby ridge crest. The moment he disappears, every sheep usually will run. Further, if a sheep is spooked so badly it gallops away, almost without fail any sheep in the vicinity will race away. Sheep do not often run at full speed. When one does, the sound alerts all others that this is no time to be wondering what is wrong.

Scenting ability is well developed, but it is not always very useful except at close range. Air currents and winds in the high country are whimsical. If sheep do catch a scent they instantly give evidence of it in alertness or flight. But they seem to know, by the way they select places from which they can see over a large area, that every-which-way breezes may not be dependable.

Hearing is also keen. But again, it is only moderately useful. As noted, the sound of other running sheep tells of danger. But a falling rock or a rock slide means little. Mountain country is full of such natural sounds. The unnatural sound is something else. A distant human voice, the rhythmic sounds of a packtrain moving in rocky country, the blowing of horses, the clang of any packtrain or hunter equipment, all are frightening.

SIGN  *(Tracks are illustrated on page 251.)*

Although hunting guides are not uninterested in sheep sign, in most situations the expanse of country is so vast that it is far easier and more profitable to look with powerful binoculars for the sheep themselves. Because of their wandering habits, tracks and droppings and beds may not mean there are sheep present on that mountain. Tracks of desert sheep at a waterhole are, of course, an extremely important clue. Tracks and gougings at a mineral lick also tell that sheep regularly use it.

Sheep tracks might be confused on some ranges with those of deer. In mud the sheep may leave a depression in the center of the track because of the spongy center in the hoof. Deer do not. The general outline of sheep tracks when prints are clear, however, show nearly straight edges, and they are blockier, larger, and less pointed than deer tracks, and almost as broad at front as at rear. In front the toes, when not splayed out as in soft earth, are more prominently separated than those of deer. In a few instances goats may be on the same range. This might be confusing. Goat tracks if plainly printed tend to be more square, and a bit indented along the middle of the outside edges.

Sheep droppings can be an indication of population, and current residence if they are fresh. They are not at all easy to distinguish from either deer or mountain goat droppings. Deer droppings as a rule are rounded on both ends while those of sheep are bell-shaped. However, droppings of deer take several forms, and those of goats are often as bell-shaped as sheep droppings. Like all of the ruminants, sheep droppings form masses or elongated shapes when forage is soft, and show as hard pellets when food is less so. Observers have often found droppings made up almost wholly of clay after sheep had been using a mineral lick.

Undoubtedly nighttime sheep beds, discussed earlier, are the most reliable sign. One who recognizes these cannot possibly confuse them with signs of any other animal.

### HUNTING

Successful sheep hunting is an art. Like many others, it is deceptively simple. There is no wide variety of techniques and methods, as there is in deer hunting. For example, you don't spook a ram out of a canyon by pitching rocks into it, as sometimes works with deer. If you are close enough to pitch a rock, any ram that had been there long ago counted the whiskers on your chin and left.

Put as simply as possible, the technique of successfully taking a sheep is to see it before it sees you, study it to make sure it is a legal specimen and a trophy of proportions you will settle for, and then get into shooting range without being seen. Any sheep that has spotted a hunter, even at a couple of miles distant, probably cannot be come upon easily within range unaware.

In any sheep terrain, from Alaska to Mexico, the hunter must be endowed first with stamina, and then with patience. Possibly one is as important as the other. Without both, success is unlikely. In almost all instances, a hunter is going to have to climb, in tough country, and the stalk may require hours. Mandatory equipment, along with proper clothing and boots, is: quality binoculars, preferably of about 9-power; a spotting scope of at least 20-power with a small tripod attached; a scoped flat-shooting rifle in a class from the .30/06 to the 7mm magnum capable when necessary of long, lethal shots.

The basic routine for sheep hunters is to select a mountain or an expanse of country that seems suitable, then ease into it inconspicuously and sit down—never stand or sit skylighted—in a place where a view of several slopes and basins is possible. The sitting spot should be where the hunter is not obvious. Then the glassing begins. Glassing for sheep doesn't mean just sweeping binoculars across the region. It means first making a slow sweep of all of it in view with the naked eye, and then a yard-by-yard study of it with the glass.

The white sheep are rather easy to locate most of the time, and the gray-faced Stones are not too difficult, but the bighorns are likely to blend well and be tough to pinpoint. The hunter using a glass may see some minute distant spot that looks interesting. He keeps coming back to it. Perhaps after half an hour he catches a movement. Or he is interested enough to get out the spotting scope. The spotting scope can bring in information about the sex and size of the sheep. A lone sheep is very likely to be a large old ram, and a most desirable trophy. However, groups of rams, three to ten, all of the same general age class, may all be trophies, and then a most careful and anguishing decision must be made.

An experienced sheep hunter does not begin planning his stalk the moment he spots a trophy. Unless the animals are close and a stalk is easy and fast, going after feeding sheep is a risky business. After a long, exhausting stalk, the animals may be long gone, and a mile away. By knowing the feeding and daytime bedding habits of sheep, one can judge from the time they are sighted about how long it will be before they lie down, or, if they're lying down, about when they'll be getting up to feed again. Sheep spotted, let's say, at 8:00 a.m. probably will lie down soon, at least within the next hour, and then stay bedded until at least noon. Sheep seen feeding at 1:00 p.m. will probably lie down shortly for several hours, but then will be up feeding and moving late in the afternoon.

Most hunters hesitate to try a stalk on feeding sheep late in the day. It probably will not be successful, and it may be a long way down for the hunter in the dark. However, the animals should be watched patiently. If their bedding location for the night is ascertained, or a guess made by the look of the terrain that it is nearby, they will probably be up and feeding right here the next dawn. Sometimes rams will select a basin in which to lie down in the daytime where there is absolutely no cover from any direction to bring one within possible range. Experienced hunters in such circumstances simply resign themselves. They keep a watch on the sheep until they finally move. Perhaps then a stalk may become possible. If not, it is better to know the general location of the animals and try again tomorrow.

When forage is abundant, on many ranges sheep do not take a noon snack, even though they usually do. If not, they may stay bedded for four or five hours. Once a hunter is certain the sheep have not seem him or are studying him with concentration, it is simply a matter of making the stalk without being seen. "Simply" probably is not the word. Once in a dozen tries the terrain may lie just right for an easy stalk. Mostly, however, no sheep stalk is easy.

The plan should always be if at all possible to circle and get above the sheep. They do not seem to expect danger from above and do not look up often. They lie overlooking a vast expanse below. Coming in from above and behind offers the hunter immense advantage, provided he does not have problems with wind direction. Even though sheep may not use their noses as much as their eyes, it's dead certain that if one winds you it will flee.

If a stalk is long, the first part can be covered swiftly, given ample cover. But the last stretch should be done with infinite patience and with cautious and thorough pre-glassing of the immediate area. Sometimes sheep get up and move a bit. They may have moved enough so in haste you stumble into them where you don't expect them. Or there may have been an animal or two unseen before the stalk began. You bumble into one of these and spook all the rest.

Practically all modern-day sheep hunters are guided. Thus they do not need to know very much except what the guide tells them. But to be successful they must pay close attention, and realize what sort of sport this is. No two stalks are alike. Meticulous plans for each must be made. Fundamentally the idea is that with a proper stalk the shot itself should be easy, at an immobile animal, and if possible not over 250 yards at most. It is the stalk that sparks the excitement and challenge. On many stalks a guide and hunter spend seven or eight hours from the time the sheep are first sighted until the shot is made.

Knowing what is a trophy and what is not is extremely important. Most guides are expert judges. It is sometimes very tricky to judge whether a head is a good or poor trophy. Some young rams among the white sheep, for example, may exhibit a full curl but still not be much. A curl that measures in length in the low 30s would never be accepted by a true trophy hunter. But one of 38 to 40 inches would unquestionably be most desirable.

Overall, sheep hunting is a physically difficult but fascinating sport. Part of the appeal lies in the wild country that is the domain of the animals. Part of it relates to the fact that, even though sheep are not rare, the number of permits for any sheep variety nowadays is limited. One may apply in several states of the contiguous United States every season for years before drawing lucky—or maybe never making it. This, too, heightens the drama. Whether one hunts, or simply goes into sheep country to see or photograph the animals, it is a good feeling to know that careful scientific management, the many attempts at reestablishment on denuded ancestral ranges, and the transplants to new ranges have been successful over the years and that without question the wild sheep will be available in at least limited numbers far into the future.

# Mountain Goat

*Oreamnos americanus*

The mountain goat, sometimes called the Rocky Mountain goat, is a collection of contradictions. It isn't a goat, but rather a very distant relative of several totally dissimilar animals of Asia and Europe that appear to be a link between the goats and the antelopes. It has been on this continent, scientists believe, for well over a half-million years, and yet less is known of its life history than of those of our other horned and antlered creatures.

It appears at casual observation to be a stodgy, clumsy creature, slow and ungraceful in its movements. Yet it lives in the highest, steepest, most dangerous terrain North America offers, calmly staring down without concern from narrow ledges on which it cannot possibly turn around, perhaps over a cliff falling perpendicularly 1000 feet or more to the next ledge. Its life is spent at the top of this continent's world, in climatic conditions under which man can survive only with most careful planning and outfitting and then only for a few days at a time. Yet the goat stoically endures day-to-day bitter weather and violent storms, and grows rolling fat on what would seem to be a meager food supply.

The mountain goat is wholly American. There is no other similar animal in North America, and none elsewhere. Scientists believe that the ancient forebears of the mountain goat came to this continent from Asia when there was, they suspect, a land bridge connecting the continents across the Bering Strait. Presumably the distant relatives of the mountain goat include such curious creatures as the goat-antelopes of Asia, the chirus, the curious goral of Siberia, the cliff donkey or serow of western China, and the better-known several varieties of chamois.

None of these is remotely similar to the mountain goat in physical appearance or coloring. Presumably the goat, isolated in its far-northern North American home, slowly evolved to fit the terrain. The white coat may have been designed by nature as camouflage in snow, yet the animal is commonly seen in snowless areas among bare rocks or even occasionally dark spruce, where of course it is blatantly obvious. There is really small need for contriving camouflage. In the world of this creature, enemies except for the terrain itself are few, and visits by man are brief and infrequent.

It is interesting that the mountain goat apparently has never been numerous—that is, abundant in the sense that other hoofed animals such as deer, pronghorn, and buffalo have been. But it also has never been scarce or rare within its range. Observations of early explorers, and modern studies and observations over many past years, tend to prove that the goat population has long remained at a modest but unendangered level, with only moderate periodic fluctuations, seldom of consequence. Possibly the awesomely forbidding habitat of the creature acts both as a protection, by eliminating or controlling populations of potential enemies, and also as a check on overpopulation by the animal itself.

Scientists admit that aside from occasional transplants of goats to new and suitable territory to launch new bands, the mountain goat is for the most part beyond the reach of modern game management. This is because its living area is also too far removed, vertically, from the common reach of man. And so it may be that this creature is one of the few and classic examples of a near-perfect balance in nature. Further, because man's influence is not expected to touch the realm of the mountain goat more that lightly in foreseeable times, this may be the one creature native to North America secure forever against possible listing as rare or endangered.

Although sport hunting has never harmed any North American animal population—under modern management techniques, indeed, it is utilized as a tool for keeping population levels tailored to available range—hunting has had and presently does have no influ-

Mountain Goat

## MOUNTAIN GOAT

COLOR: White, often shaded with yellow; eyes, horns, nose, and hooves black.

MEASUREMENTS, MATURE BILLIES: 3 feet to 3 feet 4 inches at shoulder; overall length 5 feet to as much as 6 feet.

WEIGHT, MATURE BILLIES: To 300 pounds.

HORNS: Sharp, slender, cylindrical, stiletto-like, backward-curving, at maximum to 12 inches in length, generally 9 to 10 inches; permanent; grow throughout lifetime, with annual growth rings.

NANNIES: Somewhat smaller even at maximum; horns seldom over 9 inches, but one record-book specimen taken over a half-century ago measured over 12 inches.

GENERAL ATTRIBUTES: Hair long, shaggy except on lower leg; humped shoulders; both sexes with beard on lower jaw; blocky overall appearance; calm, deliberate temperament; exceedingly surefooted.

ence whatever on the goat population. There are several reasons for this. Most important probably is that of all native big-game animals, the mountain goat is the least desirable as a trophy. Hunters after sheep may decide to try for a goat as an incidental, or to fill out a collection of trophies. However, there is so little difference in horn length among mature goats that the chances of taking an exceptional head are remote. "Exceptional" doesn't mean much — possibly another inch of horn above the norm. Further, the difficulty of getting to goat country, accomplished only by a tough and often dangerous climb, puts the animal out of range of a majority. The meat is edible, but most find it far from desirable, and useful only in a pinch.

Little use has ever been found for the hair of the mountain goat, and even if an important use were discovered, there are not enough goats to make it worthwhile, aside from the difficulty of collection. Northwestern Indians long ago made yarn from the fine undercoat of the animal by rolling it into strands. This yarn, sometimes dyed, lent itself to weaving. The source for the wool was usually animals that had died naturally, or from areas where it had been raked off by brush or rocks during spring shedding.

Another reason that the goat is of little interest to hunters is that it is really not a very challenging quarry. This does not mean it is not an interesting animal — simply that it is not especially alert, wary, or imaginative. In personality the goat is a plodder, stolid, a kind of stubborn ascetic. One writer has suggested that its lack of imagination and wariness is undoubtedly one of its greatest assets. If it spent time dwelling on the precariousness of its perches, he claims, it would quickly be a nervous wreck. Further, its plodding nature is unquestionably a by-product of its chosen habitat. Any creature in a hurry here would not last long.

No one knows just why the mountain goat has never come down from its above-timberline pinnacles and crags to probe into other areas. But it is certain that this love of the high places has allowed the animal little leeway for colonization. Apparently it has never been able or physically equipped to push its range downward. Thus only in places where it was able to move from one mountain range to another along ridges leading from one tall peak to another was it capable of enlarging its domain.

So far as is known, the original range was from Alaska southward as far as a part of the Cascades in Washington, and along the mountain spines running into central Idaho and western Montana. Over the years transplants have been made, often with great physical difficulties for the game-department personnel doing the work, from range to range within states where the animals were native. This has been heavily emphasized in Montana.

Transplants have also been made to suitable territory in states where goats were not native. Today the animals are found in their original ranges in Alaska, the Yukon, the Northwest Territories, British Columbia, western Alberta, Washington, Idaho, and Montana, plus in areas of the last three to which they have been transplanted. Alaska undoubtedly has the largest population. Within the rather restricted range in the lower-48 states, Washington contains the highest number, interestingly, possibly half as many as are in Alaska. Transplants to new territory within the United States have been made to Oregon; that project was begun in the 1950s. There is a small but stable population in northwestern Wyoming, a very few placed in mountains east of Salt Lake City, Utah, and a quite substantial population in western Colorado, heaviest in the Mount Evans and Collegiate Range areas.

One of the most interesting islands of goat population is in the Black Hills of South Dakota. The basis of this herd was formed by a few escapees from a small Canadian group placed in Custer State Park over half a century ago. Once free, they moved as if by compass reading straight for nearby 7,242-foot Harney Peak, the highest point in South Dakota, and to the adjacent Needles—the

## Range of the Mountain Goat

only two high, rough areas in the Black Hills. This herd well illustrates how the highly specialized goat is tied to high, rugged terrain. The animals over all the years have never spread outward from those two colonizing points. Populations have built up as high as 400 animals, but undoubtedly cannot ever exceed that because of lack of living room and food.

Certainly there are still left a number of places in which the mountain goat could survive and propagate, perhaps on peaks in northern New Mexico, California, or elsewhere. But the likelihood of broadening the range of the animal is slim. It cannot reach new ranges except with man's help — that is, by game-management people from the states involved. Because the goat is not avidly desired by numerous hunters, and because management personnel have more than they can handle with the more popular and abundant game animals, there is little interest in further transplants.

The goat population of the present, however, is in a healthy condition that will continue. Enemies, except for weather, snow slides, possibility of fatal falls (which do occur), and minor parasitic infestations, are minimal. Predation is low. Eagles are thought to kill a few kids. But in the sparse domain of the goat, few other predators can survive. On occasion goats are forced by blizzards to move down into or to cross high valleys. Here a wolf, mountain lion, bobcat, or coyote may attempt a kill. A few do succeed, but the goat with its rapier horns is a tenacious and dangerous foe, not inclined to give up easily.

Scientists have made some attempts to classify goats into a number of subspecies based on geography. There is little reason or need to do so. As a rule mountain goats of the more northerly range are larger at maturity than others. A few most unusual male specimens have scaled 400 to 500 pounds. There are minor differences among specimens from different latitudes and mountain ranges. But all are so similar that subspecies classification seems at best a questionable or unnecessary practice.

### HABITAT

"Mountain" is certainly the correct qualification for the favored and indeed mandatory habitat of this animal. But that word doesn't say it all. It is true that the goat does appear at times below timberline. But its classic preference is for the treeless country, where only dwarf scrub appears, and for the barren rocks and crags and short-grass mountain meadows above the line where true timber grows.

It spends much time on completely barren slopes of jumbled rock. At the bases of desolate crags there may be scattered, tough high-altitude plants subsisting in stunted fashion in the thin, flinty soil. But the rocks replace, for cover, what the forests offer to animals lower down. Portions of each day may be bright with sun, but arctic winds incessantly whistle and cut, and warmth is little known even when the thin atmosphere is cloudless.

The goat is oblivious. Its shaggy outer coat of hair may be as much as 6 or 7 inches long. It is nearly waterproof, or at least water-repellent, coated with lanolin and thus similar in "feel" to hair coated with beeswax. This outer coat is a buffer against wind and snow, and also against the dampness eternally present in much of the animal's range, such as the steep slopes along the Pacific where fog and rain are normal, not unusual, conditions. The undercoat is composed of extremely fine wool, and may be 4 inches deep. This protection is a means of adaptation to the severe habitat. The coat is gradually shed, beginning early in the brief summer, but the animals are never without partial protection.

It is true that hunters often hunt moose, sheep, caribou, and goats all on the same trip, with a bear also thrown in occasionally. But typically the terrain goats prefer is far more rugged and broken, and also higher, than that inhabited even by mountain sheep. The sheep, for example, commonly move downward during severe winters to foothill country. A group of goats may take up residence temporarily in highest timber edges or protected high valleys, but for the most part they confine themselves to the steepest talus slopes and rocky ledges. It might seem that nothing could grub sustenance from the crevices and between the rocks, but goats put on an amazing layer of fat each season, and seem not to have the slightest concern over the severity of their surroundings.

The goat, in fact, will go into high places where no sheep would venture. It is common for an old billy to stand for hours skylined atop the highest, most precarious crag in the entire vast expanse of its bailiwick. One may lie on a narrow ledge, forefeet and head hanging over the edge as it sleeps. Or it may stand or lie down atop a needle spire of rock that appears to afford no way up or down, or even room to lie at the top.

It is most interesting to realize that these animals actually *enjoy* this terrain, will not exchange it for any other, and, far from suffering in it, thrive and are placid and content. Of course, physical evolution and adaptation give them confidence. The foot, for example, is specifically adapted to the needs of living where climbing or descending very nearly perpendicular, sheer rock faces may be an everyday occurrence. The hind-foot hoof is a bit smaller than the front. Both are broad, and each hoof very nearly forms a square. Inside the hard outer portion the pad thrusts outward in convexity, rather than showing the concave form of most hoofed animals. Those spongy cushions grip the rock with astonishing traction. This enables the goat to climb and descend the steepest of cliffs without difficulty.

It was mentioned earlier that the mountain goat does not seem to be a very alert or wary creature, that it is a stoic perfectly tailored to the continent's most bleak and rugged habitats. It may be that its stoicism, its fundamental lack of fear or skittishness, has evolved because it lives in a world where nothing much happens, or at least nothing that can be avoided. It never knows the danger of the avalanche—a fairly common cause of goat demise—until one strikes; it fears no fall until it falls; it is seldom shy or worrisome of

*Mountain goats are well equipped to negotiate the precarious crags and slopes of their habitat. Their convex hoof pads form spongy cushions that grip the rock with powerful traction.*

enemies because so few ever appear. Other earthbound creatures, including man, may consider the habitat of the mountain goat a place fraught with dangers. The goat, born here, and undoubtedly of only moderate intelligence on the animal scale, must consider this upended, windswept, glacial terrain the safest place on earth.

## FEEDING

The high peaks are not only pleasant and reasonably safe for this highly specialized animal, they also offer a much easier foraging life than one would believe. To be sure, the choice of food at any given time is not very broad. But there is enough of it. Hunters have often marveled at the fact that mountain goats can make a living in the high places which seem so barren, where any timber is dwarfed and sculpted into agonized shapes by the incessant winds. This is only because the human intruder does not look closely enough.

Most abundant of the basic items of food are the mosses and lichens. These grow abundantly well above the timber. They may be short and clinging in rock crevices. But the domain is vast, and the goat can roam as widely as necessary, picking here and there. Like the other horned and antlered game animals, the mountain goat is a ruminant with a multiple-chambered stomach. It feeds for a time, then lies down to chew its cud.

In addition to the lichens and mosses, which are utilized around the year, there are dwarf willows, taken as browse. Browse makes up a substantial portion of the diet, particularly because summer is short and low browse plants are available when green succulents are not. The varied small, tough willows are a staple browse item. Added to these are dwarfed birches and aspens where present, and blueberry and bearberry brush. Occasionally some juniper is available, and when the animals move downslope a bit they are able to find pockets of high-altitude conifers, some of these also dwarfed by altitude.

So far as is known, goats are daytime creatures. They are not known to feed at night. This probably indicates that they are under no urgency to do so, and speaks well of their adaptation to what would seem to be a rather sparse food supply. It also undoubtedly indicates that they never have been harassed to any extent by enemies. They have no fear of moving about feeding in daylight. They are up and browsing placidly well before the sun, and continue to midmorning or after.

Nothing hurries this animal. When it sets out to eat, it potters along, pauses to look off down into a valley or at another ridge, consorts casually with others of its kind unless it happens to be a loner, pokes about here and there grabbing a bite, moving a step or two and ferreting out whatever is handy. If the wind is a gale, it doesn't care. If snow swirls, it continues to feed as if unaware. But goats don't like rain. They may be forced to accept it at times. Usually, however, they will retire to some cave or overhang to wait until the shower passes.

Sometimes in winter they will seek windswept areas purposely, to find forage where snow has been whisked away. Or they may go to somewhat lower elevations where the conifers and aspens furnish food. This seldom is a long trek and can hardly be considered a migration to a winter feeding range. In the short spring and summer, grass explodes from the edges of the snowbanks. On slopes where winter slides have swept brush and trees clean, grass takes over with the spring, or at least by the second summer. These patches are important locations for feeding.

Well over half of the summer rations are composed of grasses and alpine weeds or forbs. The greenery of the summer-leaved shurbs such as bearberry and willow add quantities of semi-soft foods. If aspen is present it is much sought, summer and winter. In live-trapping operations in Montana for transplants, one trapper for some years used aspen most successfully as a bait in his corral-type traps.

Most of the middle of the day is spent resting, sleeping in a cool spot, which in summer may be a patch of ice or snow, or a high crag where the cool wind whistles, or on a ledge or beside a cliff facing the north. There is no reason to hurry. The only urgency is to get moving again in midafternoon early enough to stoke up for the night. Feeding continues until dusk begins to draw down, and then the animals bed down for the night. Water is seldom if ever the worry it is for big-game animals in many other habitat situations, nor are regular trips to a drinking spot necessary. Snow or snow-melt puddles or rivulets are always present.

## MOVEMENTS

Day-to-day movements concerned with foraging are not ordinarily extensive. They are directly related to the amount of food available. Goats have been observed spending several weeks in the same area, and seldom more than a half-mile from some apparently central resting point. If food becomes scarce, they wander more. In fact, most of the movement of goats during any given day, and over an entire season, is dictated by the food supply.

In a few instances of transplants of a group of goats, the animals have wandered far. One such group was "lost" by observers who flew over the region looking for them. They were thought to have succumbed, but two years later they were discovered inadvertently when a plane survey of other game was made. The animals, with newborn additions to the group, had apparently followed high spines for many miles and were in another area entirely. Why this migration or wandering took place, no one knows.

In fact, there is still much to be learned about the habits and life history of the mountain goat. Its home among the high crags makes constant observation over long periods difficult. Seasonally the pursuit of forage generally takes the animals lower down from their summering area. Deep snows are the cause. As noted earlier, they may move up periodically, to find places to forage where wind has cleaned the snow away. But the general movement is usually downward.

It is slow, simply a matter of seeking less snow on south-facing slopes where food is more easily available. This is definitely not a migration to a specific and ancestral winter range. If a winter happens to be mild by high-altitude standards, the goats stay put. In a few places to which they've been transplanted there is no need to move much lower at any time, and so they are found year-round on the same areas of a peak.

As a rule, the beginnings of spring find them at their lowest altitude. Here late-winter food is usually most plentiful, and here the first greening of spring begins, and gradually moves up the slopes. The goats move with it. However, this entire trek may cover only 1000 to 2000 feet in altitude, with side wandering along the ridges. Most observers believe that 10 or 15 miles in a year covers the range of the average animal. Some may be born on a high mountain and never travel more than 5 or 10 miles in any direction in their entire life span.

On occasion the need for salt urges a group into a fairly long, periodic trip. Game biologists have found what are apparently ancestral mineral licks that have been used possibly for centuries. In Montana, for example, such a spot was discovered by a big-game live-trapper high above the Middle Fork of the Flathead River. He built a pole trap here, with a trip wire to close the gate, and baited with a combination of salty minerals concocted by first testing what the earth contained here that had so long attracted the goats.

Soon animals were coming regularly, and were trapped. Some were marked with colored streamers so they might be observed later perhaps, to find out how far away they lived. The trapper came to believe that several groups of goats from various places in these mountains had long utilized this spot. Some of the marked goats were later seen, apparently "at home," almost 20 miles away. Whenever they felt the need for salts, they made the trip to the lick.

To illustrate the difficulty of trapping and transplanting goats, and why so little of it is done, the ones caught here were subdued cowboy-style, and a U-shaped length of garden hose forced over the horns. The horns are vicious weapons. A big goat could easily kill a man who did not use utmost care. In a pen a billy has driven a horn through a 1-inch pine board. Sturdy mountain horses brought to the site, which was 28 miles from the nearest road, were fitted with specially built twin panniers, one hung on either side. A securely roped goat was placed in each.

Down the mountain they went by horse a short distance to the edge of the brawling Flathead River. Here they were transferred to a big rubber raft, and floated downstream in a hair-raising dangerous run to a ranger station back in the mountains. At that point a small plane flew them out one at a time to a lower-country pen where they were held temporarily and then trucked to the new release site.

In bodily movements the goat is a most deliberate and seemingly careful mountain animal. It is not much of a runner even when pressed. When disturbed it begins a lumbering trot and then breaks into an awkward gallop. It covers ground at fair speed, but relies chiefly for safety upon escape into upended cliffs where pursuit by an enemy is hardly possible.

In ordinary travel, each step in broken areas is selected with care. Moving at a stiff walk, the animal makes certain the trail ahead is maneuverable. To a goat, however, that can mean a narrow ledge with sheer rock wall above and below. It traverses such places slowly, and also will walk like a tightrope artist along a shard of broken cliff to pass across a spot where no other passage is possible. Often in a tight spot the goat will turn to face a cliff, reach up with forelegs and hook its feet over a ledge above, then pull itself up. Or it may back very carefully and slowly off a ledge it has started to walk along where it discovers a dead end. Most interesting of its maneuverings is the act of turning around on this kind of ledge. It rears up, and standing on hind legs only, faces and presses against the cliff and slowly turns, then drops again to all fours.

Although its running gallop is slow, when the mood strikes it the goat can make surprising leaps for its bulk, from crag to crag or across rough places, covering 10 feet or more. Old lone billies love to pick out bedding places that would make a human observer shudder—sometimes pinnacles barely large enough to lie down on, occasionally so small part of the animal hangs off or overlaps.

Nonetheless, goats do make mistakes. It is believed that falls are fairly common, and rock slides and avalanches kill a good many. In fact, probably these natural disasters are the main control on the goat population. As noted, a few fall to predators. Predation may be a factor, it is thought, when the animals are forced down into lower areas where forest begins, and where such large predators as grizzlies or wolves may lurk. However, a mature mountain goat is a determined fighter when the need arises. If the stiletto horns can be slammed into an enemy, the goat is the victor. There are records of bears killed by large billies and of wolves put to rout.

When moving downslope in steep places, a goat commonly passes over near-perpendicular slants. It does so by jumping downward from one tilted rock face to the next, the grip of its splaying toes and cushioned hooves easily holding its weight as long as some momentum continues. Because of their experience in severely broken rocky country and their proclivity for passage in precarious places, when they do get down into timber, and into areas where blowdowns lie in jackstraw piles, they rather comically often walk the logs some yards above ground rather than trying to push through from below.

Aside from the daily feeding travel, and retirement to caves or other protected places during heavy rain and to cool places to rest, the mountain goat is basically a homebody. It may wander around looking for a dry spot of fine earth, paw out a small depression, and wallow in the dust, or stiffly plod along to a puddle for a drink, or make a trek to the salt lick. But as long as forage to fill its belly is present, the goat has little interest in discovering what is on the far side of the mountain.

### BREEDING

Of course a billy recognizes a nanny, and vice versa, but hunters have long known that it is all but impossible to distinguish between the sexes at rifle range or even closer. It is so difficult and chancy, in fact, that it is not possible to set seasons on males only. A group of goats, with some individuals smaller than others, is probably composed of females and kids. A large, lone animal with an especially pronounced hump is probably a mature billy. The horns of the female are usually shorter and more slender, but unless comparisons are possible, the modest size of even the largest horns make correct sex judgment uncertain.

The problem of distinguishing between sexes is one reason that the hunting season for goats is almost always set in late summer — August — and very early fall. Throughout summer most of the adult males have stayed by themselves, usually as loners, although there can be exceptions. Thus a big lone goat is probably a billy. But when the rut comes on, about November and running on into December, they leave solitary ways and begin to seek companionship.

Evidence of pugnaciousness now shows in the male personality. A male may rake bushes with its horns, and brace any other male that crosses his path. At the rear base of each horn there is a gland that secretes a sticky, odorous substance. Both male and female have these glands, but those of the male are larger, and now as the rut begins they become distended. The goat rubs the glands against rocks, presumably to mark his presence.

Battles between males are not usually severe. Occasionally an especially crotchety billy stabs a sparring antagonist fatally. Most battles are simply simulated. Antagonists walk stifflegged and haughtily around each other, spar a bit, and then break off. But the horns are used dagger-fashion meanwhile, and serious consequences may and do occur.

The billy makes no attempt to collect a harem. He simply moves in on a band of females and youngsters. If, as sometimes occurs, a mature male has stayed with a small band of females and young during summer, there is trouble instantly. But most of the groups — never very large, composed of three or four to seven or eight — are nannies and immature animals, from young of the past spring to males two to three years of age.

The billy may pursue a single female, or consort with two or three. He is possessive with these, but soon breeding is finished. Ardor cools. Bands may gather, now larger than at other times, to spend the winter. Or the same groups may continue to consort. Only the older billies seem inclined to revert to solitary ways again. They may hang on the fringes of a band, or go their own way again. Possibly the low incidence of severe battles among the males during the rut is a crafty part of nature's scheme. If the males battled as violently as, for example, bull elk often do, there is little question that with the goat's rapier armament at least half the males would be killed every breeding season.

### BIRTH AND DEVELOPMENT

Most of the females bred during any rut are not less than 2½ years old. Others may be as much as seven or eight, and possibly a few still older. Goats can be aged fairly accurately by growth rings on the horns, each ring designating one year. Although much is still to be learned about the life history of the mountain goat, a specimen with a dozen annual growth rings on the horns is considered old indeed. Goats held captive are not a good criterion. They never have done very well in captivity.

Approximately six months after the females are bred, the kids are born. A nanny living among a group draws apart and seeks a safe place for the birth. This is usually a secluded rugged spot hidden away from the others and from any possible enemy. Single births are the rule. Twins, however, are by no means uncommon. Some researchers believe the incidence of twins may be related to the quality of the habitat.

The little goats weigh 6 or 7 pounds and stand slightly more than a foot high at the shoulder. They are extremely well developed and precocious; they gain their feet often only minutes after birth. A kid may begin nursing its mother during the first hour of birth. Already it seems playful, jumping and walking around a few square yards of territory. By the time it is two to four hours old, it is able to follow its mother short distances.

The mother still clings to the rough hiding place as much as possible. Forage is likely to be good now, for the births occur in the May-June period, when new grass is beginning and there is a richness of juices flowing again in all available forage. The nanny is ever watchful, a determined and vicious antagonist if any predator attempts to take the kid. She stays away from the band for several days, but then emerges with her offspring and joins the family band she has left, or perhaps throws in with another.

No more than a week passes as a rule before the kid attempts to eat plants on which it sees its mother feed. Mountain goat kids are exceedingly playful, with each other and each one individually. Like their parents, they have no fear whatever of the high places. They will race along a sharp ridge or over the rocks without the slightest consideration for the awesome cliffs that fall away beside them. It is possible some young may fall to their deaths, but presumably such accidents are not common. Golden eagles are thought to prey to some extent upon the kids. Even an eagle attack is defended with spunk by the mother, or later on by any adults of a group.

If the band has had to winter some distance down the slopes, the slow movement toward the summit passes the short weeks of summer. Many groups, however, have not moved far if at all, and a fairly large gathering, of a dozen or more mixed nannies and kids and young billies, commonly spends an entire summer in a comparably small area. Observers in settlements far below have now and then spotted the same group high above day after day for weeks at a time.

By July and August most of the kids are fully weaned. They

remain with the group, probably feeling the need for companionship and some sort of direction. The group organization is a
loose one. Animals may scatter out to feed, seldom traveling in
quite such meticulous single-file movement as is common among
sheep. If some disturbance puts the band to flight, it's every goat on
its own, selecting whatever path seems best to it. The kids may
follow their own mothers, or by fall not be quite so closely tied.

Now fat and with winter hair growing, the young seem puzzled
by the heightened activity of the rut. But once that time is passed
the young animals and nannies winter together as usual. Some of
the young males, even the long yearlings, may wander off by themselves. Others may feel stronger ties and stay with the band. Thus
the simple life of this intriguing animal completes another cycle in
this stark and rugged land that also is the fount of its simplicity.


### SENSES

It may well be that this existence, reduced to basics, avoids the
need for sharply tuned senses. Not that the mountain goat lacks a
certain alertness and excellent development of the senses. But there
is really no need here for the awesomely acute sense of smell with
which the whitetail deer is gifted, or for the eaglelike eyesight of
the pronghorn. Or perhaps a better view is that, though the goat
has the keenness of fundamental senses, there is seldom urgent
need to use them.

Researchers believe that the goat has excellent eyesight. Hunters
agree. Yet what the goat sees, such as a moving hunter far off below
it, doesn't seem very important. On occasion a hunter has reported
getting close to a goat and having it move toward him out of curiosity. Unfamiliarity is not necessarily interpreted as danger. Goats
fleeing from hunters often gallop only until they are well into the
maze of broken crags. Nothing can follow them here, they seem to
feel, and so there is no longer any hurry.

Hearing is also presumably well developed. But the high mountains are full of sharp noises—the clap of thunder, the falling of rock
shards, the roar of a slide, the clatter of pebbles that suddenly roll
from an ill-balanced resting place and set others free. Thus noises
also are not invariably signs of danger. They are part of the natural
phenomena of the surroundings.

Probably the sense of smell is also well developed. But here
again there is not often much scent to catch that is disturbing. Further, the high peaks are alive with whimsical breezes that seem to

blow from all directions at once. There is no reason why a mountain goat should be disturbed, for example, if it caught a whiff of a human intruder. A grizzly or a wolf would be different. It may have had experience, even ancestrally and the instinct passed down, with these. But a hundred generations of goats may never have smelled a man.

An interesting sidelight on the use of the senses concerns the daily habits especially of the big old billies. After feeding, one will move up to lie at the top of the peak or very near it. Daytime thermals rising from below move any scent of danger up to it. Sounds, as mentioned, don't seem important, and those of fallen rock or rolling stones are invariably below. The animal can see over a vast area below and around it. Thus there is very little to be afraid of or nervous about. Nothing can harm it from above—there isn't much of that! Unfortunately for the goat, many a crafty hunter realizes this and when stalking makes his climb to come upon the trophy from above.

### SIGN (Tracks are illustrated on page 251.)

Hunters, photographers, and wildlife enthusiasts need not look very hard for signs when looking for goats. It is too easy to use binoculars or a spotting scope and locate the animals themselves from below by carefully scanning a mountain. However, one who has gone to the trouble to get up where the goats live should know what signs they leave.

Tracks are rather similar to those of mountain sheep. While sheep prefer a somewhat less rough terrain than goats, especially at their highest altitudes, both sheep and goat tracks may appear in the same region. The track of the goat is quite square, as is that of the sheep. However, the inner edges of the impressions left by each toe are, to the practiced eye, straighter than those of sheep and the toes often splay outward farther. Length of an average adult track is roughly 3½ inches. Nonetheless, tracks of sheep and goat are easily confused.

Droppings are also easily confused with those of mountain sheep, and even with deer, although deer are seldom present in goat range. Those of the goats are generally a bit smaller. Like the others, they show different forms depending on diet. Summer droppings when the animals are eating grass and green weeds are in a rounded mass 4 to 5 inches long. By late summer when forage is harder, pellets may be seen but they adhere in clusters. By winter when browse and dry food make up the diet, separated pellets are formed.

It has been noted that goats hide out in caves in rainy or sometimes in extra-severe weather. Sometimes beds may be in shallow caves, too. Droppings and a definite bed with dusty perimeter in a cave or on a ledge indicate that goats may use or have used the area. But here again, sheep have similar habits. By and large, the most prominent sign of the goat is the white splotch of the animal itself showing against rocks of a high peak.

### HUNTING

Every goat hunt begins by getting up into the mountains where the quarry is presumed to range, invariably on horseback, and then glassing for that most obvious sign, a lone goat or a group of them. To be sure, they are not easy to sight against snow. But the black horns do stand out to a careful, meticulous observer using a good glass. Further, seldom will the terrain be so entirely snow-covered as to give total camouflage to the animals.

The quality of the various hunting locations is roughly as follows. Alaska is best—that is, with the highest goat population, possibly as many as 15,000 animals. The goat does not range throughout Alaska, but is found chiefly in the mountains of the coast beginning in the lower Panhandle and reaching northward, and then to the area above Anchorage, and out into the Kenai Peninsula. Goats have been transplanted to Kodiak, and to some islands off the Panhandle. This is mentioned because all too often hunters have the idea goats are everywhere in Alaska.

British Columbia rates second. The Yukon and the Northwest Territories are both just fair, and the same is true for Alberta. Washington has a good population, Oregon a modest one, Idaho a fair one. Montana probably rates next to Washington. Colorado is estimated to have a goat population of several hundred. Other U.S. populations are token. And, of course, it is by no means easy to acquire a permit. Most are by application and drawing.

Almost all goat hunters are guided. A guide may be mandatory, depending on where one hunts. A guide is worthwhile whether mandatory or not. Selecting a trophy is tough for a tyro. If the horns appear to be as long as the distance from their bases to the end of the goat's nose, it is without question an excellent specimen.

Actually the only truly difficult part of goat hunting is getting to the shooting spot. It is seldom difficult to get within range and still keep under cover, in the stand-on-end country of the animal's domain. The physical demands on the hunter are the tough part. When a goat is located, or a group, and a target is selected from far below, usually the technique is to watch until the billy lies down. Thus most hunts are launched early in the morning, and the animals are spotted while feeding and moving.

Once they have been located, the hunter can be reasonably certain they won't range far away. The hope always is that the hunter can spot where the chosen animal lies down along toward mid-morning. It is virtually certain to be anchored right there for several hours following. The climb and the stalk then begin. Best technique is to circle wide to keep thermals from carrying scent upward, and to get above the bedding ground. Some expert archers have stalked goats in this fashion to within 15 or 20 yards with the animals wholly unaware.

On occasion after it has been decided that a certain animal is of trophy proportions, the stalk requires such a long time that midafternoon comes without the shot being made. And from the vantage point above it may well be that there are obstructions so that one cannot see the animal. Successful close-in stalks may still be made. But most hunters play it safe at this juncture. After the arduous work of the climb, they take no chances on flushing the quarry into terrain where they can't get to it. They wait until the animal arises and begins the afternoon feeding period. The chance is then good that it will move into view and offer a shot.

There are two main cautions in goat hunting. One is to be sure to carry a rifle with ample power to put the goat down to stay. These are tough creatures. Another is to watch carefully before accepting a shot, to make certain the goat won't tumble off a ledge and either become irretrievable or break its horns.

Whether one hunts the mountain goat or simply desires to observe it distantly or to photograph it, the knowledge that it appears secure and forever unendangered in its towering world in and sometimes above the clouds is a satisfaction. Further, even though this creature is seemingly one of the least alert and intelligent of our big-game animals, it has one quality no other can match. It is the most brilliantly surefooted of all horned and antlered North American animals. It is also uniquely and perfectly tailored to a world that undoubtedly will never be quite completely understood by man, because it is too big a challenge for all but a few to enter, and then never on fully intimate terms.

# GRIZZLY BEARS

# Grizzly

*Ursus arctos horribilis*

# Alaskan Brown

*Ursus arctos middendorffi*

The grizzly bears are the most formidable and dangerous animals on the continent. In largest form—the Alaskan brown—the grizzly stands in size at the top of the world list of large carnivores. The only competition for that place it might possibly have is the polar bear. Without question the grizzly is the world's largest meat-eater living entirely on land.

Primitive Americans, early explorers and settlers, and modern hunters and wildlife enthusiasts all have been awed by, intrigued by, and curiously drawn to the challenge of these huge, unbelievably powerful creatures. No other North American mammal is so unpredictable, so irascible in temperament. None is so wholly without enemies of consequence

The grizzly is the kind of wildlife personality that seems fashioned purposely by nature as a basis for endless legends, tall tales of the frontier and of the remote hunting camp. Indians from the earliest times revered the grizzly, chiefly because they feared it. The big bears figured prominently in various primitive rituals and beliefs. An Indian who managed to subdue a grizzly and take its hide was a

193

Grizzly Bear

legend in his time among his people, a hunter without peer, due the highest respect.

There is indeed a kind of super-macho romance connected with these great animals. Interestingly, no other North American animal quite so succinctly illustrates the rule of nature that the larger the animal, especially among those that eat meat, the fewer its numbers. And it illustrates another rule: The larger and more powerful and aggressive the carnivore, the more swiftly it is dominated and brought to severe decline by man.

Basically this is because of man's fear, both of the animal itself and of its depredations upon his stock, and because as civilization nibbles inexorably at wilderness there simply are very few places left where such a large and aggressive creature can make a living. Although over a substantial portion of their remaining range grizzly bears are still on the game-animal list, there is no question that their long future is bleak.

Over vast areas of their original range they are totally extirpated. In remote northern areas of western Canada and parts of Alaska they are still numerous and not presently endangered. Trophy hunting will not bring the grizzly to extinction, because at least in these modern times hunting can be meticulously controlled, or outlawed altogether, which well may occur before the next century. Usurpation of the remaining wilderness areas that are presently home to the grizzly is the real danger. And unfortunately, unlike horned and antlered game, the grizzly cannot very well be transplanted to new areas to launch fresh regional populations. It is not that adaptable, and besides, it has nowhere else to go.

When the first white men of colonial times had pushed westward into what are now the central states, they discovered the grizzly as far east as Ohio. It is easy to imagine the awe and fear of pioneers, already acquainted with the occasionally dangerous black bear, who suddenly came upon one of the great grizzlies of the interior. The Spanish had already found the grizzly well down the Sierra Madre mountains and their brushy foothills in north-central Mexico, and later white explorers were to encounter them there in numbers. They also inhabited Baja. The Mexican grizzlies were the smallest of the lot, but had a reputation for irritability and ferocity. This same grizzly ranged northward into portions of our present-day southwest.

Grizzlies were well entrenched all along the Pacific coast, throughout all of the Rockies, and over the Great Plains. Interestingly, although the big Alaska browns were not known during

THE GRIZZLY BEARS

COLOR: **Grizzly,** varied, from near-black to blond, usually brown with silvery-tipped guard hairs. **Alaskan brown,** varied shadings from very dark to blond, but without silver-tipped guard hairs, most specimens brown to tan.

MEASUREMENTS, ADULT MALES: **Grizzly,** overall length 6 to 7 feet average, some slightly longer; height at shoulder to 3½ feet. **Alaskan brown,** much larger, 8 to 9 feet long, 4½ feet at shoulder.

WEIGHT, ADULT MALES: **Grizzly,** from 450 to 800 pounds. **Alaskan brown,** 800 to 1200 pounds, occasional specimens to 1500-plus.

FEMALES: Smaller, roughly at maximum about the minimum for adult males.

GENERAL ATTRIBUTES: Dished-in facial profile and hump over shoulders distinguish the grizzlies from black bear; very short tail; extremely long claws on forefeet (longer than hind claws), longer and less curved on Alaskan brown than on grizzly; awesomely powerful build; prominent, heavy, curved canine teeth; aggressive; always potentially dangerous.

early American history, it is believed that the bear called at one time the California grizzly was possibly the largest and most powerful of all the grizzly tribe, at least south of Alaska. The plains grizzly, which was actually the same bear, was also large and powerful and dangerous. This is the grizzly that followed the buffalo herds and was known to kill an adult bull with one smack of a paw and a bite in the neck. Early westerners were forced to brace many of these giants, and a goodly number of men were mauled or killed in encounters.

It did not take long to decimate the grizzly population below the present Canadian border. The demise of the buffalo took most of the dependent plains grizzly with it. Later, stockmen and the so-called sodbuster farmers obviously could not tolerate such a large predator, and accounted for the stragglers. Grizzlies were gone from much of their original range within the contiguous states a hundred years ago. It is believed that within the past fifty years there has not been a drastic lowering of the population in that region. But everyone recognizes that very few are left, and those in only a few places.

In mid-1975 the U.S. Fish & Wildlife Service listed the grizzly within lower-48 borders as a threatened species. That classification

Alaskan Brown Bear

pertains to an animal that may in the foreseeable future become endangered. A meager scattering remains in the Rockies in Colorado and northward, but most of the remaining animals south of Canada are in three regions: what may be termed the Yellowstone ecosystem, which takes in Yellowstone Park plus parts of Wyoming, Montana, and Idaho surrounding it; the Selway-Bitterroot region of Idaho and Montana; and northwestern Montana.

Token hunting south of Canada may still be allowed for a few years to come. Outside of controlled areas, like Yellowstone and Glacier National Parks, the only significant grizzly population from a hunting viewpoint is within the Bob Marshall Wilderness Area in Montana. Presently in that wilderness and surroundings the annual kill, whether by trophy hunting or by known poaching or for predation control, is limited to twenty-five bears. In 1975, to push protection of the grizzly south of Canada, the Boone & Crockett Club, keepers of official records of big-game animals, made a ruling that grizzly entries from south of the Canadian border would no longer be accepted. The Mexican grizzly, incidentally, is either extinct or on the brink of extinction. A few, perhaps two dozen, may be left.

North of the U.S. border the picture is better. British Columbia has a substantial grizzly population, and western Alberta has a fair number in the northwest, in the Peace River and Smoky River regions, and along the eastern slope of the Rockies. The Yukon Territory is home to a stable grizzly population, of a strain not as large as some others but known for its tough cantankerousness. In the Northwest Territories the animals are unthreatened. Alaska has probably the highest population, estimated at 10,000 to 12,000 animals, and unthreatened.

Scientific classification of grizzlies in Alaska has been confused for many years. At one time the confusion extended south of Canada. Naturalists and taxonomists split up the grizzlies into dozens of subspecies, chiefly based on geographical incidence. In early-day observations of grizzlies, color differences were to some degree puzzling to certain naturalists. One bear might be nearly black, but never with the sheen that the coat of a black bear often has. Another might have guard hairs conspicuously tipped with silver, or in younger specimens even yellowish, with the main coat dark brown. Still others ranged through various shades of brown to nearly blond. Eventually, however, it was agreed that the grizzlies south of the Canadian border were really all the same bear.

When interest in the huge brown bears of the southern Alaska coast became intense some years ago, and knowledge of them grew,

# Range of the Grizzly and Brown Bears

Grizzly Bear
Brown Bear

they, too, presented a puzzle for scientists. Color among these bears also is highly varied, from very dark through varying shades of dark brown to tan to quite blond. But their enormous size seemed to set them apart. Scientists insisted that these bears of the Alaskan coast, and their sometimes even larger relatives on Kodiak Island, commonly called the Kodiak bear or Kodiac grizzly, were of at least one and possibly more than one species. Along the fringe of range between the outsize coastal bears and the inland dwellers there is, of course, intergrading. For some years it was anybody's guess which bear was which.

Presently it is acknowledged that all of the grizzlies are of a single species, *Ursus arctos.* However, most references, including the Boone & Crockett record book, which could hardly allow the enormous coastal browns to compete with smaller inland grizzlies, consider that there are two subspecies: the Alaskan brown, *U. a. middendorffi;* and the grizzly, *U. a. horribilis.* The latter ranges inland throughout most of Alaska except the extreme northern coast and the southern coast. On the southern coast in a swath along the

# COLOR PHASES OF THE GRIZZLY BEAR

*Bald Phase*

*Blond Phase*

*Dark Phase (Silvertip)*

*Brown Phase*

Alaskan Peninsula and on coastally southwestward and south to the border, and throughout some of the coastal islands, is the domain of the largest of North American bears, the Alaskan brown.

Oddly, the Alaskan browns are not commonly as irritable and aggressive as their smaller relatives, the grizzlies of the interior. Certainly both are potentially dangerous. But the smaller bears inland are often downright ugly in disposition. They have been known to stalk hunters, and to rush to attack with no special provocation. Fishermen after salmon and trout in streams along the southern Alaska coast sometimes carry whistles and blow them to alert brown bears along the streams to their presence. Usually the animals will move off when disturbed. It is important not to surprise one at close range, which will almost certainly spark a charge.

Only a comparatively few people, mostly hunters and wildlife photographers, have seen the big browns and other grizzlies in the wild. It is difficult to conceive of their astonishing size and power. A big grizzly habitually rears upright, standing tall on its hind legs, when alerted and uncertain of what has disturbed it. In that pose, it is 8 or 9 feet tall, and if it were to reach up to claw at a tree it might leave claw marks 12 feet from the ground. The hide from a large specimen, when spread flat on the ground, may measure as much as 9 feet from claw tips to claw tips of the front feet. Each claw is at least 4 inches long.

In the records, trophy grizzlies are judged by skull dimensions. Several skulls of Alaskan browns in the record book are almost 20 inches in length, measured without the lower jaw. Most are close to 18 inches. Width runs from 10-plus to very nearly 13 inches. Imagine adding flesh, hide, and fur to such a skull. It would hardly fit into a bushel basket. All the record-book specimens, incidentally, are males.

Men have always been mesmerized by the power of these great carnivores. Notes of explorers and others tell of observing big grizzlies carrying off large kills such as bull elk and buffalo. Several hunters together cannot drag a downed bull elk, but a large grizzly handles one easily. Many years ago the early Spanish in America were intrigued with the idea of matching grizzlies with bulls. Near the earliest settlements in what is now California, it is said that bears for the purpose were roped from horseback by several riders — which must have been a dust-up to put any other horseback endeavor imaginable to shame — and dragged to enclosures. The result was, according to historical record, generally disappointing. Seldom was there much of a contest. A slap of the grizzly's paw often smashed the bull's skull on its first charge. A half-dozen bulls might be dispatched by the same grizzly as fast as they could be turned into the arena.

Much has been made in fiction and in some less than authentic nature writing about the roaring and bawling of the grizzlies, which would seem to imply that these are noisy animals. It is true that fighting adults do snarl, and that one making an attack may roar, probably a natural sound of anger and ferocity. Wounded grizzlies, and sometimes those in high anger, utter a frightening bawl. A disturbed grizzly may snort and snuffle as it tests the wind or eyes some possible interloper. It will growl menacingly, utter low woofs and coughs, and pop its great teeth together in anger or suspicion. These sounds may presage a charge. Cubs whine and whimper fairly often. But most of the time grizzlies are quiet animals.

They are also for the most part loners, except for female and cubs or yearlings together, and during breeding season. Each goes its wandering way. When several bears happen to come together, as in a stream to catch salmon or on a slope lush with wild berries, they appear to try not to get in each other's way, and even pretend not to look at each other. However, there is definitely a caste system. When an old, outsize male appears, the others move off, unless another male elects to dare the king to battle.

### HABITAT

Except when it is necessary to get together because of a forage concentration or the mating time, there is no reason for the big bears to consort. Such large animals need roaming room to make a living, and of course this requires a large expanse of terrain that is truly wilderness. Thus the habitat of the big bears is almost entirely beyond the day-to-day touch or influence of man. Obviously, the grizzly that happens to move into the fringes of man's domain, as on a mountain cattle ranch of the west, is certain to get into trouble killing stock, which triggers its own destruction. But most grizzlies have a strong affinity for privacy, and with such large animals this means living in the wildest and most remote places.

On its original vast range, the grizzly's habitat varied widely, from the hardwood forests and stream bottoms of the central states, to the wide-open plains where small thickets of brush along streams might make bedding locations, to the forested mountains

of the Rockies. But as this range was whittled down the only bears
left were those in the mountain regions. The grizzly (*horribilis*) is of
course still today generally an animal of the high country.

One who has visited off-road areas of Yellowstone and Glacier
National Parks can get a good general idea of what grizzly habitat is
like within the small range still existing south of Canada. In portions of western Alberta and throughout much of British Columbia
the habitat is not especially different, except that as one moves
northward there are many more open slopes and areas of only scattered timber, or even of high, rolling mountain country where
brush such as willow is abundant but trees stand only in scattered
groupings.

In the Yukon and Northwest Territories grizzly country is like
this, and so is some of it in Alaska; it is a mixture of timber and
mountain meadows, of river courses dense with low brush fringed
by larger growth, and in the far north range massive brushy slopes
rising to towering jumbles of rock. The mountain sheep, the caribou, and the moose of the northwestern portion of the continent
share their habitat with the grizzly.

It must be kept in mind that the inland grizzly does not simply
select a place, a kind of habitat in which it likes to live. It can exist
in today's world only in remote wilderness areas, but even more
important possibly, these areas must be able to support the animal.
They must offer a forage potential fitted to the needs of the bears.
Thus, unlike the mountain goat, for example, which seems unable
to live anywhere but among the highest crags, and the antelope,
which is specifically tailored to wide-open plains, the big bear—as
it originally demonstrated long ago—is capable of adapting to any
of a variety of altitudes and widely varying habitats, as long as
there is enough food available to keep its belly full.

The Alaskan brown bear is a case in point. The well-known
writer Jack O'Connor once spoke of the Alaskan brown as simply "a
fish-fed grizzly." Although all grizzlies are omnivorous, a diet
mainstay of the coastal browns is fish, salmon and trout that run by
millions into streams tributary to the ocean. This habitat is somewhat different from that farther inland, and certainly not at all like
the Rockies domain of the few remaining lower-48 bears.

Here stream courses are dense with low growth. There are endless open slopes where deep grass and spongy moss grow. These
lead, of course, to the uplands, where timber begins to take over.
Yet here too there are awesomely dense places of tall brush and
scrub trees. On the grassy slopes in some places a bear can be spot-

ted at long distance. But it is not the terrain, the habitat, that ties the bears here. This race was able to evolve because of the stable food source. Because enemies are unknown—except for the occasional hunter—the open places hold no fear for the animals.

In other words, the grizzlies are hardly products of a specialized habitat. Very similar bears—authentic grizzlies of the same scientific name—are inhabitants of various mountain areas of Europe and Asia, and the forests and plains of Siberia. The only restriction on colonization of the grizzlies of the world, apparently, has been climate. They obviously prefer cool climes, although some, such as the Mexican grizzly of the Sierra Madre, tolerated warmer weather than most, and one variety native to the Atlas Mountains once long ago had a counterpart in Africa. The point is, specific habitat is by no means as important as sustenance. Theoretically at least, a grizzly could make do almost anywhere, if it had at hand the wherewithal to stoke its mighty furnace.

### FEEDING

Although the grizzly is usually spoken of as a carnivore, because it will eat all the meat it can get, the fact is that if it were not omnivorous the animal could not have survived on earth for all the centuries that it has been here. There is simply not enough meat available, at least meat the bear is capable of catching or finding, to sustain so large an animal around the seasons.

Thus grizzlies make the most of what may be termed seasonal crops, such as berries, fresh green grass, runs of fish, eggs of nesting waterfowl, and large animals such as caribou when killable during a migration. It is obvious that the bulk of the forage will be made up of what is most abundant in a particular geographical area, or at a specific time of year. In Yellowstone Park, for instance, the few grizzlies present for some years made a regular restaurant out of garbage dumps. This forage was plentiful for some months during the heavy tourist season. So-called renegades have been notorious since early settlement as stock killers. They learned to kill sheep, for example, or followed cattle herds, taking whatever they needed. It is no trick at all for a grizzly to move in on a range critter, catch it, and kill it.

Occasionally a grizzly may be out at any time in winter, traveling far to seek forage. These are exceptions. Most den up, and so the feeding year of the grizzly may be said to start in early spring—about April or early May—when it emerges, ravenous, and begins

*The grizzly uses its strong claws to tear open dead logs, feeding on rodents and grubs it finds in the rotting wood.*

the search for sustenance. Now new grass is sprouting, there are roots and tubers to be unearthed, and varied kinds of tree bark are abundant and edible. The bears stuff themselves with vegetation. They graze much like cattle.

However, they are fundamentally meat eaters and the vegetation is simply a make-do. All the time they are grazing, they are ever alert for the scent of meat. In spring this is likely to be carrion, dead big-game animals that had too difficult a winter. The bears have no compunction about how ripe the dead moose or caribou. Anything available is used. This is also the time of year when numerous large animals are weak, partially starved from a severe winter, a period when the old or ill make easy targets.

Of course any healthy animal — deer, mountain sheep, caribou, elk, or moose — that happens to let down its guard in bear territory may be rushed and slapped down before it can flee. In a race the bear, though fast for short distances, is no match for a healthy horned or antlered animal, but if it gets within close range its rush may be deadly. Spring is also the period during which the young of all big-game animals on the range of the bears are born. Grizzlies make a serious business of attempting to hunt down lambs, elk and moose calves, and deer fawns. No one knows just how effective these hunts are in terms of percentage of young devoured. Much depends on terrain and abundance of the prey. Undoubtedly, where the bears are plentiful, predation on young of big-game animals is substantial. The bears may not be able to scent young calves and fawns, which exude little odor, from any great distance, but they sense that this is the time, and when parents are in the vicinity they crisscross the region intent on tender young prey.

Meanwhile grazing also continues. The coastal brown bears may forage far and wide to begin. They may find carrion on the beaches — dead fish and seals perhaps — or they may be up in the highlands seeking weak or dead big-game animals. All this adds to the diet of vegetation. Then as the spring turns to early summer the grass shoots up higher and most of the bears will be in the valleys or the low coastal areas continuing to graze like cattle.

The inland grizzlies of Canada and Alaska are fond also of small mammals such as ground squirrels and marmots. These are present in large numbers on the slopes. They are out for only a few short months during summer, before going back below ground again. The bears actively seek them, digging them out, even after they have hibernated. The long claws of the grizzly are perfectly designed for digging, and for snatching hapless small mammals from under rocks or among talus. An entire slope may be pocked where a bear has diligently hunted ground squirrels. It is meat that the big bears prefer.

When a large game animal is killed or a dead one discovered, the bear eats its fill and then caches the remainder, commonly scraping earth over it. Brush or sticks are also sometimes used. The bear is not choosy. Dirt serves as well. Gorged, the animal then retires to a nearby thicket if one is present, and lies down to rest, digest its meal, and watch the cache. It may even flop down atop the mound of the cache, and woe to any interloper that comes that way. Black bears often share range with grizzlies, but they have a healthy respect for their outsize relatives, and will flee at sight or scent of one, whether near a food cache or just in passing.

In certain habitats in fall grizzlies are able to feed heavily on acorns, piñon nuts, and other wild nuts. Bark of alder and willow also is eaten in quantity as the animals begin to lay on all the fat they can. In other words, the big bears are opportunists, grabbing any good chance that comes their way. All of them eagerly consume fish, but it is the Alaska browns along the coast that are most definitely tied to the runs of salmon and trout.

In a few places there are spring runs of rainbows inland, and of suckers and numerous other stream fish. But by and large, fish are more incidental to the diet of the inland grizzlies, whereas the coastal browns' livelihood to a large extent depends seasonally on the fish runs. It is even conceivable that their great size evolved over many generations partly because of the rich fish diet they have always had at hand for several months each year. They not only attend the fish runs, but also hunt with great concentration all over the tidal flats, when tides recede, to pick up the bounty of marine life left stranded in tidal pools or on the mud flats.

By about the middle of July the salmon come into the coastal streams by tens of thousands, and there are also runs of Dolly Varden and other trout as well, some from out of salt water and some farther inland up the streams. The huge bears know the timing and begin gathering along the rivers and creeks as the first fish show. They continue to congregate as the runs come to peak. Air surveys have shown at times as many as fifty to a hundred big bears in a single watershed network near the coast.

Many written accounts have spoken of the big browns as rather nonaggressive animals. This would be wryly amusing to many a salmon-cannery worker or official tally taker of fish in coastal streams when runs begin. In some cases these officials have the job of counting salmon in certain runs and setting the time when the commercial fishermen may go to work on them. None of these people, and few others who have lived in the range of the big browns for years, consider them the least bit docile. Annually almost without fail there are maulings or deaths from encounters with the enormous bears.

Most of these occur on the fishing streams during the heavy feeding on salmon. Some are due to irritation of a sow with cubs at sight of an intruder. Some others are simply due to the short temper of an individual bear. They do not even truly associate with each other while fishing. Several may be working a stretch of stream, but each—except females with young together—stays to itself and seems to try to avoid even noticing another, as if each is attempting to stay out of trouble. Invariably there is an outsize male somewhere in the vicinity. When this king bear appears, the others scatter, full or not, unless some irascible upstart foolishly elects to make a challenging stand.

The salmon are caught by bears standing in the water, on a shallow riffle which puts the fish at a disadvantage, or below a falls which stops the run or concentrates the salmon before they leap it. The agility of the bears as they splash and whirl and feint at fish is astonishing, considering their bulk. Individual bears may do their fishing with slightly differing techniques, but the consensus among observers is that they do not swipe a paw into the water and flip a fish out onto the bank, as has been shown in some artist con-

*Brown bears feed on salmon during the annual runs in coastal streams.*

ceptions. Rather, the salmon is pinned between the forepaws and then seized in the mouth, or it is simply seized in the awesome jaws as it struggles up a riffle.

Smaller bears working a stream already fished by others ahead may pick up fresh scraps and leavings in their eagerness to feed, and then finally begin fishing. A big bear will put away six to a dozen husky salmon before slowing down. Some especially gluttonous individuals, after sating first hunger, merely chop out a big hunk in the middle of a fish, drop the leftover ends, and go to a fresh catch. Others seem to have an uncanny eye for the roe-filled females, discard or pass by males, and seize and rip the bulging egg sacks from the female's belly.

Some of the bears eat while standing in the water, others catch a salmon and carry it ashore. The caste system among a group, based apparently on size and age, dictates that when a stream location is being fished by the old male tyrant or king of the clan, others beneath him in stature must wait, or move to a new location. Observations by numerous scientists, photographers, and hunters indicate that the salmon, which die after spawning, are not eaten as carrion. They may litter a stream bank and fill the air with their stench, but the bears then spurn them, and move off seeking other forage. Some runs continue well into the fall.

## MOVEMENTS

Most of the movements and travel of grizzlies are concerned with the daily task of getting enough to eat. The individual range of each animal is directly related to the food supply. Bears after salmon, for example, may stay within a small area for some weeks, making their daily trips to fish. When the slopes are a welter of wild berries, a grizzly may have no need or urge to wander, foraging day after day over possibly no more than a mile of aimless travel as it gorges on the fruit. But when such seasonal supplies are gone, the animal must broaden its search.

In a habitat where a daily living is not too difficult, the average grizzly probably does not roam over more than a plot of 8 or 10 square miles, possibly less. In shortage seasons, it may wander much more widely, within a circle having a diameter of 25 miles. Further, adult males may move about rather aimlessly, climbing a high ridge, retreating to a valley to potter along a stream course, almost without noticeable direction. When first out of the den in early spring, and again late in fall prior to denning, some bears may have to roam widely to find adequate food. However, as a rule before denning up the bear is larded with fat to tide it over winter, and thus may not be inclined to waste energy on aimless exercise.

There is some question whether the grizzly should be classed as diurnal or nocturnal. It is a little of each. Given ample easily acquired forage, most movement is by day. By dusk the bear finds a bed in willows or a conifer thicket, and sleeps until dawn. In lean times, or when grizzlies live in proximity to much human disturbance or intrusion, they feed and move around as much by night as by day, and possibly more by night.

All grizzlies, inland and coastal, are fond of following trails. Old roads, if present, and game trails may catch their attention. Soon these become bear trails. Some lead arrow-straight for hundreds of yards. If more than one bear is in the area, as is common in the coastal Alaska range, animal after animal may follow the same trail, as range cattle do, until it is worn deeply into a slope. However, the grizzly is in no way migratory. It does not change from summer to fall and winter range, as, for example, elk or mule deer may. It may switch its range simply because of a seasonal shortage of food, but the new one is never ancestral nor necessarily the same each time a shortage occurs. Again, these animals are simply opportunists.

The grizzly is so bulky that it appears, as it shuffles along flat-footed, to be a kind of immense bumbler. Not so! Angered or frightened, or in a charge after living food, or man, a grizzly can attain a speed as fast as a moose or even a deer—perhaps up to 35 miles per hour—though it cannot sustain this pace for long. It moves in a plunging gallop that appears astonishingly easy and even, considering its bulk, almost graceful. When an old male sets out to travel, perhaps with destination known, it may walk with plodding determination, unhurriedly. Or it may break into a trot, or an easy lope. Grizzlies have been observed running at that gait for several miles, seeming not to tire at all. Long, easy runs are not the rule, however. Unless put to flight, there is seldom that much reason to hurry.

Although the grizzly is a fine swimmer, only very rarely are there adults capable of climbing trees. This is because of their immense bulk, and their claws. Though long, the claws are not curved enough to allow a secure hold. Black bears, of course, easily go up trees; their much shorter claws are deeply curved. Grizzly cubs are known to climb occasionally. Ordinarily the claws of the inland grizzly are more strongly curved than those of the Alaskan brown. As grizzlies grow to adulthood, the claw curve lessens. Their great bulk would require a solid grip indeed to allow them to haul themselves up a tree trunk.

### DENNING

One of the most purposeful movements of the grizzly is its early-winter search for a denning place. Bears are not true hibernators. Their metabolism continues at a rate only moderately less than before denning. They den up and sleep, but are not in a suspended state and can be aroused rather easily. A den may be prepared early in fall. If not, then by mid-September or on into October each animal seeks a proper place and makes its den. Most den sites are selected on a north slope. It is believed this choice avoids having water from melting snow run into the quarters, and also ensures that winter snow will plug the entrance and make the den snug and warm.

A cave may serve as a den, but usually the bear digs into the side of a slope, under an overhang, among blowdowns or under large tree roots. Some dens contain bedding material of branches and leaves. By the time the den is ready, or at least by the time the first hard storms are due to arrive, the bear becomes drowsy and is in a mood to curl up in its cave and go to sleep. Some researchers believe denning is triggered by the first severe snowstorm. The sleepy bears may be out and moving sluggishly around, their digestive tracts now empty. When the hard storm strikes, all go into dens at once.

Possibly so. Whether that is merely a regional occurrence that has been observed or a general pattern for all grizzlies, no one knows. It has even been suggested that grizzlies wait for the big snowstorm so that tracks to the den site are obliterated. Conceivably there may be some such instinct, each animal wanting to be sure it is well hidden away. It is difficult to believe, however, that fear is the impetus. They have nothing to fear from other animals. Possibly the bears realize a heavy snow will close them in. Or maybe it is simply that a light storm doesn't have any effect on a big bear, but at denning time a hard storm helps it make up its mind.

At any rate, depending upon latitude the grizzlies, wallowing in fat, perhaps several hundred pounds of it, are denned up anywhere from late October to November or early December. Not every one stays denned. Individuals may be aroused and do some winter wandering. Here and there a bear may den up only intermittently, coming out during warm spells. When April arrives, spring is on its way and the long sleep is about over. Late in the month, or in early May—again, latitude makes some difference in timing—the big bears awake and move out of their dens. They are empty, and the prodigious fat of fall is all burned up, so the first urge now is to find food. By the time the transition to an active life has been achieved again, and the fat is partially replaced, the breeding season is at hand.

### BREEDING

This is the only time of the year when adult bears consort. The females may be ready to be bred any time from early June on through the middle of July. Probably latitude influences the time to some extent. Not all come into heat simultaneously, of course. Further, females must be fully adult—that is, four or five years of age—before they breed, and each adult female breeds only in alternate years, some even every third year. Considering the fact that a grizzly, of either sex, has a life expectancy in the wild of probably not over twenty years, and usually less (though captive grizzlies have lived past thirty), the average female will breed only five to eight times during her life. This low potential production rate per female helps avoid overpopulation of so large an animal.

Although grizzlies are short-tempered during breeding season, it is known that very occasionally two large males may breed the same female and somehow avoid trouble with each other. Because the breeding season lasts several weeks, probably some males mate with more than one female. Much is still to be learned about the intimate habits of these large bears. However, individual males may continue a romance with a single female for several weeks.

During the mixing of the sexes, playful wrestling and nuzzling is now and then evident. The pairs forage together and show fondness and moderate affection. But as the season advances, ardor fades. The pairs drift apart, the older males once again becoming crotchety, irritable loners living as far from others of their kind as possible within a given domain.

### BIRTH AND DEVELOPMENT

The development of young grizzlies—and black bears, too—from the time the mother is bred until birth is one of the most interesting arrangements that has evolved in nature. No one is certain just why the complicated sequence developed, though there are some at least reasonable theories. Most of these bears over eons of time have lived in severely cold climates, and the breeding season is in spring to midsummer rather than fall. The young, if born after what would seem a logical gestation period compared to many other large creatures, would therefore arrive in midwinter, in some cases even before the bears go into dens. Obviously, they could not survive.

This is especially true because baby grizzlies are unbelievably small and helpless at birth. They are blind—that is, with eyes snugly closed—and they are covered with short hair, brown as a rule for the Alaskan browns, and gray for inland grizzlies. The cubs number one to three, and in rare cases four; usually there are two. Coming from a mother weighing 400 to 800 pounds, each weighs at maximum roughly 1½ pounds, sometimes less. They are no more than 8 to 10 inches in length.

When the female is bred, the fertilized egg cells make only a start at development, which is arrested thereafter, and they then remain in a kind of state of dormancy, unattached to the uterine wall. That attachment, of course, is necessary before formation of the embryo can proceed. This unusual process, which occurs in a few other of the world's mammals, is termed "delayed implantation." Actually it is a process that assures at least a fair chance of survival of the young.

Sometime in the late summer or early fall the uterine attachment

is consummated and the embryos begin to grow. By this arrangement the female is certain to be denned up well before the helpless
young are born. It is a kind of guarantee that the young will be born
inside the snug den, and thus well protected. The gestation period
runs somewhere between six and eight months. The female, having
denned sometime between late October and mid-December, bears
the cubs during the January-to-March period. By the time she
leaves the den in April or May, the cubs, fed on her rich milk during
the weeks in the den following birth, are ready to follow her, eyes
open, more fur grown, and feisty as can be.

Some naturalists have theorized that the mother is so sound
asleep in her den that she is not even aware of the coming of the
cubs. This is very doubtful. The birth of such tiny babies from such
a huge animal is certainly not difficult, and just may be part of nature's plan. But undoubtedly the mother cleans them and snuggles
them against her in her drowsiness. Instinctively they find the milk
source and really get excellent care — which is to say, just what they
need, food and warmth.

The youngsters grow swiftly in the den, and once out of it
follow their mother and romp with each other, exuberantly playful,
and continue swift growth. By midsummer they are ready to imitate their mother and try eating anything she does. She allows them
to chew on ground squirrels she catches, and the coastal bears that
fish for salmon carry the catch ashore to waiting and often frightened cubs, the big salmon possibly flopping vigorously. Soon the
cubs overcome shyness, and once they've had a taste, they are well
initiated.

By fall the young bears are sturdy, well filled out, and have
grown a heavy coat of fur. They are constantly under close super-
vision of their mother, a ferocious, hair-trigger protectoress, from
the moment they leave the den. Enemies are few. Oddly, the most
serious danger is from other bears — males. An old male especially
will kill cubs if it has the opportunity. In fact, trappers have sometimes used young bears as bait to catch old males. The mother,
however, does not make it easy for the male. Even though she is
much smaller, she instantly shows snarling hostility to any male
that comes near, and will charge as quickly as she'd go after a
human intruder.

The young of the year stay with the mother constantly on
through the fall, now beginning to do some foraging on their own.
They become fully weaned before denning time, when mother and
cub or cubs go into the same den together. This also appears to be

part of the grand plan. Compared to most other young, bears develop rather slowly and seem to need parental support for a longer period. Since the female breeds only every other year, or even skips two years, she can continue to mother her young into a second year.

The partly grown young bears continue to stick together and with their mother through the second summer. Some of them stay on until they are going on two years old, and a few even into the third year. On the average, the young den with their mother only during the first winter. That spring after emerging they begin to grow apart. This second spring the female is probably ready to breed again and start a new family.

### SENSES

Experienced hunters are probably the keenest judges of the senses of animals. The successful hunter must thwart the animal's varied senses in order to come within range of it. Grizzly hunters have long known that the sense of smell is the first defense of the big bears. When they are searching for food, ever testing the breeze, they pick up the smell of carrion, for example, at extreme distances, and home straight to it. A whimsical breeze in mountain terrain that suddenly touches a stalking hunter on the back of the neck will instantly alert a bear at long rifle range and put it to flight.

Probably this sense developed with priority because it is the one most useful to the animal in making its daily living, and keeping in touch, regardless of the cover it may be in, with the world around it. Hearing is also sharp. But sounds do not disturb grizzlies as scents do, unless the sound is highly unusual. A bear foraging along a stream hears rushing water; one in the mountains is used to the sound of falling rock, or thunder claps. Even a gunshot, unless in the immediate vicinity, is not especially disturbing. The whistles carried by fishermen along coastal streams in Alaska where the big browns fish alert the animals and cause them to move off simply because this is an unusual, unknown sound. In some cases they may even learn to associate it with man's presence.

Eyesight is poor. The eyes are comparatively small. Undoubtedly eyesight has never developed highly for distance vision because it is used so incessantly for rather close work. Motion is instantly picked up by a watching bear, but it may not know, unless a scent drifts to it, what the moving object is. A low-hunkered, stationary hunter who stays utterly immobile may be carefully studied and passed by. Unless a scent reaches the bear, it is not certain what the hunter is. At close range, of course, vision is excellent. But at close range the other senses also can zero in to bring multiple stimuli. All told, the sense of smell is the grizzly's keenest one, constantly whetted by use in its daily routines.

SIGN *(Tracks are illustrated on page 252.)*

It is obvious that an animal the size of a grizzly is certain to leave ample sign. In a few instances, where both black bears and grizzlies are on the same range, an inexperienced observer might confuse tracks and other signs of the two. Most grizzlies, however, are so much larger that there should be only minor confusion. And the differences between tracks in particular of the coastal Alaskan brown and the inland grizzly are distinguished not only by size difference but by the geographical location of each.

Bear tracks of adults leave, in good imprint material, the entire flatfooted impression of the hind foot. The forefoot track—the physical aspects of the forefoot are quite different—shows the toes and front pad, but does not always show the small, rounded imprint of the heel pad. It is the claws of the forefoot that are so long, in the grizzly. The length generally shows plainly, or at least where the tips make an imprint far out from the toes. This easily distinguishes them from the shorter, curved claw prints of the black bear.

Track measurements, of course, differ according to the size of the bear. Average adults should measure about as follows: inland grizzly, hind foot 9 to 11 inches to ends of toe prints, greatest width 5 to 6 inches; Alaskan brown, hind foot 15 to 17 inches by 10 or a bit more in width; black bear, hind foot 7 to 8 inches long by 3½ to 4 inches wide. An obscure fact little known to wildlife observers is that the so-called big toe and little toe on a bear are exactly reversed from the same on the human foot. In some materials the little toe barely leaves an imprint, and sometimes none at all.

A walking bear shows the hind-foot imprint a short distance in front of the forefoot print on the same side. Occasionally an individual bear when walking may overlap hind-foot and forefoot prints. At a gallop individuals may make slightly differing patterns. As a rule the hind feet are well out ahead of the forefeet; the two hind-foot tracks are in line, one behind the other, and the forefoot tracks are close together but slightly staggered off to one side. Looked at straight-on from behind, the galloping bear appears to run much like a dog, the rear end not quite lined up with the front end. However, gallop patterns of individual bears commonly differ.

As noted earlier, grizzlies like to follow trails. Most of these they make and continue to use, sometimes for years at a time, even following generations walking them. At other times a trail begins with an old moose trail or an old trail or road cut by man. Streamside trails are broad and well packed. Trails in grass, as on the coastal slopes or tundra, are much like old wagon trails. The feet on each side wear a rut and there is a ribbon of grass left in the center. Now and then a trail may be discovered where bears have meticulously stepped time after time precisely into the pad tracks they or other bears have left before. With much travel, these trails, especially in soft or moist earth, are rhythmically pocked along each rut, each track hole several inches deep.

So-called "bear trees" have been the stuff of frontier tales since the first grizzlies were known. Supposedly a big bear selects a tree in a prominent place near a trail, so other passing bears will see it, stands on hind legs, reaches up as high as it can, and rakes the bark. The next bear tries to outdo it, and so on. This, so the tale goes, leaves a kind of challenge, the biggest bear telling the others to beware. Of course this is just old-timer talk to impress the tyros. Bears rub their backs and bellies on big trees, often coming to the same one habitually. They rear up during the process, seize the trunk and rake it, and even bite at the bark, leaving tooth gashes as well as claw marks. After a tree has been rubbed and clawed, another bear, snuffing around it, may also use it, just as a dog or coyote sniffs at a tree where another has urinated, then does likewise. This is how the bear tree is established.

Trees with bark ripped away, chiefly conifers, sometimes with the trunk entirely girdled, are a different kind of sign. These indicate that a bear has been after the soft layer and its oozing juice below the outer bark. On occasion one may also find a grizzly bed. These may be simply lie-up spots in brush, or they may show that the bear has raked together branches or moss to make a soft place to take its ease. Dens may be spotted occasionally, but most are hidden away where a casual observer is not likely to find them. Plowed-up areas where a grizzly has been digging tubers in a low place or digging out a colony of ground squirrels on a slope are both obvious signs, the latter plain enough in the open to be spotted through binoculars at a considerable distance. Food caches have already been mentioned. When one is located, it's a good place to be shy of unless you are hunting, and then it pays to be alert, for close examination may bring a charge from a watching owner.

Droppings also are easily spotted sign, especially on feeding grounds where an animal has spent some time. Droppings are large, and take several forms. Fruit, grass, and fish diets will make them formless and very soft, reminiscent of cattle manure when they're eating fresh green grass. A meat diet will show lots of hair in a much firmer scat. Such droppings are long and round and over 2 inches in diameter. All of the signs mentioned are ones wildlife observers, photographers, and hunters should be aware of. Fresh sign of several varieties means that one or more grizzlies are certain to be using the area.

## HUNTING

Grizzly hunting is closely controlled everywhere nowadays. Because it is strictly trophy hunting, there is no sense whatever in taking a small specimen. Judging what is a top trophy and what is not quite is a job only for a competent, thoroughly experienced guide. Indeed, all grizzly hunts nowadays—this includes, of course, the Alaskan brown—require guide and outfitter services. Some hunts on the Alaskan coast are made by boat, most of them during the spring soon after the animals leave their dens. The craft, on which hunter, guide, and cook live, is the means of transport. Coastal areas are scanned by glass, and the hunter and guide are put ashore by wading or via a small boat to hunt on foot. Some other hunts in the interior are fly-in, and others via pack train. These may occur either in spring or in early fall.

The most important equipment for a grizzly hunt is a rifle of adequate power. Although many large bears have been downed by good marksmen with a rifle such as the .30/06 using a heavy bullet, nowadays the much more powerful large-caliber magnums are a far better tool. A hunter should give himself every chance to put the animal down for keeps with the first shot. A wounded grizzly hiding in willows or other cover presents a seriously dangerous situation to both hunter and guide.

Regardless of where the hunt is held, it is never easy. In mountains the climbing is arduous. Along the Alaskan coast, weather that is considered "good" may be by standards elsewhere abominable, always damp and chill. Walking in the moss and the tall grass and at times through fantastically dense cover is exhausting. Twenty or thirty years ago it was easy enough to book a grizzly hunt into territory where little or no hunting had occurred, and bears were enormous and plentiful. One may now find areas where they are plentiful enough, but virgin grounds are all but gone, and because of cropping of the largest, oldest males, chances of record-size specimens are not as good as they once were.

As noted earlier in this chapter, no one is certain how long grizzly hunting will be allowed to continue. With miserly and astute management of the resource, it may still continue for several decades. There are attempts underway here and there to so regulate grizzly hunting that a sportsman would be allowed only one in a lifetime. A somewhat similar arrangement is in use for token populations of other large game animals in some states. If a hunter gets a moose permit, let's say, he cannot apply again, regardless of whether or not he makes a kill, for two, three, or five years, whatever the law states. Although the one-in-a-lifetime rule might be rather hard to enforce, it would certainly encourage true trophy hunting. No sensible hunter would settle for a so-so specimen, especially not at what it costs nowadays — several thousand dollars — to make a hunt.

There is nothing especially complicated about grizzly hunting techniques. If one is physically able to stand up to the hunt, it is a matter of riding horseback and glassing constantly, or walking and glassing. The open slopes, and the harder-to-scan low places with brush and tall vegetation, must be long and carefully studied with a glass to be sure of spotting the quarry. Guides always hope the animal will be at a substantial distance. That way the animal can be studied and sized up, and if it doesn't look big enough it is passed up. But if it is a shootable trophy, then a stalk can be planned to get within range, which means anywhere from 100 to 250 yards. Come upon at short range, a grizzly may charge, and no guide wants that to happen — not only from the standpoint of danger but because it may not be a desirable trophy yet might force a shot in self-protection. Also, at close range the bear may bound into cover and, alerted, get away or be much more difficult to track.

Of course, sign is always in mind. The places with the most sign get the most attention. However, because grizzlies are so large, and because the inland tribe particularly may be anywhere in a wilderness setting, a constant lookout and glassing are the chief methods of locating game. It is considered advantageous — and safer — always to try to get above the quarry during and at the end of the stalk if the terrain will allow it. Keeping the wind in favor is of course the main concern. With an animal finally decided upon and the stalk completed, the hunter should always take plenty of time to settle down, get his wind, and select an aiming point with utmost care before making the shot.

Grizzly hunting is a dramatic endeavor, always spiced with danger. The challenge of hunting so large an animal is undeniable. Without question, however, the grizzlies still left on this continent have an uncertain future. Those of the far north undoubtedly will be here in at least modest numbers for many years in the future. But it can be reliably predicted that grizzly hunting will see more and more restriction, and ever more careful cropping of the existing population. Overhunting certainly can be harmful to the species nowadays. That is not likely to occur, because of enlightened management. The basic problem faced by these huge bears is one of wilderness living room. Man's so-called progress incessantly chips away at it. Whether there will be any of it left a few decades hence is difficult to predict.

# Black Bear

*Ursus americanus*

No other large North American wild animal has been more enmeshed in the skeins of the country's history and its legends, nor has any appealed more to American imaginations, than the black bear. The prowess of the colonial hunter was rated, in the final analysis, by his success with bears. Daniel Boone staked out a monument of sorts on the spot where he "kilt" his first "bar." Bear fat was used to grease boots, sometimes even hair and wagon wheels in a pinch, and even served as cooking oil. Hides made robes that were status symbols. Bear steaks and mulligan swirled their aromas throughout many a log cabin.

If boys were bad, a bear might get them. If they were good, they could sleep on the bear rug with the head and claws on. If the bears were exceedingly fat in fall, the winter would be long and severe. If they appeared from their dens early, it would be a mild and good growing year. The pigs, and old Bossy, must be watched on a crisp fall night to make sure bruin did not raid and carry them off. In summer beehives also bore watching, if there was to be honey for the home folks and not for the confounded bears.

Black Bear

Nursery tales were filled with cute cubs, and with terrible boar bears hard to rhyme with that chased cool hunters who dispatched them with supreme bravery amid much black-powder smoke. Grandpa's bear stories held listeners enthralled by hearth and campfire. Cute, cuddly teddy bears have long been playmates and security symbols for kids. And in modern times movies and TV shows have disgraced beardom and their producers by giving bears human traits and intelligence and the gentlest of personalities.

There have been circus bears, dancing bears, leashed bears begging pennies for itinerant fiddlers and accordion players, bears exhibited walking around and around smelly cages at roadside zoos. Then there was Smokey, the orphan cub from New Mexico that grew up to become nationally renowned for urging citizens not to set fire to our forests. And far from least, there are the Yellowstone Park bears, which countless tons of printed flyers have warned millions of visitors for decade after decade not to feed or fool with—and the term the same bears put into the language, "bear jam," which means a lineup of cars blocking the highway for anywhere up to several miles, formed by tizzying tourists feeding and fooling with them regardless, and occasionally getting cuffed and chewed on for their lack of sense.

It is little wonder that the black bear has always been such an important wildlife symbol. Although it is the smallest of the continent's bears, it has always been the best colonizer. In its adaptation to many varied habitat and climate situations, the black bear in some ways might be compared to both the whitetail deer and the cottontail. Almost everywhere that early settlers and explorers went, they encountered this animal.

Presumably the black bear originated in Asia and entered North America long ago when, as geographers believe, there was a connection of land across the Bering Strait. Whether or not that is true, these bears colonized all of Alaska except the far north and parts of the Peninsula, and all of Canada to where the forests disappear in the north, except minor plains expanses of the south-central prairie provinces. Within what are now the contiguous states, black bears managed to dwell happily and push forward practically everywhere except over the wide-open plains of the Great Basin, the treeless country of eastern Oregon, and parts of the southwestern deserts. The original range continued far on down into Mexico, over both eastern and western flanks of the Sierra Madre and the pine and oak forests of some desert mountain ranges.

Obviously this vast range, to which the animals adapted over thousands of years, took in almost every conceivable combination

## THE BLACK BEAR

COLOR: Highly variable geographically; eastern Canada and U.S., glossy black, with or without white area of varying size on chest, muzzle and part of eye area paler to brown; western U.S., Canada, Alaska, cinnamon to brown to tan to occasional blond color phases common, plus black; Alaska glacier bear, a subspecies (*U. a. emmonsii*), smoky to iron gray to bluish to near-black, muzzle brownish; Kermode's bear (*U. a. kermodei*), islands off west-central British Columbia, rare, white, nose grayish-sand, claws white, foot pads brick-reddish, eyes brown.

MEASUREMENTS, ADULT MALES: 4½ to 6½ feet overall length, rare specimens 7 to 8 or even 9 feet; height at shoulder, average 3 feet, some less, some slightly taller.

WEIGHT, ADULT MALES: Average 250 to 400 pounds, exceptional specimens 500 to 600-plus.

FEMALES: Smaller on the average by about one-fifth.

GENERAL ATTRIBUTES: Coat when at best has glossy sheen; very short tail; face straight, not dished as in grizzly; shoulders without hump as in grizzly; claws short compared to grizzly, and well curved; shy, not naturally aggressive, but occasionally dangerous.

of terrain and climate. The saw grass and palm hammocks of the Florida Everglades, the mountains of Maine, the hardwood and mixed forests of what are now the central and Great Lakes states, the Rockies and their broad foothills, along the Pacific coast except southern California—all these were home to the black bear. Climate apparently was no barrier, and nor for the most part was altitude. Blacks are common in many places in the southeast in near-sea-level swamps, and also at 6000 and 7000 feet in all mountains. Hunters have bagged them and seen them much higher, to 9000 feet and above, well up toward the timber line, although probably they do not actually live at or above the timber line.

Because of its highly diverse diet and unrestricted tastes, the black bear can live—and has lived—practically anywhere. However, the one barrier to range expansion appears to have been where forests ran out. This is a forest or woodland creature. Unlike the plains grizzly that followed the buffalo, the black bear, unless broad stream bottoms thick with timber and brush were present for it to follow, never has been able to adapt to wholly open country.

Also unlike the grizzly, the black bear has been able to adapt rather well to man's presence. As an animal personality, this bear possibly has a keener intelligence and more cunning than its larger relatives. It is decidedly a shy creature, with an uncanny ability to keep its private life private. Its shrewdness in finding places to hide even on the very fringes of settlement is in many ways comparable to that of the whitetail deer. Today black bears live within short distances of very large cities, where habitat is suitable and food available.

In spite of its adaptability and its secretiveness, the black bear has suffered a serious population decline compared to earlier times. Certainly the species is not remotely endangered. But it has nonetheless disappeared from large areas of its original habitat. There are numerous reasons. In a few instances, particularly in colonial times and on to the mid-1800s, hunting pressure, chiefly hide hunting, depleted bear stocks locally. As human settlement progressed, bears in the vicinity of settlement were systematically destroyed because of their exasperating inroads upon livestock of all kinds, from sheep to pigs to cattle to poultry. Because blacks are extremely fond of sweets, bee raisers in many places — Florida even today is a classic example — always have had to take severe measures. A single raiding bear can put a bee man out of business in a night.

The most important influence on black bear populations was clearing of the forests, which drove the black bear from tens of thousands of square miles of its original range. It needs roaming and foraging room, and thus must have fairly large blocks of unbroken woodlands or wild lands in order to survive.

Today, black bear populations outside the contiguous states rate about as follows. In Alaska, very high; across the far-northern areas of Canada, substantial populations in the Yukon and Northwest Territories; in British Columbia, a good population; in the northern portions of Alberta and Saskatchewan, also a good population; in Manitoba, only fair to good; in Ontario, excellent; in Quebec, plentiful; in New Brunswick and Nova Scotia, good; in Newfoundland and Labrador, some.

In the eastern states, Maine has a high population, New Hampshire and Vermont are fair, New York is fair to good, Massachusetts and New Jersey have a paltry few left. Pennsylvania rates quite high — a surprise considering human population. Virginia has a fair number left in its western forests; North Carolina has quite the opposite pattern, with most bears in the tidewater region. South Carolina, West Virginia, and Tennessee have only a few animals left, and in Kentucky they are probably all gone.

The Great Lakes states — Michigan, Wisconsin, Minnesota — are still home to a large but slowly diminishing population. The

# Range of the Black Bear

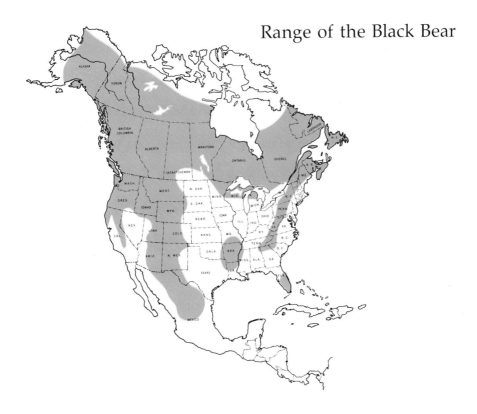

Ozarks, once home to a good number, now hardly count. Missouri has a few, and Arkansas has made transplants but certainly isn't a bear state.

In the south, Florida still has possibly a thousand animals all told, Georgia a few, Mississippi possibly a few. Other southern states are questionable. Texas still carries the black bear on the game list but has none except a token population in the far-west Guadalupe Mountains.

It is in the Rockies and the northwest that the highest black bear populations remain south of Canada. Here Washington has the most of any lower-48 state — in some areas to nuisance proportions. They are anathema on timber-company lands, where they destroy hundreds of acres of young planted conifers by eating the inner bark. Oregon and Idaho have large populations, with Montana and Wyoming next in line. There are a surprising number still left in northern California, a few in Utah, and a fair to good scattering in Colorado, New Mexico, and Arizona.

Because of its vast range, the black bear was a perfect candidate for the "splitters" among the taxonomists to whack up its population into endless subspecies. They divided it into numerous races, based on minor physiological differences that were possibly the result of geographical and climatic influences rather than genetics. However, except for two distinctly different races, there is no reason to be concerned with these, and indeed it is probable that the majority of the continent's black bears are a single variety that needs no closer delineation.

In the days of early western exploration it was believed, with some logic, that the brown and tan bears so common particularly throughout the Rockies were of a different species entirely. The so-called "cinnamon bear" was the subject of much interest in those times. However, it was soon observed that a black sow might be trailed by a brown cub and a black cub, that shades of color were even more varied than had been thought, and that all of these were simply color phases of the same bear. Individuals can be light tan, dark tan, chestnut, cinnamon, and even pale blond. These last darken with age. It is indeed interesting that very few brown black bears have ever been recorded from the eastern half of the country or from eastern Canada. An occasional one turns up, but it is rare. Blacks of the east, much more commonly than those from the west, often have a patch of white on the chest. This may be a snow-white area a foot across, or only a few white hairs.

The two striking exceptions of subspecies are northern. One, which lives on a few islands in a very restricted range along the coast of central British Columbia, is a strikingly beautiful animal, often pure snowy white, with the muzzle sandy to gray-beige, the eyes brown, the soles of the feet reddish brown, and often the claws white. This bear, usually called the Kermode black bear, *Ursus americanus kermodei*, is not an albino, but a "sport" of sorts that apparently breeds true. It is a rare creature, fully protected.

The second notable subspecies is the blue, or glacier, bear, *Ursus americanus emmonsii*, also with an exceedingly restricted range. Its color is from pale smoke to bluish silvery gray to dark iron gray, and in some specimens a rich near-black gray. Its home is a section of coastal Alaska, in the St. Elias Mountains and along Yakatut and Glacier Bays. Named both for its color and for the fact that it lives amid numerous glaciers in awesomely rugged mountains, this handsome animal is elusive and rather rare. It may be less rare than supposed, since its forbidding habitat has kept hunters from collecting many and scientists from studying it in depth.

Whether or not the black bear should be considered potentially dangerous to man depends upon which writers you read and to whom you talk. Some writers and outdoorsmen scoff at the idea of danger from black bears. They claim, correctly, that blacks are shy and furtive, are wont to disappear like smoke at the slightest intrusion, would rather run from a man than stand and fight, and are quick to learn, unlike many other carnivores, from varied frights such as being chased by dogs or shot at by hunters. Therefore, they say, there is no reason whatever to fear them. But the facts hardly prove this conclusion. More people have been mauled, and killed, by black bears than by their large relatives. This may be because there are more blacks, and over a greater range. Nonetheless, it should impart a message.

To be sure, black bears are not very aggressive unless aroused. They are not as a species especially irritable or quick-tempered. What they are is individually wholly unpredictable. Berry pickers have been hurt, and even killed, by blacks. This may occur because the bear suddenly feels trapped or startled, or simply because it doesn't want any other creature sharing its forage. Sows with cubs are notoriously edgy and often vicious, which is understandable. Old bears, injured bears, even extremely hungry bears, are irritable and cantankerous. A bear startled at close range may fly into a protective rage. **Any** black bear deserves respect as potentially dangerous. One of the problems, in places like Yellowstone Park, for example, is that the average urban dweller whose knowledge of bears is limited to Smokey and cuddly teddy bears has no idea how strong and fast a bear can be. A yearling cub weighing under 100 pounds can knock a man flat with one easy swipe, or snap his neck with one bite of powerful jaws and long canines.

Along with unpredictability, black bears seem to have in them a kind of devil-may-care vandalism syndrome. They appear, exasperatingly, to take some perverse pleasure often in simply wrecking anything that comes handy. Combined with this is their curiosity. In campgrounds, aside from bedeviling garbage cans, blacks are prone to ripping up tents and smashing anything that lies around. In some instances food draws them and they bite into canned goods and smash ice chests. They commonly break into woodland cabins, and have been known to try this even while the owner is present. Like the trained dancing bears of the old roadshows, they are clowns of a sort, but they are not always funny.

Ordinarily the black is a quiet animal, uttering vocal sounds only when irritated, or making love, or mumbling to offspring.

# COLOR PHASES OF THE BLACK BEAR

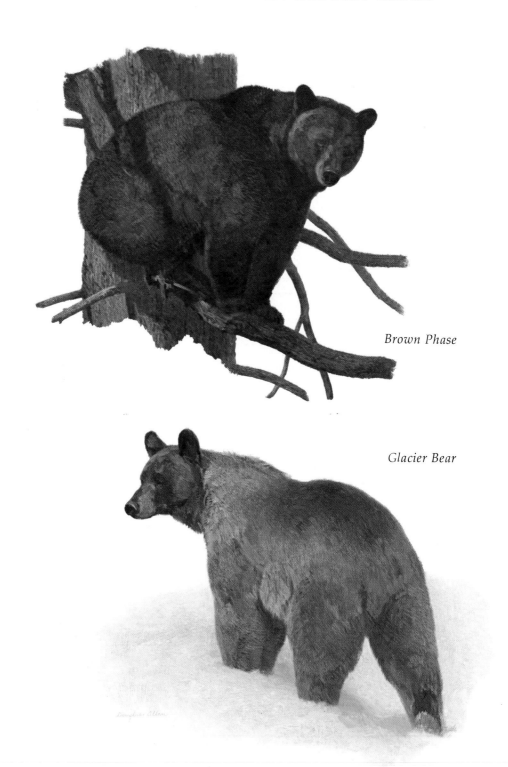

*Brown Phase*

*Glacier Bear*

*Kermode Bear*

*Cinnamon Phase*

Large bears may bawl or roar, snuffle, make grunting sounds. When suspicious a black may rear up and snort and grunt. When it begins to cough, growl, and snap its teeth together, these sounds should be read as signs that it probably intends to run only one way — toward the intruder, with purpose. A wounded black on occasion utters a hair-raising moan. Little cubs may let out diminutive bawls when scared, and they whimper and whine to their mother. However, many a woodsman who has been in black bear territory for years has yet to hear one utter a single sound.

One reason may be that except for cubs and mother together, or male and female consorting during mating, black bears, like other bears, are loners. The adult males stay to themselves all year except for mating season. On ranges near settlements, the big boars are inclined, probably because of long experience, to stay in the thickest, most remote cover, except for forays and raids outside. It may also be that bears are silent most of the time because they have no enemies among other wildlife, and thus little reason for bluff or rage. Large blacks may attack, and even eat, young blacks. But aside from man and his dogs, or the rare occasion when a big bear might be hurt while trying to down an antlered game animal or starve because of a mouth festered from porcupine quills, black bears are safe from hazards other than internal parasites. In territory where grizzlies occur on the same range, they brook no interference from blacks. The black bear that sees or smells a grizzly doesn't waste time growling or bluffing. It flees.

### HABITAT

Perhaps the best way to define the fundamentals of black bear habitat is to say that this is an animal requiring cover, with at least portions of it dense. This includes a broad variety of range. Some bear hunters in Florida, Georgia, North Carolina, and Virginia might think of the bear as a swamp animal. The Everglades and Big Cypress, Okefenokee, in Florida and Georgia, the tidewater swamps of North Carolina, and Dismal Swamp in Virginia have bear populations still today. Yet westerners think of the black as an inhabitant of mountain forests and meadows.

The black bear was originally so adaptable that it was able to live happily in both swamps and high mountains as well as in intermediate forest zones. The reason some of the southern swamps still are home to it, even though it may be scarce in upland portions of the same states, is that the near-impenetrable swamps are last stands, remote, with only moderate intrusion by man, and capable of furnishing enough food.

Black bears will venture from their woodlands into open areas, but not very far. It is common to observe a big black in the mountains of Wyoming or New Mexico moseying about in a high-country meadow, eating grass or remnants of a long-dead elk, or grubbing for small rodents. But these meadows are simply openings in the forest, each rimmed by mixed aspen and coniferous forest. Typical of optimum black bear range east of the Mississippi are the mixed forests of Maine, Pennsylvania, northern Michigan, and portions of Ontario, where pine, spruce, and other evergreens mingle with poplar, birch, maple, and varied oaks.

Brushy stream courses bordered by alder and willow tangles, or fringed with serviceberry, black haw, chokecherry, and similar fruit-bearing shrubs invariably are used heavily by bears within their forest domain. The dense thickets of spruce in portions of Canada and the jackpine and poplar plains and wild-hay meadows of the northern Great Lakes country also are home to the black bear. In the Rockies, the wild river courses and their hemming slopes, thinly or densely forested, serve perfectly as bailiwicks, and along coastal Alaska and British Columbia the streams with dense thickets plus the grassy slopes nearby sustain this bear in settings much like the home of the Alaskan brown.

Basically it is not so much the specific type of habitat that keeps the black bear contented as it is the amount of forage present. Given places to hide in peace, room to wander without too many frights or disturbances over a big block of country, the black bear can adapt to almost any surrounding — as long as there is enough food present to keep its belly full. Where man has settled the edges of large forest tracts, black bears don't mind at all living in proximity. They are drawn to these fringes because of the windfalls of garbage and other sustenance that result from man's presence. But a bear cannot abide a small woodlot, as a whitetail deer may. It needs room where it can make its presence either unknown or at least not obtrusive, and where, when harried, it can retire to tangled thickets and still eke out a living.

### FEEDING

Given cover and room to roam without constant disturbance, food is the key to where the bears must be. Although classed as a carnivore, the black could not possibly have been so successful a species had it not adapted to a broad menu. Black bears will eat meat whenever they can get it. They are not the least bit choosy, either. A healthy live forage animal, a sickly old one, a dead one so ripe the carrion smell permeates the forest breezes for hundreds of yards around — the bear isn't finicky.

A nest of baby mice is slurped up grass and all. The nest of a wild duck on a marsh edge is gobbled, perhaps full of eggs partly incubated, or of just-hatched young; if a parent can be seized, so much the better. A newborn fawn, also its mother if a sneak attack is successful, an elk growing old and feeble, a pig from a forest-edge pen raided in darkness, the dog that barks at the raid, even a young bear of its own kind — all are accepted without qualm as bonuses to be seized when opportunity is presented.

Those are just for starters. Black bears love to claw apart rotten stumps and logs and lick up the ants swarming from nests inside them, taking the ant eggs as gourmet tidbits and never overlooking beetles and grubs. If a log is flipped over and a small salamander wriggles, it is also snapped up. Frogs, snakes, turtles, fish alive or dead, the raccoon that is after them if it can be grabbed, anything that crawls, swims, runs, or flies is fair game for the black bear.

Curiously, however, all these items, which might be lumped into the "meat" category, are actually only a small part of the average black bear's diet. It must be presumed that probably hundreds of thousands of years ago these carnivores were unable to supply their food requirements solely as predators. Even the teeth, which are thought to have evolved from a quite different arrangement long ago, are so designed that the two large pairs of canines for seizing and tearing are complemented by flat-topped molars at the rear of the jaws that serve as grinders for vegetation and other soft forage.

Thus the black bear and its larger grizzly relatives, large creatures that require a high daily intake to keep their big engines running, slowly adapted eons ago to omnivorous foraging. At least the ones that survived did. And over the broad expanse of geologic time, the animal that succeeded in expanding its range over almost the entire continent was able to do so because it developed a physical system and metabolism that could be fired by any forage available.

It is interesting that the large true predators — those that evolved on another tangent and were geared to meat only — have been the first creatures of the earth to decline drastically, and they often were and still are animals of rather restricted ranges. The African lion did well for centuries because forage animals of large size were always abundantly available and it was able to kill them with ease. But it could not spread its range to places where such forage was meager. The gray wolf of North America, at one time present over a vast range, could not sustain a high population level when its living forage declined because of human intrusion, and it could not live with man because it was too destructive to stock. The black bear, conversely, although badly affected by encroachment of civilization, still can eke out a living on the fringes because it can live on and will eat practically anything. The lesson in species survival is intriguing.

The black bear more than any other North American animal seems to love sweets. It raids bee trees in the wild, plunging right in, often until face and shoulders are covered with angry bees, but still the bear continues to gorge on honey until it is sticky from jowls to elbows. Now and then it also eats the bees. Blacks cannot resist fruit, and wild fruits in season are a mainstay of diet. Wild black cherries, chokecherries, and pin cherries are favorites. It is common in bear country in New England and the Great Lakes region to find cherry trees with limbs torn off, and masses of bear dung full of pits below them. Chokecherry and wild plum thickets in the west get the same treatment. Hillsides everywhere that blueberries grow, and in some wooded lowlands the now rare huckleberry swamps, are literally combed by black bears.

In the old logging country of New England and the Great Lakes, cut over a hundred years ago, there are many places where apple trees either were planted near log camps or grew from discarded cores. These, and apple trees on abandoned farms, are favorite feeding places in late summer and early fall. Commonly a bear climbs a tree, even in somebody's backyard in the western mountains or back-country New England, and rips the tree all to pieces as it carelessly gorges with apples, and knocks more to the ground where it can get them later. Needless to say, these bears, if caught at their orchard raiding, don't last long.

Vegetable gardens and some small crop fields in bear country also take a drubbing. Patches of sweet corn are totally destroyed in one night unless the owner stays alert with his gun. Melons are a delight to any bear that lives nearby. So are tomatoes, pumpkins, and even row vegetables. So also are fields of barley or green wheat plowed near forest edges. There is by no means the problem with bear raids on crops that there was in frontier days and even early in this century, simply because there aren't as many bears, nor as many crops located on the fringes of bear territory.

Wild nut crops are avidly enjoyed by black bears. These are, in fact, of inestimable value to the animals in fall because they are rich in fats and oils. Acorns, beech nuts, and in parts of the west piñon nuts are staples that help the bears put on thick layers of fat before denning. Not every year is a good acorn year, and some varieties of oaks bear only every two years. Because oaks of one kind or another grow almost everywhere within black bear range south of Canada, they are extremely important to bear survival. In off years when the acorn crop is low, blacks have to work harder for a living, and are consequently sometimes irritable and more likely to get in trouble with human neighbors.

Black bears are also insatiable bark eaters, eagerly devouring the inner bark of a number of trees, among them some hardwoods such as maples. However, the conifers, particularly pines, get most attention. Timber companies, in the west particularly, look upon the black bear as an exasperating nuisance and expensive pest because at times it destroys thousands of young trees in new plantings. Varied tubers, of sedges, cattails, rushes, and numerous other plants, are dug for food, particularly in spring. Also in spring and early summer great quantities of green grasses of endless variety are consumed. When first out of hibernation, in fact, black bears in some places eagerly graze new green grass. In Ontario, for example, hunters sometimes quietly walk old log trails during a spring hunt. In these openings new grass shoots up quickly and bears soon find it.

During spawning runs of fish, black bears go after them with concentration. However, they are by no means as expert anglers as the grizzlies. In southern Canada and the lower United States they hang around creeks and larger streams when suckers and carp run in quantity. They are sometimes able to grab quantities of these near stream obstructions or where a small creek is packed with them. Hunters have high success by scooping up spring-run suckers and piling them on a bank for bait. Blacks are also hunted along the Alaska-coast salmon streams much as the browns are. But for the most part the black bears take their fish, such as spawned-out salmon, dead or dying, and others mostly trapped in shallows, where they are easy to catch.

It would be nearly impossible to list everything that goes into a black bear's stomach. It will eat almost anything, dead or alive, in the entire plant and animal world. This is really the secret of the animal's success on this continent. Seldom does a black bear simply go hunting for a specific kind of meal. It shuffles along, nosing here, nosing there, digging, clawing, ripping, overturning, sniffing, accepting anything that it finds. On occasion the finding is easy, as a whole hillside blue with berries, or a big moose turned to carrion by a hard winter. If no such bonanza is at hand, the bear keeps moving, picking a little of this, a little of that, endlessly stoking its nonselective stomach.

## MOVEMENTS

Most movements of the black bear are directly related to its daily search for food. If there is an abundance, a bear may stay within as little as a square mile of range, but only as long as the abundance lasts. Much of the time its wanderings will encompass at least 5 or 6 square miles. In times of scarcity at least double that may be necessary. In addition, black bears apparently like to travel and wander, poking here and there much like curious travelers. There is no migration as such. A black bear may go to slopes where blueberries are ripe, even several miles from its spring and early-summer home. Or in spring it may follow low places where quick-growing plants of which it is fond, such as skunk cabbage, emerge in profusion. A beech grove within a mixed forest may draw bears from some distance when mast is abundant. But there is no definite winter and summer forage or definite seasonal movement over any appreciable distance.

Old males are inclined to travel more than females and cubs. They're drifters who make the rounds, but meanwhile stay away from other bears except during mating time. Occasional fights between males occur, but no individual is eager to brace another unless it is extremely hungry, or hurt and irritable. Nor does the black bear have a strong home feeling. It may live out its life, if food is ample, within a short distance of where it was born. Or it may wander off many miles for no good reason and never return to its original home range.

Now and then a bear shows up in a location where none has been known for years, and hangs around. Just why, no one knows, and probably the bear doesn't either. Hundreds of bears have been live-trapped and moved, in parks and in settled areas where they have become nuisances. There are few instances of them returning, even when released only 20 miles or so distant, although very occasionally they have apparently felt strongly enough about "home," to have returned from long distances.

Blacks are strong swimmers. There are untold instances of them swimming in large lakes for several miles to reach an island seen from shore. Why, only the bear knows. A cabin built on an island in a large back-bush Canadian lake, where the owner felt sure no bear would ever bother him, may have its door smashed in or its windows demolished and the interior vandalized by a bear from the mainland that went looking, as black bears will.

Blacks are also excellent climbers. Grizzlies, except some very young individuals, cannot climb trees because their claws are so long and straight. Possibly their bulk also is a handicap. A black bear has shorter, closely curved claws that cling to bark expertly. An adult black, when pressed, can shinny up a tree almost at a run. Blacks also climb trees casually, after fruit or nuts, and sometimes probably just because they enjoy it. They have been observed up in a big tree dozing in a broad crotch, paws dangling, and at other times simply looking around as if pleased with the scenery. Coming down a tree, the bear has to move rear end first, sliding and grabbing with its claws. While still a few feet above ground, it lets go and plops down. Very occasionally a treed bear will jump, anywhere from 15 to 30 feet, landing rather awkwardly but without apparent harm.

Much has been written about whether blacks move chiefly by day or by night. A common belief, repeated over and over, is that they are by nature diurnal but when harassed by humans become nocturnal. This is mostly nonsense. A black bear moves whenever it pleases. In campgrounds panhandling bears rummage in the garbage buckets at midday and at midnight. They may be observed pottering along a stream course by day, or seen on jeep trails far back in wilderness areas in the middle of the night.

It may be that bears on the fringe of settlement switch to almost complete nocturnal habits as a measure of furtiveness. However, black bears taken by hunters out of fly-in spike camps far back in the Canadian bush, in places where they've never seen a human or smelled one, and bears far back in the mountains of the west, living in total seclusion, habitually come out very late in the afternoon just before dusk to feed on a pile of carrion left from a winter-killed elk or deer. The last hour of daylight is invariably the best hour of hunting. Conversely, the same bear may be found fiddling around on a slope at midday—if it happens to feel like it.

The gaits of the black bear are several. Undisturbed, it ambles along flatfooted in a rolling, almost aimless manner. It also walks swiftly, head swinging, at times, and when in a hurry or frightened it breaks into a swift gallop. Going all-out, which it can do for short bursts, it may reach 25 or 30 miles per hour. Its slower gallop covers much ground, and can be maintained for much longer distances. In front of a dog pack, a big bear with stomach not overloaded can run for hours, doubling and circling, pausing to whack a dog here or there and then moving on. Some never are treed or bayed before wearing out the dogs.

After feeding full, the black bear makes a bed and dozes several hours. The bed may be in a thicket of brush, under a blowdown, or just anywhere that is comfortable and secluded. It does not habitually use the same bed more than once. Occasionally a bed will be a mound of leaves or grass scraped together for greater comfort, but most of the time the animal is not very particular. Some of the more interesting bedding places of black bears are those out in the open. They have been seen lying sound asleep on a rock ledge that overlooks a valley where they have been gorging on carrion or dead and dying fish in a stream. It is also not unusual to see a bear lying in the sun high on a mountain slope, even up atop a big flat rock spang in the open, forelegs dangling over the edges.

In areas where they have established goals, such as a slope where they sleep and a valley where they feed, or along a stream course traversed often, they wear broad, distinct trails from point to point. These are seldom as common or deep-rutted as those made by the big Alaska browns and some grizzlies. Probably the most active time for the black bear is when it is first feeding in spring and must hunt hard to fill up, and late in the fall when it is constantly gorging and laying on fat before entering its winter den.

### DENNING

The amount of fat a bear puts on, when food is abundant, to see it through the long winter sleep is phenomenal. An extra 100 pounds is common, and twice that in northern areas is not especially rare. Many wildlife enthusiasts, and hunters, are under the impression that the black bear, and grizzlies, hibernate. They don't. When a bear dens up for several winter months, there is no drastic change in its metabolism. It becomes drowsy, and goes to sleep.

Much is still to be learned about the precise physical aspects, and what triggers the sleepiness. Temperature certainly is a factor. Southern black bears, undoubtedly with the instincts dating from the early evolution of the species, may go into a den for only a week or so, or only a few days, or intermittently during winter. Some may be less active but not den up at all. In far-northern regions black bears may enter dens as early as mid-October and stay denned for five months or more, emerging in April or as late as early May. In more moderate winter climates the den stay is shorter, from about mid-November until March or early April, or even less. Conceivably the urge to retire to a comfortable, warm den and sleep through the severe weather is an instinct toward survival acquired long ago. Winter is the time of scarce forage. The energy required to keep alive — if enough food for keeping alive were available during the difficult winter season — might defeat the purpose. The bear would die because energy expended in cold while gathering a livelihood would overbalance the intake of food.

By putting on fat in the fall, the bear is able to go to sleep and wait out the difficult time. Its body temperature drops, but not much. Its breathing rate is only slightly slowed. It goes to sleep, but is never in a state from which awakening is difficult. During warm spells, bears may come out of dens, groggily wander about, then go back. When the first of the drowsy season comes on, there is an interesting sequence the bear follows quite instinctively. It apparently feels too dull and drowsy to eat for a few days. During that short fasting period the entire digestive system is of course emptied.

However, it would hardly do for the stomach and all of the intestines to be flatly deflated for so long a period. Thus the bear takes on some roughage as padding, commonly needles of conifers if they are available, dead grass, or fallen leaves. A substantial portion of this material passes through the stomach and intestines and lodges in the lower bowel, where it forms a firm stopper of sorts. If the bear entered its den with stomach gorged and intestines full and went to sleep, masses of excrement would be piled inside the den. The swiftly shriveling stomach and intestines, with the lower bowel stopped up, avoid this.

Dens are selected in a wide variety of locations. A cave serves well, or a hollow beneath a blowdown. A hole under a cut bank may be chosen. Some blacks dig dens in the side of a slope, under tree roots, or among rocks. Still others, less finicky, may simply curl up beneath a low-hanging evergreen and let snow cover the branches, or even make a bed in dense brush or high dead grass. Females use more care in choice of den site as a rule than males, presumably because it is in the winter den that the young arrive.

When the animals first emerge from dens in spring, they have lost some of their fall fat, which has been burned up during the long sleep. They drink water and eat soft foods. Fresh sprouting green grass, full of liquid, is often taken in large quantity right at first. Its juices, plus water if easily available, apparently soak the contracted, empty digestive system and purge it, getting it in working order again. By the time the bodily functions are geared up once more the bears are feeding heavily, and now the urgings of the mating season are at hand.

BREEDING

Only during early summer each year do males and females consort. The period during which females are ready to be bred begins as a rule in June. Not all allow attentiveness of males at the same time, and so the breeding season lasts sometimes through all of July. During that period one male may stay for several weeks with the same female. This may be the only female he finds. Or after a short period the male may wander off to look elsewhere, thus servicing more than one sow.

Black bears may be crotchety and antisocial at other times of year, but during the mating season the boar is an ardent swain, nuzzling and licking the female, following her constantly, feeding sometimes nose to nose. The two may rear erect and embrace. They paw each other and occasionally wrestle playfully and seemingly with great affection.

Females are fully adult before they are able to mate. A female cub born in a den in February or March of one year will not breed until she is in her third summer. Then, possibly because young bears need parental care longer than many wild animals, she skips at least one year, coming into heat again two years later when she is free of her youngsters and they are on their own.

The growth of embryos in bears is quite different from the system among most other mammals. After fertilization, the female's egg cells do not begin immediate development, and do not attach themselves to the uterus until several months later, in fall. Just how this system evolved, and why, no one is certain. Bear cubs are extremely tiny at birth, and helpless—almost, one might say, premature. Delayed implantation (embryo development) may be to assure that the female is denned up cozy and warm before the cubs arrive, so that they are not brought into a bitterly cold world where they could not survive.

It may also be that the habit of denning is matched to the season where food is scarce, as has been noted. Youngsters could not possibly learn to take solid food in dead of winter. Thus with the heavily fattened mother giving warm milk in a weatherproof den, both she and the young are able to wait out the winter and the coming of spring forage. Man may believe he could have planned all this better and simpler — as by having mating season in fall and obviating the need for latent embryo development. Be that as it may, the unique arrangement seems to have worked well, and with high success, for bears over many centuries, and the "why" will always be only supposition.

### BIRTH AND DEVELOPMENT

Baby black bears are almost unbelievably small. It seems preposterous that a 350-pound mother bear should give birth to young that can be held two at a time in the hand of an average man. Each weighs from 6 to 8 ounces. Many females giving birth for the first time produce only a single cub. If so, from then on twins are the rule, and triplets not rare. Seldom are there more, but regular litters of four to six have been known.

The litters are born with eyes snugly shut. The cubs are covered with very fine hair so short that they appear naked, but in the warm den they have no trouble worming down into their mother's long, dense fur. Whether or not the mother is deeply asleep during the birth no one is certain. Probably she is only drowsy, is at least aware of the birth, and is able to clean up the offspring and snuggle them to her. One of the most intriguing physical attributes of the mother is the placement of her teats. Two are located between her hind legs, and four more are on her chest. Is this arrangement a safeguard to make certain the tiny cubs, born to a less than wide-awake mother, find milk, or are some of the extras standbys in case a whole litter of small bears occurs? Such are the puzzles of wildlife.

Most cubs are born during January and February. About six weeks later, give or take a few days, the youngsters have their eyes open and are beginning to be a bit frisky, but of course so far their only knowledge is of their mother and the interior of the den. A couple of weeks later, still unsteady on their legs but weighing ten times what they did at birth, they follow their mother from the den and begin to learn about the outside world.

Black bear cubs are often an exasperation to their mother. They are like bubbly, exuberant small children, forever teasing and chasing and rough-housing each other, climbing, and tumbling into everything, and bedeviling their mother. Now and then the mother, though exceedingly protective in face of any danger, and always suspicious of disturbance or the presence of another bear, finds it

*A yearling black bear cub.*

necessary to bat a cub with a swipe that sends it flying and crying.

The small bears continue to nurse, but soon are picking at any food they see their mother eat, and sharing with her any kill or forage discovery she makes. They climb trees agilely now. In fact, at sign of imminent danger—or what the mother suspects may be danger—she herds them together and sends them scurrying up a tall tree. Boar bears that happen to pass by have no compunction about killing a cub. But woe to one that tries it. The mother flies into a violent rage and will fight instantly.

By late fall the youngsters begin to look more like replicas of adults. They are weaned but loath to leave their mother. At denning time, they go in with her, and all sleep together congenially. When spring arrives and all leave the den, family ties begin to fray. Very occasionally young bears may stay on into the fall with their mother, but the majority begin lives of their own during that second summer.

### SENSES

The most highly developed sense of the black bear is smell. Like almost all creatures that live in a habitat that has much dense cover, it is important that the bear be able to pick up scents at long distance. A keen sense of smell is also important in locating numerous varieties of food. A black bear zeroes in on carrion from a half-mile away when the breeze is right. It can locate abundant ripe fruit the same way, and easily select by smell the types of vegetation that make up the bulk of its diet.

Hearing is also good. Many nature writers equate keenness of hearing with ear size. By this measure, a mule deer would be able to hear better than a whitetail deer, whereas probably their hearing abilities are about equal. Nonetheless, among bears, the black does have the largest ears, and it does have extremely sharp hearing. Again, this sense undoubtedly has developed to a high level because the animal lives in and hides in heavy cover. A bear must always be listening for disturbing sounds. The furtive and secretive black bear, bringing both senses of scent and hearing to fine tuning, is well aware of what is constantly happening for several hundred yards around it, and thus can drift off unnoticed when its suspicions are aroused.

Its eyesight is not very good. Possibly its small eyes are near-sighted. It sees movement readily, but does not quickly identify motionless objects unless it can smell them. In its daily foraging, extra-sharp eyesight over distances is not any great advantage, and in cover it cannot see far anyway.

### SIGN *(Tracks are illustrated on page 252.)*

In a forest where the ground is carpeted with pine needles or other matter that does not readily accept imprints, a black bear moves silently without leaving any sign at all. But a bear that lives in and feeds over a specific domain invariably marks its presence plainly. Tracks show in mud, dust, or snow. The bear walks flat-footed. It is the hind foot that leaves the print rather similar to that of a human barefoot track, except that the claw marks show in front of the toes and the little toe and big toe are transposed in placement compared to the human foot. The print of the front foot shows the pad or ball of the foot, plus toes and claw marks, but may or may not show the small, rounded heel.

The only track with which a black bear print might be confused is that of the grizzly. However, among tracks of adults the grizzly is far larger, and the stride is longer. Tracks of adult blacks of average size are as follows: forefoot, not counting the heel, about 4½ inches long by 3½ to 4 inches wide; hind foot, overall, 3½ to 4 inches wide by 7 inches long. Walking or bounding, the hind-foot prints are ahead of those of the fore feet.

One of the most interesting "track" signs of the black bear occurs on the bark of a tree here and there, of species that have fairly smooth, soft outer bark, such as poplar and birch, maple, aspen, and the smoother-barked nut bearing trees, for example, beech.

When a bear climbs one of the these trees, each claw sinks into the bark. The wound bleeds but eventually heals and in time leaves a scar, usually black or at least dark on lighter-hued bark. At first glance these old bark scars, which with age become rounded and broadened, look exactly as if they were imprints of the toes. Of course all they mean is that a black bear was there sometime, several seasons previously. But if such scars are numerous they may indicate that this is perennial bear range and that a search for fresher sign is worthwhile.

Blacks also rake trees with their claws. Rough-barked evergreens commonly have claw marks, fresh or old. Bears may make them when climbing, or they may simply rear up and claw a tree. They also rub against certain trees, especially when shedding, and wear the bark smooth. These trees may also have claw marks. Torn bark where bears have ripped it open to lick juices or eat the soft inner bark, shredded rotten stumps or logs where they've sought ants and beetles, broken limbs on wild fruit trees such as wild cherry—all mark where black bears have been foraging.

Any sharp-eyed woodsman is ever alert to all these signs. He also watches for bear trails. They appear only in special places— along a stream, perhaps, or in a habitually used bedding place near a feeding area and the abundant food. Bears coming to garbage dumps or carrion, perhaps a dead big-game animal, where they feed daily for some time, make well-packed trails that are easily seen. Hunters look for copious droppings. It is easy to judge from these whether the bear has been using a place regularly, or recently. Soft foods—fruit and grass—form manure that is also soft and left in large piles. More solid foods, as meat, tend to make droppings firm, 1 to 1¾ inches in diameter and in pieces several inches long.

### HUNTING

Every hunter always gets excited when he spots fresh bear sign during an open season. But most of the time, aside from relaying the message that a bear lives here or recently went through the area, it is not likely to pay off with a rug on the floor. It is estimated that at least 90 percent of all black bears annually bagged are taken as incidentals by hunters after other big game when bear season also happens to be open. Deer hunters, because they are the most numerous and because deer and black bear commonly use the same ranges, collect most of them. Thus, most of the hunting is not done "on purpose."

There are two chief methods of purposely hunting black bears. One is with dogs, the other is with bait. Tough, highly specialized big hounds are mandatory for bear hunting, and several are needed. There's no denying that hunting with hounds is a most dramatic, and also exceedingly rugged, sport. But because a trained pack is the basis for this endeavor, plus location in an expanse of habitat that has a large enough bear population to make it worthwhile, the only sportsmen who ordinarily pursue this hunting are the dog owners and their friends, or those who book hunts with an outfitter who specializes in running bears with dogs.

In some states no dog hunting is allowed. Where it is legal, obviously there are not very many dog packs. It's expensive to train and keep the dogs. It also takes a lot of one's time, and quite a few are killed by bayed quarry. There are, however, a number of outfitters, particularly in the west, who specialize in this hunting. It is fairly expensive, and also chancy. Here and there a booker advertises guaranteed hunts. These may or may not be legitimate. A no-bear-no-pay guarantee is usually all right. The outfitter gambles, knowing he has good dogs and a good territory. But there have been a lot of shenanigans over late years in the bear-hunt-with-dogs game. A booker who guarantees a bear, period, is one to stay shy of. In some of these cases bears live-trapped or bought surplus from zoos and kept in pens are released just before the hunt. However, a legitimate run with dogs is sporting indeed. It is not necessary to explain the technique here, because it is invariably done with a guide and pack.

Hunting over bait is one of the most successful methods of black bear hunting. This is done almost entirely in the spring, as soon as the hungry bears have come out of their dens. Here again, most bait hunts are booked with an outfitter. He puts out or finds a bait, perhaps a dead big-game animal that died during winter, an old horse or cow destroyed and placed in a location where bears will find it, or maybe a pile of freshly netted suckers from a stream. At least one astute guide is known to use gallons of cheap strawberry jam, dumped and smeared over a crisscross pile of down timber. It is not as expensive as buying an old decrepit cow, it is easily transported to a good site, and as it dribbles here and there it makes the bears work over a number of visits to get it all.

Garbage from camps—for example, winter lumber camps in the Canadian bush—also serves for bait. Many winter logging camps may house dozens of men and work horses all winter. They are abandoned before ice-out. Guides often take hunters to these camps, for bears hang around them after coming out of dens, eating grass that sprouts and leftover grain, licking salt, and digging in the dump.

Baiting, or hunting over a natural bait, is also not legal everywhere, and for that matter, there are spring seasons in only a few states and provinces. Still-hunting along old log roads in spring is sometimes successful. So in fall is riding horseback in mountains, glassing for bears, or prowling along stream courses. But still-hunting for black bears, especially in fall, is a long gamble. Very occasionally a stand beside a well-worn bear trail may bring good fortune. Along the Alaska coast blacks are hunted the same as browns (see the chapter on grizzly bears) along coastal rivers or from a boat cruising the shoreline.

Even in territory where black bears are plentiful, purposely hunting one without dogs or bait is never very productive. They are simply too shy, and a man cannot cover enough ground to be at the right spot at precisely the right time except by total chance. Even when hunted with dogs, and in some instances with a score of hunters spread out taking stands where a jumped bear may pass within range, the gamble is still long. Many a bear offers an exciting run, but is never seen. In addition, many a good dog has been killed, sometimes half of the pack if they are tenacious and have bayed a bear that won't tree, before hunters can get to the racket and dispatch the quarry.

Nonetheless the black bear is a prime and exciting game animal. Happily, even though black bear range is only a remnant of what it was originally, and the number of bears likewise, this animal is in no danger, nor is it likely to be in the foreseeable future. It is one of the most interesting of all North American game animals. For those who would hunt it, or photograph it, or simply try to observe it in the wild, it also deserves a healthy respect. A clown the black bear may be, but ever a totally unpredictable one.

# COMPARISON OF TRACKS

## Hoofed Animals

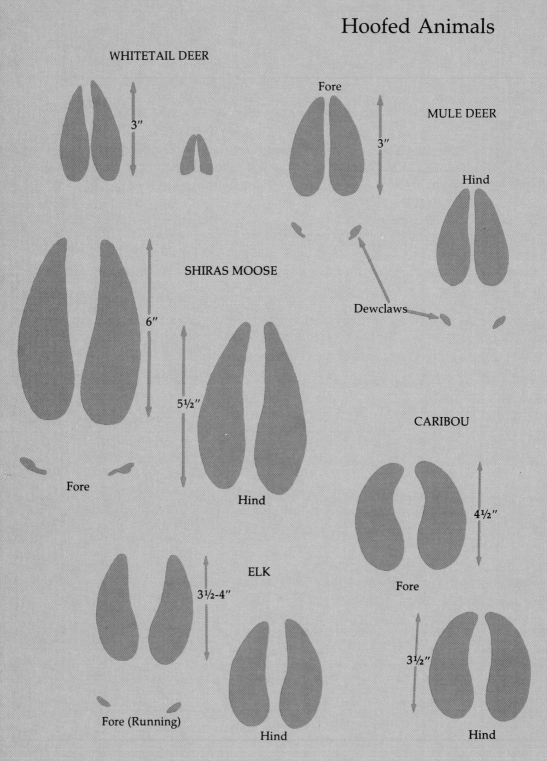

WHITETAIL DEER

3″

Fore

MULE DEER

3″

Hind

Dewclaws

SHIRAS MOOSE

6″

5½″

Fore

Hind

CARIBOU

4½″

Fore

ELK

3½-4″

Fore (Running)

Hind

3½″

Hind

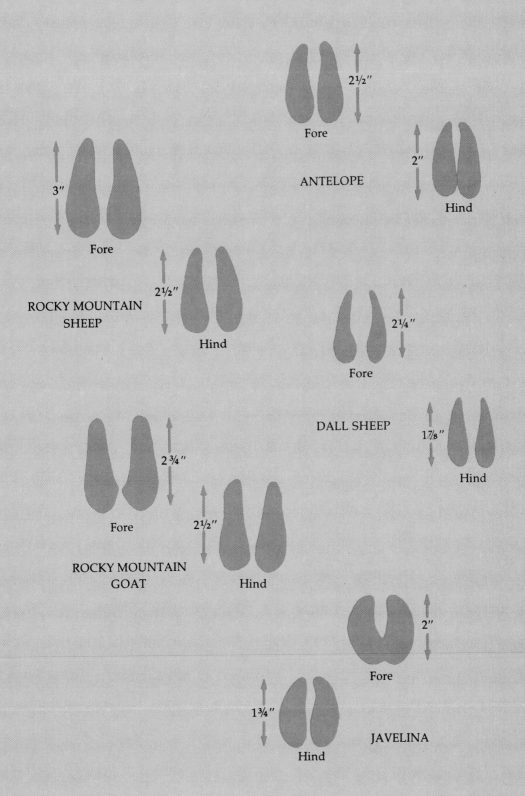

2½″

Fore

ANTELOPE

2″

Hind

3″

Fore

2½″

ROCKY MOUNTAIN
SHEEP

Hind

2¼″

Fore

DALL SHEEP

1⅞″

Hind

2¾″

Fore

2½″

ROCKY MOUNTAIN
GOAT

Hind

2″

Fore

1¾″

JAVELINA

Hind

# Bears

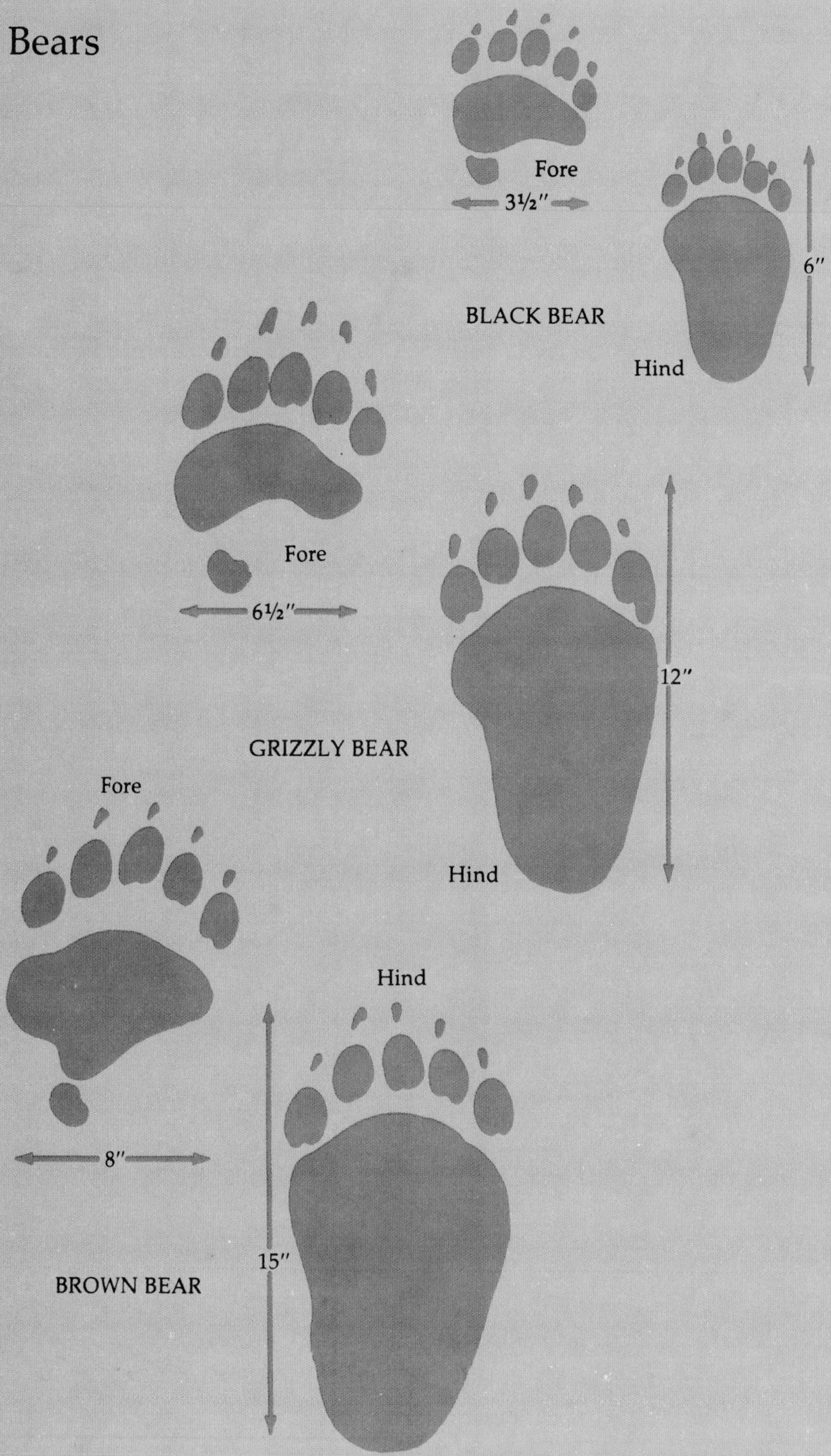

Fore

3½"

BLACK BEAR

6"

Hind

Fore

6½"

GRIZZLY BEAR

12"

Hind

Fore

Hind

8"

BROWN BEAR

15"

# Cats

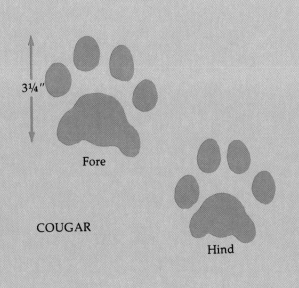

3¼″

Fore

COUGAR

Hind

2½″

Fore

BOBCAT

Hind

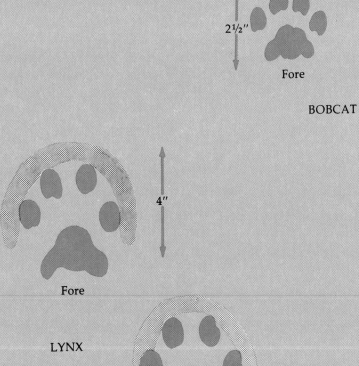

4″

Fore

LYNX

Hind

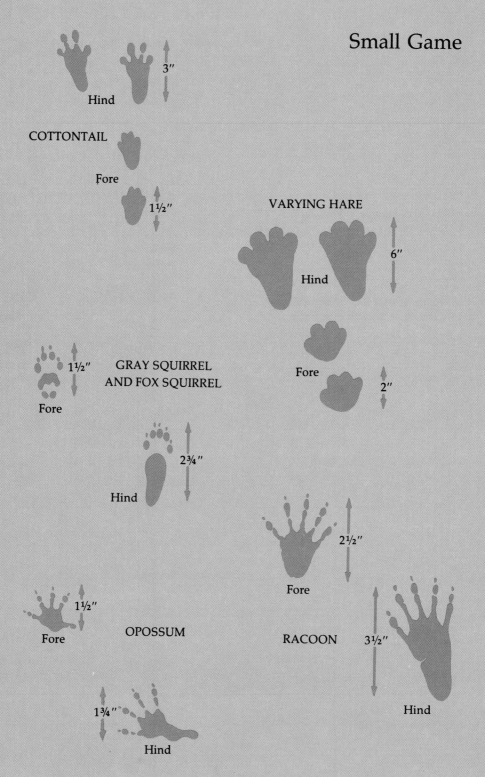

Small Game

Hind

3"

COTTONTAIL

Fore

1½"

VARYING HARE

Hind

6"

Fore

2"

1½"

GRAY SQUIRREL
AND FOX SQUIRREL

Fore

Hind

2¾"

Fore

2½"

1½"

Fore

OPOSSUM

RACOON

Fore

3½"

Hind

1¾"

Hind

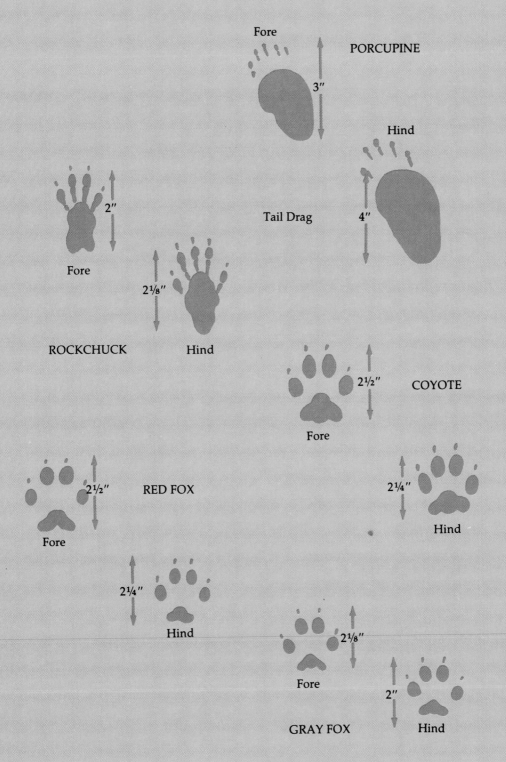

Fore

PORCUPINE

3″

Hind

4″

Tail Drag

2″

Fore

2⅛″

ROCKCHUCK    Hind

2½″    COYOTE

Fore

2½″    RED FOX

2¼″

Fore

Hind

2¼″

Hind

2⅛″

Fore

2″

GRAY FOX    Hind

255

# Mountain Lion

*Felis concolor*

Mountain lion" is the name by which this animal, the largest unspotted, long-tailed cat of North America, is known today to most people. It is not an especially apt name. It has come into common modern usage chiefly because most of these cats still left on the continent are found in the large, wild forested expanses of the western mountains. Originally, however, colonists and later settlers and explorers in widely separated locations might not have known what animal others referred to in chronicles of the frontier that were filled with tales and legends concerning this big cat. It was known by numerous names—cougar, puma, panther and its corruption "painter," catamount, and many others.

Local names galore were born from the vast original range over which the creature had spread and the astonishing variety of habitats to which it had been able to adapt in the process. The first known written account of what is presumed to have been the cougar was by Columbus, telling of sightings in coastal Central America. Coronado's 1540 expedition in the southwest also notes the animal. Undoubtedly some of the first of the big cats seen by white men in present-day U.S. territory were prowling the swamps of Florida and the deserts and mountains of the west. When explorers of varied origin first touched land on the Pacific coast, they discovered the mountain lion. The same was true in eastern Canada.

Indeed, wherever pioneers pushed into new territory, from all of the east coast to all of the west and from what is now southern Canada to the bottom of Mexico, the tawny cat was present. Mountains, deep swamps, wooded stream courses meandering across plains, deserts of dense cactus and thornbrush all were home to it. In fact, this enormous range over all but the northernmost quarter of the entire North American continent, wherever ground cover grew for it to hide in and hunt in, was only a beginning. Known by scores of differing names in English, Spanish, Indian, and even French, *Felis concolor,* "The cat of a single color"—without mottlings, stripes or spots—had prowled its way down through the centuries clear to the southern tip of South America. Of all land-dwelling mammals, it had colonized and long held the greatest expanse of territory.

In North America particularly, it was not able to hold its vast possessions long. A creature of the truly wild places, in need of large hunting areas and exceedingly shy of disturbance, it could not tolerate the presence and competition of the white man. Conversely, neither could the newly arrived white man tolerate in his intimate domain a predator so large and so deft at the hunt and the stalk. As settlement inexorably reduced lion habitat, as settlers competed with the lion for its natural food, the deer and similar large forage animals, the cougar was driven back, yet was still ever on the fringes of human domain. As game dwindled, easily killed livestock was placed in ever growing numbers at its disposal. Quickly it acquired a taste for horses in particular, and for sheep, pigs, and calves simply because they were available and easy to catch.

Because of the pressure brought to bear on them by shoot-on-sight settlers, by government trappers, and by the swift shrinking of suitable habitat, the lion was gone from most of its eastern haunts by the turn of the last century. In various places lions had been bountied since early Spanish days. From the beginning of the cattle business cattlemen had instituted bounties throughout the west. States continued them. Yet there was still enough western U.S. wilderness and more in Mexico to sustain a moderate unendangered lion population. Within recent years the mountain lion has received much attention, and protection, from game-

Mountain Lion

## THE MOUNTAIN LION

COLOR: Varying shades of light brown, from yellowish to reddish; in some areas grayish; very occasionally melanistic (black); without spots; face usually darker than body color, on sides of muzzle, nose bridge and forehead, but with front of muzzle white to grayish; underparts gray-white; whiskers white, eyes yellow, tip of tail darker than body, to black; geographical races differ in richness or paleness of overall coloring; seasonal differences also, richer in summer, grayer in winter.

MEASUREMENTS, ADULT MALES: Overall length 7 to 8½ feet including tail, rarely to 9 feet, the tail 2½ to 3 feet of the total length; height at shoulder 2 to 2½ feet or occasionally slightly more.

WEIGHT, ADULT MALES: 135 to 175 pounds average, exceptional specimens over 200 to a maximum of 275-plus.

FEMALES: 35 to 40 percent smaller.

GENERAL ATTRIBUTES: Solid, unspotted color, long tail, large size; slender build with comparatively small head; ears without tufts as in the smaller, short-tailed lynx and bobcat; loose-appearing skin of belly; short, smooth fur; shy, secretive personality; very graceful movements.

management people. In almost every state, bounties have been removed and it has been placed on the game-animal list. This allows regulation of hunting as to method, time of year, and number that can be legally taken, and also allows total year-round protection in states where the animal's existence appears precarious.

Officially today the mountain lion is considered to range in suitable wild habitat over much of British Columbia, southern Alberta, parts of western Saskatchewan, southward throughout the Rockies and the Pacific Coast states, border to border across southern Texas, spottily in the southern swampy expanses of the Gulf States, and in southern Florida, as well as over much of Mexico. However, the official range doesn't tell the most interesting part of the modern mountain lion story.

Periodically sightings are made that appear well authenticated in widely separated places from which the lion was presumably long ago extirpated. Reports come out of Canada's Maritime Provinces. Others originate periodically in Maine and other New England states. Massachusetts has officially pursued several scattered reports over past years, and game biologists are convinced the few sightings and tracks have been authentic. New York State, the

Appalachian region, and isolated locations in the Ozarks have all reported the presence of an occasional mountain lion.

This big cat, one might think, could not possibly reside near human habitation without its presence immediately becoming known. But it is superbly equipped to lead the secretive existence, moving on padded feet without sound, sifting like smoke through the heaviest thickets and forests available, hunting by night and lying up by day in rocky crevices or on slopes dense with brush, ever attuned with astonishingly sharp senses to the slightest indication of man's near presence.

To illustrate the uncanny ability of an animal this size in keeping its local existence unknown in suitable circumstances even on the fringe of large urban areas, an incident in Texas is a classic example. Careful studies of the lion in Texas had previously indicated that the animal was endangered there, with a probable total population of no more than fifty animals. These were in the arid southern so-called Brush Country near the Mexican border, and in the neo-frontier Big Bend Country of far-western Texas.

The central-Texas Hill Country 200 miles north of the border traditionally is a mohair and sheep area. Large predators such as coyotes and bobcats are not tolerated and are rarely found. Lions have been unknown there for decades. Yet that year lion tracks were discovered on a ranch of modest size but with dense cover, within a few miles of San Antonio, which with environs totaled over a million people. Lion sightings had been reported for several years in the ranch vicinity, but were scoffed at. Eventually, however, residents were astonished when two adult male lions were trapped. In 1975 another big lion was shot by a deer hunter in another part of the Hill Country where lions are unknown, and in 1976 one was struck by a car at night near the village of Ingram, where mountain lions have been unknown almost since frontier days.

Thus no one can say with absolute certainty precisely where mountain lions still range. Doubtless the places where they still exhibit well authenticated populations and are occasionally and successfully hunted as game trophies form the important islands of population. Various estimates have been made as to how many mountain lions still exist north of Mexico. Numbers have been set at 200 or 300 east of the Mississippi, 5000 or 6000 west of it. These are strictly guesses. Counting mountain lions is like counting mirages.

By estimating the hunting domain of a lion, dividing the figure into the suitable square-mile habitat in a state, and then applying

# Range of the Mountain Lion

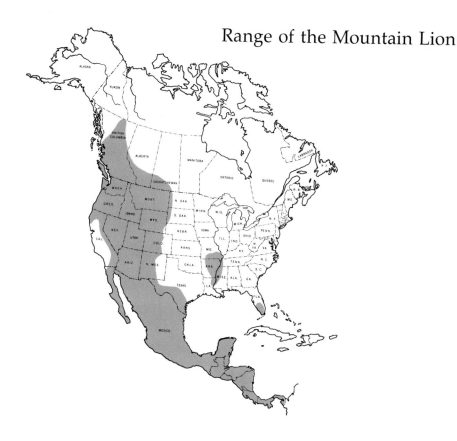

figures of bountied kills or sport-hunting kills, a rough estimate can be made of how many lions may be — or *might* be — present. However, there are scores of outdoorsmen who have spent a lifetime in sign-spattered cougar country without ever glimpsing one alive and free in the wild. Thus population estimates, though perhaps helpful in management, are just that — estimates. Some wildlife-management specialists suspect that the cougar is slowly making a minor comeback in certain sectors of the east, perhaps partially adjusting to life on the wilder fringes of human settlement.

Numerous geographical races of mountain lions developed over the centuries because of their vast range. Such differing populations usually evolve because of isolation from others, in a more or less specialized habitat. At least thirty have been named, split about evenly between North and South America. Many of the subspecies are based mainly on size and color differences, with minor physiological differentiations. There is little reason for the layman to be concerned with them. The mountain lion, cougar, or puma is for any practical purpose the same animal wherever it is found. In general the largest individuals have evolved in the extremes of the range, both north and south, that is, in colder climates of the north in the United States and Canada, and at the far-southern portion of South America. Mountain lions of the tropics are decidedly smaller.

Throughout the long history of the relationship of people and pumas, from the times of ancient Indians even to the present, so much legend, ritual, and yarn spinning has accrued relating to these cats that it is difficult to separate truth from fiction. Added to the puzzle is the true mystery of the cats themselves. Everyone, it seems, knows *about* the beast—but those few who know the most about it admit that they actually know very little. Probably no large animal has done a more thorough job, by its retiring habits, of fending off familiarity.

Indians of various tribes on both continents anciently revered the lion, used its hide for very special leather, wore and made decorations and ceremonial icons from skulls, teeth, hides, and claws. Ancient Incas used thousands of their slaves in hunting drives to gather abundant pumas. Many native peoples ate and relished the mountain lion. In fact, within recent times—even as late as the 1940s—back-country "crackers" in Florida would flock to a southern swamp village when word was out that a lion had been killed, hoping to get a piece of the meat, which was considered a delicacy. In scattered locations in Mexico natives have always watched closely for circling buzzards that might indicate a lion kill, so that they might attempt to rob the cache left after the predator had eaten its fill.

Tales of mountain lions attacking humans and trailing woodsmen, hunters, and mountaineers for miles are legion. Are they true? Some are. Numerous trailing instances have been well authenticated, but conclusions have invariably been that curiosity, or some unknown attraction of following a trail, was the reason. It is doubtful that a predatory urge was ever the motivation. Nonetheless, there are a very few well-documented cases of attack without provocation.

The all-time classic, presumably, was the killing and partial devouring of a boy years ago by a cougar in Washington. As recently as the mid-1970s a New Mexico resident was mauled during an apparently unprovoked attack. A few provoked attacks have been recorded. What may have happened in colonial times is now impossible accurately to assess, but it is believed that in more recent times, within the past century, there have been possibly two dozen people killed by cougars.

Regardless, the big cat cannot be considered truly a dangerous animal. Hundreds have been hunted with dogs, treed, and approached without danger. Many of these have been roped alive by an experienced hunter who climbed up after them. In rare instances, possibly, a lion may make an error of judgment, believing a human to be a forage animal. The bulk of experience with the cougar in all of its range indicates that it is an extremely shy wilderness character to which human scent is frightening, one that would prefer to run or even give up rather easily rather than fight man, its only serious enemy. That a creature so extraordinarily powerful should have with so few exceptions so successfully and intentionally avoided mankind for several centuries, while being crowded endlessly by human incursion, would indicate that the puma is basically a retiring and inoffensive predator.

Most Indians, who knew the big cats on the whole more intimately than we do, must have thought so. They greatly admired the hunting prowess of the mountain lion, its power and quick skill in killing adult deer and other large animals. Some of them prayed to it, hoping to have its hunting abilities bestowed upon themselves. Probably the most striking evidence of the reverence in which the cougar was held by many earlier peoples, and a measure of its importance in nature's scheme in their view, is still to be seen in Bandolier National Monument in New Mexico. It is a sculpture carved in native stone by ancient ancestors of modern Indians. It is believed to have been a shrine of sorts, a pair of mountain lions standing together.

### HABITAT

It is not possible to give a specific description of the mountain lion's habitat. Like all animals that have been able to adapt to highly varied conditions of terrain, vegetation, climate, latitude, and altitude, no one description of its usual surroundings fits the larger picture. Nonetheless, certain general characteristics are apparent in all situations. For example, the lion, like all cats, stalks its prey and then makes the kill with a brief, swift rush and pounce. It must therefore have cover in which to hide while hunting. Thus mountain forests, densely vegetated swamps, and the thornbrush and cactus of deserts all answer the purpose.

However, and obviously, proper forage must be present in ample quantity. Therefore where a puma lives is a bit like the puzzle about whether the hen or the egg comes first. Although the lion has been known to eat snails and catch mice, because of its size it must have available large prey animals. It is pertinent to note here the difference between predators with an omnivorous inclination, such as the bears, and the wholly predaceous creatures of which the mountain lion is a classic example. A black bear makes do nicely on a vegetarian diet when meat is not readily available. The lion must have meat, in large quantities. And it does not relish carrion. Thus, whereas the bear, a complete opportunist, may visit a dead and rotting elk until every consumable ounce is eaten, and then eat grass, the lion is rigged by nature to endlessly need fresh kills.

Only because large herbivores — deer especially — were able to spread their range so broadly was the lion able to follow. Otherwise it could never have adapted to the swamps, the high mountains, and the deserts. Further, because large, antlered and horned prey animals require a rather large living area, and are restricted in numbers to what a range of given quality will support, the lion must roam widely in order to make a living. Even when the prey is extremely abundant, deer perhaps overpopulous with as many as fifteen, for example, to a square mile, the predaceous lion cannot hope to successfully stalk and kill each one it sees.

So it might be said that the mountain lion can be anywhere that ample cover exists for its hunting, but with the qualification that it is restricted to places where prey animals of large size have colonized first. Because in general the large prey creatures require large wild expanses in order to forage and propagate successfully, the lion must have an even larger wild expanse in order to glean its living from them. Thus the mountain lion invariably is found most numerously where there are large, unbroken wilderness expanses affording ample cover for its secretive ways, and for a goodly supply of its prey.

To be sure, the habitat picture is drastically changed from what it was before settlement. Then lions might roam almost everywhere. Now they are forced, with some straggler exceptions, to remain in the few suitable true wilderness situations still remaining. However, as long as food and undisturbed prowling cover are available, the lion is not choosy about its general habitat type. Mountain lions have been found high above timberline, to as much as 13,000 feet altitude. The Everglades and Big Cypress swamps in Florida still sustain a modest population. The deserts of the southwest and Mexico are still havens.

In the Rockies, where the major cougar population is now confined, the big cats favor the most rugged and remote canyons. Hunters running dogs after them can well attest that the best lion country is invariably the most difficult of access. Forested areas slashed by steep cuts faced with jumbled rock slides, pinnacles, and ledges are typical lion habitat.

FEEDING

These regions are also typical habitat for mule deer and elk. Of the long list of prey animals found in the diet of the cougar throughout its North American range, deer are the most important. Undoubtedly this is because deer, both whitetails and mule deer, are the most numerous large animals present. It might seem to a hunter who doesn't always get the deer he goes after even with a long-range rifle that the wary creatures would present insoluble problems to the lion. Studies have shown that on good deer range, a lion traveling its hunting circuit makes a kill at least once each week, sometimes more often. That is at least fifty deer per year. Certainly the lion, like all predators, is an opportunist. If an easy kill of some other animal is presented, hunger is sated then and there. Regardless, the lion is a severe predator upon deer, and deer are constantly targets of its hunting efforts wherever they are available.

Nature writers of less than ample field experience, and many of the modern "instant ecologists" who have lately discovered "the environment," are fond of claiming that a predator such as the mountain lion, unlike the sportsman who selects the best trophy, takes only the weak, the sick, and the old, and thus is a boon to natural herd management. This is utter nonsense, as many studies of lions have proved, in some instances where researchers spent weeks living on the trails of their subjects and tabulating kills.

It is true that the lion will seize opportunity to make an easy kill. Certainly this will account for deer or other prey that happen to be partially incapacitated. But just as the big cat seizes these opportunities, it seizes any that are presented. Whatever deer a lion spots when it is hungry, in a situation where it senses that a successful stalk may be made, it makes the attempt. Some alert, vigorous deer in fine health are successful in escaping. Some aren't. Out of fifty deer taken in a year, it is probable that most are in good health. They are the ones most active in feeding and moving about and thus more often present themselves as targets of the stalk. Many are among younger deer, simply because they are somewhat less wary. Conversely, many are prime, trophy bucks that just happened to be victims because a mountain lion noticed them.

Inept nature writing and disgracefully faked movies have fal-
sified the manner in which the lion makes its kills on large animals.
More often than not, the story or film scene is of the cat lying
hunched and tense on a limb high above a well-worn deer trail, or
on a rock ledge beneath which deer pass. As the unaware prey
moves into range, the lithe cat makes its spring. Flying through the
air with forepaws outstretched, claws extended and fangs bared in
a snarling mouth, the lion slams atop its prey, smashing it to the
ground.

It is possible that some lions sometimes have happened to be
lying on a branch or a ledge and have grabbed the chance to jump
upon an unsuspecting deer. Lions often lie on ledges to rest. They
seldom climb trees, however, unless after food up in the branches,
such as a porcupine, or when chased by hunting hounds. A lion
that habitually tried to waylay its quarry would inevitably starve to
death. Almost all kills of large animals are made by a belly-to-the-
ground stalk, after the creature has been located by scent or sight, or
by zeroing in one or the other or both senses when a sound has
alerted the cat.

During the stalk every bit of cover is utilized by the cat to cover
its movements. It may keep moving parallel to a trail along which a
mountain sheep or a deer is traveling, slowly narrowing the rush
distance. Unlike the wild dogs, cats are not geared to long chases at
high speed. The lion moves with astonishing agility and power in a
short burst. But like the housecat stalking a bird on a lawn, it stays
low, gets close, then in a violent and beautifully coordinated rush
closes the distance and leaps. A lion has been observed moving in
on feeding deer hunting as it invariably does, into the wind, in a
mountain meadow where only foot-high tawny grass was available
for cover. With the end of its long tail twitching, eyes burning,
forepaws fully extended and head flat down between them, the cat
crept along, freezing for long moments immobile, moving at intervals without the slightest sound. When within only a few yards it
catapulted into action—the awesomely powerful, swift rush, the
leap to land on the shoulders and neck of a deer.

The mountain lion is a brilliantly designed killing machine. Like
all cats, it has retractable claws. Sheathed in their soft packaging,
they are never worn dull from contact with rocks or hard ground.
They are curved like talons. When about to make the final rush on
stalked prey, the lion gets all four feet well placed under it. The
claws are now extended so that they get a turf grip to help hurl the
muscular body ahead.

There are five toes on the front feet, four on the rear. However,

*A mountain lion, after stalking its prey on the ground, pounces for the kill.*

the "thumb" toe and claw of the forefoot is of little practical use. When the kill leap is made, the hind feet are commonly used to rake the flanks and belly, but it is the forefeet that are most important. The claws on one foot sink for a grip across the shoulder, and the other set of claws rips into the deer's nose and head, in an instinctive attempt to pull the head around and backward. Meanwhile the great canine teeth set in unbelievably powerful jaws sink into the spinal region. Sometimes the combination of the downward bite and clence of the jaws, plus the twisting of the deer's head, breaks the animal's neck instantly. Teeth may even slash the spine in two.

Of course the technique of each kill varies, according to the situation presented. An interesting physical attribute of the big cats — and smaller ones, too — is the unusual development of the bones of the shoulders, specifically the clavicle. Whereas the wild dogs are fashioned for running, seizing prey with teeth, and ripping at it, the cats are designed across the shoulders for immense striking and gripping power. The strike of a big lion at the end of its leap often involves such force of impact that a deer, not expecting it or braced against it, is knocked over.

By no means every stalk ends successfully. The quarry senses danger and flees. Now and then a lion gives up without any final rush, aware that the prey has been alerted and that it cannot succeed. Or a deer, occasionally badly mauled, breaks free and runs. The lion fails to catch it. Many times a lion goes hungry because it fails in its attempts to kill a large animal. Then it must grab whatever is handy or possible. Stomach analyses have shown rabbits, mice, varied small animals. Ravenous lions have even tried skunks and coyotes, though apparently not with relish.

Young of elk or moose are fairly easy kills. But apparently the cougar is not skittish of attacking the largest of antlered game animals. Lions have been known to kill adult elk and moose. On occasion when opportunity is presented, wild turkeys furnish a feast. In a few locations, for example along the Mexican border in the southwest and in Mexico, southern Texas, and southern Arizona, where the javelina or peccary is fairly abundant, individual lions form a particular taste for them. This may be simply because the little desert pigs are available, and fairly easy to stalk and kill.

As mentioned earlier, domestic stock on occasion is turned into mountain lion food. The cats seem inordinately fond of pigs, once they get a taste, and of sheep on a range, probably because they are easy kills. The lion also is renowned as a horse and colt killer, habitually turning down a chance at cattle when horses are on the same range. However, even large steers are not too difficult for a lion to handle. Stock killers seldom last long. Ranchers or government trappers go after them with determination.

A seemingly favorite meal for the lion is the lowly porcupine. Again, this may be because it is easy to catch. Females are known to climb and knock porcupines out of trees to cubs waiting below. The quills present a danger that can be severe. Apparently lions learn to flip a porky over and rip open the soft, quill-less belly. However, it is all but impossible for the cats to eat a porcupine without eating quills or getting them into lips, tongue, or parts of the mouth. Curiously, an abundance of quills, possibly softened to harmlessness in the digestive tract, are often found in lion scats. But now and then a lion gets its mouth full of quills that fester and finally kill it, either by infection or by starvation because the animal cannot eat.

Odd as it seems, the porcupine therefore may be considered one of the few potential enemies of the mountain lion. In isolated instances, a lion may also be an enemy of its own species. Males kill kittens now and then, even eat them, and an old lion may kill and eat a smaller, younger lion that gets into its territory. In the tropics, jaguar and lions may cross paths and do battle, but the heavier jaguar can hardly be considered an important enemy, and may even be whipped by the more agile puma. Probably more often than one might believe a lion is injured severely during the attempt to kill a deer, elk, or other big-game animal. Injuries of this sort, by falls over ledges or by horn or antler damage to the attacking cat, are well authenticated.

Once the kill of a large prey animal has been concluded, if it has occurred in the open, as in a mountain meadow, the carcass is dragged to a hiding place in brush or timber. A big lion is capable of moving even an adult bull elk, or a horse. Usually, although not always, the belly is ripped open first. Lions are especially fond of blood, liver, heart, and entrails. After eating its fill, the animal scratches sticks, grass, or rocks over the remainder, covering it in a cache to which it will return several times. If the weather is cool and the meat stays in good shape, the animal may make trips for a week or more until it has cleaned up all edible parts. Even bones are stripped of meat by licking action of the rough tongue.

Of course not every cache is revisited. If game is abundant, a lion may forsake cached meat for the excitement and hot pungent taste of the blood from a fresh kill. The cats are unpredictable. Ordinarily an individual will kill only when hunger dictates. Now and then, however, one goes on a killing binge, downing several deer for which it has no need, or wiping out a band of domestic sheep apparently just because they're easy.

## MOVEMENTS

Except for the wandering of a male seeking a female, practically all of the travel of the lion is concerned with keeping its belly full. A predator that insists on fresh meat cannot be casual about hunting. It may not gorge every day, but it must keep roaming, making its hunting circuit endlessly, if it hopes to sustain itself by its prowess as a hunter of other living creatures.

It is believed that most of a lion's hunting movements are nocturnal. However, this is probably another of those half-truths born of the difficulties of observation of retiring, secretive animals. Animal callers operating at night have now and then called lions. Animal callers even more often have had a lion respond in broad daylight. Most of the very occasional sightings of lions in the wild have been made in daytime, although some lions have been seen crossing roads or trails in vehicle lights at night and rarely one has come into a hunter's camp at night. Females are known to take youngsters on daytime learning-to-hunt expeditions.

Probably the truth is that a lion hunts whenever it feels like it, moving both day and night as the urge strikes. It does hunt much by sight, but it sees well in very dim light and it may instinctively know that stalking prey is easier at night. The rarity of sighting mountain lions in the wild may be because they do most of their moving and hunting nocturnally, lying up to rest by day.

The size of any individual lion's hunting ground is determined by the abundance of game within it, and also, especially in the north, by the season. A traveling cat requires more food when the weather is cold, and in addition food may be scarcer. A cougar ranging in high mountains on the summer range of mule deer, for example, has to make adjustments when the deer herd moves lower to its winter range. In some instances the predators may follow the deer, in which case hunting may be easier because the winter range is smaller as a rule, and the deer more concentrated.

Probably any lion moves several miles each day. Various studies indicate that most individuals travel an average of 5 to 10 miles a day — or night — consistently. A female with young still in a den must restrict her hunting range, coming back within each twenty-four-hour period to the den. When the kittens begin to hunt with her, she is also moderately handicapped. She cannot roam at will. During the period of raising the young a female unquestionably combs her bailiwick intensively, and is forced to depend more on a variety of forage. Males are not so restricted and therefore usually roam wider, covering at times as much as 20 to 25 miles in a single night.

Like many predators, even down to the diminutive weasel, the lion hunts more or less in a large circle. There may be much wandering meanwhile. The entire hunting area may be 50 to 60 miles or more across. But each individual has staked out a domain and unless driven out stays within it, coming back time after time to the same places within it, and time after time making the same general hunting circuit. There are advantages for the lion in this system. The larger the hunting area, the less severe the pressure upon the prey animals.

After a kill, the cat may quit roaming for several days and stay in the vicinity, going back to feed at its cache. It has been etimated that 10 pounds or less of meat will fill up a large cougar. Trappers of long experience believe that certain lions will rest after gorging and not eat for several days, then go back to the kill for more. Travel and meal frequency are, of course, interdependent. In what is probably the best study ever done on mountain lions, *The Puma, Mysterious*

*American Cat,* by Young and Goldman, published by the American Wildlife Institute some years ago, the authors relate the experience of a hunter in Colorado who was trailing a lion on its hunting route.

With dogs, he stayed on the trail for eleven days. During that time the lion, a female that when finally taken dressed out at 160 pounds, killed two adult bighorn rams and a buck deer. Whether other kills were made in remote places shortcut by the dogs was not known. After each ram kill, the lion apparently had rested for a couple of days, going back to feed until each was almost wholly eaten. The hunter was able to catch up to the lion after the deer was killed. His estimate was that this lion had made a kill and gorged on the fresh new one every three days. If most lions follow a similar pattern, that would total at least 122 kills annually!

The cougar is not migratory, although it might at times seem to be. When one shows up where none has been known before, it is undoubtedly for one of several reasons. Perhaps food has become scarce on its previous hunting ground; or its chief forage has moved, as in a mule deer winter migration; or possibly competition from other lions has caused it to seek a new home. Young lions must scatter as they grow to adulthood to establish their own roaming grounds, even though in some instances it is known that several, of the same sex or both sexes, occasionally hunt the same region and even feed communally.

Because the puma is a constant traveler as it goes its hunting rounds, and each animal is quite individual in habits, it is not possible to state precisely how much roaming it does as a species, or guess why certain lions make certain trips. For example, occasionally a lion will cross an open flat several miles wide, traveling from one mountain range to another. This belies its nature of keeping to cover. In southern Arizona one was discovered bedded and resting out the day in the shade of a single bush out in the middle of an open desert expanse between ranges.

When traveling on a hunt, a mountain lion walks, meandering, casting about for clues to game with all its senses. A low-to-the ground stalk may be swift, or awesomely patient. As mentioned previously, the big cat is amazingly swift for short bursts. Individuals have been known to catch an alerted and running deer within a couple hundred yards — and the deer itself is swift. But the lion cannot keep up such a pace. It is a fantastic jumper, bounding when pressed from ledge to ledge 15 to 20 feet with ease, and on occasion even farther. Game biologists who have built supposedly predator-proof fences around pastures containing such animals as desert bighorns for breeding stock—fences above 8 feet high, of net wire and electrified at the top—have found to their exasperation and enlightenment that a determined lion goes over the top with ease.

A lion ahead of dogs can leap to a tree limb 15 feet above ground, or leap out of a tree when need be from a height of 30 feet or more without damage. Like most of the cat family, the cougar dislikes getting into water, but it is an excellent swimmer when the need arises—and whimsically sometimes when there seems to be no need at all. Pushed by hounds, a lion will occasionally swim a stream or a pond. A few have been observed casually swimming large rivers without any pressure from hounds or hunters.

### BREEDING

Some of the movements of the mountain lion, particularly of males, are concerned with the frequent search for females ready to be bred. With few exceptions pumas are solitary creatures, except for females with young, or occasional immature animals of like or differing sex ranging together. At the earliest they do not breed until they are two years old, and may not until they are three. There is no seasonal mating period. Though most young have been observed in spring, trappers in various parts of the range have recorded taking pregnant females around the entire year.

Mountain lions are therefore similar in breeding habits to domestic cats. The female has regular periods of heat. As soon as a litter of kittens is born, she is ready to be bred again. Observations in zoos have filled in much knowledge of such details. The heat period lasts for roughly nine days. Obviously, when a male picks up the scent of a female in breeding condition, he is diverted from his prey hunting and his travels are centered on finding a mate. These hunts for females ready to be bred cause trouble occasionally among males. If lions are fairly abundant on a given range, several may track the same female.

Statistics kept for many years of hundreds of lions killed by trappers and others in several states indicate that the sex ratio is close to even. In some locations females have been slightly more numerous than males, and vice versa. The 50-50 ratio is undoubtedly general. This is certain to mean that several males at a time will be aware of any female nearby that is in heat. Battles between males ensue. Most researchers doubt that many of these fights are violently severe or determined, although some may be. A few fatalities have been authenticated.

Whichever male wins the contest claims the female. Again, this is quite similar to the habits of domestic cats. However, it does not mean that the first male to breed the female is the only one. Later she may accept several other males, if any are in the territory. Or a male may stay with or near a female for several days, with frequent breeding. Possibly competition among breeding lions is heightened because many live rather long lives. Although the average life span is thought to be about seven years, numerous individuals both in zoos and in the wild have been known to more than double that.

During mating periods, it is fairly well agreed among scientists who have diligently pursued the matter, mountain lions utter the same general types of sounds as domestic cats, except with much greater volume. Although lions are most of the time exceedingly quiet, nonvocal creatures, the matter of the "scream of the catamount" is likely to bring on heated argument among any group of hunters, predator trappers, or even zoo keepers who have substantial knowledge of mountain lions. For over two hundred years this argument has gone on. Modern outdoor magazines hardly ever get through a year without a pair of opposing I-was-there stories, one claiming the puma screams like an anguished, terribly frightened woman, the other just as adamant that it never utters such a sound.

Supposedly the hair-raising shrieks have frightened scores of campers, woodsmen, and dwellers in remote places—or so many have attested. Some of these sounds probably were not lions at all, but the wails of mating owls. Some others may have been imagined, or sworn to simply because it seemed like a dramatic tale. However, zoo personnel who have had daily contact with numerous mountain lions over many years agree that the females at least do "scream" during mating periods. The male may or may not do likewise, but it does utter a sharp whistle.

It is indeed curious that there should be such lack of thoroughly authenticated information about the screaming of pumas. Pet lions purr loudly when petted, exactly like housecats except louder. Cornered or treed lions sometimes growl, and invariably hiss and spit when closely approached. Reliable observers agree that cougars do "yowl" and "caterwaul" at various times, much in the manner of domestic cats.

## BIRTH AND DEVELOPMENT

Mountain lion kittens mew like any other kittens, and the mother reassures them with a low grunting sound. As they grow to playful size, when alarmed they sometimes utter a shrill whistle. Cougar kittens, like most baby animals, are extremely appealing little creatures, weighing a pound or less at birth. They are quite different in appearance from their solid-color parents. The coat is spotted, and the tail has ringlike markings. Most of the world's cats have spots or stripes as adults. It may be that the markings of mountain lion young are an indication of ancient ancestors that did not grow up to be of a solid color.

The kittens are born a few days more than three months from the time the female is bred. Like domestic kittens, at birth their eyes are closed, but begin opening after ten days and are fully open within a couple of weeks. They are born in a well-hidden place; the mother hopes to avoid intrusion by other lions, particularly males that might kill the young. The den may be just that, in a rocky cave or beneath a protected ledge. Or it may be under the roots of a big tree or beside a down log. In mild climates the hideaway is simply in the midst of an extremely dense thicket of brush.

It is doubtful that the female breeds every year. Scientists believe a litter every two or three years is normal. However, as previously mentioned, kittens may be born any month in the year. They are exceedingly playful, romping and tumbling with each other and grappling with the mother's tail or paws when she is in the den. They nurse the mother for at least a month, often longer, although she may try to wean them after four or five weeks. If she does not, even though they begin eating meat when roughly a month and a half of age, they will continue to nurse until they have half their growth. Few are allowed that privilege.

Average litters contain two kittens, with three, or one, not uncommon. Occasionally larger litters are born, with four, five, even six young. By the time the kittens are two months old they are usually as large as a big domestic cat, 8 or 10 pounds. But they do not grow even from babyhood very swiftly. At six months a young lion will weigh three or four times as much as at two months, averaging up to 35 pounds or more. Then it begins quickly to fill out and look more like an adult. When it is a year old if in good health it may weigh 60 or 70 pounds. Meanwhile, as it grows the markings on its coat become less and less distinct and finally disappear.

When the kittens are small and still in the den but ready to eat meat, the mother at first brings food to them, or in some instances urges them to follow her to the kill, if it is not too far. Then she returns them to the denning place. By the time they are fully weaned and well able to travel, at possibly six months of age, the youngsters are beginning to feel the hunting instinct on their own. The female

*A mountain lion kitten, one month old.*

may take only one on a hunt, and allow it to try a stalk and kill, although she may have to help in the kill. They all make foraging trips together as the youngsters grow. They learn from their mother, the trips become longer, and the den site is forgotten. When a kill is made, mother and youngsters all feed on it together.

As a family group, ties are fairly strong. If danger threatens, such as a hound pack on the trail, the female may make a stand to try to fight them off. But if the hunter following the dogs shows up, the cats usually scatter, running and treeing. Young mountain lions that begin playfully hunting each other as babies around the den site soon switch to using the stalking tactics they've been perfecting on prey. But they are not eager to leave the mother and go it alone until they are at least a year old. Undoubtedly they depend too much on her hunting abilities. Occasionally young lions twice that age still run with the mother. If they persist until she is ready to be bred again, she irritably chases them off, and each starts a life of his own.

### SENSES

Like all cats, the mountain lion is equipped with exceptionally keen eyesight, because its livelihood depends upon its stalking ability. Although the big cat is colorblind, living therefore in a world of varying shades of gray, it sees extremely well in the dimmest light, in what to the human eye would be classed as total darkness. The eyes, which in bright light become mere vertical slits, are equipped with literally millions of light-gathering cells. In darkness the iris opens until the entire eye seems to be pupil. The eyes are slitted in bright light because of their extreme sensitivity. When a bright light is directed into the eyes of a lion at night, they glow brightly, as do those of all night-feeding animals, even deer. Conversely, the human eye, far less well supplied with light-gathering cells, does not glow in a light at night.

Stationary objects are difficult for the cat to identify. But it masterfully detects the slightest motion. However, in all animals it is difficult to tell at what point one sense is aided by another. For example, the sense of smell in the cougar is keen, but by no means as sharp as that of the trailing animals such as wolves and coyotes. At closer ranges than the wild dogs it uses scenting ability in conjunction with sight, and of course hearing. It may pick up the smell of a deer drifting downwind, move in until it can see the animal, then bring both senses to bear. Hearing is also sharp, and all three senses are utilized as a battery during any hunt.

The lion also has most extremely sensitive whiskers, each with nerves at the base that relay messages. Thus a cougar creeping through brush in darkness "feels" for openings with its whiskers, slithers through narrow places without a sound because it is aware of the proximity of every twig. Unquestionably this acute sense of touch is an important asset to the stalk.

### SIGN *(Tracks are illustrated on page 253.)*

Because the lion is so seldom seen, familiarity with its sign is especially important to the student of wildlife and to the hunter. Seeing the tracks of a puma in soft earth near a desert spring, or in dust at the mouth of a cave, or in snow high in the Rockies, is as close as most observers ever will get to the animal itself, and therefore they have high interest and significance.

It is not always easy for the casual visitor to wilderness areas to distinguish between the tracks of the wild dogs and wild cats. Except under unusual circumstances, cat tracks do not show the claw marks. The claws are kept retracted. Most wolf and coyote tracks have definite toenail imprints. The toe prints of the cat are usually more distinctly separated from the heel print than those of the dogs, and they also form a wider and more rounded arc out in front of the heel-pad mark. The heel print usually is in addition larger and much more distinct than that of the dogs.

The tracks of an adult cougar can hardly be confused with tracks of the smaller wild cats, such as bobcat and lynx. They are on the average at least 3 and as much as 4 to 4½ or more inches long for each foot, front and rear, with the print of the front pad wider than it is long, and also wider and somewhat larger than the print of the hind foot. Conceivably, in portions of Mexico and Central America, the tracks of lion and jaguar might be confused. However, an adult jaguar is a larger, heavier animal, with correspondingly larger track. In some locations, where snow is deep, a lion may leave marks of its dragging tail. This is a specialized sign and seldom observed.

Like all cats, the lion has a habit of covering its scats, scratching a slight depression, depositing the droppings, and covering them with scratched-up dirt or leaves and twigs. However, it may also simply deposit droppings on a rocky place with no attempt to cover them. "Scent posts" are common, and a sign lion hunters seek. These are small heaps of earth as a rule, scratched together, upon which the animal urinates. Another lion that comes upon this scrape will pause and also urinate on it, and sometimes claw up more dirt. In scientific studies, and in trapping, urine collected from a captive cougar has often been used on scratch spots to freshen them and draw other lions to them.

Now and then one may happen upon what has been a meat cache, or even upon one with parts of a kill still in it. Most of these are hidden too well, however, for hikers or casual travelers in lion country to find them. Droppings, though quite obvious and easily identified, also are not often discovered or recognized, except by hunters and trappers seeking lion sign in a specific territory. They are large and are usually full of hair and of bits of bone from the kills. In form they may be large pellets of varied shapes, or a continuous, long scat with deep corrugations in it at unequal intervals. Droppings may be on or near the scent mounds, as well as covered elsewhere.

The lion, like the domestic cat and other wild cats, rakes its claws on tree trunks, presumably to sharpen them. Although a schooled trapper or hunter might spot this sign, it is by no means distinct; the scratches are not as deep and plain as those made, for example, by bears. Thus this sign is rarely noted by average observers. When a lion is walking, the average stride of each leg is about 2 feet. Quite often the tracks are blurred and confusing because the hind foot is brought forward and set down almost exactly into the impression of the front foot.

This instantly tags the puma as a stalker. The front foot is carefully placed to avoid any slightest sound. This is a safe place into which the following hind foot is instinctively set. When a lion track shows plainly for some yards, the direction is ordinarily in a fairly straight line, not meandering or dodging and darting from side to side.

HUNTING

Tracks and the scrapes of the mountain lion are what hunters seek for evidence that a lion is using a particular territory. There are only two methods of lion hunting that have even remote chances of success. The most common and generally most productive is with a pack of specially trained dogs. On occasion an excited and less than well-informed sportsman has come upon cougar tracks and decided to trail the animal down. Only by the rarest plain luck is such an endeavor successful.

The second method of lion hunting that has ended successfully in recent years for a scattering of outdoorsmen is calling. The call used is a standard coyote or "varmint" call, mimicking the squall of an injured rabbit. In order to have any chance at all of calling success, the hunter must be positive a lion is resident in the area to be hunted. The caller takes a stand where he can watch broken approaches, for example in a remote canyon, and begins blowing the raucous call. If a lion happens to be lying up within hearing distance, it may come to investigate. The thrill is tremendous when this does occur. However, of numerous callers who have tried this, only a very few have been successful. It is a gambler's game.

In almost all states and provinces today the hunting of the mountain lion is carefully controlled, with season limits, one-lion bag limits, and even stipulated areas that may or may not be hunted. In country where a substantial lion population is present, a few experienced lion hunters, some of them former or present government predator trappers, keep and train hound packs, and offer their services as guides to hunters who wish to book a hunt.

Thus there is really no hunting by individual sportsmen nowadays. It is just too expensive to keep and train the dogs. Most booked hunts are also quite expensive, and success, though chances are fair with an experienced outfitter, is far from certain. The sport is exceedingly rugged. Nonetheless, the chase is thrilling. Some sportsmen book lion hunts not to kill a lion but simply to enjoy the wild experience of the chase. Sometimes a lion that doesn't tree, or leaps out of a tree and is caught by dogs, swiftly kills several of them. It is capable of swatting and slashing to death a whole pack. Curiously, however, a mountain lion will run from even a small, yapping cur dog, unless it is a female with young. For some reason, with few exceptions the big cats have no pluck when it comes to standing ground before a dog.

Much has been written about the personality of the cougar as a stoic, and sometimes as a downright coward. "Coward" is hardly the word. Left alone in the wild, it is by no means one. Rather, it is a shy and supremely secretive creature without notable enemies, one that likes to be left alone. Only man and his dogs seem to unduly disturb this animal as true enemies. Stoical, on the other hand, the lion certainly is. Scores of instances are recorded of lions treed or trapped sitting calmly and without undue fuss seeming to accept their fate. Perhaps this is in some degree a reflection of the amazing patience and discipline the cat displays in its hunting.

Much has also been written over recent years decrying the hunting of the mountain lion, and the placing of it on the list of game animals. Those who pursue this tack, though perhaps sincere, are in error. Before the mountain lion won its place as a game animal in state after state, it was indiscriminately killed, usually with bounty. To stockmen it is, properly in the case of individual lions, intolerable.

The bounty, and the lack of protection as a game animal, long allowed continuous persecution of the big cats. Now in all but a few locations the mountain lion has come into its own as a game animal, a status that gives it haven. By the careful and meager cropping of surplus animals through trophy hunting, the lion population is kept in control, stock killing on wilderness-fringe ranches and public forest grazing lands is held to a minimum, and the great cat is able to maintain an unendangered status.

Further, in areas where the mountain lion is not abundant enough to allow token hunting—which is all it gets anywhere nowadays anyway—all hunting can be, and in most instances has been, stopped. This system is one that state and federal game-department personnel have fought for over many years. It assures that this large, handsome, and graceful cat of the wilderness places still left to us will continue to be a mysterious part of the native fauna of the continent, the basis for legend, argument, and fireside tales for as long as those wilderness retreats are still with us.

# SHORT-TAILED CATS

## Bobcat
*Lynx rufus*

## Lynx
*Lynx lynx*
*(Lynx canadensis)*

The short-tailed wild cats are among the most intriguing of North American animals. Although the long legs, extra-large feet, and long body of the lynx give it a rather ungainly appearance, the better-known and more compact and close-coupled bobcat is a stunningly handsome creature. Between them the ranges of these two cats practically blanket the continent, so they cannot be said ever to have been very far removed in total — especially the bobcat — from man's environs. Yet the incidental sighting of either animal in the wild has always been a rare and quite special experience. Both are masters of the art of crafty secretiveness.

Because the vast range of the bobcat coincides with the most heavily settled portions of the continent, it is by far the best known of the two cats. Rather curiously, it has also stamped its presence upon American history, lore, and tradition with an emphasis quite out of proportion to any fundamental usefulness it has ever had for man, and far out of proportion to the meager intimate knowledge of it and its habits ever gleaned by the average American.

Bobcat

Even far back in the period of early settlement and exploration, when the lives of wild animals were an important influence upon and part of the daily lives of men, few people commonly saw or knew much about these cats. Usually the presence of a bobcat was guessed at only by a pad outline indiscreetly printed, or by a sudden hideous caterwauling at night from a woodlot, or by the scattered remnants left from poultry deftly and silently slaughtered in a weed-surrounded roosting shed out behind the barn.

The pelt of the bobcat has never been an especially important commodity, its flesh has never been relished, and it has been important as a game animal only to a relatively small group of specialists with trained hounds, and more recently to a greater number of animal-calling enthusiasts. Nonetheless, from earliest times the bobcat—or wildcat as it was more commonly called—somehow managed an astonishing word-of-mouth press. If a young fellow was tough at rough-and-tumble fighting, he was said to be able to "lick his weight in wildcats." That, indeed, would take some doing, for the bobcat is strong and determined when cornered out of all proportion to its size.

An old adventure story of the last century quotes one Seth Barnes as "seizing aholt of a wildcat and wishing to the good Lord he mighten leave go." A turn-of-the century hunters' joke has it that two lads had trapped a small bobcat and managed somehow to get it into a burlap bag. They told this to their father, who commanded them to release it. A nearby neighbor swore he had heard the bobcat squalling, "Turn me loose! Turn me loose!" But one boy, when questioned, said, "No sir, that warn't the cat, it was my brother, onct he'd opened the bag!" And a hunter who raced in to help when his six-hound pack got mixing it with a cat they'd bayed on the ground was quoted in an old newspaper account as swearing he had "once fit three buzz saws and come out better."

When land was first cleared and the stumps pulled in parts of the east and the Great Lakes region, wild hay grew in newly formed forest-opening meadows to feed livestock of the pioneers. Low places, small swales, quickly burgeoned thick with tall marsh grass and such shrubs as red willow. A man with a scythe invariably cut around these useless patches. Cottontails and rodents swarmed in the newly opened havens, and found ready homes in the taller vegetation of the swale "holes." These also made prime hunting and lay-up places for bobcats. A common name for such cut-around waste places in a meadow was for many years "catholes." It is still not especially uncommon in Florida, for example, when a develop-

## THE SHORT-TAILED CATS

COLOR: **Bobcat,** variable, from reddish-brown to tawny gray on face, back, sides, outsides of legs, overlaid with variable darker markings, sometimes black, in spots, broken bars, or blotches; close around eyes, chin, underparts generally white, but commonly and highly variably flecked, mottled, barred, or blotched with gray to black; tail with several dark bars across top and broad black bar or spot atop bordering white tip. **Lynx,** usually much paler than bobcat, gray to pale yellowish or tan, these several shades often intermingled; face ruff gray to white with black markings; ear tufts and tip of tail black.

MEASUREMENTS: **Bobcat,** highly variably by latitude and among individuals; adult males, overall length anywhere from 24 to 48 inches, shoulder height from 15 to about 22 inches. **Lynx,** averages slightly taller than bobcat and 3 feet in overall length.

WEIGHT, ADULT MALES: Although the lynx is commonly envisioned as larger and heavier than the bobcat, actually average weights are quite similar, from 15 to 25 pounds, with exceptional animals to 40.

FEMALES: Usually slightly smaller.

GENERAL ATTRIBUTES: Short tail, 4 to 6 inches, lynx tail invariably shorter than that of bobcat; more or less prominent face ruff and ear tufts, both usually more pronounced in lynx; variably spotted coat; large feet; extremely secretive habits.

ment is opened on the edge of a timbered swamp, to hear tales of a bobcat scrounging its living, killing stray housecats and poultry on the fringes of a suburb.

The range of the bobcat covers a sizable swath of southern Canada border to border, sweeps down across all of the area of the contiguous states wherever there is proper cover, and continues south throughout most of Mexico, excepting the southern tropical lowlands. Obviously the bobcat has always been an able colonizer, anciently having spread over western mountain forests, the wooded swamps of the southern United States, the snowy woodlands of the northeast, and the thicketed cactus and thornbrush deserts of the southwest. It is at home along wooded stream courses in numerous areas of the plains, and is absent only in the more heavily cleared and cultivated interior where forage and cover are unsuitable to its secretive way of life.

In early days of settlement, the lynx, fundamentally a northern species of the snowy forests, was present in modest numbers down through much of the Rockies as far south as portions of Colorado, and even meagerly existent here and there in the central states. Its basic range, however, has always been over the forested vastness of most of Canada and Alaska. A few specimens turn up occasionally nowadays in northern New England, the northernmost sectors of the Great Lakes states, in the northern Rockies states, and in the mountains of Oregon and Washington.

The lynx, a deceptively ungainly-looking animal whose graceful movements and astonishing agility belie its somewhat homely at-ease stance, actually never has been what might be classed as a true game animal. Perhaps because of its northern environment, its fur is long and soft and has served as an important commodity since the early days of trappers in the far north. Lynxes were—and are—caught both in leg traps and more commonly in snares. Occasionally a lynx is hunted with dogs, or called with a predator call. But the range of the animal outside areas of heavy human settlement, and the deep snow, on and in which it easily maneuvers with its outsized, well-furred feet, have protected it from any severe sport-hunting pressure. Hunting hounds have difficulty in deep snow. Now and then a big-game hunter in the north country gets an incidental shot at a lynx as it ghosts through the timber, and here and there it is run with a dog pack purposely for sport. But it is dealt with in this chapter not because of any special game qualities but simply because of its rather close relationship to the much more abundant, wide-ranging, and better-known bobcat.

Some of the renown of the bobcat stems from the fact that it is a nuisance predator here and there, a bad actor where lambs and kid goats and even their adult parents are concerned. It can be a vicious killer in a wild turkey roost, for of course it is a superb climber. Deer and elk fawns are easily taken by bobcats. Many naturalists have stated unequivocally that the bobcat is no danger whatever to adult deer. This is simply not true. It may be that the bobcat does not regularly kill deer, but numerous kills, particularly in the north in winter snow, have been well authenticated.

The lynx has never gotten into much trouble with man as a predator simply because the preponderance of the lynx population is well outside the important areas of livestock operations. It does kill deer, however, in portions of its range where they are available, and is even known to bring down caribou, mountain sheep, and moose calves. Interestingly, the name given to the lynx by early French trappers referred to its prowess as a predator upon deer— *loup-cervier,* or "deer wolf." However, the name is probably a somewhat fanciful exaggeration, for over the major portion of its

## The Lynx

range the lynx has no deer on which to prey, and the mainstay of its diet is the varying "snowshoe" hare.

The lynx is, in fact, dependent for its very survival over much of its range upon the level of the hare population. All rabbits and hares are strongly cyclic. The population builds swiftly for a few years, often until the animals are unbelievably abundant, then debacle strikes, a vast die-off occurs, and only a meager hare population is left. Nature writers are fond of relating the striking population-level relationship between lynx and hare as shown by records of the Hudson's Bay Co. When the varying hare cycle was at peak, so invariably was the lynx population, indicated by pelts turned in by the trappers. When the hare cycle fell drastically, so did the lynx population, but always during the year following the big die-off of hares. Obviously, with a chief food source removed, the major share of the lynx population starved, and what were left failed to reproduce efficiently, a situation that occurs among most animals on starvation diets.

In some portions of its range the bobcat also feels the pressure of forage cycles. This is true, for example, in the northern sectors of the Great Lakes states, where snowshoe hares furnish a substantial part of bobcat diet, and in the southwest where jack rabbits and such rodents as pack rats rise and fall drastically in population because of fluctuating wet and dry years. But the bobcat has suffered the greatest permanent losses in numbers over the past few decades because of destruction of its habitat by the inexorable push and sprawl of human progress. Further, in some heavily populated states it has been hunted hard by both hound enthusiasts and predator callers.

In addition to sport hunting the indiscriminate killing of bobcats as nuisances—and for bounty—has long been a tradition in numerous states, especially where poultry and small livestock such as sheep and goats are big business. Bobcats were even bountied as far back as colonial times. The combination of all these pressures, over many years, and especially in populous states the swift destruction of habitat suitable for both cats and their forage, have made the bobcat a rarity today in numerous places where once they were rather common. Even though bobcat hides are not especially desirable in quality for the fur market, except for trimmings, a spurt in all fur prices during the early 1970s for some reason disproportionately increased the value of bobcat hides. In Oklahoma, for example, up to $125 was paid for a single large cat hide during the winter of 1974.

For a great many years the bobcat—wildcat and bay or "red" lynx are common names colloquially—was accorded no protection whatever. It was considered, and still is in some states, simply a varmint. However, with a drastic decline in numbers, one benefit has been the calling of attention by sportsmen, game managers, and conservationists to the plight of the animal. In a number of instances sportsmen have urged that the bobcat be accorded full game-animal status. In others it has at least been placed among the furbearers. Today a majority of the states set a specified hunting or trapping season on the cat, with the remainder of the year closed. Some stipulate methods by which bobcats may be hunted or taken. Thus the wildcat is slowly gaining status. In Minnesota even the importance of the lynx is recognized with a stipulated season.

Like the mountain lion, the bobcat has developed numerous modestly different local populations scattered over its broad range. A number of geographical races, or subspecies, have been named. However, none is distinctive enough or physiologically different enough to be of much importance to the hunter or casual observer of wildlife. Cats of northern climes are in general larger than those of warmer latitudes. Conceivably this may be due to survival of the most powerful, healthy specimens over many years in habitat situations of rugged climate, occasionally scarce forage, and a mandatory dependency at least part of the time upon larger animals for food.

The sometimes-used name "bay lynx" and the scientific species name *rufus* are not proper descriptions of the bobcat in many areas. Desert specimens are commonly very pale yellowish to gray. But color variations are not always easily related to general color background of the habitat. In parts of the north, for example, individuals with a distinctly gray base color are as common as those with a reddish cast. For that matter, in a two-kitten litter one may be grayish and the other reddish when they get their full coats. Body markings also vary widely. Some particularly handsome specimens have jet-black spots and bars on the belly and insides of legs against a snowy-white background.

Except for brief mating, and the period while young are with a mother, the bobcat leads a solitary existence. Its large, yellow eyes with black pupils, like those of all cats, give an indication that the animal is chiefly nocturnal. In bright light the eyes become slitted. However, it is a mistake repeated all too often in popular nature writing that the bobcat is exclusively nocturnal. It may be likened in many respects to the domestic cat, which hunts and moves and rests as momentary whimsy dictates.

Unquestionably the bobcat is predominantly nocturnal. Nonetheless, as animal callers have discovered, it comes to a call—usually the injured-rabbit sound, which is something of a standard—almost as readily in daytime as at night. This indicates that it is on the prowl for food, or it could not respond. There are hundreds of well-authenticated instances of cats rushing to a call, or being sighted skulking after prey, at all times of day, even on a hot noontime in desert terrain.

Like other cats, the compact little bobcat is a stoic of sorts. It is seldom given to panic, and now and then exhibits a wide streak of curiosity. Callers have related how they sat blowing a predator call in daytime, happened to glance around, and there was a big bobcat, sitting on its haunches within 30 paces or so, staring at the caller as if wondering what this is all about. Even a bobcat on the run in front of hounds will often potter about seemingly unhurried unless close-pressed, climb a tree and leap out, leave a tangle of tracks in a brushpile or a jampile of down logs. Hunters and others hiking in the woods occasionally glimpse a bobcat bounding away, yet now and then one will pause in flight to turn and peek out, looking back at the human intruder.

In a trap the cat often displays the same personality trait of stoicism. One bobcat, caught by a single toe by a trapper trying to obtain a live specimen, had not tried to pull away, but simply sat watching as the trapper approached. It was offered a drink of water in the white plastic top from a water jug, pushed near it with a stick. It drank without apparent unease, then put its paw on the container when the trapper tried to draw it away.

## HABITAT

One of the reasons bobcats are so seldom glimpsed in the wild is that they are cover creatures. Like all cats, their hunting success relies mainly on the silent stalk and the quick rush and pounce. This is most easily accomplished in brush or other tall vegetation, or in forests with a heavy understory. In addition, most of the forage of the bobcat also dwells in cover. Ground-nesting birds such as quail and grouse, cottontails and snowshoe hares, and most of the smaller rodents all require close and ample ground cover. In the large scheme of things, all such creatures are in their way aware that they are forage for predatory animals. They are therefore adapted to food available in areas of substantial amounts of vegetation. It serves them also for safety in hiding—yet in turn allows the meat eaters to utilize the same cover in order to make their well-screened stalks.

The bobcat is therefore perfectly tailored to, and in addition tied to, the mixed forests, the brushy stream bottoms, the moss-hung swamplands of the south, the cactus and thornbrush jungles of the southwestern deserts. Over the centuries, as it presumably broadened its original range, it was able to probe insistently into almost endlessly varied climates and vegetation types, but it could not settle, as did those runners and roamers the wolf, the coyote and some foxes, on open plains or vast sweeps of grass alone.

Nor can the bobcat survive in more than the most meager numbers in environments such as the tall coniferous forests. These are bereft of forage creatures, and to a large extent—except along stream courses—of ground cover in which to prowl and stalk. In some localities, however, the cats thrive in country with only modest vegetation but a jumble of rocks. In these instances, the rocks form the hunting cover, and the forage animals—ground and rock squirrels, and numerous small rodents that live on the low inbetween grasses and other vegetation—also are comfortably at home here.

There is, therefore, no such thing as a "typical" bobcat habitat. There are only basic needs that any given habitat must furnish. In the Great Lakes region and New England some of the best bobcat habitats are in the so-called "cedar swamps" or "greenswamps" situated in the valleys and along streams. These are not literally swamps. They have only a scattering of spots that hold water or are more than moist or damp. They are generally lowland stands of cedar, tamarack, or balsam, or all intermingled, with willow, birch, poplar, and alder interspersed. The snowshoe rabbit is the chief drawing card here, plus chipmunks and varied small rodents and birds.

In the west, broken country of rocky ledges cut by small streams and dotted with brushy patches and draws are prime bobcat habitat. In the south, the pine and palmetto lowlands and hammocks, the dense hardwood bottomlands, and the lake and pond edges fringed by moss-hung live oak and cypress are classic bobcat habitats. It is an interesting commentary on the basic needs of the bobcat for large expanses of hunting cover stocked abundantly with prey species in variety that the center of bobcat abundance has long been in the southwest, particularly in southern Texas, New Mexico, and Arizona, and the deserts and foothills of northern Mexico.

This land of long drought and sudden deluge, of spines and thorns, vicious heat and sometimes bitter winds, this in some parts utterly barren-appearing sweep of the funneling southern portion of North America, is a deceptive place, to the uninitiate an enormous dreary and lifeless expanse of presumably useless real estate. Ah—but its bleak outward appearance protects the unsuspected secret of this land: the most varied and teeming fauna on the continent.

Few wildlife enthusiasts are aware that the center of abundance and variety of the wild cats of North America is here. The jaguar, lion, bobcat, and ocelot; the tiny, house-cat-sized miniature of the ocelot, the margay; the low-slung, lean jaguarundi—all were here originally, and in varying numbers and areas of the region still are today. Of all the continent's wild cats, only the lynx lacks presence

## Range of the Bobcat

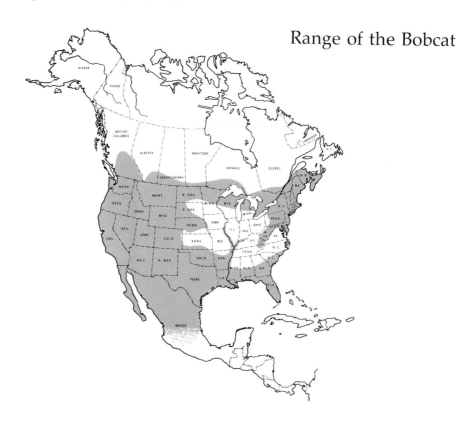

here. The basic reasons for this amazing gathering of the cats in southwestern North America were the tremendous numbers and variety of forage creatures, and a virtually perfect and congenial habitat in which the cats might hunt them down.

### FEEDING

Hunting live prey is a daily concern of both bobcat and lynx, and accounts for a major share of their time. How much rest a cat can take from hunting food is of course directly related to the abundance of forage available, in variety, in numbers, and in size. In practically every part of its range, a staple item of bobcat diet is the rabbit, cottontails almost everywhere, those and the larger marsh and swamp rabbits of the southeast and some central states, the

## Range of the Lynx

varying hare all across the north, and the several species of jack rabbits wherever their habitat and that of the bobcat coincide.

Although the rabbits make up a very substantial percentage of bobcat diet, as noted previously they are cyclic everywhere. Thus the cat must be willing, and able, to utilize a broad spectrum of other living forage. In this respect the bobcat differs from the lynx, not so much because the lynx is unwaveringly selective and partial to hares, but because over the preponderance of its range the variety of forage animals available in quantity to sustain it is extremely limited.

The wildcat is more fortunate over most of its range. If rabbits become scarce, although the bobcat population may drop, it seldom does so drastically because a number of other forage possibilities are usually present. Various mice, rats, and shrews live in the northern woods as well as in warmer habitats. Kangaroo rats and pack rats, both active at night in western terrain, are easily caught. At least they present little difficulty to the stealthy cats. Squirrels and chipmunks are readily eaten whenever they can be caught. Porcupines are standard fare where they are abundant, although bobcats occasionally get into difficulty with quills. In most instances they are adept at ripping open a porcupine's belly and avoiding quills.

Birds, particularly the larger game birds, are avidly stalked and eaten. Ground-nesting ruffed grouse and woodcock in northern forests, and quail, especially the western quails in desert scrub, are all favorite prey. Blue grouse of the west, rather naive birds, offer easy kills, and the spruce grouse of southern Canada and the western mountains, a rather stupid bird, is effortlessly collected. Tree-nesting birds are not immune to the attention of the bobcat, which is an agile climber. In the forests of northern Mexico, for example, colonies of whitewing doves, red-billed pigeons, and the noisy chachalaca are prime delicacies.

The bobcat is rather fastidious about having its meat fresh. On occasion it will kill a rather large animal, such as a young deer or in the southwest a javelina, and, having eaten its fill, make a cache of the remainder. But this small cat seldom makes enough return trips to finish the kill while the meat is still fresh. Only under the duress of severe hunger will a bobcat eat carrion, or sample wild fruit or vegetation, and then only reluctantly. Thus, large kills are in most instances partially wasted.

Sometimes a bobcat goes on a killing spree. Groups of roosting wild turkeys are now and then targets for massacre. So are flocks of domestic poultry in rare opportune circumstances. Lambs, kids, and adult sheep and goats now and then figure in a killing binge. As mentioned previously, bobcats do kill deer. Fawns are easy for them to handle, and so are adult deer of moderate size, particularly in deep snow. With its big, furry feet and light weight the bobcat maneuvers in snow more easily than its prey. However, only in most unusual situations are bobcats any real menace to a deer herd.

The bobcat is physically a truly tough customer. Part of this stems from its excellent muscular development and strength, and part from its amazing determination. In any kind of battle a bobcat is a startlingly vicious, able, and tenacious performer. For example, hunters with hounds know better than to allow all but the largest battle-tested dogs to tangle with a cat. The speed with which a bobcat can handle its sharp claws, all four legs raking, ripping, and

*A bobcat on a killing spree will attack groups of roosting wild turkeys.*

grabbing at once, plus teeth slashing, is unbelievable. A cornered cat in a fight with a hound tries to roll onto its back and rip the dog's belly. When one stalks and flings itself upon a deer, it is just as determined. What it lacks in weight it makes up for in ferocity.

This fierce and even irascible disposition is apparent in the numerous attempts that have been made to tame bobcats. Very occasionally a kitten collected before its eyes were open has been raised to become a moderately congenial pet. The majority of attempts, however, even with kittens, wind up with sullen, short-tempered half-tame cats thoroughly disagreeable to deal with by the time they are half-grown.

To illustrate by a rather unplesant example the total "wildness" and stubborn determination of the bobcat, an animal handler who furnished on several occasions both wild coyotes and bobcats to movie crews has divulged some of the tactics used. It is well known in this trade that far too much cruelty is routinely involved. Even portions of some of Hollywood's most loved and popular wildlife films in years past were filmed by such practices, although no one ever willingly admits it. At any rate, this man explained that to lift a coyote of average size out of a cage and tether it to a hidden stake for filming, all he did was to keep moving one hand in close in front of the cage to fix the attention of the animal inside. Then the lid was slowly opened by a helper, and he quickly seized the coyote by the scruff of the neck. It was instantly cowed and docile while held thus.

"To get a bobcat out of a holding cage," he was quoted, "you have to reach in with a noose on a long pole." This device is arranged so the rope forming the noose runs on up the pole. It can be jerked snug and held that way, with the animal out away pole-length from the handler. "Once the noose has been fought onto the cat's neck, the animal has to be choked almost to unconsciousness before you can ever get near it!"

This, of course, is a matter of fighting for its life. But a bobcat is just as determined and tenacious and wildly all-out in full drive when it makes a kill of an animal that matches it in weight or outweighs it. A raccoon, for example, often on a par for weight, is an extremely strong animal for its size, and also a tough antagonist, but bobcats regularly kill and eat them. In fact, the wildcat is an opportunist. Turtles, frogs, muskrats, beaver—any living creature it can handle is fair game and is eaten when need be. Curiously, although cats are traditionally skittish of water, bobcats have been known to rake spawning fish from a creek. Incidentally, although they dislike getting wet, they swim adeptly if they must.

The more or less dappled coat of the cat, and its base tones of gray to reddish, blend well among brush and vegetation and in dappled light and shadow. During a slow, patient stalk, a bobcat close-crouched to the ground is all but invisible. Its eyes are efficient in darkness, and its whiskers are extremely sensitive to the touch of nearly objects unseen in darkness. It is all told a beautifully designed and tremendously efficient killer. The curved, retractable claws are constantly honed on logs or tree trunks to keep them needle-sharp. Padded feet carry the cat silently. The lithe muscles and legs long in proportion to body size catapult it at the end of the stalk. It hurls itself upon its prey in a wild swirl of perfectly coordinated, blurred, ferocious motion.

### MOVEMENTS

If food is plentiful, or a large kill is made, the hunting cat fills up and then may lie up for a whole day, or even longer. A bobcat at rest is utterly relaxed. But fundamentally this is a restless creature. Its entire life revolves around the hunt. As soon as its stomach begins to get empty it is on the prowl again. Almost all of its movements, except for those concerned with mating, are focused upon the gathering of live forage. The same, of course, applies to the lynx, which is an equally perfect stalker and killer.

Its shy, secretive nature causes some spur-of-the-moment quick travel for the cat. The intrusions of man, or of dogs near settled areas, instantly put a bobcat to flight. It doesn't wait as a rule to see the source of disturbance. It slips silently away, and if the need arises, runs with a bounding, dodging gait. Not that enemies are numerous. An adult male may kill young, but the bobcat is simply too rough a customer for other animals to brace, and too quick and agile at slipping away should a bear or lion appear in its territory.

Indeed, only man and dogs dangerously harass it. When pressed by dogs, a cat will duck into a cave, or climb a tree when it tires. It cannot sustain a speedy race for very far. But it is adept at tangling its trail. It may tree and let the hounds bay below it until it gets its wind, then make a flying leap and run again. Old hands at cat hunting know that there are special places in any bobcat's domain where it will invariably go.

In northern Michigan a group of hunters ran cats with hounds each winter for years in the same territory, chiefly for the sport of the chase. The only way to bag a cat before the hounds was if it treed and stayed until the hunters arrived, or if it could be waylaid at some known crossing. In that area the swift Pigeon River cut through the forest where many a run was launched. There was a place on the river where a fallen tree made a bridge, precarious and slippery when snow and ice were on it, but a perfect crossing for a hard-pressed cat.

Invariably any cat jumped in the area—year after year—would if hard pressed eventually make a run a mile up the river, regardless of which side it was on, and cross on the slippery log. This strikingly illustrates how intimately a cat knows its bailiwick. It was also at once an indication of the distaste the cat had for getting into the water to cross, and an example of its instinctive knowledge that greater safety lay across the river. The dogs could not cross on the log. If they tried they'd probably fall off into the swift, bitter-cold river. The men, on snowshoes, could neither wade nor, removing their webs, dare the log route. Alas for the cat on occasion. When it took off beeline up the river, every hunter knew it must feel hard pressed and was heading for the log crossing. If a hunter running through the forest on snowshoes beat it to the spot, the ambush was laid and the hunt concluded. That happened every year or so, but most of the time the crafty bobcat won.

Hunting range of any bobcat—or lynx—depends primarily upon the abundance or scarcity of forage animals. As indicated previously, the cats will climb trees to get at birds or animals, but the preponderance of their hunting is done on the ground, for prey that spends at least most of its time there. In habitat such as the Texas brush country near the Mexican border, where most years pack rats and rabbits are abundant, a couple of square miles may contain a cat for months at a time. On the average individual range is larger, to perhaps 5 square miles. In habitat where variety of food is sparse, or population of the mainstay of diet low, the hunting range may be much greater, to the point where the animal may wander as much as 50 miles.

However, each cat does have a home feeling, and a territorial base, unless forced to leave it to make a living. On its hunting rounds it may spend a week, or longer, traveling a more or less constant route. That is, certain locations, such as a brushy draw, a stream course or waterhole, a rocky area of ledges and slides that have proved to be prime pay-off spots for food on a previous round, will be visited each time. This habit also plays into the hands of hunters. In snow country, for example, hound men habitually check specific draws and stream courses after a fresh snowfall. Sometimes a cat hunting the region will leave its fresh tracks so regularly the hunter can just about predict the day a fresh trail will be laid at a given point.

The daily, or nightly, travel of any bobcat in reasonably productive hunting territory averages, again based on abundance of prey and how successful each stalk, from a mile to 5 or 6 miles, seldom more. It doesn't have any specific "home" in terms of a bedding place where it rests. If a short hunt proves unusually successful and the cat fills its belly, it may lie up right there, on a rocky ledge, under a windfall, in a thicket — just anywhere that is warm or cool as the need demands and where it will be comfortable and hidden. Perhaps this one time it spends two resting periods in the same place, but only because a comfortable place happens to be convenient and the forage handy. Basically, however, it is a nomad, lying up between hunts wherever it happens to be. In its habitats there is never much problem in finding a desirable place.

Most of the time while on the hunt the cat walks, ever intent not to miss a sight, scent, or sound that may mean a meal. Like most cats, its instinctive foot placement is with care, each hind foot brought forward in turn at each step to fall upon the track — or partially so — left by the front foot. This assures silent movement. Now and then a cat trots along while hunting. When prey is sighted distantly, or runs, the cat may run, bounding in long leaps, 6 to as much as 10 feet at a time.

Most of the time, however, it is a prowler. It knows it cannot

*A lynx stalks a sleeping rabbit in its form.*

outrun many prey creatures. It sneaks, stalks with belly to ground, or circles to ambush an intended victim. Rabbits are often pounced on, after a silent sneak, as they hunch asleep in their forms. In varying hare country, a cat commonly lies in wait along a well-used trail in a cedar swamp, patiently watching for a meal to come hopping along. Now and then a cat watches from a rock ledge or the low limb of a tree to drop upon prey passing beneath. However, most of its hunting is more active. Waiting is too chancy. Hunger is always urging.

### BREEDING

Although the need to hunt keeps a bobcat—or lynx—constantly traveling, the still stronger urge of the mating season usually steps up the pace of movement and broadens its range, at least that of the male. The breeding season differs slightly according to latitude, but occurs predominantly for both bobcat and lynx during the first quarter of the year. There is undoubtedly still much to be known about the sex lives of these wild cats. The males are of course able to breed at any time of year, and the females come into heat periodically. Nonetheless, January, February, and March are the months when, presumably, almost all sexual activity takes place.

This is the period during which the males yowl and scream with cries that might well be frightening to anyone who did not know the origin and reason. Their vocal "singing," usually at night, is quite similar to the evil-spirit sounds made by domestic male cats intent on locating a female ready to be bred, except that the volume is much greater, and the repertoire broader. It is believed that this anguished caterwauling is to let the female know that a male is in the vicinity. Females at times make a less intense but unmistakable and repetitious low-pitched yowling sound when in heat. This, in turn, may be a sign to a wandering male that his attentions will be tolerated.

Males during this time of year travel widely, far less intent on hunting prey than on hunting female company. It is believed that a male may wander anywhere from 10 to 25 miles seeking a mate, unless he happens to find one on the way. There is not much in the way of attentive and graceful courtship, and the mating is often a noisy affair. The male is no gentle swain. Nor is he in the least faithful. As soon as mating is consummated, the tom is quickly on his wandering way to more conquests.

Fights between males are not common. Undoubtedly the squalling and screaming of an amorous male is in part a way of staking out his rights to a breeding territory. The night music lets other males within hearing know that they are on uncertain ground. But the males are far more interested in finding mates than in battling each other. As the male wanders about, he may breed several females, as many as he can discover that are free and willing.

From the discovery of young cats occasionally in late summer or early fall, observers believe that at least part of the females may be bred again after weaning one litter, or else that females missed on the first round are discovered by eager males and bred later on. Most kittens, however, are products of the traditional late-winter mating.

### BIRTH AND DEVELOPMENT

Approximately two months after mating, the female searches for a suitable denning place. A variety of locations suffice—a rock crevice that is protected, a hollow log or tree, a dense thicket, the protection formed by the tangled roots of a blowdown. Both bobcat and lynx require only that the birth place be protected somewhat from severe weather, dry, and hidden from disturbance. Females seek secluded places instinctively to hide from any danger, especially from males, which have no affection for their offspring and often kill them if they find the site.

The number of kittens differs. There may be as many as four, but the average litter is two or three. The young are variably marked with black spots and blotchy markings against a brownish background. The background color varies between lynx and bobcat and geographically among bobcat kittens. Like domestic cats, the kittens are born with eyes sealed. When after about ten days the eyes open, they look pale blue, also much like those of most domestic cats, but they change color in a few weeks as the youngsters grow.

Wildcat kittens are handsome little fellows, playful and appealing. But from the moment their eyes open they hiss and spit and growl, running through in miniature most of the sounds they'll make in volume as adults. Like the contented mother that nurses them, they will also soon learn to purr in pleasure. This sound is similar to the purring of a housecat, only greater in volume.

After a day or two of close care of the newborn young, cleaning and nursing them, the mother leaves periodically to hunt again, feeding herself and presently bringing tidbits to the kittens. The youngsters weigh half to three-fourths of a pound at birth, but grow swiftly. Soon they are trying pieces of meat, small birds, and rodents brought by their mother, and by the time they are approximately eight weeks old they are weaned and are eating a diet of meat like their parent. They are playful, enter into mock battles with each other and with their mother. She brings live rats, rabbits, or other small prey whenever possible, allowing the kittens to play with them and thus learn their first lessons in killing their own food.

The spotted coats have been lost by the time the young begin forays away from the den with their mother. They are now full-fledged scale-model wildcats. As they grow, the mother becomes less and less tolerant of them. This doesn't particularly upset them, for after young cats, trained by their parent, have made their first kills there are seldom strong family ties. As a rule by fall the youngsters will be about half-grown. Instances are known among both lynx and bobcats of young staying all the first winter with the mother, or at least until mating time for her.

Sometimes these family groups hunt together. Lynx families strongly evidence this trait, often for a full year. Or in fall the mother may leave the young and wander off on her own, while they stay loosely together for some weeks, or all winter. Most families, however, begin to break ties by late fall. It will not be long now until each young cat must stake out a hunting territory of its own.

When each is a year old it matures to breeding age. All family ties are sundered. Each cat assumes the solidary, wandering life.

### SENSES

It is now that the early training while hunting with their mother, observing her kills, and making their own first kills, plus lessons learned from the numerous unsuccessful stalks and rushes, become all important to survival. By now each sense is keenly honed, and the cat recognizes the comparative value and useful development of each.

Although all senses are sharp, cats are designed for sight hunting, as opposed to the wild dogs that follow scent trails. Their eyes are large and set straight forward in the face with the bridge of the nose flatter than that of fox or coyote. This arrangement indicates that sight is all-important to them. It is also a design of nature in animals that stalk close to pounce upon their prey.

Any slight movement calls the attention of either bobcat or lynx — the flutter of a small bird, the sudden turn of a leaf in the smallest breeze. Motion equates with possible food, and these cats miss little that moves within sighting distance. Because sight is so important to them, curiosity — always associated with cats — is a strong trait. This is an obvious combination: whatever the cat sees it must be curious about, else it would miss endless opportunities. One extremely successful bobcat trapper designed a set with a small square of white cardboard, a hole punched in the center, tied to a string. The string was secured to a branch above and a short distance past the trap set. The set was made so only one approach could be taken by a cat. Any slight breeze made the cardboard twirl or swing. Curiosity brought a passing cat close to investigate. Numerous variations on the theme have been used — a few feathers tied to a string hanging near the trap, a squirrel tail used in similar fashion.

Hearing is also well developed. It is interesting that most predators that live in more or less dense ground cover have sharp hearing. It allows a silent retreat from any possible danger, but more than that, keen ears enable a cat to detect the smallest sound that may mean living food. Hearing is therefore a kind of direction finder for the eyes. Of course both senses are automatically used together. A movement instantly swivels the eyes into intent focus, but meanwhile ears are alert to help substantiate what has been detected by sight, and vice versa.

The cats have only a moderately developed scenting ability. A bobcat can trail close-in along a fresh trail of prey, or pick up scent in the air from large animals nearby. But the sense of smell is by no means as sharp, or as necessary, to the cats as to the true trailers, the wild dogs. The nose does play an important role, however, in picking up knowledge of other cats in the same region, and also during the mating season.

Old hands at trapping bobcats have often managed to take one alive, a male if possible, and have kept it in a cage with a bottom arrangement made from tin slanted and then bent into a kind of trough at one end. Beneath the end of the trough portion, under the floor, is a small catch container. Urine is caught in the container and used at a trap set. It is hideously strong-smelling, and no cat in the area can resist examining such a scent post.

### SIGN *(Tracks are illustrated on page 253.)*

Although a cat will readily recognize the urinating place of another, there is no sign left for hunter or wildlife observer to recognize, and undoubtedly the scent also would be missed unless extremely copious and fresh. Droppings of lynx and bobcat likewise seldom leave evidence of their presence, because cats have the habit of covering them. Nonetheless, there are instances where they fail to, or the earth where the stop was made is too hard to use efficiently.

Scats aren't easily confused when out in the open with those of coyotes and foxes. In arid country they sometimes take the form of elongated pellets, or the entire scat, 4 or 5 inches in length, may be pinched at several places. Occasionally in firm earth scratchings are noted where a cat has covered its dung, or at least tried to. These scratch marks usually will be in a circle or half-circle around the spot, and the claw marks rather thin. Conversely, a coyote may deposit dung, then scratch several strokes with its hind feet, but not to cover the droppings. Cat scratchings are made with the forefeet and are useful sign, when present, chiefly in combination with tracks. That is, if the tracks are not plainly printed, the scratchings may clinch the identification.

It is doubtful that tree scratches ever are a very important wildcat sign. Presumably these are made during claw sharpening, but seldom are they emphatic enough to draw attention. The track is the most important sign. It is not always easy to distinguish between wild dog and wild cat tracks. Positive identification depends on the material in which they are printed. In deep snow, for example, identification can be confusing.

Where prints show plainly, bobcat tracks show quite positive characteristics. They are by no means as large as mountain lion tracks; they are larger than tracks of feral cats, if any might possibly be present. No claw marks show because cat claws, unlike those of the dogs, are retractable, and are kept sheathed in their fleshy, furred scabbards during travel. Further, cat tracks are much rounder than dog tracks. And if a track is very plain one should look closely at the print of the center pad of the foot. The foot of the bobcat has a slight U or V in the front center of the pad. This shows in perfect prints as a kind of minor notching.

Other close-scrutiny track characteristics of the bobcat are as follows: front-foot print sometimes slightly wider than that of hind foot; center pad of hind foot a bit smaller than that of front foot; average track size of adult from about $1\frac{3}{4}$ to $2\frac{1}{4}$ inches wide, and a bit longer, though often not much, than wide. Lynx tracks are substantially larger, even though the animal may not be. The large feet are fashioned for snow travel, and the toes are spread wider. A lynx track may be very close to 4 inches wide, but is more commonly about 3 to $3\frac{3}{4}$ inches. Length of stride or bound is not a very accurate criterion for either animal because these dimensions vary greatly.

### HUNTING

Until the advent and popularity of the predator call, bobcat hunting was entirely a highly specialized hound sport. It would be utter folly to go into the forest or desert with a gun and hope to bag a bobcat for a trophy simply by prowling around hoping for a shot. Thousands of outdoorsmen, many of whom have spent their lives outdoors in bobcat country, have never seen one alive and roaming at will, partly because the cats are most active at night, but mostly because they are far too adept at staying out of sight.

There are a few guides and outfitters who nowadays offer bobcat hunting with their specially trained hound packs. However, most hound enthusiasts addicted to bobcat chases aren't in it professionally. A hunter who is able to book a hound hunt, or to arrange to go with someone who has bobcat hounds, doesn't really need to know much about the techniques of the sport but just follow directions of the hound-pack owner. It is an exciting and dramatic endeavor.

Most bobcat chases are run in the north, in snow country.

Hounds as a rule are big and rugged. They need to be to run in deep snow and heavy cover. The usual procedure is for the dog owner first to scout his bailiwick thoroughly. He comes to know where a cat, or several, range. He learns their habits—which places they cross streams, what coverts they hunt on each round, where they cross a hiking or vehicle trail.

Nowadays in much of the northern forest region the beginning of a hunt is done from a vehicle. Let's say that a light, fresh snow has fallen during the night. The hunters load up their dogs and cruise back-country trails, in state or national forests or other wild country, watching for a fresh track. They know the types of crossings cats habitually use. Driving very slowly, it is not too difficult to spot a track. In fresh snow it is certain to have been made after or during the snowfall. A good cat hunter watches the weather and knows when the snow began and stopped. Out at dawn, sometimes a track can be picked up that cannot possibly be more than an hour old. This means that almost without fail the cat will be lying up within a half-mile or so of the crossing.

One good hot-trail dog is brought out on leash. It is allowed to test the track. If it is eager to go, the hunters probably will decide to release the pack, which may be only a couple of hounds or as many as half a dozen. Great efforts have been made, in most instances, to be certain dogs are "deer-broke," which means if they jump a deer they won't chase it. Deer usually are present in bobcat range. Most dogs love to chase them, and the habit has ruined many a cat hunt. If a track seems a bit cold to the test dog, and a cold trailer is in the pack, it is given a smell. Sometimes a cold trail is run. But in large wild areas hound men are reluctant to turn loose a cold-trailer, or a pack on a cold trail. The cat may not be jumped for hours.

When a chase is launched, the hunters, often on snowshoes, follow and keep listening. They can tell by the hound voices when the cat is jumped. They spread to likely points to try to intercept the chase, or race on their webs with great physical effort to try to get ahead of the run. However, the cat may circle, or backtrack. It is never even remotely possible to guess how a chase may end. If a cat is pressed hard and trees, stays treed long enough, and the hunters or any one of them are fast enough, the trophy may be taken. Often as not, however, an all-day operation, the cat tangling up the trail time after time and losing the dogs, winds up with hunters utterly exhausted, the cat still alive and probably smirking in contempt—and the dogs scattered far off in the forest and having to be hunted until well after bitter-cold dark by the hunters.

The late Carl Allen, who was for years a master cat hunter with his own hounds in northern Michigan, had his dogs trained to backtrack when they were lost or the trail was lost. He'd leave his old hunting coat in the woods near the place where the run had started. On many an occasion a chase launched at dawn was given up at dark, and the hounds picked up the next morning, curled up in the snow by the coat, hungry, frazzled, and sad-eyed.

Cat hunting with hounds in the west is sometimes done on horseback, and is similar in some respects to lion hunting. In the swamps of the deep south procedures are similar to snow country except for the drastically differing terrain. Larger dog packs are employed as a rule in the south and southwest than in the snow country of the north, where a couple of good hounds are traditional. A good many avid bobcat hunters, incidentally, never shoot the quarry. They just love the chase. If the cat is to be bagged, some northern hunters use a shotgun and heavy shot for possible running shots in a way-lay situation. Others in various parts of the country carry a .22 or .22 magnum to dispatch a treed or bayed cat.

Calling is a sport in which the average hunter has much more opportunity. Some calling enthusiasts use only a camera, some just call to "watch the cat come," and some collect cats for hides or trophies. The call used is the so-called predator or "coyote" call, mouth-blown, that imitates the anguished cry of an injured rabbit. There are also tape and record players with the same sounds, to be played. Some callers like these, but they are not legal everywhere. Nor, in fact, are mouth-blown calls. There may be regulations, for example, in some areas against using them at night.

Recorded instructions for calling are available from a number of firms, and there are printed instructions with each call. The basic points are to wear camouflage, and to select a calling area carefully, preferably after having checked it for sign. The stand from which to begin calling should also be carefully chosen. Cats invariably come to a call sneaking through cover and do not like to cross large open spaces. However, a caller should have a reasonably wide view. Bobcats seldom run toward a calling sound, as coyotes or foxes may. They prowl and potter, often coming in very slowly and secretively, stalking their presumed prey.

The caller blows a series of squalls, then waits a few minutes, and repeats. For bobcats one should stay on a stand at least half an hour. If by then there are no results, a move to a new stand should be made. It should be well outside hearing range of the first calling, perhaps a half-mile to a mile distance. Night calling with headlamp and shooting light usually gets the best results, although bobcats also come to a call readily by day.

Ironically, overhunting of bobcats for bounties and as undesirable varmints in years past may in the long run have turned out to be an influence toward the good of the species. It was not until these handsome small cats of the wild places became scarce in the more populous states that pressure was brought, almost entirely by sportsmen who enjoyed the chase, or watching reactions to a call, to offer the bobcat some protection. Predator bounties, fortunately, are now in total disrepute as a game-management tool. They serve no purpose whatever, except to cost money that might be better used for other purposes. They are also a wide-open invitation—proved endless times—for plain thievery, among those who fake records of more predators than they've taken, and among the county or state employees who concoct dishonest records and pocket the money.

The bobcat has moved up a rung or two in status. Few areas now offer bounties on them. They have standing in most states now either as furbearers or as full-fledged game animals. Unquestionably the move upward to protected game-animal status will catch on in future in more and more states and provinces. Bobcats—and the lynx chiefly because of its lesser contact with civilization—are not candidates for the endangered species list, at least in the foreseeable future.

# FOXES

## Red Fox
*Vulpes vulpes*

## Gray Fox
*Urocyon cinereoargenteus*

The foxes have been an important part of sporting history since ancient times. Because of their running abilities and their craftiness at contriving escape, they long ago became the chief targets of the chase, a course, often run not so much to take the fox as for the pure joy and excitement of its pursuit. No other animal ever became such a status symbol as the red fox, coursed by royalty and the wealthy in England and Europe and finally in this country. The pomp and protocol of riding to hounds after a fox became an intricately detailed social ceremony.

But along with the red coats, the fast horses, the chase masters, the whippers-in of the hounds, and all such blueblood arrangements, foxes have always been in this country the favorites of hound enthusiasts of the one-gallus hill-country variety as well. Many a bet has been laid among a group on a hilltop beside a crackling evening fire on whether Rattler, Old Blue, or Bawler would open first or be the one to run the fox to ground. And many such a group of country cronies has finally heard the chase come to a stop, with the wily fox having at last given the mixed pack the slip. "Time to douse the fire and go home," someone might announce. Many a nagging country wife has found excellent fodder in her foxhound-loving husband's helling around the woods at night.

Although foxes, both red and gray, are hunted for fur by various means, their status as game animals has always been based chiefly upon the drama of a run before the hounds. Yet the sporting scene is not the only claim to fame of the foxes. In earlier times animals as daily neighbors of man quickly were tagged with specific identities. The fox was the sly creature that slipped through a tiny hole in the fence and made a raid on the chicken coop, or dragged off the old gray goose. So slick was the fox at turning such tricks without getting caught that "sly" and "foxy" became synonymous.

Children by thousands went to sleep in earlier times while their mothers read tales of the prowess of smirky-visaged—but somehow lovable—Reynard, who managed so astutely to outwit his enemies. Or, on occasion in the stories Reynard was, conversely, the villain, concealing his true identity until the last dramatic moment by holding his brush before his face.

Indeed, the fox as a personality type assigned by man worked its way unalterably into folklore, into song and story and even comedy, such as the old cartoon character for kids, "Foxy Grandpa," a jolly sort full of tricks who always fooled the boys who were intent on playing pranks on him. The fox has also figured in the droll stories passed around among sportsmen. Deadpan and believing these themselves after endless retelling, they relate the one about the hard-pressed fox that hopped into the farmer's wagon or atop the cow's or sheep's back and rode away from the hounds in fine and astutely planned security. Or how the fox criss-crossed among the cows in the pasture so that the pursuing hound was overwhelmed with cow scent and lost the trail, whereupon it stood watching and grinning after them. Or the one about the fox that carried eggs one by one from the hen house, never breaking a single one, then dined on them regularly, two for breakfast each morning, at its leisure.

Foxes are indeed crafty and intelligent animals, even though man has with his love for tall stories often exaggerated their cleverness. One reason for the lasting interest in foxes is that their range is so immense that throughout the history of settlement of this continent almost all people had and still have experiences with them. Although there are pockets from which one or the other or both foxes have been eliminated or nearly so by the press of civilization, their ranges still blanket almost all of North America.

Red foxes are found over practically all of Alaska and Canada, ex-

Red Fox

Douglas-Allen

## THE FOXES

COLOR: **Red fox,** variable, from yellowish to deep reddish, darker along the back shading lighter on sides to a whitish belly; tip of nose black; lower sides of face, throat, chest, and tail tip white; pale to whitish inside ears, but outside of ears along tips black; feet and lower legs black; tail except for tip darker than sides, often with dark to black hairs intermingled; several color phases—black, black with silvery hair tips, the "cross fox" a yellowish phase with darker band lengthwise of back and another across the shoulders; several color phases may occur, especially in the far-northern range, in the same litter. **Gray fox,** much of body grizzled gray; ears and area around them, a "collar" below the white throat, the flanks, and outsides of the legs rusty orange red, often quite bright, sometimes flecked with black hairs; insides of legs, belly, and chest white; tail black on top with hairs raised ridgelike, gray along sides, commonly rusty beneath, with black tip.

MEASUREMENTS: **Red fox,** overall length 3 to 3½ feet, at least a third of that the tail; shoulder height 15 or 16 inches. **Gray fox,** overall length averages about the same as red fox, with tail-length ratio the same, and height at shoulder generally similar.

WEIGHT: Both species fairly similar, varying by range from 5 or 6 pounds to twice that, with the red fox at maximum and also on the average usually somewhat heavier than the gray.

GENERAL ATTRIBUTES: The exceptionally bushy tail, cylindrical in shape, black feet, and white tail tip easily distinguish the red fox from the gray with its black-top-maned tail with black tip, and its gray (never red) back and upper sides; the narrow face and sharply pointed nose of the foxes are distinctive; red foxes often hunt open fields, grays seldom leave cover; the gray fox is the only member of the wild dogs that is capable of climbing trees.

cept portions of the plains of western Canada. Southward over parts of the plains within the United States and throughout western Texas the red fox is missing. Its range stops somewhat above the Mexican border. But it is present almost everywhere else within the lower-48 states. Most authorities agree that it was not native to eastern Texas, but was introduced there by hound men for the sport of the chase. It is present today in limited numbers in eastern and central Texas. It is also well established in the southeastern United States, from which at one time it was presumed to be excluded.

Basically the gray fox is an animal of rather temperate climes and might be considered predominantly southern. It is found, often in surprising though rather secretive abundance, over all of the southern United States and far down into Mexico coast to coast. Northward it ranges up the west coast at least to northern Oregon, and into the central Rockies and the western states over parts of Nevada, Utah, and Colorado. Broadly westward from the Mississippi River it is found clear to the Canadian border and slightly above in the Dakotas-Minnesota region. Populations are sparse to substantial across the Great Lakes region and New England, and in fact everywhere over the United States east of the Mississippi River.

Both red and gray foxes have been divided into geographic races or subspecies. The red is resident over much of Asia and Europe, but the division into American and European species did not stand up in modern times. All red foxes are now considered of the same species, and the subspecies, of both reds and grays, which differ slightly in size or color from place to place, are not important enough to be of concern to sportsmen and observers of wildlife. By and large, reds in most places are a bit larger than grays on the same range. Also, northern red foxes are usually substantially larger in the far north, and in the north-central and eastern states than in the west.

There are other foxes on the continent. The kit, or desert, fox and the swift fox, both westerners, are very small, some specimens weighing no more than a good-sized cottontail. They are by no means abundant nowadays—in fact, they are endangered—and are certainly not in the game-animal category. The beautiful arctic fox, with its white and "blue" or smoky-gray phases, is not a true fox, but a closely allied animal that at times is important to the fur trade but hardly can be classified as game.

Even though the red fox has an exalted place in the social world and has long been much touted as a game animal, it has by no means had all factions on its side. And the gray fox, curiously, was never very popular with hunters until recent years when animal calling came into wide use. Both foxes got themselves into trouble early in their relationships with man because they are predators. They not only picked off domestic poultry at every opportunity, but have for many years been accused of decimating game-bird and small-game populations. This brought bounties down on their heads.

Not very many states nowadays still offer bounties. The bounty as a control on predators was discredited by game-management research years ago. In Michigan, for example, where red foxes were blamed by some hunters for all but wiping out the pheasant population, it was discovered that over a period of several decades as

## Range of the Red Fox

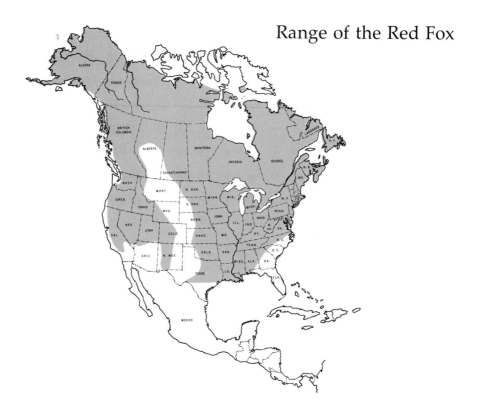

many bounties were being paid for foxes as during the early years of the practice—and yet they were as numerous as ever.

Further, the bounty system on all predators and in all states has always been notoriously corrupt. Often the bounties were paid by a county clerk who knew everybody in the rural community. A few years ago one local clerk and cohorts in a small Michigan community were found to have paid bounties in a single year on several thousand foxes. One wag noted that had those foxes actually existed, the whole country would have been knee deep in them. The fact was, they existed only on paper.

In some wryly comic instances where a fox had to be brought in and shown to the clerk as proof that the bounty payoff was legitimate, crafty old hands would fetch in an animal some days dead. The paymaster would demand that the body be removed pronto, and the same fox might be used several times and several bounties collected. Some small-time racketeers carted scores of foxes across state borders, collecting in several bordering states on the same animals.

# Range of the Gray Fox

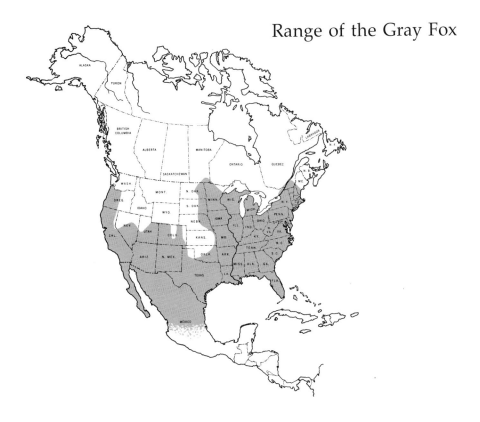

Crooked bounty shenanigans aside, thorough research discovered that the fox, regardless of how abundant, was incapable of controlling a game-bird or small-game population. Granted, a fox will seize a pheasant if it can catch one. But small rodents are far easier prey. One biologist in a now-famous study actually walked over 1000 miles of fox tracks in winter snow, in pheasant country, working at the project a little at a time over several years. He was thus able to spot the kills the animals made during their travels. Most kills could be identified by the surrounding sign. Along the entire mileage of fox tracks only a small number of pheasant or other bird kills were discovered. It is now well known that loss or degradation of habitat is the chief factor in game-bird population control, and that except in a scattering of highly unusual situations predation is a negligible factor.

Today in almost all states foxes are classed as either game animals or fur animals, with a stipulated hunting or trapping season. In a few states there is no closed season and thus no protection, but bounties are pretty much an outmoded management method. In general, fur prices dictate how much attention foxes get from trappers and some hunters. In certain areas the avid hound men would not think of killing a red fox. Some small clubs of hound enthusiasts even try to persuade others to leave the foxes alone. They like to have a substantial number for their runs.

The feeling about the gray fox is different. Although grays are run with hounds, most avid fox hunters hold them in contempt. The gray fox has the rather astonishing ability to scurry up a tree as handily as a squirrel. It will run briefly, and then tree, or even den up. In a tree it can be killed easily enough, if fur is the object of the chase, but the sport is what most enthusiasts are after. If it fails to tree or run into a hole, a gray fox will often head for areas of horribly dense brush or swamp tangle, where it slips agilely through cover big hounds can manage barely or not at all. Thus it is the red fox, a real runner that can't climb and must contrive its getaway by sly trickery, that is the quarry of the hunter with hounds.

The red fox was the basis for the fox-farming business, for furs, which was important some years ago but not so nowadays. The most prized pelts were from the so-called silver fox. This color phase was bred—and the "platinum," a farm-produced phase—for some time because of the beauty, value, and popularity of the fur. Actually the wild silver color phase is a melanistic (black) animal on which the outer guard hairs of the pelt are tipped with silver. During periods when fox furs are valuable the silver fox is a great prize for the trapper. For some reason it is extremely rare in the wild except in the more northerly portions of the range.

The phase called the "cross fox" also is a rather rare and comparatively valuable find. This curious color aberration is a reddish-yellow animal commonly with dark guard hairs scattered over portions of its body. Along the back there is a swath of black or very dark brown running from neck to rump, and another similar swath crossing it across the shoulders. Some red fox color phases are simply black—melanistic—without silvery-tipped guard hairs. A few look intermediate gray. Always the white tail tip, however, easily distinguishes any of the phases from the gray fox.

Fur hunters and trappers many years ago coined the name "bastard fox" for the gray-hued red fox. There is also the "Samson fox," a red with a deficiency in the hair follicles so that the long guard hairs of the pelt fail to grow. Pelts of these woolly animals are valueless. Presumably the name used for this curious aberration originated far back in history. Supposedly Samson outfitted foxes with flammable material tied to their tails, lighted it, and set them free to race through grain fields and set fires. The foxes were heavily scorched during their flight, but the bursts of flame racing through the fields also put the Philistines to flight. The foxes with "scorched" coats thus became "Samson" foxes. Although prime red fox furs have always had fair value for trappers during the high peaks of the fur trade, hides of the gray never have been very valuable or popular because the fur is rather coarse and thin.

### HABITAT

Because the range of the foxes covers almost all of North America, it is obvious that they tolerate a broad variety of surroundings. Red foxes are found in Arctic snows and the stunted forest areas of the far north, in the New England woodlands, in the farm fields and woodlands of the midwest, in the lowlands of the south, and in the mixed farm and brush and even rain-forest expanses of the Pacific coast. Gray foxes live out their furtive lives in tangled swamps of the deep south, in the laurel thickets of the middle south, in the forests of New England, and in the cactus and thornbrush of the southwest.

However, between these two species there is a notable difference in preference of habitat type. Basically the red fox is an edge animal. It may live and hide in dense forests, as in Canada and portions of its eastern range, but it does most of its hunting along the edges, the lakeshores and stream courses, the open swales, on the west coast and elsewhere in forest burns, and everywhere around farm woodlots and fields.

In fact, it is believed the red fox became much more abundant and began substantially spreading its range as the country was settled, the forests cut and fields planted. It is along the edges, over fallow or crop fields, along small farm creeks and in woodlots that a heavy crop of rodents, a mainstay of diet, may be harvested. The red fox also is a rather bold little predator, an animal personality with full confidence in its ability to outwit enemies, which are chiefly dogs, hunters, and trappers.

It cannot be said that red foxes dislike wilderness regions. They have colonized millions of acres of them. However, their populations are always less in true wilderness simply because the food supply is less abundant. In other words, the red fox gets on quite well with man's civilization, and indeed is often discovered living a cleverly masked existence right on the fringes of large cities.

Thus the red fox may be classified in general as a creature of fairly open terrain. A mixture of forest and farming country is virtually perfect for it. Pasture lands, especially with weedy or brushy fence rows, weedy cover in draws, and intermittent woodlands, furnish prime red fox living quarters. The vegetation type is not as important, nor for that matter the climate, as the potential of a habitat for raising abundant forage. The red fox seems always to be willing to make a bargain with danger if the grub stake is high, secure in the knowledge that it is equipped with the wits to cope.

The gray fox is a fundamentally different personality. It is far less bold, shyer, not as confident, and adapts less well to heavy human settlement. It is an animal of dense thickets, from the deep, moss-hung southern swamps to the spiny tangle of cactus, mesquite, and varied thornbrush of the southwestern deserts. In open forest situations it is at home, but invariably there is ample understory for hiding and hunting.

The gray is not as strong or willing a runner as its relative, or perhaps it is not as inclined to trust its flair for trickery against the push of danger. A red fox commonly streaks across a wide-open field in front of hounds. The gray fox takes to the most impenetrable brush, cane brakes, or shintangle. Even then when only moderately pressed, or tiring, it takes to a tree or to a den among rocks, or temporarily utilizes what it hopes is the safety of the burrow of some other animal.

There are, of course, exceptions in the case of both species. In the Hill Country of south-central Texas, for example, gray foxes are plentiful on ranches, living among patches of scrub live oak and shin oak and mesquite, with much well-grazed land intermingled. Nonetheless, almost without fail there are rocky canyons and draws dense with brush to which they can retire when danger threatens. Even though habitat preferences of the two foxes are distinctive, both can and do use to some extent the preferences of the other. It is obvious that both types serve as havens for the small prey which offer them livelihood.

### FEEDING

More important, foxes have an exceedingly broad range of diet. A tasty mouse from a barley field or a fat pack rat from a cactus clump may be a gourmet dish to a fox. However, if these are not consistently on tap, wild grapes, some varieties even dubbed "fox grapes," do nicely, regardless of the old tale about Reynard and the grapes he couldn't reach and decided he didn't want anyway because probably they were sour. Juicy magenta-colored "apples" from the prickly pear cactus commonly replace the grapes for the desert gray fox. A host of varied edibles suitable for the nonselective tastes of a fox are invariably to be discovered wherever either red or gray may be, and whatever the season, and whether it has been one of leanness or abundance. The foxes are not picky. They calmly make do, and apparently with relish regardless of the fare.

The main diet of any fox at any place depends upon the season. Their adaptability and opportunism is what originally allowed them to colonize such a vast territory. Mice and rabbits are basic food items. But during grasshopper season in crop country many a fox gorges on them. Other insects also are eaten as the chance is presented. When wild fruit is abundant, the foxes take it—wild blackberries in the north, dewberries in the south, wild strawberries. Gray foxes in Texas are fond of hopping up into a scrub persimmon shrub—a different variety from the tall persimmon trees of the south—and at ripening time gobbling the black, super-sweet fruits. They also gorge on the larger persimmons from trees.

The red fox, which is not capable of tree climbing, reaches up or leaps up to strip chokecherries from bushes, is fond at times of low-growing blueberries, and gleans wild black cherries and grapes fallen to the ground. In the process of seeking fruits, it may seize a frog or a small bird, and eat grubs or even earthworms after a heavy rain that brings them out of the ground. In spring and summer the nests of birds are commonly destroyed by both foxes. Eggs are gulped down shell and all, or young birds are eaten.

Anything remotely edible and sustaining periodically makes up part of the diet. Foxes commonly eat moderate quantities of grass. Various nuts that can be chewed down, such as beech nuts, are relished, and gray foxes in the south are known to like peanuts grubbed from crop fields. Live foods such as ground squirrels, rats, mice, and rabbits, however, are the basic fox diet whenever and wherever they can be caught. Nor does either fox species have much difficulty catching them.

Foxes seldom make a stalk the way the bobcat does. Their sight, scent, and hearing are all keen. A fox has been observed trotting zigzag across a meadow hunting mice, pausing to cock its ears and listen, gaze riveted nearby. It may stand on hind legs momentarily to see better. Then it comes to all fours, takes a careful step, and simply makes a sudden dive. The ease with which foxes catch mice and other small rodents is amazing.

There is a limit, obviously, to the size prey a fox can handle. For example, a fox of average size is seldom capable of doing in a full-grown wild turkey, an exceedingly strong bird which will weigh more than its attacker. It can handle birds the size of grouse, and domestic chickens. A fox family with young almost grown, all hunting together, occasionally slaughters a chicken flock, killing apparently for the excitement of it, dragging some birds off and eating bits of them but unable to clean up the total kill.

Game birds such as quail, pheasants, and grouse, as noted earlier, are not important staple items in fox diet simply because they are difficult to catch and other food is usually more easily available. Along marsh edges foxes now and then raid muskrat communities. Exceptionally large red foxes in the north may even tackle a deer fawn. That's a tough assignment. Usually when sign indicates that a fox has been feeding on venison it is from one that has died a natural death or one wounded during hunting season that later died. Foxes of both varieties commonly eat carrion. The red fox has a habit of making a food cache of leftovers and coming back to it sometimes. The gray is not as well noted for this habit.

Most of their hunting for food is done at night, but neither gray nor red fox is by any means entirely nocturnal. Much depends on the abundance of food, the strains of hunger, or the whim of the individual animal. It is not at all uncommon for outdoorsmen to glimpse a red fox trotting across a field or along a brushy draw in full daylight. The gray is not as often sighted because it is more inclined to stay in heavy cover. However, animal callers using the predator call that presumably imitates the squall of an injured rabbit call in gray foxes quite often in the daytime, and the red fox also may come to the call either day or night.

In the winter in the northern range, incidental forage such as fruit and insects is unavailable. Now the fox must work hard to make a living, and this is the time when its hunting prowess as a predator is most evident. It may discover old fruit beneath snow, or pick away at such items as rose hips showing above the snow. But now is the time when its attention is focused chiefly on living prey such as cottontails, snowshoe hares, and mice and other small rodents that it can dig from beneath snow in the matted grass of fields. Carrion also may become an important food source now, particularly for the red fox in northern areas. A dead deer is a real find, and the cold weather keeps the meat from becoming intolerable. However, in northern winters it is necessary for foxes to range wide and hunt long hours.

## MOVEMENTS

In fact, the travel required to keep its belly full accounts for the major physical activity of all foxes. The size of the individual range varies, of course, according to the food supply. In a southwestern desert expanse, for example, during a year when pack rats, kangaroo rats, and desert cottontails are all on an up cycle, living is easy for a fox. It may be able to stay well fed and never roam over more than a square mile of territory, and in some instances even less. However, the home range of any fox is usually larger than that. It may cover several miles. On one ranch in Texas a gray fox known for a bad limp in one front leg came to a predator call one evening at a stand roughly 3 miles from the spot where what was apparently the same animal had been called in the previous evening.

Most observers believe that a range of 10 square miles is about maximum for individual foxes making their hunting rounds. Probably the travel distance for a single night of hunting seldom is longer than a straight-line 5 miles, although the fox may do a lot of zigzag wandering during the trek. Like most predators, when a fox has sated its hunger, it rests. Thus, if hunting success is good, either gray or red may require only an hour to fill up and then take a snooze. If things are difficult, the animal may find it necessary to hunt all night, and perhaps even to continue intermittently during the day. Again, the foxes are opportunists; even though full, one may continue hunting, or come to the squall of a predator call, simply because of the predatory instinct.

Sometimes hunters or hounds interfere with the foraging travel of a fox. To a red fox, which puts on a real run, this interruption can be an exasperation. It must run, full or empty, until it loses its pursuers or the hunt is concluded in the hunters' favor. Some of the tricks displayed by red foxes before hounds well illustrate their craft and intelligence. The animal, once it lines out and knows for certain the dogs are on its trail, may enter a stream, running in the water in either direction. It may even swim, although neither of the foxes do so except in time of dire need. The gray will usually go up a tree or into a den of some sort to get away from dogs, but the red does neither. In earlier days when there were many stone and rail fences throughout the eastern half of the United States, a red fox commonly hopped up on one, ran along it, then leaped far off to ground to run again, thus confusing the dogs.

There are endless tales about how Reynard "outfoxed" the hounds, many no doubt exaggerated. It is claimed that several foxes occasionally criss-cross their tracks to puzzle pursuing hounds. Reds do run up slanted blowdowns and leap off, dart through hollow logs, and sometimes circle around to come in behind dogs that are chasing them. Red foxes have been observed on occasion running on abrupt tangents back toward a hound pack, but wide of

*When pursued by dogs, a red fox often darts through a hollow log and circles behind the pack.*

it, then standing to watch, to see when and if the dogs unravel the trail before running again. The craft of the red fox under pursuit is what has made it over long centuries such an admired game animal.

Both red and gray foxes walk, trot, or run in rather similar fashion. Both often hunt at a slow trot, possibly moving at 4 or 5 miles an hour except when they scent, hear, or see forage. The gray has a bounding running gait, and the red may streak off in a straight-out, low run, or lope in galloping fashion. The legs of the red fox are a bit longer than those of its relative. As noted, it is also the better runner, with the greater inclination and endurance. However, when going all-out, both species attain roughly the same top speeds on the average, around 25 miles an hour or a bit more. Some hunters believe a red fox can do better than that, with bursts to 40 and a steady run of as much as 30.

An old tale about the gray fox is that it climbs trees easily because it has retractable claws like a cat. This is patently false. The nails are somewhat curved, but are short and not retractable. It has also been written in numerous places that a gray fox can climb only a slanting tree. This also is false. The fact is, no one is quite sure exactly how this agile little animal is able to go up a tree as swiftly as it does, but it is actually capable of going up a perfectly straight, large-trunked tree.

*The agile gray fox may evade an enemy by climbing a tree.*

The Burnham Brothers of Marble Falls, Texas, well-known animal callers and call manufacturers, discovered a unique way to demonstrate the tree-climbing abilities of the gray fox. At one time they had an old border collie that loved to chase foxes. They'd take a stand hunkered down in a likely spot, and surrounded by several large oaks. One would hold the dog still and flat on the ground while the other called.

Observers taken along with them were witness on several occasions to what occurred. When a gray fox came trotting in, the Burnhams, covered with camo clothing and headnets, let it come until it was within mere feet. Then they yelled and gave the dog a push. The dog was instantly within its own length of the fox, which invariably turned all but wrong side out and went up the closest tree. On a large oak, apparently it was able to hook its nails into the rough bark and simply catapult itself up to the first branch. From there on it would go clear to the top if it elected to, with no difficulty whatever. Hunters who have long chased gray foxes know that they will often run up leafy trees and hide among foliage. Although this climbing ability is interesting, it is not a clever way for a fox to attempt to save its hide. A gray has been known to stand on a bare limb, when that was all that was offered, barely out of reach of a leaping dog and in plain sight of surrounding hunters. That makes it exceedingly vulnerable.

The red fox, generally considered as more crafty and intelligent than the gray, also makes itself unwittingly vulnerable at times. In snow country, when it tires of hunting or daylight comes, it may bed down right out in an open field, or with only a bush or two nearby. With tail curled around to cover feet and nose, it goes to sleep—and a still-hunter glassing the fields can spot it instantly because of its striking color contrast against the snow.

Red foxes seldom take refuge from bitter weather in a den. The gray, which prefers more temperate weather and is used to hiding or resting in rock crevices or other denning places, often retires to these protected spots during cold snaps or during a blizzard in its more northerly range. This is not actually hibernation. When the weather settles or it gets too hungry, it moves out to hunt again.

The movements of foxes are generally wider in fall than at other times of year. This is not because there is a greater need for food, but because families begin to break up at that time. Each fox must now stake out its own hunting area and home. To be sure, there are often several using the same general area, but a dispersal period during fall pushes family groups widely apart because of the basic and instinctive need to make certain each has hunting room. During this period foxes "on the loose" may move 20, 30, even 40 miles from where they were born. The dispersal distance depends to a great extent upon the food situation, and upon the current fox population of the area. It is these fall dispersals that over many centuries influenced foxes to broaden their range to the utmost tolerable potential.

## BREEDING

There is a second roaming time. This occurs in winter when foxes begin to seek mates and pair off for breeding. This period occurs from late December among reds to February among grays. Males travel widely if necessary in order to find a mate. Foxes have a musk gland atop the tail which exudes a strong odor not pleasant to the human nose. The gland of the gray fox is much longer than that of the red, but the musk of the red fox is decidedly stronger. This distinctive smell undoubtedly identifies individual foxes to others, and is used year-round to let the animals know of the presence of others. Undoubtedly it plays a part in the location of mates.

Like most of the wild dogs, foxes are quite ardent about their lovemaking and remain mated and together from the time of mate selection on through the year until the breakup of the resulting family. There are vicious fights now and then between males vying for the same mate. But when the matter is settled mates are inseparable, the pairs running together. At this time of year hunters in snow country discover paired tracks making hunting rounds. The animals are also at this time unusually vocal.

Foxes are capable of uttering a wide variety of sounds. During mating season the female usually makes a whining or crying sound in answer to the yap or bark of the male. Sometimes they bark back and forth to each other even when only a short distance apart. Much of the barking of foxes is heard during mating. The sound is a short, sharp yap repeated several times in series. Later on in summer they may bark also, when the young are beginning to try to hunt and the family must keep in touch.

Both red and gray foxes also hiss and growl. The growl of even the most pint-sized gray fox heard at close range for the first time is a hair-raiser. Animal callers after grays often have the experience of a fox coming in close at night and then becoming suspicious, yet reluctant to leave. It will stand unseen in the darkness and growl with a volume that one would imagine could only come out of a ferocious animal twenty times the size. It is believed this tactic is an attempt to frighten the "unknown" into showing itself. The fox won't come closer, but wants to know what's going on.

During the several days the female is in heat, mating occurs several times, but only with the chosen mate. A denning site is now selected. Red foxes are inclined to look for old burrows once used by woodchucks or badgers out in open fields or on ridgesides from which there is a broad surrounding view. The site is sometimes, but not always, quite well concealed, and there are usually several entrances, or exits, with trails leading to them from several directions. Fox dens used year after year are often appropriated each season presumably by different pairs that happen to find them.

Gray fox dens may be in rocks, or also old burrows. The female does the selecting for both species, cleans up the place and readies it for the family soon to arrive. On occasion a gray fox may make its den in a hollow log, or even above ground in a hollow limb of a tree. Fox dens are usually lined with dry grass or other nest material available, the chambers may be enlarged, and the animals begin to use them well before the birth of the young. Ordinarily the female stays inside the den while resting, and the male stands watch nearby, dozing intermittently as it lies on a ledge or a hummock or ridgeside from which it can view the vicinity.

### BIRTH AND DEVELOPMENT

The young are born approximately 7½ weeks after the mating. Depending on latitude, they arrive from about mid-March to as late as May in some instances. The number of young is highly variable, but on the average the red fox's litters are larger than those of the gray. An exceptional red fox litter numbers as many as ten, that of the gray perhaps five. Most litters of both are smaller.

Baby foxes are born with eyes sealed shut, weigh only 3 or 4 ounces, and are dark-colored and almost hairless. They are unable even to crawl when newborn, but within several days they begin to move about a bit. During the first couple of weeks the female must stay with them almost constantly. The male hunts and brings food to her. The eyes of the little ones open during this period. By the end of the first month the young foxes are comic, fluffy, active youngsters, and the mother leaves for brief forays. At roughly five weeks of age the kits begin to take their first brief trips outside the den entrance for a look at the world they'll soon enter.

For a time the mother leaves only for short periods. It is interesting that the instinct of the young tells them not to stray. They are exceedingly playful, are busy every minute tumbling and biting at each other. But they are also alert instinctively to danger and will scurry into the den if frightened by any unusual sight or sound. Actually foxes both young and adult have few natural enemies. Hawks, owls, and eagles account for a few young. Other wild dogs of larger size, the coyote and wolf, and also the wild cats, kill foxes if the opportunity is presented. But apparently the fox is not relished as food by any other animal. They are prone to a number of diseases, the chief one as concerns man being rabies.

During the weeks while the swiftly growing offspring are flexing their muscles around the den vicinity, the female extends her hunting trips somewhat. Both parents fetch food for the young, and in time begin to bring in living creatures when that is possible. These the youngsters learn to kill and rip apart. It is a basic of their training for the predatory life.

When they are roughly two months old they are left at the den much of the time by themselves. The parents resume hunting for long periods. They must hunt in daytime as well as at night to keep themselves and the litter fed. But now the mother rather automatically weans the kits because she is away for hours at a time, and when she returns they are eager for the forage she and the male bring in.

At the end of the third month the young foxes are ready to start testing themselves on hunts with their parents. Trips for the entire family grow longer; when half-grown foxes learn to make kills of their own and to sample the variety of food eaten by their parents. By late summer or on into the fall the family begins to break up. The young drift off more and more, individually or as a group, or part of them hunting together. Finally they have dispersed each on its own, and the parents, with no ties now to hold them, also drift away from each other. Neither may be a total loner over the next several months, but there will not be the close relationship between adults again until another mating season begins.

### SENSES

It is difficult to say which of the senses of a fox is the most important or most highly developed. Probably the sense of smell is the most useful in its daily hunting, and it is astonishingly keen. But scenting ability, which allows trailing prey by scent by all the wild dogs, is but a part of the battery of senses that are all brought to focus in the art of making a daily living.

Numerous nature writers and wildlife researchers have stated that a fox can hear the squeak of a mouse at astonishing distances. When the intriguing sport of animal calling began to develop and became popular on a national scale, foxes were the chief targets simply because they ranged in modest to abundant population over most of the continent. Foxes are rather easily called, except for individual animals that have had bad experiences with callers.

Hundreds of successful animal callers can attest that the lowest-volume squeak can be picked by a fox at many yards.

In fact, it is common practice to use a predator call that mimics the sound of an injured rabbit in a loud squall as a long-range appeal. Then, when a fox has raced in close but is hesitant to come closer, a mouse-squeak call is employed. It is blown so quietly that a man at 10 yards cannot hear it, but a fox often picks up the sound and moves stealthily in from 50 yards or more distant. One caller, with a camouflage net thrown over him, had a gray fox tiptoe in close and then pounce on him as he squeaked the call.

A superior sense of smell is of course the basic need for trailing or locating hidden prey. But hearing may take over at close range and is almost on a par with scenting ability. These two senses can in fact sustain a fox when it cannot see at all. On a Texas ranch, for example, a workman with a .22 rifle in his pickup saw a fox trotting up a trail toward him. It came closer and closer until it was only a few feet away. Thinking it must be rabid, he picked up the rifle and shot it—and was chagrined to discover that the fox, fat and apparently in good health, was totally blind.

Ordinarily, eyesight of foxes is excellent. Like other wild dogs, they are colorblind. This is not necessarily a handicap and perhaps may even make their simpler world of sight more easily deciphered. The eyes, as in all dogs, are set well focused ahead because of the need to trail and to watch prey distantly. The eyes of the gray fox are dark, those of the red fox yellow.

**SIGN** (*Tracks are illustrated on page 255.*)

The presence of foxes may occasionally be indicated by their yapping bark. In snow country and during snow season fox tracks are evidence, but in other seasons and over much of the domain of the foxes tracks are not readily spotted. The animals are not heavy enough to leave an imprint as plain, for example, as that of the coyote, and the material over which they travel, such as dry leaves, earth, or grass, does not register the imprints.

Where tracks may be seen, they are not especially difficult to identify. The trail laid down by a walking red fox is very nearly a straight line. That is, each footprint is almost, but not quite, straight ahead of the last one imprinted. When the animal runs, the hind-foot imprints are ahead of those of the forefeet, spread apart and staggered, with the forefoot imprints almost one behind the other. Gray fox trails appear slightly more staggered at a walk, although the bounding imprints are similar.

The footprints are much like those of a small dog. The forefoot is rather widely spread, the hind foot hardly at all. The red fox forefoot print is about 2½ inches long, that of the hind foot slightly smaller. Gray fox tracks are usually a bit smaller, but the pads of the individual toes make larger prints than those of the red fox. Now and then an observer cannot decide whether a fox or some cat such as a housecat or a small bobcat has made the tracks in question. The distinguishing characteristic is the lack of claw marks in cat tracks, because the animals walk with claws retracted, whereas the nails of foxes invariably leave their marks.

Sometimes fox dens give ready evidence of the presence of foxes. Red fox dens are the most likely to be spotted, because so often they are in fields, or on an open ridgeside. Gray fox dens are in most secluded places as a rule.

Probably the most quickly spotted signs of either fox species is its droppings. Foxes leave their scats conspicuously along a trail or road, in plain sight. They are much smaller in diameter than the scats of the coyote, on the average each segment 2 to 3 inches long, and tapered on each end.

What the individual animal has been eating affects the color and consistency. Hair and feathers are commonly evident. In fruit season fruit pits and seeds may be. Climbing gray foxes usually show more evidence of seedy fruits having been eaten. In the southwest, where the ringtail and gray fox consort on the same range, the ringtail scat can be distinguished because the animal invariably deposits it atop a rock, even a very small one. Scats of similar size to those of foxes, but with a preponderance of insect carapaces in them, are probably signs left by skunks.

HUNTING

Unquestionably the most popular method of fox hunting nowadays is calling. This is because it allows almost anyone to pursue the pastime. In most gray fox country it is easy to find a hiding place and bring the fox in close to the caller. In calling reds, the country is often more open, longer shots can be made, and one must select hiding places more carefully. Most callers agree that the red fox is warier than the gray.

The basics of calling are simple. The hunter calls at one spot for perhaps twenty minutes, then moves at least half a mile. In snow country one should dress in a white parka and even cover the gun with white tape. Elsewhere standard camouflage clothing should be worn, with net gloves and headnet of camo cloth a good idea. A variety of arms may be employed, depending on the situation. Some call foxes just for the experience, or to photograph them. Others are after fur. Fur hunters should use a bullet that won't spoil the pelt, and place it carefully. At long range a good choice is the .222. Shorter shots can be made with a caliber such as the .22 magnum. In either case it is best to employ a scope for meticulous bullet placement.

When a calling stand is selected, if any breeze is moving the caller must be facing into or across it. Even then a fox will circle to get the wind on the caller. Still days or nights are best. The hunter should move to his chosen stand very quietly and carefully. Some start calling with a loud squall to cover a lot of range. However, others start with a mouse-squeak type call, just in case a fox happens to be close. If there is no result, then the loud call is blown in a series. When a fox is spotted coming in, if it is a red it may streak right across open areas. A gray will zigzag through cover as a rule.

All fox and predator calls have instructions with them, and there are calling instruction records to study and books on calling that will be helpful. For those who do not wish to blow a call, tape players with tapes of various sounds that appeal to foxes are numerous, also with instructions. For night calling, where legal, a headlamp and a bright spotlight must be used. The headlamp, with beam uptilted so only a glow is cast on the ground, is used to pick up the eyes of a fox or its shadowy movement. Then if shooting is to be done, the bright light is turned on the quarry.

Hound men, of course, look down their noses at callers. They love to run their dogs, and many of them are not much interested in killing the fox. This is a dramatic sport, but of course it is only for those who can own and keep and train dogs, or have friends who do. It is doubtful that one can locate many guides throughout the country who specialize in booking hunters for fox runs with dogs. The other hound sport, of the club sort with horses and dressage and all the ceremony, is exceedingly restricted to memberships, and there is not much of this royal hunting presently in the United States.

The real purist fox hunters are those who walk fox tracks when snow is on. This hunting is almost entirely for red foxes. The technique has been fine-honed by a few enthusiasts who wear white and camouflage their rifles in white. This is a matter of picking up a fresh fox track and following it, pausing often to use binoculars to scan the fields and woods edges. Sometimes a fox can be picked out bedded down and asleep. Or it is seen actually hunting. Every speck of cover must be used; movement must be slow and glassing acute. True, no great number of foxes is taken thus, but the challenge and difficulty of the hunt make it thrilling.

A very few hunter groups, particularly in the northeast, organize fox drives. Several hunters meander through a woodlot without making undue racket, hoping that any fox bedded down in the area will move ahead and try to slip away out the far side, where cohorts placed downwind are waiting. This is occasionally a successful maneuver, an enjoyable undertaking for a group, and good exercise, but it is no easy way to collect fox hides.

That technique also is aimed chiefly at the red fox. Still hunting or driving gray foxes in most of their haunts is a waste of time. The cover is too dense and the animals too reluctant to show themselves. Sometimes, of course, dens can be located that grays habitually use in winter. As previously mentioned, they use the protection of dens more than reds do. A stand within sight of a den may pay off with a trophy. Hunting grays with dogs that push them hard is easier than the same with red foxes. The gray tires quickly and dens or trees and is often quickly dispatched.

Foxes of both species have demonstrated over many decades that they are tenacious creatures are easily brought to dangerously low populations by trapping, hunting, bounties, or even poisons. Little by little they have won full-fledged game status over much of their vast range, with seasonal protection. It is unlikely that the fur market's demand will ever put excessive pressure on them, and their depredations upon domestic poultry and stock are so inconsequential except in extremely isolated individual instances that no severe pressures are brought upon them by their more numerous human neighbors. The foxes are in no way presently endangered, and it is virtually assured that these intelligent, interesting animals will still be featured alive in the wild as well as in song, story, and tall tales for as long as there are rodents to pounce upon and wild grapes available that may or may not be sour.

# Coyote

*Canis latrans*

This wild dog so thoroughly a part of the history of the western United States was named *coyotl* by the Aztecs. The Spaniards and Mexicans changed this, in their tongue, to "ki-*o*-tay," gently accenting the second syllable. By the time the western cowboy had conveniently abbreviated what to him was prissy "foreign" pronunciation, the word became "*ki*-oat," heavy accent on the first syllable.

The coyote currently sports a thoroughly confused status both among those who know it intimately and among those who don't. It is despised by many a rancher wholly frustrated by federal big-brother regulations that too thoroughly protect it. It is unreasonably revered and beloved by romantic, city-dwelling, faddish wildlife fetishists, most of whom have never seen or heard one yet clamor loudly against any rational control. The calmer folk in the middle know the ubiquitous coyote as unquestionably one of the most interesting wildlife species on the continent.

The coyote is the smallest of the North American wolves. In some parts of its range it is occasionally called the "brush wolf" or "prairie wolf." It is less than half the size, on the average, of the true wolf—that is, the gray or timber wolf, *Canis lupus*. It is slightly smaller than the red wolf, *C. niger*. Yet curiously, because of its wily tenacity and adaptability, in modern times it has been vastly more successful than either of the larger species.

The gray wolf, once supremely abundant over virtually the entire continent and divided by taxonimists into more than twenty subspecies, today is believed to be wholly extirpated from the contiguous states, except for a few remnants in the west and southwest, all questionable, and for a known population oasis in the northern Great Lakes area, chiefly northern Minnesota. Canada and Alaska have substantial wolf populations in some areas, and a few are even hunted as game animals. But the gray wolf situation today—and undoubtedly for the long future—is such that this big predator cannot remotely be viewed as a game animal.

The outlook for the red wolf is far more precarious. This interesting animal, which few casual wildlife observers of today have ever even heard of, let alone seen, was once abundant in both its tawny and black phases from Florida to Texas and over much of the Mississippi Valley region at least as far north as Illinois. Today it is believed extinct except for a population of possibly less than 100 animals in several small pockets along the Texas-Louisiana border. Even on the fringes of these it has so thoroughly intergraded with the abundant coyote that researchers fear that few pure-strain animals may remain.

Attempts are being made to try to establish a captive and semicaptive breeding population of red wolves and thus perhaps reintroduce them to certain areas of their original range and save the species from extinction. The intricacies of the program are intriguing. The live trapping in itself is a delicate and complicated procedure, to make certain the animals do not injure themselves. They have been trapped and tranquilized simultaneously by attaching the tranquilizer potion to the trap; the animal chews it and thus is dosed.

A team from the so-called Red Wolf Recovery Program, launched in 1971, then tries to determine positively whether the animal is a true red wolf, a coyote, or a hybrid. Skull X-rays, measurements, and weighing help in identification. Possibly more important are sonographic voice prints that are made of the howls of each animal taken.

Red wolves are being bred in a Washington State zoo, and a pair was released in 1976 in the Cape Romain National Wildlife Refuge,

# The Coyote

Bull's Island, South Carolina. This region was once part of their native range, and it is hoped they may adapt to it and breed there. Eventually, the program people believe it just may be possible to reestablish a wild breeding population in a few carefully selected locations. At best, if successful over future years, this will mean an expensive, brink-of-extinction existence for this animal comparable to that of the whooping crane.

Meanwhile, the wily coyote could hardly have been doing better. It made its name, and assumed arbitrarily assigned uncomplimentary human characteristics, during the shoot-'em-up days of

## THE COYOTE

COLOR: Variable, from reddish or yellowish tan to distinctly pale gray, grizzled especially on upper parts by black-tipped guard hairs; darker sometimes in wavy lines along back and top of tail; tail tip very dark; chin, throat, and underparts pale to whitish.

MEASUREMENTS: Overall length rather variable by local range or latitude, averaging, adult male, from 3½ to 4½ feet, with the outstretched tail 1 to 1½ feet of the total; height at shoulder 1½ to 2 feet or more; females slighly smaller as a rule.

WEIGHT: 20 to 30 pounds, usually less than 30; exceptional specimens, chiefly northern, authenticated very occasionally at 50, 60, 70 pounds.

GENERAL ATTRIBUTES: Coat coarse, shaggy, rough as compared to softer fur of fox and wolf; face and nose narrow, pointed, sharp, foxlike compared to broader, more powerful snout of wolf; size midway between fox and wolf; ears sharply pointed and distinctly erect when cocked; intelligent mien; general build, body and legs, slenderer than domestic dogs that may resemble coyotes; extremely wary, canny, tenacious.

the early west. Readers of endless western stories know well that when the white hat—or the black hat, as the case might be—is braced by an antagonist, one or the other is almost certain to exclaim, "Draw, you mangy ki-oat, and I'll spread yore innards from here to the corral!" Or something like that.

Mangy the coyote often was, and is. But the term "coyote," used derogatorily by the usually fictional cowpoke in a fuss, was intended to indicate that the gent at which the epithet was hurled was a low-down, sneaky, shifty varmint. And further, that he was a sniveling coward.

Why the coyote was tagged with such traits has never been quite clear. Shifty it is, if by that one means sharp, crafty, and awesomely adept at dodging traps and poisons. Sneaky it may be also, if this is synonymous with getting in and out of scrapes—as in raiding a flock of sheep, perhaps—and getting away with a whole hide. Cowardly the coyote is also, if judging by general human standards the better part of valor is to fade away from danger and run rather than make a stand.

In fact, the coyote is indeed a runner. It has been running for many decades until, from its main launch point on the western plains and the southwestern deserts, it has quite literally overrun practically the entire continent. During the early exploration and later throughout the heyday of western open-ranged cattle and the historic cattle drives, the coyote was thought of as strictly a western animal. Later as notes of wide-flung observers were pieced together it was discovered that probably the original range before the intrusion of the white man extended from parts of Mexico and California eastward to eastern Texas, thence northward over all of the territory north possibly into Wisconsin, and then in a huge triangle between there and northern Alberta and back down to northern California.

This eliminated the upper west coast, most of Canada, all of Alaska, and the entire region east of the Mississippi River and some area west of it in the Ozarks and Louisiana. The elimination of the gray wolf, which was an enemy of the coyote and killed it on sight, when opportunity arose, may have been an influence that allowed the coyote to enlarge its range by filling that void. It has been claimed here and there that coyotes and gray wolves occasionally interbreed. Most scientists believe this is highly doubtful. The wolf at any rate disappeared as the buffalo did, and further because of incessant persecution—or control, whichever side one takes—by stockmen.

It seems almost believable that the coyote followed, or moved with, human settlement. Possibly it actually did, or was at least assisted by settlement. Whatever the influences, the more man extended his presence, the more the coyote appeared along its environs. By the time the Alaska gold rush was over, coyotes were well established there, where they had never before been known. By the early decades of this century they were fairly common eastward in the Great Lakes states as far as over all of northern Michigan. They were abundant enough there by the 1950s so that sportsmen specialists wearing snowshoes and following burly hounds avidly hunted them in winter.

During the period from the 1930s onward there were reports of coyotes as far east as New York and New England. There was much argument and guessing as to the true identity of the doglike creatures occasionally seen in those regions. Subsequently some were proved to be "coy-dogs," crosses between the coyote and domestic dogs. Coyotes have long been known to occasionally romance dogs when they live near them, and the crosses were and are not rare. But more and more of the eastern animals proved eventually to be authentic coyotes.

Presently the coyote has long been well established from a vast portion of Mexico and Central America clear to the Arctic Ocean and the bottom of James Bay. Its range blankets British Columbia, all of the U.S. west coast, and most of southern Canada at least into Quebec. All of the U.S. west is covered, plus the Ozarks, the Great Lakes region, and eastward. Although not abundant in most of the east, coyotes have been reported all the way from Maine to Florida, and are moderately common in New York State.

This astonishing modern colonization would not seem so striking if it were not for the fact that over all these years, from the day of the early trapper and then the stockman to the present, landowners often aided by government programs have tried, at times rather desperately, to eliminate the coyote, or at the very least to reduce its numbers. It is now admitted in most scientific circles that elimination is probably not possible, and that reasonable population level control probably is, but not without a constant battle. Cowardly? The astute animal seems more likely an expert in future planning and coyote demography!

Arguments of the self-styled wildlife experts that a high coyote population does no harm and that nature will balance things are, in our modern day, when man has already irrevocably changed any semblance of natural balance, ridiculous. Control attempts have long been in vogue. At one time when the virulent 1080 poison was in use, ranches in southern Texas, for example, had huge hunks of 1080-injected horse meat staked out at intervals. This method was partially successful in control, although many coyotes soon wised up. This poison was subsequently outlawed because it was progressive. Anything that ate whatever was killed by it also died, in chain reaction. The so-called coyote-getter, a baited pipe set into the ground that, when the bait was tugged, shot a dose of quick-acting poison into the coyote's mouth, also proved effective, and much more selective. The federal government in 1972 outlawed this also on federal lands.

Hunting from small planes, a rather effective control method, was in addition made illegal almost everywhere. Both were eliminated because of outcries from emotional self-styled environmentalists who knew utterly nothing firsthand of the problems. Coyotes that had at least been kept under modest control made a tremendous population upsurge almost everywhere. Schemes to use pregnancy suppressants and impotency compounds were toyed with.

It must be emphasized that neither landowners nor wildlife managers have ever wished to wipe out the coyote population totally. The animals act as vital control agents themselves, on jack rab-

# Range of the Coyote

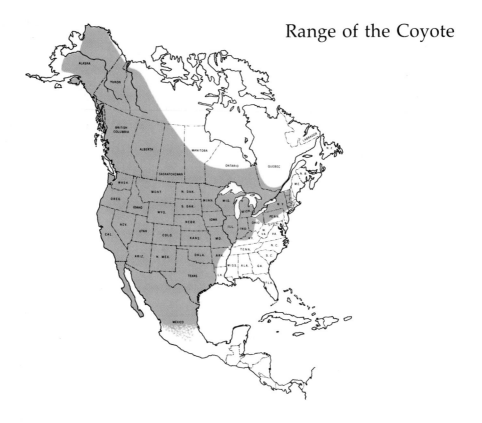

bits that at high cycles rob a range of an astonishing percentage of stock forage, and on numerous rodents. Indeed, it has been rather well proved in careful studies that not all coyotes cause serious depredations. Much depends on their food-supply situation and their location. It is well known, however, that *individual* coyotes definitely become stock and game killers. Landowners and wildlife managers alike favor the individual-elimination approach, plus basic overall control to keep coyote populations from eruptions that are certain to cause trouble.

Some of the endless and intricate studies that have been performed are interesting. One, a federal-state cooperative effort, was launched in several western states in 1974 and continued for several years. On one study area in New Mexico, for example, where predator numbers were found to be low, nonetheless the loss to coyotes of the sheep crop was a whopping 36.8 percent just during the study period. A twelve-month Montana study showed that 82 percent of sheep lost during the period were killed by coyotes, and that 75 percent of them were healthy animals. The New Mexico study was done by fitting lambs and adult sheep with what are known as mortality transmitters, which work by a motion-sensitive switch. While an animal is making any movement at all, there is no transmission signal. If there is no movement for a three-hour period, the signal begins. This allows researchers to quickly home in on the location of the animal, which is presumed to be — and invariably is — dead.

It is not difficult to tell from tracks and from the manner of kill what predator was involved, and, by amount of hemorrhaging under the skin at the wound site, whether or not predation is the cause of death or if a predator simply found an already dead animal. Many such studies unfailingly prove that coyotes are indeed a serious menace, especially to sheep and goats.

In the Hill Country of Texas, for example, a mohair goat raising region, predators had long been under severe control, but began to reappear when control procedures were outlawed. In a single night during 1976 one rancher lost more than forty kids to coyote depredation, and over a period of several weeks more than ninety sheep. The theory that coyotes take only weak, old, or sick animals is, as all stockmen know, nonsense. So is the false notion that a coyote kills only what it needs to eat. Many studies have shown that mutliple kills, if easy, are the rule.

In some studies on antelope, coyotes have been let off the hook as a controlling influence on substantial populations. One eastern-Montana study is an example. Conversely, in western Texas where the antelope population is not high, transplants of several hundred antelope to new range by the Parks and Wildlife Department had their kid crops literally wiped out by uncontrolled coyotes, and big northern coyotes in some regions of the northwest and east literally slaughter adult deer herds during periods of deep or crusted snow.

One curious occurrence regarding coyote depredation is that in instances of heavy populations on cattle ranges, particularly in the southwest and Mexico, although the coyotes cannot down adult cattle, they run among them incessantly, sometimes in groups, snapping chunks from their tails. In warm climates especially, infections begin and some of the cattle die, offering more forage for their tormentors.

Far more serious, rabies, to which coyotes are prone, is sometimes spread by them. During the winter of 1976–77, Laredo, Texas, had a serious outbreak of rabies, with dozens of city dogs infected, and a number of people bitten. It was established that the epidemic began with coyotes, which are so abundant in the brush lands around the city that they often brazenly forage within it, and have even been seen in the middle of the downtown area.

Over recent years in Los Angeles and its outlying towns and communities, coyotes have become both abundant and bold. They commonly have grabbed cats and small dogs and carried them off as forage. In one instance a family of coyotes was seen trotting along Sunset Boulevard. The Federal Wildlife Research Center in Denver, Colorado, which has done extensive research on coyote problems, claims that every major western metropolis today has its quota of the animals in residence. No other sizable predator has been able in modern times to so vastly enlarge its domain or to so successfully adapt and scheme to live partially by the fruits of man's civilization.

In many states bounties have been placed on coyotes for years. The bounty has proved a costly failure everywhere on all predators, with built-in opportunities for crooked shenanigans in collections. Fur prices and their fluctuations undoubtedly might have a more profound effect. During the early and middle 1970s, for example, wild-fur prices began to edge up and finally by 1975 and 1976 had skyrocketed. The coyote pelt, never much in demand or for that matter very useful or desirable because of its rough texture, became amazingly valuable. Coyote populations in some places were pared down by trappers and animal callers. If pelt values continue on a high and stable basis, or new uses are found for the fur, some of the coyote problem might be solved.

Certainly there is little chance of the coyote becoming a food item in demand. Long ago some Indian tribes used to eat them. The same peoples also considered dogs a delicacy. However, any modern white man who has ever inhaled the stout odor of a coyote, or skinned one, is not likely to bring it to the kitchen. The canny coyote, whatever human friends or enemies may do or say, is on this continent for keeps, for as long as we are here and probably long after. For that matter, no one would want — no one does want — the eerie song of the coyote removed from evenings and dawns over the long plains and deserts, and the woodlands to which it has adapted. Considering the massive expanse of its present-day range, anyone almost anywhere willing to go to a bit of trouble or travel can experience the thrill of listening to that wild sound.

## HABITAT

It is in fact that vastness of the coyote's domain that makes difficult or impossible a concise description of its habitat. Over its original range the coyote was a creature chiefly of the brush and cactus of southwestern deserts and the grassy sweeps of the open plains. It might be said aptly that the coyote never has cared much where it lived, as long as forage was available. Because, like all dogs, it is a runner, a chaser, a trailer, open spaces with long views were natural for it, and so were the dense mottes of thornbrush broken by patternless openings that typically represent American desert country.

Yet that does not give a true picture of where the coyote lives, because, to repeat, it can live anywhere a living is afforded. Today in the immense expanses of eastern New Mexico, for example, representative in many parts of it of poor cattle range, the coyote does well. In southern Texas along and spreading out from the Mexican border, a country of undulating, seemingly endless reaches dense with the low growth of cactus and chaparral, coyotes are extremely abundant.

In the grassy valleys of stream courses in the Rockies — prime examples are those within Yellowstone Park, with the valley of the Madison River typical — the coyote, usually in a pale-gray color, thrives. Representative of the habitat where Great Lakes states hunters have long pursued coyotes are the mixed forests of the northern Lower Peninsula of Michigan. Here the virgin pine was cut a century ago and was replaced by second growth that eventually became a mature forest of poplar, birch, and maple mixed with various evergreens — balsam, hemlock, cedar, jack pine.

A native from the deserts of southern Arizona or from the long country of rippling grass and grain in South Dakota could hardly visualize a coyote roaming such woodlands as those of the Great Lakes, or of the similar habitat of New York State. A trapper from the early fur days who had often gone to sleep on the peopleless plains to the yipping and wailing of prairie wolves could hardly believe the sight of coyotes in the settled, brushy canyons surrounding Los Angeles, or for that matter in the rain forest of the Pacific Coast, or the scenic but forbidding reaches of vast mountains and valleys in Alaska.

In the northern U.S. Rockies, coyotes in moderate numbers commonly laze out the summers at timberline, while others of their tribe are earning their livelihood far below in the foothills. Others are hiding in stream-slashed woodlands of the Ozarks, or panting in the heat of western Oklahoma's all but treeless terrain. Indeed, notwithstanding the popular concept of the coyote's homeland as set forth in western story and song, the fact is that there is really no "typical" habitat niche that it fills.

### FEEDING

Rabbits and rodents are the mainstay of living forage for the coyote, and they, too, are tied to no "typical" habitat. Coyotes chase snowshoe hares in the high-country west, and in the wooded states of the north and northeast. They have been living on jack rabbits for centuries, from the deserts of Arizona to the plains of the Dakotas and eastern Montana. The cottontail, as amazing and successful a colonizer as the coyote itself, is eaten by coyotes all the way from the Mexican border to the hilly woodlands of Missouri and the thickets of southern Canada.

Mice and various rats also have served to sustain the coyote and help it broaden its range, as land clearing and settlement made it possible for them also to expand and multiply. In portions of northern Mexico, for example, a coyote might live some seasons within a square mile and keep its belly full of pack rats, which make huge stick-mound nests with a burrow maze below them in prickly pear cactus clumps. Coyotes in packrat range, called in by animal callers, and killed and opened to discover what they had been eating, commonly have been found with as many as seven or eight still-undigested adult pack rats already in their stomachs.

Ground squirrels, in the sage country of Wyoming, for example, are often unbelievably abundant. It is no trick for a coyote to gorge on them. Nor is it difficult, from the coyote's viewpoint, for it to catch mice. One animal observed and photographed working a grassy stream meadow in Wyoming was seen to catch and devour six field mice while moving scarcely 50 yards, and within a mere fifteen minutes. No doubt the mice were plentiful that summer, but the coyote nonetheless gave a startling exhibition of its skill at catching them.

Although the coyote is fond of rabbits and rodents, and serves to some extent as a control upon their numbers, just as it seems not to be particular where it lives as long as food is available, so it also cares little what it eats. Or at least, although it undoubtedly has preferences, and enjoys hunting and staples, it will accept practically anything that is available. Though called a predator, the

*A coyote pounces on a nest of field mice. Rodents are favored items in its varied diet.*

coyote is wholly omnivorous. There is little question that its all-inclusive taste is the attribute that has allowed the animal to move into and sustain itself well on such an enormous and varied range.

In watermelon fields in Oklahoma, coyotes occasionally make serious inroads. One pair of coyotes known to be raiding and based on a prairie dog town in New Mexico also suddenly raided the garden of a nearby rancher, stripping tomato vines and a sweet corn patch, and then nosed about a corral and barn, chewing on the girth and stirrup straps of a saddle.

Wild fruits are eagerly eaten, anything from cactus fruits to wild cherries. Domestic sheep and goats, as mentioned earlier, are routinely utilized. So, when obtainable, are chickens and other poultry. The latter, of course, are simply incidental opportunities. Fish when catchable are relished, and crayfish, turtles, and frogs serve as the animal happens upon them. Snakes also are occasionally eaten, and of course birds of all kinds, adults, nestlings, and eggs.

Carrion is standard fare. Sometimes the coyote is blamed for killing calves, deer, and even elk that were dead before it found them. The enormous number of birds and animals large and small killed by automobiles along highways today has been a windfall for coyotes as well as buzzards and other carrion-eating creatures. It is common to see coyotes patrolling some main highways in the west where the kill of various animals is high—and also to see coyotes that have met the same fate while foraging. A hungry coyote will even feed on a dead member of its own species. A severe winter forces many a coyote to feed heavily on carrion. In turn, winter is the time when carrion is often most abundant, from game animals and livestock that have succumbed to cold and disease.

Although adult deer or antelope are difficult for a single coyote to handle, unless in deep snow, these crafty creatures are well known for ganging up. An illustration of their intelligence is strikingly evidenced when two or more hunt together. One or two may start a chase, while another or more than one lies in wait to take up the relay. A coyote cannot catch an antelope, running all out, but several running relays sometimes push one until it is exhausted and falls. Many times coyotes have been observed tricking jack rabbits by doubling up. One circles the rabbit while another jockeys sneakily into a position out ahead where it can intercept.

Another illustration of their cunning and intelligence is the way they sense that they may be able to dine on leftovers. In southern Colorado a hunter wounded a deer and was trailing it when he found coyote tracks also on the trail. Looking ahead, he saw distantly in an open area two of them with the deer down and finishing it off. A coyote has been known to trail a larger predator, such as a bear or mountain lion, to pick up leftover scraps or raid a cache.

Like foxes, the coyote will eat grasshoppers when they swarm on the plains. They also now and then eat grass, and grain, even when not pressed by shortages. In the southwest, mesquite beans are a staple at times. In other words, wherever found the coyote is a fulltime opportunist, with no guilt complexes about stealing from other creatures or backing off when suspicious that trouble may come from insistence. Certainly such tactics do make the coyote seem in human view sneaky and cowardly, but then, they have served its tribe exceedingly well.

Most students of wildlife refer to the coyote as nocturnal. That is only partially true. The major share of its hunting is done at night, probably because the animal's senses are so acute that it can hunt as well then as by day, and has the advantage of darkness to cover its movements. However, coyotes even in good times for them often hunt by day. This was proved emphatically when animal calling, with the coyote one of its main targets, became popular. Thousands of them have come on the run in daytime to the simulated squall of an injured rabbit. Anyone who has driven or hiked or hunted extensively in coyote country knows well that it is not at all uncommon to see one or more trotting nonchalantly along across a stretch of desert or plain, swinging here and there with nose low to pick up the scent of prey.

Even though this animal will eat almost anything, it is predominantly predaceous. One of the basics of the wildlife management not always understood by the casual observer is that though predators such as the coyote do serve as controls on small forage pest animals, curiously they in turn are almost totally controlled by their prey. When rabbits and rodents are on a high cycle, invariably coyotes thrive and multiply swiftly. The abundance of living forage builds healthy animals and then prolificness is thus enhanced. But superabundance of forage creatures is immediately an indication that they soon will see a sharp decline.

In 1957, for example, unusual rains came to most of the southwest after a severely damaging drought of almost seven years. Cottontails, jack rabbits, pack rats, cotton rats, and all other small animals, plus quail, literally erupted in unbelievable population peaks. These vegetarians quite literally mowed down greenery, which had also experienced explosive resurgence. By the end of the first growing season the predators, coyotes among them, gorging on this bonanza, were swarming also.

As the growing season ended the demand for food was so great among small creatures that rats, for example, were stripping scrub mesquites of bark from the ground to 6 to 8 feet above. The next spring the coyote upsurge doubled again. But by now the fall-off in forage was of disaster proportions. Yet somehow the abundant coyote population managed, and there were so many that breeding momentum during another spring produced a new high crop. By now the forage creatures were at low ebb, and a year later there was an utter crash in the coyote population.

Starving coyotes, with competition for livelihood severe, produced small or no litters, and adults were decimated as the debacle progressed. Such up-and-down cycles are well documented among wild animals. They are one cause invariably of increased predation by coyotes upon domestic animals. The incidence of individual stock-killer coyotes rises even during the normal levels of population whenever their natural food declines.

### MOVEMENTS

As with all animals, and especially predaceous ones, the matter of keeping a full stomach accounts for most of the coyote's travel. A square mile might do, depending on foraging conditions. However, the coyote is a lean, strong, agile creature; at a deceptively fast but easy trot it is capable of covering much ground, is intensely attentive to every sight, sound, and scent in its bailiwick, and on the average utilizes a much larger living space. Several square miles is normal, given a good food supply.

Except during mating season coyotes, like most dogs, seem to get along reasonably well with others of their kind, and so wanderings outside a home place are usual. If one meets another, the introduction is likely to be pleastant enough, perhaps a nose-touching and general sniffing. When food is scarce, of course the area patrolled increases in proportion. In forest and high-country situations, for example, the variety of food may be less, and the travel range much exaggerated. Trappers who have come to know individual coyotes by tracks with distinguishing characteristics have occasionally authenticated their visits to baited sites many miles apart.

The "shuffle" that occurs when families of young break up and move into territories of their own spreads the range, and induces individuals to keep moving until they settle where it apparently pleases them. Marked young have been found 50 to 100 miles from the tagging site the following year. A coyote having a difficult time making a living may travel region of 50 to 100 square miles.

Coyotes have been observed simply walking slowly, sniffing bushes or rocks here and there, even uncharacteristically with tail aloft much like a dog. But the trot is the basic gait, tail dropped or partially. The speed is approximately 10 to 12 miles an hour. It can be sustained endlessly. An observer watching the animal move along a trail or zigzag through brush cannot help being impressed with the effortlessness and the astonishing amount of distance quickly covered. Meanwhile, the animal is ever alert, ready to cock its ears, halt and watch distantly, or pounce on small prey.

The agility and instant reactions of the coyote are remarkable. Animal callers often are able to observe these. A coyote coming to call will suddenly cross the track of the caller left moving to the place where he hides. In a flash the animal wheels and is gone. Fast-sequence still photographs, and movies, have shown the astonishing agility when danger is sensed at close range. A coyote comes on the run toward the squalling rabbit call. It circles swiftly, within only a few yards, to try to get the wind on the location of the sound. The camera shutter begins clicking or the movie camera whirring. Literally in midair in the middle of a long bound, the coyote swaps ends, head swiveling meanwhile to keep eyes glued to the sound location. In a tawny blur it is gone.

At a lope a coyote probably moves along at 20 to 25 miles an hour. When pressed, it can do better than that, up to 35 or 40. This speed is impressive enough but the stamina of a coyote, for example before dogs, is incredible. In the heyday of coyote hunting with hounds in winter in northern Michigan, a few years ago, a group of hobbyists based at Indian River would go out on a bright, cold morning looking for fresh tracks that crossed a sideroad where a snowplow had made it possible to drive a vehicle. When a suitable track, fresh enough, was found, the dogs were turned loose.

Listening for the direction of the chase once the coyote was jumped, and studying a county map, attempts were then made to cut off the coyote by intercepting, a mile, or 2 or 3 miles, away on another trail. Men were posted here and there in likely crossing places. Often a chase continued all day, fresh hounds released and exhausted ones taken up. The hunters might give up toward dusk, winding up 15 or 20 miles from starting point, and no telling how many circling, wandering miles in between.

On one occasion a coyote was jumped by the dogs near Wolverine, a small village approximately 45 miles south of the Straits of Mackinaw. By nightfall the hunters, picked up periodically by vehicles and leapfrogged from place to place, were near Mackinaw City. The dogs, known to have run this far, were lost and the hunters returned home. Next day one of them got a call from someone in the Upper Peninsula. The dogs, barely able to walk, had been found there. The coyote had run all day, then finally decided to make a beeline across the frozen Straits and lose itself in the dense Upper Peninsula forests. It succeeded. The hounds were over 50 miles from where they had jumped the coyote.

When traveling the forage route, a coyote simply beds down wherever it feels the urge and is full enough to cease hunting. It seldom goes into a den hole or cave. It is content to lie down in the brush, or in heavy grass in snow country, just wherever moderate protection is afforded. When hunting, as mentioned earlier, several coyotes may travel together, a whole family of young and parents, or several adults that have joined forces, or, much of the year, a mated pair. There are also loners, some of which may have lost a mate or are still not mated, or for whimsical coyote reasons prefer the lonely life. On the whole, however, these are moderately gregarious animals, acting in the wild much the same as a group of neighborhood dogs.

## BREEDING

The breeding season, of course, sees heightened activity and travel, and to some extent a let-down in wariness of danger. Apparently there is no strict pattern of mating. That is, some pairs that have accepted each other at their first mating may remain paired for a lifetime, or until one or another dies. Others run together for a year or more, some only until a family is raised and grown and dispersed. Now and then a male may mate with more than one female and not be very attentive. Or one may be something of a rake and look for a new mate each year.

The loner male now and then gets into a battle with another male over a female. On the whole, however, the general pattern of coyote lives is for young adults to find and select mates, and then to stay together. The mating begins in most latitudes about January or February. During this time, because the animals are especially active, hunters in snow country who are specialists at this endeavor eagerly get into the woods. Mating time farther south is not always the same; it may even bit a bit later, or at least extend farther toward spring.

From the time of breeding until the young arrive is about two months, or a few days more. This places the majority of births during April. The period during which almost all females come into heat is spread over not more than eight weeks. Nature's scheme to make sure the race is perpetuated is seen in the fact that the males are in a period of "rut" for almost twice as long. Thus latitude and altitude differences, and normal and abnormal weather in any given year, allows the breeding of practically all females. This may be one of the reasons the coyote is such a capable and tenacious colonizer. In addition, a coyote a year old is able to breed. If it occurs that one does not find a mate, then of course it is two before another opportunity occurs.

Some persons with interest in but little experience with wild-life are under the impression that the famed "song" of the coyote is an accompaniment to the mating season. The animals do mutter and whine and growl to each other during that period. But the famous serenades of coyotes are a year-round part of their lives. Evening, during the night, and dawn are the dominant times it is heard. However, any unusual sound may launch a coyote into running through its unique repertoire.

The serenade usually begins with several short, low yapping barks and then sails into a high-pitched howl that may span two octaves, with whines and barks intermingled. Many a listener has believed that a half-dozen animals were all "singing" simultaneously, when only a single one is carrying on. The performance is difficult to describe because the various sounds are so intricately interwoven. Once heard, however, it is never forgotten, nor is there any other animal sound—from fox or wolf for example—that is remotely comparable.

In country where coyotes are abundant, when one or a pair begins, it is common to hear others from several compass points join in, as if saying, "We hear you, and we're right over the hill." Interestingly, as many an animal caller has learned to his frustration, when a call is blown one or more coyotes may instantly launch into their routines, even at times very close to the caller. Many a tyro caller has had his heart begin thumping and has hunkered down close, believing the animals are coming on the run. What they are actually doing is laughing derisively. When coyotes begin to bark and howl at the sound of a call, it means, "We know you're there and we aren't going to be fooled!" At any rate, though the presence of coyotes on any range, and even their general abundance or lack of it, can be ascertained by a listener to their evening, moonlight, and dawn serenades—and even at times during daytime—the sound has no special relationship to the mating season.

After mating, the pair begins to prepare the den site. It may be a den used previously by the same pair, or either one. The female may dig a new den, or even several before she is satisfied. Or an old burrow of a badger or a fox den may be taken over and enlarged. Now and then coyotes den in forests in large hollow logs, or among the protective spreading roots of a blowdown. A below-surface den, however, is the rule. The animals are strong diggers, but must utilize soil not too hard and rocky. The den tunnel may be as much as 2 feet across, and extend anywhere from a few feet to 25 or more. At its end the nest chamber is enlarged, but it is not lined with grass or leaves, as fox dens often are.

The site for a den may be selected on a slope, or the bank of a stream, or out on the open prairie where an eroded cut allows digging into it high on a protected side. Dirt from a dug den is hauled back to the entrance and heaped around it outside. The den itself is kept clean, the animals coming outside beyond the den entrance, or pausing before entering, to deposit their droppings.

## BIRTH AND DEVELOPMENT

The coyote is at times an astonishingly prolific animal. Although the average litter is fix or six, a great many litters are much larger, ten or a dozen. Several naturalists have noted as many as fifteen to nineteen births at one time. Such large litters, of course, occur only among parents in excellent health and with optimum feeding conditions.

In most coyote families the dog stays nearby but apart from the female during a brief period before the birth of the young. From there on, though he has little if anything to do directly with his offspring, and is not tolerated right away, he must bring food to provide for the family. The baby coyotes are blind and unable to move around at all for a few days. Before they are two weeks old their eyes open, and now they begin to crawl about the den chamber. Their bodies are lightly clothed in very short grayish or brownish fur.

With a large litter, the female at first can do little hunting, but soon she makes short forays. The male meanwhile leaves his food offerings at the den entrance but is seldom welcome farther than that. When the youngsters are about 1½ months old, they make their first tentative ventures outside. They romp playfully, and as they grow they cement a strong family bond. They may wander briefly, but find their way back along their own trail by scent. These instinctive lessons in trailing are a first evidence of what will soon come.

Both male and female coyotes regurgitate partially digested food for the growing young, in this manner making the first steps in weaning them from the mother. Soon they are tearing at rabbits or mice or carrion brought to the den. When they are roughly two months of age the male begins to see more and more of them without objection by the female. In a short time the whole family goes hunting together.

Of course the pups are all feet at first. They don't really have any idea of what they are up to, except they know that following parents, falling down, yipping, and running hither and yon are fun. Presently, however, the smells and sightings of possible food excite them as much as their parents. They watch the successful hunts of the adults and presently are making kills of their own, at first in a bumbling fashion but with ever increasing fierceness and adeptness. The den where they were born has long been forgotten. They do not return to it—or seldom do—after full weaning.

By fall they are partially grown, gangling sub-adults. Some families may continue hunting together much of the first winter. Among most groups, the young wander off to establish new hunting grounds of their own. This is partially an instinctive dispersal, to be sure there is enough food to go around. A good many youngsters don't make it through those first weeks or months alone. They are fairly easy prey for dogs and hunters, and naive about calls unless they have been with parents that have had bad experiences and thus shun those sounds. Many are killed by other animals, or perhaps struck by vehicles while crossing highways. By the end of the year most families are fully scattered, and it will soon be time for adults to start once more the annual process of making certain their race continues.

### SENSES

Because the coyote is a trailer and chaser, rather than a stalker and pouncer like the wild cats, unquestionably its sense of smell is its most important equipment for making a living. This sense is uncannily keen. The animal can easily follow a trail even of small rodents. It can scent one out from heavy grass or other cover, or even in a burrow below ground. Its nose incessantly monitors the slightest breeze, censors it for possible danger and picks up knowledge of distant prey. The animal is exceedingly adept at the close stalk as well as the chase. It may not be able to actually catch a jack rabbit in a chase, because the rabbit dodges too agilely. But a coyote will trail such prey, then make a flat-bellied crawl the last few feet, and with a rush and snapping of strong jaws take it in.

Coyotes are also equipped with superior hearing. The squeak of a mouse, the call of a distant quail, the whisper of brush against a hunter's clothing—it misses nothing. Between scent and hearing it has a dual battery of monitors that feed endless information to it. In addition, eyesight is on a par with hearing. The eyes of a coyote are somewhat different in shape from those of the foxes. Yellow in color, with a dark center, the pupil is round instead of slitted vertically. The eyes are set for excellent straight-ahead vision, like those of all long-trailers and chasers. Distance as well as close vision is superb, and this serves perfectly because of the open character of much of the animal's hunting ground, the plains, the deserts, and foothills.

**SIGN** *(Tracks are illustrated on page 255.)*

The "yodeling" of the coyote might be considered a sign of sorts, telling of its presence. The sound, however, is not always heard where the animals are present. Oddly, in places where they are constantly disturbed by having man as a neighbor, and where they skulk like tawny wraiths in the dusk on the fringes of human domains, they learn to keep quiet, the better to conceal their presence.

Coyote tracks are commonly seen in the southwest, in trails along ranch roads and arroyos where the dirt is soft enough to take their imprint. They are also plainly printed in snowy portions of their range in winter. Elsewhere—in woodlands, for example—the ground is not as likely to record their passing. The tracks can be mistaken for those of a dog, which they resemble, except that in most places dogs would not be roaming where the coyote dwells.

Nail prints show plainly in proper materials, such as wet ground, and the front foot print is larger than the rear, the track measuring when plainly imprinted about 2½ inches long. When moving at a trot, the tracks appear in series of two, one not quite behind the other, the hind-foot print of each pair ahead of the front. At a moderate run or lope, they resemble the pattern made by dogs, each group of four prints canted slightly at an angle, again with the hind feet making prints one and three.

Droppings are habitually deposited along trails or old roads and especially at the juncture of two trails. It must be remembered that the size of individual coyotes differs substantially, and thus both tracks and scats may. However, average-sized adults leave droppings several inches long and at least an inch, sometimes more, in diameter. Where rabbits and rodents are in good supply, this diet staple shows up in the scat, which is compacted with hair. Quite often there are scratches left in dirt where a coyote has paused to leave droppings or to urinate, made with the hind feet, exactly as domestic dogs now and then mark their stopping places.

HUNTING

In the northeast and the Great Lakes region, as noted earlier, specialists run coyotes with hounds. Hounds must be large and heavy to stand the hard going in snow, and the long runs. The average hunter today has little opportunity to pursue this sport. It requires keeping and training the dogs. Also, just feeding a couple of 80 pound dogs gets to be expensive. A very few hound owners set up hunts for coyotes and charge a guiding fee. On the whole, however, this is a specialists' sport. It is by no means a surefire proposition. More often than not a good run is all the hunters and dogs get.

Another kind of hunting entirely has been practiced on the plains, again by those able to keep and train the dogs. This is running coyotes with greyhounds or whippets. This also of course is a specialists' game. On occasion several ranchers or farmers join forces in a kind of small club, split up the expense of the dogs, and run them as they have time and opportunity. In Kansas, Oklahoma, and western Texas, for example, this method is still used today by a few enthusiasts. However, more and more fences, for instance in Kansas, have put a damper on this sport. On some large Oklahoma and Texas ranches where a single pasture may contain several thousand acres, it is still practiced by a few who can afford it.

Greyhounds do not follow a trail, but run by sight. Thus the coyote must first be jumped and then the dogs are slipped. Many of the dogs used are crossbreeds, partly greyhound and partly wolfhound or other long-legged, fast dogs. A scent hound may be used to follow a fresh track and jump the coyote, at which time the other dogs are set free. Or, as in most instances, hunters cruise around in 4WD vehicles until a coyote is sighted, and then the dogs are put down. They are faster than the coyote, and if they don't lose sight of it in brush or rocks or gullies, they rather quickly overtake it. The coyote begins to circle, and they cut it off as it tires. Hunters rush to the scene to dispatch the coyote before the dogs tear the hide.

Numerous coyote hunters simply cruise open country in a 4WD watching for targets, then try long shots at them with a flat-shooting rifle such as the .243 or .270. This is a popular method on the plains and across the southwest, but not feasible in any forested country. A scope-equipped rifle is mandatory, and so are binoculars. Now and then a hunter who likes his exercise simply walks plains areas, glassing for coyotes. This covers too small an expanse of country to be very practical, except for the exercise involved.

For years ranchers across the plains and southwest hunted coyotes from light planes, mostly to rid ranges of an excess supply.

This does not give a jumped coyote much chance at all, and though it may be considered "sporty," using a shotgun for example from a ground-skimming plane, it can be highly dangerous to the hunter as well as his quarry. In most places this approach is currently illegal.

The bulk of coyote hunting today is done with a call. This allows anyone who lives where coyotes are nearby to participate. It is inexpensive, effective, and exceedingly dramatic. Some calling enthusiasts go out armed only with a still or movie camera. A few handicap themselves by using only bow and arrow. Rifle hunters, with fur valuable nowadays, employ a rather light rifle, such as the .222, and accept only close shots so the bullet can be meticulously placed. The .243 or 6mm is also an example of a good arm for this. No rimfire caliber should be used. The coyote is too tough a target. A scope and binoculars are part of the equipment.

The basics of coyote calling are identical to those for calling foxes. For night calling, which is not legal everywhere, a red headlamp and spotting light are an improvement over the standard white lights. Because the wild dogs are colorblind, they seem hardly aware of a red light on them, which probably appears to them a subdued gray illumination.

Coyote calling is an extremely intriguing sport, whether you go out to collect hides or simply to watch them come to the call and shoot photos. But be assured that they catch on fast. In an area where much calling has been done, where a few animals have seen the caller and run away, or have scented danger from the call location, or been shot at and missed, it is common to hear them chortle derisively when a call begins. Or one moves out of brush several hundred yards distant and stares, then slinks back into cover. Some callers believe that in places where calling pressure is heavy, parent coyotes, by example, pass along to progeny their caution about going to the sound.

The coyote is indeed an intelligent animal, not in the least endangered in our time by man's ever more dense usurpation of the land. It does need to be controlled in some places, but as has been said, no one, not even landowners nowadays, want the coyote totally removed from the scene. There is little likelihood that it ever will be. Scientists estimate that the coyote has been on earth at least five times as long as man. In just the paltry few hundred years that the white man has been here in North America, even with awesome pressures on its populations, the coyote has done almost as well as he has, and perhaps from its viewpoint even better.

# Raccoon

*Procyon lotor*

Most children and many adults assume that the raccoon is a lovable little woodland personality precisely as it appears in animated movies, books for youngsters, and nature writings that endow animals with human characteristics. The raccoon as casually seen in the wild certainly is an appealing creature, and as a pet when very young seems mischievous, lovable, and comical. It is an extremely intelligent animal. It is also a tough and cantankerous personality—even as a rule in captivity when grown—well able to take care of itself against high odds, an unbelievably vicious fighter when the need arises, brave, tenacious, and amazingly strong.

Thus it seems almost to have a split personality. Many a hiker has peered into a hollow stump and looked into the burglar-masked, sharp-nosed face and wide, dark eyes of a raccoon that looks almost cuddly, or watched one wander along a creek, poking here and there with its forefeet, using them much like human hands, turning over a stone to savor a crayfish, rolling along in a shambling gait, butter-fat, innocent-appearing and playful. It is no

355

Raccoon

Douglas Allen

wonder that human traits and lovable qualities have attached them-selves to this creature. But anyone who happens to corner a husky coon and attempts to befriend it would soon discover that trying to pet a wildcat could hardly be worse.

Since the time of early white settlement on this continent, the raccoon has been an important and usually honored woodland neighbor. Its pelt was one of the most common and valued of early-day furs, because it was easily acquired and heavy when prime in winter coat, and thus warm as well as durable. The coonskin cap of the colonists, the explorer, and of course Daniel Boone long ago became an integral part of American legend and lore.

Although the raccoon is eaten today only by a scattering of country people and hunters, long ago it was a staple of sorts, usu-ally roasted. A roast raccoon is indeed delicious. Many are ex-tremely fat, especially in fall, and old-time cooks invariably first parboiled the dressed animal, then removed as much of the fat as possible. After that the meat was browned, buttered, and roasted in an earthen pot in the old wood stove or fireplace. It is dark, but not strong, and made a superb and welcome meal whenever available.

The fat of raccoons was an important side product in early days. Settlers and small farmers greased boots with the fine oil and used it as a lubricant for varied purposes, and poor turn-of-the-century farm boys occasionally daubed it on a recalcitrant cowlick when readying for a local hoedown. Thus very little of the "coon," as it is usually called for short by hunters and country dwellers, was wasted.

In the early decades of this century the faddish raccoon coat was tremendously popular, for those who could afford it, for both men and women. It was a trade mark of the 1920s among college boys, and country kids at that time trapped coons all fall and winter and in good years got as much as $10 or $15 each for the largest, primest hides.

Over intervening years from then until near the present the market for raccoon hides had its ups and downs, mostly the latter. For a number of midcentury years raccoon hides brought little or nothing. Then in the early 1970s the wild-fur market boomed again — oddly, it would seem, what with the more extremist environ-mentalists decrying the appearance of any wild fur draped on a human. By 1975 and 1976 coon hides were bringing anywhere from $15 to $30. Trapping and coon hunting for the country lad, and indeed for his dad also, were once again not only enjoyable sports but money-makers.

## THE RACCOON

COLOR: Moderately variable, darker to lighter, from yellowish or reddish gray to plain gray to nearly black with gray undertones; underfur normally reddish to dark, outer long fur grizzled or white-tipped; underparts, lower legs, and tops of feet paler, gray to yellowish to whitish; black "mask" across the face and eyes and running from forehead down bridge of nose, contrasting with whitish or very pale remainder of face and sides of nose; nose pad and soles of feet black; tail circled with several black rings, tip black.

MEASUREMENTS: Highly variable by latitude and local races, but average maximum overall length 30 to 36 inches, with tail approximately 10 to 12 inches of that; average shoulder height, 1 foot.

WEIGHT: Extremely variable by latitude, race, and time of year, that is when extremely fat in north in fall; average span from 10 to 20 pounds; 25 to 30 not rare in some areas; unusual specimens with fall fat up to 40, 50, rarely 60 pounds.

GENERAL ATTRIBUTES: Face mask and ringed tail are distinguishing characteristics; a strongly built, tough, intelligent animal with endless curiosity about everything in its surroundings.

During the years when coon hides had little value, there was relatively little pressure on them from hunters and trappers. Only the dyed-in-the-hide hound enthusiast who loved to stumble around the woods at night on a coon chase gave the animals much trouble. Consequently, raccoon populations in many states boomed to nuisance proportions. The upswing in hide prices was welcomed by both game managers and farmers who suffered from too-numerous raccoons and their depredations.

The rascals avidly eat field corn and sweet corn patches in the milk or ripe and hard, and love to cut up patches of melons. They raid fruit trees on occasion and now and then get into trouble in a poultry yard, and in rare instances in the west and southwest large specimens have locally become astonishingly destructive killers of sheep and lambs. These, however, are rather rare instances. For the most part the raccoon has gotten along without irritating its human neighbors unduly. It has also been a master at learning to live with them.

Although most urban dwellers are unaware of it because the raccoon is chiefly nocturnal, there is hardly a city or village that does not have a resident raccoon population along its fringes and even

# Range of the Raccoon

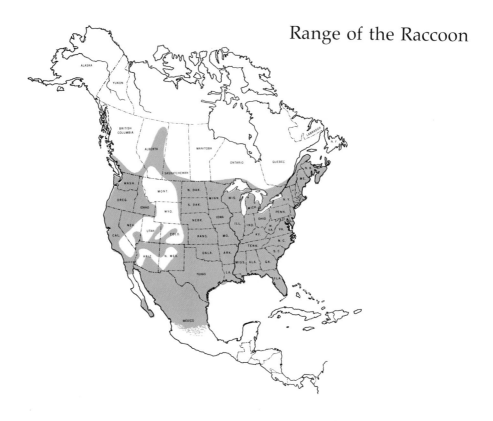

within its environs. Practically every farm woodlot and creek course also has its quota, often more than in the wilderness places.

The range of the raccoon is vast, throughout almost all of Mexico and Central America and all of the lower U.S. states except in parts of the Rockies and the deserts of the southwest. The animal reaches across a thin swath of southern Canada, and its range bulges northward in a triangle into portions of Saskatchewan and Alberta. There is a modest transplanted population in southern Alaska.

Only two other native animals could possibly be mistaken for the raccoon. One is the slender, small, big-eyed and big-eared ringtail cat of the southwest. But the rings on its long, handsome, bushier tail do not completely encircle it on the bottom, and it is at a glance a quite different, strikingly beautiful and slim little animal. The other is the coati, or coatimundi, with its long, slender tail, ringed but with short fur. It is fundamentally a Mexican and Central American animal, with a straggler fringe population above the U.S. border in southern Arizona and extreme southwestern New Mexico.

Taxonomists have split the raccoon into numerous subspecies, generally based on minor differences in various places across their immense range. To the hunter or casual student of wildlife these are not important. Raccoons in the northern Great Lakes region, in New England, and in the Northwest are often astonishingly large. In fall they put on huge amounts of fat to help them over severe winters, and the weight of a big fellow killed in late fall is often half fat.

In northern Michigan or upper New England a specimen weighing 30 pounds or more is not at all rare. The few that have been authenticated in the 50- and 60-pound range are obviously unusual specimens. In parts of the south, for example in far-southern Florida, some raccoons are miniatures of only a few pounds. Color also varies throughout the range. Many northern animals are very dark along the back, almost black. In fact, an occasional melanistic specimen does turn up. White (albino) ones are more common, though also rare. In desert areas raccoons are often pale in color, apparently the better to match their surroundings.

Many a camper knows all too well what a nuisance raccoons can be. Even in a back-country camp they are invariably bold, bumbling about and trying to get into everything, and usually doing a masterful job of it. They use their forepaws like hands, and with amazing dexterity. They can take the tightly fitting lids off tin containers, open an ice chest, and unlatch a cabin door, and have been known to sneak into an open car window and open the glove compart to get at oddments such as mints and chewing tobacco. One even carried a bottle of whiskey out of the vehicle of a Texas camper in the Big Bend Country, and managed to get the cork out. What happened afterward went unrecorded.

Hunters with hounds know the raccoon at times as much more than a quasi-comic pest or nuisance. An old boar can be an exasperating yet sporty quarry, and he can also be a danger to dogs. For example, one that has been run before and knows the trickery of escapes is as astute as any red fox and as full of chicanery. It will climb a tree and leap out to hold up dogs that must work out the puzzle. It will wade a creek, swim a river upstream or down, whichever might be less expected, climb and jump when feasible from one tree to another as far as it can go, then come to ground and run again. Walking logs and blowdowns, or rail or stone fences, it eludes and confuses pursuing hounds.

The danger occurs when a hard-pressed raccoon takes to water and eager dogs follow. The animal is an excellent swimmer. It will seize a dog by the head and either climb atop its head or tread water and push the dog's head under. A big coon is awesomely powerful for its weight, and many a burly hound has been quickly drowned by one. In fact, now and then several are drowned by a single old boar. In a fight on the ground a single dog is often no match for a big raccoon. Even two or more wind up well slashed before they finally subdue the determined antagonist—if they do.

During a fight with dogs a raccoon even sounds ferocious at times. It may remain quiet, but now and then it will hiss and growl with emphatic menace, make a grating barking sound, and even in high temper let out a bawl that gives both dogs and hunters pause. It sounds as bad to handle as a black bear, to which it is distantly related.

Probably the best-known facet of raccoon personality is its insatiable curiosity. It pokes into every conceivable cranny, picks at and puzzles over every iota of debris in its bailiwick that it doesn't instantly identify. A shiny can or bottle carelessly flung onto the edge of a lake by a littering camper the raccoon painstakingly retrieves and examines. At one campsite where litter was deplorably heavy, a visiting raccoon was watched from a tent as it picked up one after another a dozen or more pop-top can tabs. A pet raccoon persisted on moonlit nights in trying to trap with both hands the glint of moonbeams on its water dish, and seemed perplexed to always come up with nothing. Trappers have long used this innate curiosity to lure coons into reaching for a leg-trap pan to which they have attached a shiny object.

The most valuable trait the raccoon possesses, so far as its own success and well-being are concerned, is its apparently limitless adaptability. Obviously, given its vast range, it has been able to get along, and multiply satisfactorily, under highly variable conditions, not only of habitat, but also in relation to human settlement and progress. It is an interesting commentary on the status of the raccoon that numerous game experts and wildlife biologists are convinced that there are as many raccoons present in North America today—some millions of them—as there were when the pilgrims first tried roast raccoon along with wild turkey for their first Thanksgiving dinner. Indeed, some believe there are more.

### HABITAT

The adaptability of the raccoon to such diverse habitats as those found from Central America to Canada, from Florida and Texas to

*Taking to the water, the raccoon will drown a pursuing dog by climbing on its head.*

New England and the Pacific Northwest, is based on three attributes of the animal: its ability to tolerate a wide range of temperature; the fact that though it is classed as a carnivore it is wholly omnivorous; and its compactness and modest size, which allows it to sustain itself individually on a comparatively modest range.

One of nature's immutable laws is that the smaller an animal, the less living room it needs. This is obvious because the amount of food necessary to keep it in health is proportionate to size. Further, whereas a strict carnivore, such as the mountain lion, must range a large territory in order to find enough large-sized forage to kill, a smaller animal that is only partially carnivorous, taking meat or getting along without it, needs no large individual bailiwick. Its population therefore is always larger. Also, the omnivorous creature able to adapt to a broad temperature and latitude range can be comfortable in any number of different types of habitats. And it can spread out from one to another, enlarging its range to the limits of its seasonal temperature tolerances, because no single member of its tribe requires more than minimal living space.

Thus the raccoon, from wherever it started its progress anciently, moved long, long ago into every conceivable habitat type where a livelihood was available. Basically, however, because it also anciently formed a habit of sleeping in hollow trees and of climbing trees to rest or escape danger, it has clung for the most part throughout its range to woodland and forest areas. In addition, and perhaps because of its broad-spectrum diet and the fact that so many varieties of foods are obtainable near water, the raccoon is oriented toward lake shores, stream courses, the fringes of swamps, and even the sparsely vegetated dunes and beaches along our marine shores.

There is an interesting correlation here. It is along the lake shores and the stream bottoms that the preponderance of the hardwoods and deciduous trees grow, as opposed to the stands of evergreen conifers. Not only are mixed woodlands and deciduous-timber stands places where forage of the widest variety is most abundant—again as opposed to the rather barren conifer or predominantly coniferous forests—but also it is the leafy hardwoods and softwoods that most commonly furnish dead or partly dead trees with hollow trunks or limbs which serve raccoons as hiding, resting, and nesting places.

It is true that the hollow tree so much a part of the lore of the raccoon is by no means plentiful nowadays. Cutting of bottomland hardwoods throughout the south, for example, to make room for more and more soy beans has decimated many virgin stands, and selective cutting even in farm woodlots long ago removed most dead and dying trees. The ingrained habit of consorting in the leafy woodlands and forests has nonetheless persisted among raccoons, and they have adapted as usual to finding new resting and nesting places when their ancestral favorites are unavailable. Undoubtedly the bounteous food supply in these ecosystems based on the lake shores and stream courses and their environs have kept raccoons tied to them.

Swamp regions and their edges, typically in the south, furnish homes for raccoons. Areas such as the Texas Hill Country, laced by clear streams coursing its steep and rocky canyons where brush, cedar, and oak grow, harbor dense raccoon populations. Brushy stream edges and shelter belts in the Dakotas, a quite different habitat, support this animal. So do the north woods in Wisconsin and Maine, along with the small woodlots and crop fields of the central farm states.

In a few parts of the range the raccoon has spread into expanses of territory that are nearly treeless and have little water. Portions of

Arizona, New Mexico, and Texas are examples. Here they have adapted to rocky ledges and caves, and the secondhand burrows of other animals. As long as food is at hand, the raccoon is able to live quite happily, finding seeps of water in canyons or rocky catch basins, and puddles collected in depressions from rainfall.

### FEEDING

Perhaps the eat-anything habits of the raccoon stem from its insatiable curiosity. In the beginning it must have been willing to try strange items, and apparently it has found little in any of its diverse habitats that is especially distasteful. Along Florida beaches that fringe the big southern swamps, raccoons putter about in the mangroves and along the sand at night, combing them for mollusks, which they deftly open, for dead fish, and for live ones now and then that a wave sends to them or that are trapped in tidal beach pools and are a cinch for catching.

Along a freshwater lake shore, crayfish are a favorite item. The raccoon wades and flips over stones and expertly seizes them. If minnows or small fish are unwary, into the gullet they go, too. In some places raccoons are a menace to nesting waterfowl. They gobble up the eggs, slicing each expertly in two, and the young, and during the flightless molting period of adult ducks cut down a number of them. They are well fitted for swamp foraging, wading when the depth is right and swimming when it isn't. Muskrat houses are systematically broken into when the opportunity is presented; the young are eaten and the adults also if the raccoon can catch them.

Most foraging is done on the ground, simply because the variety and abundance makes this easier. However, many a coon climbs to investigate a bird's nest, taking eggs or young, reaching a deft hand deep into hollows in limbs in case a nesting bird may be present. Frogs are of course a tasty item along waters and in moist meadows. After a rain that sends earthworms and nightcrawlers to the surface, these are eagerly raked in. Numerous varieties of insects add morsels — crickets, grasshoppers, the grubs in a rotted log, ants. If in tearing into an old log the animal discovers a quick little salamander, a flash of that facile forepaw and down it goes. Whenever a rabbit or its nest is found, or mice discovered, the raccoon crunches them avidly.

Although meat is eaten with relish whenever it is easily available, the preponderance of the diet of most raccoons is vegetable matter. This is simply because so much more is at hand and it can

*With a deft swipe of its agile paws, a raccoon steals a bird's egg from a tree nest.*

be had with little effort. Grasses in spring, all varieties of wild fruits, domestic fruits, nuts, including abundant acorns in fall, various grain crops, especially corn when it is in the milk stage but also later when it is hard and ripe, melons, even potatoes dug from the hills—all these are fodder for any raccoon that finds them.

A family of raccoons attracted to a corn patch can be extremely destructive. They seldom finish an ear they've started before going to another, breaking down the stalks meanwhile and in general leaving a shambles. Now and then a raccoon is tempted to try for a chicken. With its amazingly dexterous "hands" it can reach through a wire fence, seize an unsuspecting hen by the neck, pull her head through the wire, and bite it off almost before she can squawk. Domestic kittens are not safe from the appraisal of a marauding, bold raccoon, and of course a full garbage can, even with the lid snugly in place, is an invitation to make a mess while picking things over.

Carrion plays a part in raccoon diet also. Thousands of coons are killed nowadays along roads which they patrol for other vehicle-killed creatures to feast upon. Particularly in late summer and early fall when families of young raccoons are fattening, the naive youngsters are blinded by car lights and seem not to have sense enough to move. Now and then three or four will be seen dead on some highway, all in a group, usually near some carrion they had hoped to savor.

Much has been written about the fact that the raccoon washes everything it eats. This is a nice little legend, and has served well in folk tales and stories for children. Like many a "fact" from nature, it is a half-truth. Raccoons do like to scrub some kinds of food in water, even rubbing clean food in dirty water. One researcher even tested a theory that the raccoon doesn't have enough saliva, or possibly no salivary glands, and thus must wet its food. Others believe it simply likes the feel of scrubbing or fiddling with food in water. Even its scientific species name, *lotor,* refers to "one that washes."

However, even though a raccoon may scrub a frog that it has just grabbed from a pool, it is probably simply an ancestral habit based on its attachment to water, and may not mean anything special. Perhaps it just likes to play with a piece of food and finds dabbling it intriguing, like a human gourmet turning a rare delicacy on a fork and looking at it from several angles before savoring it. No one really knows. The fact is, unless a raccoon is at water or very near it, the animal just eats. It doesn't hurry to find a puddle to wash a beechnut or an ear of corn in, or try to carry a mouse from a meadow to the nearest creek for scrubbing.

### MOVEMENTS

It is obvious that because the raccoon is something of a glutton most of its travels are concerned with discovering tempting morsels. Now and then a raccoon is seen ambling about by day, particularly on overcast days. Basically it is a nocturnal creature, coming out at dusk and spending much of the night hunting, or moving out some nights not until late evening or even midnight, then at dawn finding a pleasant, comfortable place to sleep away the day.

The ambling gait of the raccoon is caused by its flatfooted walk, like the bear's. Because of omnivorous feeding habits, it is not necessary for the average raccoon to cover a very large territory. Nor with its short legs is it equipped to do so. Some individuals that live in lush year-round feeding locations, such as along a warm southern beach or swamp, may never wander more than half a mile from a favorite denning site. Others must cover twice that. If food is scarce, a raccoon may be forced to find a new range, or to hunt a territory of several square miles.

As it hunts, the raccoon, especially when fat, appears to waddle. Its usual gait is a meandering, shuffling walk. There is seldom any need to hurry, except when a hound takes its trail, and even then many a coon doesn't get very perturbed until the sound is close. The slow walk is insurance that it misses nothing. The rolling shuffle is caused by placing one forefoot ahead, then bringing the opposite hindfoot forward, almost beside it but a bit to the rear.

When it wants to hurry, perhaps homing in on a good smell or eager to get to a special crayfish-catching shallows, it may break into a trot. When a raccoon runs, it bounds along, placing the forefeet and then humping up and bringing the hind feet past them. Even at its best it isn't very fast. Ten miles an hour, with a top of possibly 15, is an all-out run.

During its hunting, or when chased by dogs, it climbs trees with great agility, the strong claws clinging and pulling it up. Although a raccoon loves to curl up after a foraging trip in a hollow stump, log or trunk of a tree, it doesn't go to special bother looking for such a favorite spot, unless it already knows where several are along its routes. It will go into a cave, under a rocky ledge, or in open areas into an old badger or other burrow.

Even where hollows are available high up in a large tree, perhaps where a limb has broken off and the inner trunk rotted to form a hole, many a raccoon doesn't bother to climb. It simply curls up in heavy grass during the day. Dry marsh-grass areas are favorites for this type of bed. Or perhaps it knows of an old muskrat house it has broken into. This makes a fine sleeping place. When weather is pleasant it is not uncommon to spot a raccoon snoozing high up in a tree, lying in a crotch or stretched along a limb.

In temperate climates raccoons stay active all winter. But in the north, where they invariably put on much more fat in fall than elsewhere, as soon as deep snows and severe cold arrive, and a scarcity of food with them, the animals den up. This is not a hibernation. It is simply a device for putting in time comfortably and burning up stored fat while things outside aren't pleasant. Nor does it take much cold to convince a coon. If weather is steadily well below freezing, most of them look for a hollow tree or stump, or a burrow, even the outbuildings of farms. On occasion a family has taken over the attic of a house in use, or to the dismay of both raccoons and people, tried out the fireplace chimney.

Sometimes a number of raccoons den up together. This may be a family that has stayed together all fall and into the winter, or it is believed on occasion several congenial adults may simply join for warmth and company. Hunters in winter who locate a full "coon tree" now and then collect a bonanza. Unless a winter is exceptionally severe, the animals by no means sleep all of it away. During sudden thaws in midwinter they come out and wander again, eating whatever they can find, and giving hunters much sport putting dogs down on tracks of slushy snow.

During this lazy time of winter the sleep is never deep enough so a raccoon is not easily awakened by disturbance, from dogs or hunters. It is also during this period, in some latitudes, that the breeding urge interrupts the winter dormancy and sends the males traveling hither and yon.

## BREEDING

Among raccoons there is a rather curious social arrangement based on the mating season. The male roams about, looking for any receptive female he can find. In colder climates where the animals are denned up, the male must poke here and there, never overlooking a location where a receptive female may be waiting in a den. In warmer climes, of course, his search may not need to be quite as pinpoint.

When he finds a willing mate — and she is likely to be a bit choosy and ready to let him know it — he stays with her for several days, possibly as long as a week. Breeding may occur a number of times during this interval. The restless male now leaves. If the female is in a den, she remains, and dozes off again to wait for congenial weather to arrive. Regardless of where the mating took place, she remains true to her mate — but he doesn't. He is off roaming again, looking for more mates in succession. Thus, he is polygamous but the females, in most cases, are not. It is during this mat-

ing spree, which occurs depending on latitude and weather sometime during the first quarter of the year, that the males at least do
the most wide-ranging traveling of the entire year.

Perhaps one reason the raccoon has done so well as a species is
that both sexes are capable of breeding when very young, and with
good health and luck any raccoon has a life expectancy of from 5 to
10 or more years. Numerous young females are bred in their first
year, which means they are two or three months short of being a
full year old. It is believed that the majority of males, though
capable, miss that first year and begin breeding in their second
year.

### BIRTH AND DEVELOPMENT

Slightly more than two months after mating, the young raccoons, extremely tiny little fellows, are born. Except for the fact that
their eyes are sealed, they are quite recognizable as raccoons. They
are furred, and have the same face and body markings they will
wear as adults, except not quite so plain on these miniatures of only
2 or 3 ounces. In a few days the distinctive features begin to fill in
much more plainly.

Litter sizes differ, as with most animals. Three or four is normal,
but there may be several more. Their promiscuous father is still off
wandering on his own. Unlike the social pattern among the wild
dogs, for example, the male raccoon does no helping out around the
house. The mother does all the caring for her young. If a male
should stop by and be inquisitive, she will drive him away,
because male raccoons, like male cats, sometimes kill the young.

The raccoon is more dexterous with its "hands" than any other
American animal. The young, while still blind, are able to crawl
about and hold onto each other or their mother quite efficiently.
They all sleep cuddled together in a pile in the darkness of the den.
They grow swiftly, get their eyes open when they are approximately three weeks old, and soon are climbing about, instinctively
attempting to scale the den wall. They don't succeed until they are
roughly 1½ months old. Then the den entrance from which a bit of
light enters begins more and more to intrigue them.

If the mother has selected a den in an old badger burrow, or in a
rocky cave or hollow log, the youngsters have it easy. But if they are
up in a tree there are problems. They now weigh somewhat less
than 2 pounds and like to peek out the den entrance. This tempts
them to try for outside. Seldom does one fall to the ground. They

seem instinctively to know how to cling and climb. But their growing curiosity about the huge world out there leads them to explore
higher and higher. They crawl around the limbs, and one suddenly
finds itself far up above the den and it is frightened.

Obviously the thing to do is yell for mother. Going up seemed
easy, but it looks like a tough route back down. The baby raccoon
squalls, whimpers, and whines. It still has to make it on its own
unless the mother goes up and carries it back, holding it by the
scruff of its neck in her mouth. The mother reassures all the
youngsters with whickering sounds and with soft mutterings and
chirpings one would hardly associate with raccoons. Several
wildlife observers claim to have heard adult raccoons call with a
tremulous, subdued sound similar to that made by the small
screech owl as it talks to its mate. If the young have been born on or
below ground, they play around the den mouth, and when they
wander the mother often goes after them, fetching them back one at
a time, the way a cat carries a kitten.

As they grow to fluffy, fat balls of fur and gain some three
months in age, the time to begin following their mother has arrived. The world can be a rough place at times for young raccoons.
A bobcat or a big owl or hawk may grab one. In the modern world
with its skein of highways, thousands of youngsters are struck by
cars. In farm country a dog may find a family of young and kill one
or more before the mother can rake it over and force it to run. Disease takes some. For the most part, however, they are sturdy,
healthy creatures, and eager to eat what the mother finds as they
follow her around.

With a few recognizable smells now to guide them by experience, and the inherent hunting instinct, the whole family is soon
foraging together, each gathering its own livelihood. By fall they
still may travel together and sleep together, or they more likely will
begin to separate and drift apart, dispersing so that each young
animal can search for and stake out a territory of its own. Each will
be roughly two years of age before it has reached full stature, although as noted a fair percentage of the young animals will launch
families of their own the first winter.

## SENSES

Because raccoons are principally nocturnal, their eyes contain
hundreds of thousands of light-gathering rod cells. These are the
cells that permit sight in dim light. The presence of so many of them

is what makes the eyes of a raccoon shine in a light at night, reflecting in red or green colors depending on how the light strikes. Raccoons have excellent sight, and undoubtedly their distance vision is good. However, most animals built so low to the ground and not wholly predaceous neither need distance vision nor can accommodate their eyes to far-distant objects. A raccoon is mainly concerned with what is nearby.

Unquestionably its scenting abilities are excellent also, but here again, the raccoon seldom needs to use the sense of smell for any but close-up chores. It is not a trailer, except possibly for very brief distances, and then only very occasionally. It probably uses a combination of sight and scent, plus its most unusual adeptness with which it feels objects with its forefeet, in order to glean much of its living. Probably feel, or touch, is more important in daily life to the raccoon than to any other comparable animal. Hearing is also keen, and possibly sharper than the sense of smell. A raccoon needs to be ever alert for both sounds of nearby potential food and those of more distant danger.

SIGN *(Tracks are illustrated on page 254.)*

In certain specialized situations raccoon droppings are an important sign. In northern Michigan, for example, avid raccoon hunters while out after ruffed grouse and woodcock in early fall keep on the lookout for potential coon-hunting grounds a bit later. If the year has produced a heavy crop of wild cherries, a full-bearing big black cherry tree or a choke cherry clump may have below it a welter of coon scats filled with cherry pits and skins. Each dropping is roughly 3 inches long and the diameter of a large cigar. Raccoons also deposit droppings now and then atop a log, stump, or rock. This is fairly good evidence that a raccoon has been there. However, the ringtail in the southwest invariably leaves piles of droppings atop rocks, and so in that area where both may be present confusion could exist.

Sometimes hunters walking the woods in search of raccoon den trees, or trees suitable for dens, look for hollow trunks or a hollow high up where a limb has long ago broken off, and then for scratches or claw marks on the trunk. There may also be numerous droppings nearby. The really important and readily spotted sign of the raccoon, however, is its track. There are five toes on each foot. The toes are long and slender. The print of the front foot, roughly 3 inches in length, is reminiscent in miniature of the print of a human hand. The claws show, of course. The hind-foot print is longer, a plain print of a large adult almost 4 inches long.

The print of the hind foot ordinarily shows the impression of the entire foot more plainly than that of the front; that is, the heel and instep are well printed. It looks quite similar to a bear track except, of course, much smaller. Country people have often described raccoon tracks as like those of a human baby, and there are old folklore tales of the lost child whose tracks were confused with those of a big raccoon.

Hunters looking for coon sign check the mud and soft earth along lakes and streams, or along washes where the prints might plainly indent, or in the north in winter in first snows, or later on during a thaw. No raccoon is likely to be out in deep snow. It is simply not built for plowing through drifts.

The track of the raccoon with its long, slender toes is distinctive, and not easily confused with any other. Conceivably a beginning hunter or wildlife enthusiast might confuse it with that of the opossum. However the opossum track is if anything more distinctive than that of the raccoon and easy to tell apart. It is the tracks of raccoons, and their abundance or lack of it, that hunters always check.

## HUNTING

Raccoon hunting with hounds is one of the grandest of the traditional American sports in which dogs are employed. The bird-dog enthusiast might scoff at the idea. To be sure, coon hunters are only a minor percentage among sportsmen in this country, but most of them are dedicated. This is a homely, old-timey sport, perhaps corny and old-fashioned by modern dress-up standards when many an urban-dwelling hunter spends as much on his duded-up bird-hunting garb as he does on dinner clothes. But fundamentally it is a sport that has a nostalgic aura of history about it and an atmosphere of authentic and crystal-pure countrified enjoyment.

Picture a farmhouse somewhere in the midwest back in the early decades of this century. It is a warmish, damp, still evening in late fall. The weather has been chilly enough to prime up coon hides. As darkness wraps the farmyard a hound on its chain bellows from out by the barn. A second chimes in. They are eager. They know the time of year and the kind of night when their personal lightning may strike.

The farmer in overalls finishes his supper by lamplight. His wife is putting the milk from that evening's milking into crocks to cool in the dug-dirt cellar. No refrigeration, no electricity here. Kerosene lamps, a wood stove, an old outhouse with moss-covered roof out back. The hounds are setting up a rising clamor. There's something exciting in the air. The man knows the feeling well. He steps to the old crank telephone on the wall and rings — three long, two short — for his neighbor. Every receiver on the line comes off. Listening in is a way of life.

Would the neighbor like to make a little run tonight? He would. But before the man can get his old jacket and his black knee-length gum-rubber boots on, the phone is ringing like blazes. Another, and still another neighbor, whose wives had listened in and not had the good sense to keep quiet about what they'd heard, just happened to wonder if he'd like to get a coon-hunting group together this perfect night. What they are doing really is asking if they can join in, acting as if no one had heard the original conversation.

They gather, walking, at a country road corner handy for all. Kerosene lanterns glimmer. One man has a carbide headlamp and an old single-shot .22 rifle. Each of the group is cussing at his hounds on leash to settle down, batting them with his hat or trying to get the mess of them untangled. They decide to try the creek bottom on someone's north forty. Stumbling along in the dark, but still knowing every foot of the countryside, they move off. Within seconds one man out ahead with a strike dog is having difficulty holding it. The hound is going wild. It has gathered in the stimulating aroma of a sizzling track at a fence corner.

The dogs are set free. The clamor of the chase is fearful. All these hounds are open trailers. That is, they bawl and yammer on trail. Some like silent trailers, but these gents like to hear the racket and feel the hair on the backs of their necks rise with it. Everyone hurriedly follows, once the chase direction is set. Eerie flickers of shadow and weak yellow lantern light dart across stands of tall weeds and brush and presently on tree trunks as they enter a woodlot of maple, beech, elm, and oak.

The coon is into the creek, that's sure. The dogs are milling off there, momentarily confused. The men race stumbling to the sound. One barrels into the shallow creek, slips, goes down yelping, and the woodlot rings with laughter. The soaked man is cussing and laughing at the same time. Someone produces a pint bottle of corn whiskey. That'll ward off the chill for the wet man — and shucks, why not everybody have a nip just in case he falls, too?

The dogs are off again, lining out through the woodlot. But then the wild trail song ceases and two or three dogs are barking—the tree bark; the coon is treed. Soon the group surrounds the tree and the dogs. Lanterns are held high. The carbide light, after much too-hurried effort, leaps to life. It sweeps the treetop weakly. There is the glow of an eye. But the coon keeps turning its head to avoid the light. A shot is finally tried with the .22. It's a miss.

In the darkness the coon scurries along a branch and leaps to another tree, and another. It is down and gone. The dogs realize what has happened. They begin circling. Presently they pick up the track. By now the coon is into the creek again and moving fast, but the dogs never do discover which way it went, or where it came out. The group gather, puzzled but grinning. Someone finally says, "Well, by cripe we sure give 'im a run anyways—huh?" Wet from a drizzle that has started and will probably wash out tracks, brush-scratched, they plod off, hounds leashed now, to look for another chance at a run.

Coon hounds are carefully selected by enthusiasts, shown at their own shows, and meticulously bred to get the nose of old Blue, the voice of Belle or Bawler, the weight and stamina and tenaciousness of some other much-loved hound with a reputation. A few hunters like the silent trailers because the coon isn't aware of them until they are practically on it. Some such dogs open up only when the raccoon is jumped and the real run is on. But it is short as a rule in front of quiet hounds. The coon doesn't get a head start.

A few hounds are astonishingly expert cold trailers. The late Carl Allen of northern Michigan, game warden and lifelong hound man, on numerous occasions demonstrated such a dog to unbelievers. He'd take it out in the morning after a shower had occurred about midnight that would dampen tracks made earlier. At that, many a track the dog took would be eight or more hours old. The dog would potter along, spending long periods making decisions, finally let out a bawl after perhaps an hour of persistent work, and head straight for a hollow stump or tree where a coon was asleep. This daytime coon hunting seldom happens, of course, but it is quite an experience when one has the dog that can do it.

Among the more famed coon-hound breeds are black-and-tan, redbone, Walker, bluetick, and mixtures of them. In modern coon hunting with hounds, equipment is far better than old-timers had. A good headlamp is worn by each member as a rule, the battery slung on the belt. No other light is needed, although most hunters also carry a long, powerful flashlight. If the animals are to be collected for hides, a .22 rifle, or pistol if a shooter is good enough with it, is carried by only one man of a group. When a coon is treed, the dogs are leashed so they cannot get at it to tear the hide. Headlamps shine the animal, and the shot is carefully placed in order not to damage the pelt. Sometimes a "coon squaller" call is employed. This presumably mimics the raucous sound of a raccoon bawling when in difficulty, as when caught by dogs. It often influences a coon hidden in a tree to move, to look down or to jump, so it can be seen.

Laws pertaining to raccoon hunting differ widely state to state. Some years ago there was in most states no protection. Today most states have a season on the animal, either as a game animal or under furbearer laws. Only a scattering of states allow all-year hunting, although a few certain counties are open all year while other parts of the state have a season. It is a good idea to check hours that hunting may be done. Some states allow no daytime hunting. It may be restricted, for example, to one hour before sunset or one hour after sunrise.

In Mississippi there is a season during which raccoons may be taken for food, but without a gun, and another during which according to law they may be taken for food with the use of gun and dogs. An interesting arrangement is currently in force in Kentucky, one of the traditional coon-hunt states. You may train dogs during certain times but may not take the raccoons. There is a "shake-out" season during which dogs can be run and the raccoons collected, but only by "shaking" them out of a tree, which means one hunter from a group, as was often done long ago, is elected to climb a tree where a coon has taken refuge, and literally shake it down. Still another season allows taking of raccoons with dogs and firearms.

Coon hunting with dogs is of course a sport for specialists who can afford to own and keep dogs. For many country dwellers this is not a problem, but urban hunters are handicapped, unless they hire a farm friend to keep the hounds. Few if any opportunities are open for booking raccoon hunts with a guide, although hunters wanting to experience the sport may find some hound man willing to let them go along.

Animal callers have discovered that raccoons come fairly well to a call. It is used at night, of course, and with best results as a rule along lake or stream shores, or near a corn field or other prime feeding ground which raccoons are known to be using. Sometimes the standard predator call is used, imitating the cry of an injured rabbit. However, raccoons seem more intrigued by distress calls of various birds. These utter a cry or trill to imitate a gull, or a flicker or other bird that is trapped or disturbed.

Headlamp and bright light are needed. The red-lensed lights that came into use a few years ago are an assist. The animals appear not to realize they are bathed in light, and thus are not quite so anxious to flee. Calling tapes and records and the machines to play them are also available. All tapes and mouth-blown calls come with instructions for their use. Calling procedures for raccoons are much the same in fundamentals as for fox calling.

Although there are probably fewer coon-hound enthusiasts comparatively today than there were in earlier times, simply because of our population shift to urban centers, the sport still hangs on strongly in a number of states. Hunting with hounds, and calling, is not always done nowadays with the idea of bagging the raccoon. Many pursue these pastimes just for the excitement of the chase, or watching the animals come to a call. It is certain that as long as there are coon hunters among us, there will be abundant quarry in most places for them. Happily, this interesting and most successful animal has adapted so fully to our ways where necessary, and carries on so prolifically everywhere, that the possibility in our time of its reaching the endangered list is indeed scant.

# Opossum

*Didelphis marsupialis*

The opossum might be described as a tall tale of nature that has come true. In any list of peculiar animals, the opossum certainly would rank high. Its several most remarkable attributes, if described to one who had never heard of an opossum, would hardly seem believable. It can hang by its tail like some monkeys; the tiny young ride around for weeks in a furred pouch on their mother's stomach; the hindfoot track of an opossum looks almost like a miniature human-hand print; when under stress of unusual fright, the opossum may simply keel over in a limp faint, mouth open, apparently dead.

It would be nice to be able to claim that beyond all this the opossum is an intelligent and crafty little creature. The fact is, it has an exceedingly small brain and one of the lowest IQs—if animals can be said to have those—of any of the earth's mammals. Yet here a view of the opossum as an example of stupidity on four feet runs head-on into enigma.

It would seem logical that a creature lacking much intelligence might have evolved and then quickly been destroyed because of its lack of competitive ability. The opossum, however, is believed to have been present on earth in virtually the same form as it is today for close to 75 million years. In its bumbling, dumb fashion it somehow managed, presumably, to spread anciently over every continent. But then in North America long, long ago something happened that wiped out the species here. Yet that did not deter the inexorable push of the witless little creatures.

Slowly waddling, fat and without seeming purpose, the opossum made its way from what we now call South America up into and over much of the southern portion of this continent. This reestablishment occurred some hundreds of thousands of years ago — and the homely and still-fat and unintelligent opossum might well chuckle in the persimmon patch recalling the thousands of extinct creatures it left behind. Indeed, the opossum is a valid argument that in some instances, at least, stupidity pays.

In its relationship with man there is another curious paradox. Among the various attributes that have been used to define a game animal are intelligence, wariness of approach by the hunter, and high craft in escape; all of these together give the hunter his challenge. Game animals, even by dictionary standards, are defined as "plucky," or "spirited," and the hunting of them as a "contest."

The opossum isn't spirited. It isn't very plucky, is not at all cunning, and doesn't require cunning of the hunter. It isn't very wary, and it is probably the easiest of all the game animals to put into the stew pot. Notwithstanding this ridiculously unchallenging character, the lovable old possum has been one of the most popular targets of the chase, particularly among country people, since colonial days.

It may well be that the possum won such popularity precisely because of its lack of classic game qualities. Here was a kind of Everyman's game animal, a prolific creature that over much of its range, particularly in the deep south, was invariably abundant. The fox hunter or raccoon hunter might want or need highly trained dogs. But almost any potlicker could tree a possum. The hunt was therefore relatively easy when measured against the success percentages. It is like the difference between brown trout fishing and fishing for bluegills. The brown trout appeals to some because it is such an exasperation and challenge. The bluegill appeals more widely because it is so lovably willing to be caught.

Although opossum fur has never been as valuable as the pelt of the raccoon, it was much used in earlier times, and still is used, chiefly for trimming. The opossum is invariably fat, exceedingly so,

Opossum

## THE OPOSSUM

COLOR: Body grizzled gray but variable from very pale to quite dark; deep underfur nearly white; face distinctly whitish; naked ears black but commonly pink or white-tipped; eyes black, nose pink; tail nearly naked and scaly grayish to off-white; darker toward base; legs and feet dark but toes usually very pale to white.

MEASUREMENTS: Body averages 18 inches long, tail 12; unusually large specimens to 3 feet overall length; shoulder height averages about 6 inches.

WEIGHT: 5 to 7½ pounds average; large specimens, especially exceptional males, when fat to 10 or 15 pounds.

GENERAL ATTRIBUTES: Long, soft but shaggy and rather coarse fur; narrow, sharply pointed face and muzzle; naked tail, which is prehensile—that is, it can be used as an extra grip when climbing; marsupial—female has pouch on belly in which young, born prematurely, spend early weeks of life; handlike hind feet, with one toe clawless, shaped like and used like a human thumb; defense under dire circumstance by "playing possum," lying inert and presumably dead.

and the oil in earlier days was never wasted. It was utilized as fine oil for lubricating numerous items and for making soap, and many a black and poor-white plantation family in the south years ago commonly made do with it for cooking vegetables. But aside from the pure old-fashioned fun of possum hunting on black nights in the southern river bottoms, the fame of the animal in folklore has long rested on its presumed delights as table fare.

Who has not heard of "possum and sweet taters"? This traditional dish, or simply roasted opossum, was a staple of many poor families in early America and throughout plantation days in the south. Many a modern who has sampled it suspects that the fame was built more on hunger, scarcity and lack of variety of more domesticated fare, and the ready availability of the animal, rather than on its gourmet qualities. Opossum is indeed quite edible, when much of the fat has been removed or cooked out, but it hardly rates as a delicacy.

When the opossum long ago recolonized North America, it established itself in the broad lower elevations on both sides of Mexico, and made nearly a clean sweep over Texas and all of the South. Many an oldster in his seventies or eighties, living in the Great Lakes region and New England and even down into the midsouth today, can remember when he first saw or heard of an opossum in his home country. Not until near the turn of the century did the animals break out of their southern bailiwick and begin that waddling expansion of range once more.

Nowadays the animal ranges by its own establishment over almost all of the area east of the Mississippi, with presently the exception of unsuitable north-woods domain in northern parts of the Great Lakes states, and extreme northern New England. It is found even across the border in Ontario, in the farm country along lakes Erie and Ontario.

There are opossums in eastern Nebraska and over all the central states, the Ozarks and Oklahoma, and even into eastern Colorado. To further illustrate what determined travelers opossums are, early in this century captive specimens were taken to California and either accidentally or purposely were released in the Los Angeles vicinity. Today the opossum is in residence in the western portions of the Pacific Coast states clear from Mexico to Canada.

Although opossums here and there exhibit marked color differences, they are all the same species. The average animal looks at a glance to be simply gray. Close inspection shows that the deep undercoat is usually quite white, but the hairs black-tipped. The long outer guard hairs are nearly white, or at least white over a part of their length. This of course gives the generally gray appearance. However, melanistic opossums, or at least dark specimens, are not uncommon. In these the long outer hair has no white, and is almost black throughout. Here and there a true albino turns up. But there are also color phases that are unusually pale, almost white, and these are indeed handsome creatures, if "handsome" can be applied to the opossum.

A few opossums appear brownish, but this color phase is not very common. There are variations in ear and foot hues. The ears may be solid black, or with distinct white tips. The toes, usually whitish against black feet, may be black on the ends. In northern areas opossums are seen now and then with short tails or ears. This is a sign of frostbite. It is probable that the naked tail and ears, and the fact that the opossum, though it dens up in the coldest weather, is not a hibernator, are factors in limiting its range. It is doubtful that it can spread much farther north unless evolution drastically changes it over millenniums.

Long ago the opossum wormed its way into our language because of its habit of playing dead. At one time it was believed that the opossum used this ruse to make enemies believe it was dead, so that they would then go away and leave it alone. Credence was lent

# Range of the Opossum

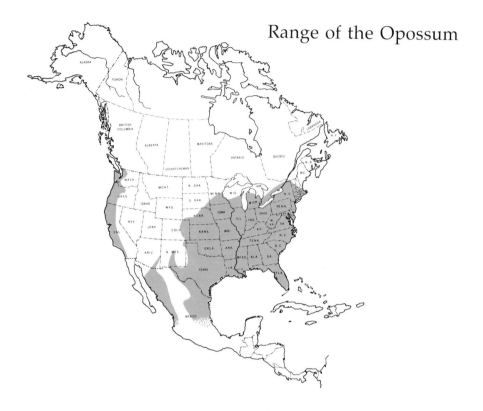

to this theory by the fact that the opossum does have a distinctive and not altogether pleasant odor that influences predators to leave it alone, once it is presumed to be dead.

This odor is not especially noticeable at close range by a person, but apparently it smells strong to a dog. Many a hound that will run possums will refuse to grab one, and many a dog that will bay and kill a possum won't touch it more than enough to be convinced it is dead. It is a curious fact that though predators kill opossums, they seldom eat them. Owls now and then kill and eat one. Oddly, the only creatures that seem to relish the opossum are buzzards, which eat them as carrion, and man.

At any rate, at one time when an opossum "played possum" and dogs wandered off and left it, hunters believed it logical that the animal simply used the ruse hoping to save its life. Modern science, however, tends to the belief that the animal doesn't make any conscious decision in the matter. A theory currently presumed correct is that when under severe stress the opossum experiences a kind of paralysis. Some substance is shot through its system that affects nerve centers in the brain.

For those who have never witnessed this unusual phenomenon, it can be described about as follows. When harassed by dogs or hunters, the animal suddenly falls on its side on the ground, utterly limp, eyes closed, mouth fallen open. It can be picked up and handled or carried, and it makes no movement whatever. It is conceivable, of course, that this death-feigning act, though involuntary, may be an intricate adaptation by nature that, combined with the odor that causes predators to spurn the opossum as food, helps protect it.

However, as curious as the playing-possum act is the fact that not all opossums evidence it. It is actually not a common reaction. Hunters who have taken hundreds of opossums over the years with their hounds agree that only occasionally does one react this way. A Texas rancher who for years has had opossums get into 55-gallon steel drums in which he burns trash says that he has long been puzzled as to why some do and some don't keel over.

"They are agile enough to leap up the outside of a barrel," he related, "and fall down inside. But apparently they need a running start, and if the barrel is almost empty of ashes one on the inside can't leap back out. When I find one and tip the barrel on its side, it will usually skedaddle immediately. However, every now and then one simply falls flat and I have to rake it out. I've watched one lie inert for fifteen minutes, begin to revive, see me watching, and faint all over again."

An opossum can bite severely and usually is willing to. In fact, it has more teeth than any other of our animals. The various wild cats have either twenty-eight or thirty, depending on species, the raccoon forty, and the wild dogs and the bears forty-two, but the opossum has fifty. When scared and backed into a corner, it pulls back its lips, hisses, and shows all those teeth.

The opossum is one of the toughest animals for its size. Since colonial times it has been more or less standard procedure for those hunting the opossum for food and hide to simply hit it on the head to kill it. It was always easy to hold off a dog or shake one out of a tree and whack it before it could get away. The .22 rifle or pistol is nowadays the standard arm for most opossum hunters, but undoubtedly some millions of the animals over the years have met their demise at the heavy end of a club.

Yet hunters long ago discovered that a simple clip would no more than stun the animal. Opossums under scientific study have been discovered by the score to have had numerous broken bones that had healed, even crushed vertebrae. Opossums "killed" by dogs or by hunters and tossed into a vehicle have been found alive and hissing viciously when the hunters arrived home. Possibly the physical toughness may actually be related to a low intelligence, which in some animals correlates with high tolerance for pain and injury. This innate toughness may be one reason for the animal's long survival and abundance.

With the upsurge in fur prices during the early and middle 1970s, opossum hides did not rise in value much compared to pelts of other furbearers. The fur is widely used, but mostly in cheap trim. In addition, as our human population becomes more and more urban, opossum hunting, although still a popular sport in rural areas where the animal is abundant, is by no means as common as it once was. Thus the opossum, which has vastly extended its range during this century, has fewer pressures upon it in our modern times. In many places it is so abundant that it is a downright nuisance. Whether because of lack of wariness and intelligence or by the simple expedient of easy adaptation, it lives congenially—from its viewpoint at least—with its human neighbors over a wide variety of latitudes and climates.

## HABITAT

Throughout its original range the opossum was most abundant along the hardwood stream bottoms and lower lands, where it found an abundance both of forage and of places to curl up in hiding to sleep during the day. Farm lands with woodlots were also perfect for it. For the most part, as the opossum extended its range northward, these same basic habitat types were its preference.

Thus, the varieties of trees may differ, and of farm crops, but wherever the opossum is found it depends most frequently and abundantly either on settled country of mixed farms and woods, or on the creeks and rivers and lakes with their bordering woodlands of hardwoods or at least of mixed hardwoods and evergreens. Deserts and high mountains are in almost all instances barriers. This is because either of inadequate food over the small range of each individual animal, or else lack of suitable places to hide and rest. Perhaps the hot, dry climate of deserts is also unsuitable.

Swamps and swamp edges and drier marshes of tall grass with scattered trees and willow clumps are home to opossums. Examples of their adaptability as long as ample food is obtainable are found in Texas, Oklahoma, and Kansas. In Texas the opossum is fully at home in the eastern "piny woods," a humid region of nowadays numerous huge impoundments. It is less abundant but at least present over the cactus and thornbrush region south from San Antonio to the Mexican border, and it is scattered here and there over the west-central plains and into the Panhandle. In those last-named areas the wooded stream and creek courses, even though some of them are dry much of the year, enable the animal to penetrate into grasslands that it might not otherwise inhabit.

Much of the same situation exists in Oklahoma, where opossums range from the mixed heavy forests of the hilly east and southeast westward over much of the more arid plains region. In Kansas thousands of possums are trapped each winter by farm boys who pick up a few extra dollars for the hides. Possums are not at all difficult to trap. Here again, in Kansas, their wanderings are in general tied to the broad wooded area of stream courses and to farm woodlots.

### FEEDING

According to long tradition, an opossum would rather eat persimmons than anything else. Legend would have us believe that practically every possum ever wedded to sweet taters in a roasting pan had waxed awesomely fat beforehand by gorging on this staple wild fruit. The fact is, although the persimmon does blanket the deep south, the midsouth, and parts of the midwest in its range, the species never was, nor is it presently, all that common, and the fruiting season is brief. A possum bent on living on persimmons would have had a tough schedule even in the good old days.

They do indeed eat persimmons, They also eat almost anything else that is remotely edible. A fox, for example, will kill a mole, but shies from eating it. A possum gobbles it down and calls it good. In some latitudes insects make up a basic percentage of opossum diet during the summer. Angleworms, small snakes, frogs, crayfish, salamanders, and lizards when these quick creatures can be caught all stoke the possum's fat belly.

Untold numbers of opossums are killed annually on the highways—probably hundreds of thousands of them in total—because the animals feed on carrion from other vehicle kills. One gentleman who loved roast possum is said to have given it up forever when he found a possum denned up inside the remnant carcass of a dead cow, having its warmth and food both from the same source.

Fruit of all kinds, wild and domestic, is eagerly eaten. Corn in the milk, and sometimes when ripe, is as welcome to a possum as to a coon. So are melons. Birds and their eggs and young are a staple. Opossums are surprisingly adept at catching mice. Now and then they bumble into a rabbit's nest and eat the young, and the adult too if they happen to be able to seize one. Very occasionally an opossum gets into trouble with a farmer or poultry raiser because it learns to kill chickens. It is by no means as handy at this as are foxes and raccoons.

During the summer various greens go into the diet to garnish the fruit, meat, insects, and carrion. As fall approaches the animals feed more and more heavily. As acorns and beechnuts begin to fall, they gorge on these fat-rich foods also. By the time winter has arrived even in the south, food is a bit less abundant. The opossum seldom needs to worry. It is now so fat that it can get through the leaner months if need be on a far more meager intake.

### MOVEMENTS

Individual opossums seldom wander very far. They don't need to, nor are they physically geared to long travel. The opossum's broadly diverse diet allows it to keep its belly full by making rather short forays over a small home area. On many occasions in winter snow an opossum has been tracked in the morning from a place where it had slept during the previous night, and found bedded down after leaving a wandering, foraging trail no more than a crisscross of 10 acres away.

Most observers agree, in fact, that given ample food an opossum may live out its life on a patch as small as 10 acres, and at the most it is not likely to roam over more than 50. In the northern part of its range travel in winter may be farther than in the south. This is simply a matter of having to move about more to find enough to eat. Most hunters agree that in fall the animals are more active and wander more than at other times. This may be because fall and winter are when hunters pay most attention to them. It is undoubtedly influenced by the fall dispersal of families, each seeking to stake out its own home, and also by the urge to fatten up for winter.

No individual is very adamant about keeping others of its tribe out of its domain. The opossum is a loner, except during the breeding season. But it isn't inclined to argue with opossum neighbors that come nosing about its home area, and any one, in turn, may mosey off across a field where it does not usually hunt, cut the

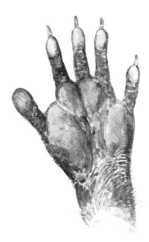

*The hind foot of the opossum is designed like a human hand in miniature.*

tracks of others, or meet them and just go along peacefully, as if with a passing nod.

During all of its wanderings the opossum moves along at a waddling gait, never in a hurry unless pressed by danger. Even then it isn't much of a runner. Carrying its usually fat body on short legs and its rather odd feet, when it attempts to run it appears almost to be in trouble. The tail switches side to side and the body rolls precariously, as if about to tip over at any moment. The tail appears to act as some sort of balance mechanism. The whole impression of the movement is awkward and comic, a study in making haste slowly.

In a tree, however, the opossum is a master of climbing. It feeds to some extent in trees, robbing bird nests or gorging on fruit, or on occasion lying on a limb or in a squirrel's nest to snooze. Even though the major share of its foraging is on the ground, because most of the food is there and easily attainable, the animal is uniquely equipped for climbing.

The hind foot is designed like a human hand in miniature. There are four rather stubby, well-padded fingers with nails, plus a nailless thumb, actually a big toe. This thumb works like one, the joint joining it to the palm designed to allow it to work opposite to those of the "fingers." This allows the foot to grip securely even very small branches when it climbs. The toes of the forefeet are more slender and widely fanned, and the animal is adept in holding with them.

It doesn't have to depend entirely on its uniquely designed feet for gripping. This is the only animal on the North American continent that has a prehensile tail. That means it can use its tail like an extra foot, to hang on with. Commonly an opossum wraps the end of its tail about a branch as it moves out fearlessly on very slender ones, in order to steady it. Or it secures the tail around a branch, then lets go with all feet in order to reach a morsel, or to let itself down to a lower limb.

An especially fat, large animal probably cannot hold its bulk by tail grip alone, but individuals of moderate weight can. The tail is also used for other interesting work. A female with small young not long out of her pouch occasionally carries the little ones clinging in the long fur on her back. She may curve her hairless tail over her back to give the youngsters a solid gripping bar to hang on to. It is said that in making a nest of dry grass in a den, an opossum pulls up mouthfuls, shoves them back toward the rear, cinches up a load in its flexible circled tail, and hauls it inside for bedding.

The opossum is not a hibernator. It does, however, den up at times when the weather is cold. The den may be in any of a number of handy places. A hollow log does fine. So does a hollow stump or the area beneath upturned roots, the abandoned burrow of some other animal, or a small cave. Dense, dry marsh grass serves sometimes. Old buildings are favorite locations, where one may squeeze in under the floor, or find a cozy nest in an attic, or a horse manger. All such places are also used by the opossum as daytime sleeping locations. Although opossums are occasionally seen waddling around by day, they are basically nocturnal. Even when one decides to den up during a blizzard, it doesn't stay long. After still, cold winter nights, as many a country dweller knows, the next morning finds opossum tracks meandering about the fields or woodlot.

When hunters are out with their dogs, unlike the fox or raccoon that may become disturbed immediately at the sound of baying on a trail, the dumb little opossum seldom pays heed. It seems oblivious that the noise has anything to do with it. Thus the dogs are likely to be practically on it before it begins to run. Even at its muddled gait it can still start out pretty well. Built close to the ground, it scurries into undergrowth hard for dogs to plow through. But it isn't much of a trickster at eluding pursuit.

Indeed, the chase is likely to be brief. The animal takes to a tree, or pops into the first hole or opening of any sort that is presented, or gets bayed flatfooted against a stump or in whatever cover the hounds have overtaken it. About the only defense it presents then is to pull back the lips of its long, sharp snout, bare that big mouthful of teeth, drool copiously, and hiss at its tormentors. It will bite when a dog makes a pass at it. But aside from attempting to look mean, it isn't much of a battler. Nor does it have the vocal abilities to squall or growl like the raccoon. Some individuals may mutter a bit with low grunting, or growl a little. For the most part, however, aside from the hissing sound which is apparently an attempt to frighten an enemy, the opossum has little to say.

### BREEDING

As if the thumbed hind foot, the prehensile tail, and the female's pouch for carrying the young were not odd enough, the opossum has a peculiarly designed breeding mechanism. The female is equipped with two wombs. The scientific generic name, *Didelphis*, "double-wombed," recognizes this fact. To serve this female peculiarity properly, the male is equipped with a penis that at the forward end is split into two parts. This male oddment has given rise to endless imaginative speculation about the mechanics of breeding in the opossum, but actually the opossum approach to breeding is the usual one.

The breeding season is not as restricted as it is among many animals. It may begin about the first of the year, and continue on until fall in the more congenial climates of the southern part of the range. In the north it is over sooner, usually by May at latest. This arrangement assures that young opossums in colder latitudes have a better chance to grow large enough to care for themselves before the severe weather of their first winter.

The males wander more during breeding season, mating with all receptive females they can find. One of the reasons the opossum has been able to remain abundant and to spread its range is that females throughout all the southern area usually are bred twice each season and give birth to two litters, the first born early in the year, in January or February, the second about June. It is believed that farther south, in Mexico and Central America, some females may produce as many as three litters annually.

### BIRTH AND DEVELOPMENT

That's a lot of opossums. Even one litter is large, averaging seven to ten but sometimes twice that many, or even more. Yet so curiously are birth and development arranged that in any litter of more than twelve or thirteen, all young above that many are doomed to die. There is no place for them, no milk available.

In the mother's pouch, which she can keep snugly closed with specialized muscles, there are either twelve or thirteen teats, the number differing among individuals. These are neatly arranged in a long U pattern. to give room for the tiny young. The baby opossums, born far prematurely, attach themselves to the teats, first come. When all places are taken, any young left over cannot survive, for this is not a share-alike arrangement.

The reason there can be no sharing is that young opossums are born only thirteen days after the female was bred. They are so premature that they still have no eyes, the ears are barely developing, and the rear legs and tails are only suggestions of what they will be. Internal organs can be seen throughthe transparent sides of the body. The babies are so tiny that it would take fifteen or sixteen to weigh an ounce.

How these naked and partly formed young manage to reach the mother's pouch, enter it, find a teat, and hook up to it is one of the marvels of nature. Scientists used to believe the mother picked up the tiny youngsters and placed them in the pouch. What actually happens is that they somehow immediately drag themselves by their fairly well-developed forelegs and feet, the toes of which are already equipped with miniature nails. Once inside the pouch, each baby instinctively locates one of the long, slender teats. It attaches itself, quite literally swallowing the end of the teat, and there it stays, hooked up and nursing as needed for at least a month and usually a bit longer. Baby opossums are the original incubator babies. The opossum is the only native North American marsupial.

The preemies grow swiftly. After they once release their milk supply they begin to explore inside the pouch, and bravely peek out now and then. Young that were too numerous to find a milk supply die within hours, and if they have actually gained entry to the pouch, the mother is able to expel them. The lucky ones remain in their snug home until about eight weeks old. Then at mouse size they begin to venture outside, but return if disturbed.

At this stage, when the mother travels about, foraging, the young cling to the fur of her back, and to her tail when she swings it over her back, and go along for the ride. But soon they are off beginning to sample solid food. Natural attrition is fairly high among the young during the premature weeks and from then on until they are foraging on their own. Of a full pouch quota, only five or six to eight or nine of a large brood may reach the crucial two-month stage.

*Baby opossums cling to their mother's back when she travels about in search of food.*

Family ties are not very lasting. In fact, opossums are among the speediest of animals in turning out families and getting them launched. By the time the young are roughly twelve weeks old — which adds up to only 3½ months from conception — the family of youngsters begins to scatter, each going its own way and staking out a home and hunting ground for itself.

### SENSES

The opossum's sharp nose has just as sharp a sense of smell. It does not need to scent food at long distances, however, but only close at hand. Conceivably it may home in on carrion at longer distances, following its nose. Apparently the sense of smell is not much concerned with danger, or else the rather dimwitted little creature just doesn't pay attention. It seems not to scent pursuit or at least isn't perturbed until the last moment.

Observation of opossums leads one to believe that sight is poor. Or perhaps it is simply that it is good enough close up but not needed over more than modest distances. Hearing is sharp, and probably is an assist during foraging. The animal may be able to detect sounds of approaching danger, but if so it usually either fails to properly interpret them or else just doesn't pay much attention.

## SIGN

The only sign left by the opossum that is of much importance is its tracks. When a den is located, a handful of leaves or grass scooped up at entrance may show evidence of hair, and hunters occasionally check likely sites this way to see if they are in use. But the track is so distinctive that it is easily identified. However, an opossum wandering in a woodlot or field does not leave footprints unless there is snow or it happens to cross a soft spot of ground.

Thus hunters, or others seeking tracks, generally look along the edges of ponds and streams, or else go out in the morning when snow is on the ground to check likely places where an opossum may have been foraging. The tracks are printed usually in pairs, a hind-foot and a forefoot track almost side by side, but the hind print slightly behind—left front and right hind together, and vice versa.

The toes on both front and rear feet are quite long. The front print might be described whimsically as spidery, but with the palm portion showing quite well. The hind print is the unmistakable one, because of the unique design of the foot, discussed above. The thumb, or big toe, print is positioned as it would be in a human hand print, but even more canted or angled back and downward away from the palm. The end joint of this big toe is rather round and blunt, and as noted earlier without a nail.

The three longer "fingers" in the center of the odd hind foot make their print close together as a rule, and with the nails leave a comparatively long impression. The fifth toe or "little finger" is held off to the side away from the other three. The prints of the five toes of the front foot leave a more evenly spread print. The forefoot track measures on the average about 2 inches across the toe prints.

Opossum tracks are unmistakable because no other American animal has feet of similar shape. When the opossum is walking, the distance between the pairs of tracks is anywhere from about 6 to 10 inches. In soft snow tail marks often accompany the giveaway footprints. In some places the tail may leave a regular dragging depression, or it may only touch here and there. Opossum droppings differ widely in consistency, and are not distinctive enough in shape to be of much use as sign.

## HUNTING

There seems to be no halfway feeling about opossum hunting. Dedicated coon-dog men, and fox hunters who follow their hounds, have nothing but contempt for the opossum. It is a plain nuisance and exasperation to them because most dogs unless exceptionally well broken will run an opossum the instant they hit a trail. This interferes with the purpose of the chase to these specialists and ruins an evening for them. Conversely, the old-time possum hunter just loves to get out on a dark, quiet night in the south, or in the hills of the Ozarks, and make short chase after chase. In good possum country on a good night a whole sackful may be bagged in a few hours of struggling and falling around the woods.

There is another category of hunters who are not choosy. These are the ones who enjoy the combination hunt—take 'em as they come, a coon here, a possum there. They are willing to compromise and just enjoy themselves. These undoubtedly make up the majority of the opossum-hunting group, for it is hardly possible in good range to unleash hounds and not have them run one animal as readily as another. These mixed-bag dog men just go out at night and let the dogs cast about in likely places until they hit a track.

The few specialist possum hunters still around are mostly even in this modern day confined to the south. Farther north most are raccoon hunters whose dogs run opossums incidentally. When the old hands start out, they take the dogs to a place where they've seen opossum tracks, or where they know the animals are abundant, or where opossums are known to have been feeding—near that fruit-bearing old persimmon tree, for example.

Dark, still nights are favored. The accouterments are few and simple, the old coal-oil lantern is now as passé as button shoes. The usual light is a headlamp of the type that can be turned down dim or up to extra-bright. One of a group of hunters may carry a powerful flashlight. Seldom does more than one hunter carry a weapon, and it is a .22 rifle or pistol. Even an old single-shot .22 is sufficient.

The short, noisy chase is often accompanied by much crashing and falling of the hurrying hunters charging through brush and woodlands, by yelling and laughing as they make for the tree where the dogs have the quarry bayed. This is a classic fun sport, not a terribly serious endeavor. Sometimes the opossum is shaken out, but more often the dogs are leashed as they stand leaping up the tree trunk and bawling their primitive song over the success of their trailing. Then the light is shined on the treed possum and it is dispatched.

Here and there young country-dwelling hunters like to roll out at dawn of a crisp winter morning and look for opossum tracks made during the night. Sometimes the farm dog, of almost any mixed-up variety that has a fair nose, is allowed to work out the track. But in snow it is easy enough to follow and the young nimrods soon find the place where the animal has denned for the day. It may be prodded out, or the old forked-stick trick employed to twist into its fur and hide and haul it out. However opossum hunting is done, it is always a plain, old-fashioned pastime couched in the long tradition of early days in America.

It is certain that hunting will never decimate the opossum population. Many wildlife experts believe that the curious little animal is still not through its North American colonization. They believe it possible that in due time the opossum may virtually blanket practically all of the lower states and make incursions farther into Canada to the limits of its ability to cope with the winter cold.

Some even suspect that over coming centuries—not much time to a possum—it may evolve ways to adapt to the weather and range even farther north than seems presently possible for it. Whether or not this occurs, it is a safe bet that the dumb little possum will be on stage in numbers, waddling its way across the scene when many of the more intelligent wildlife characters have long been retired to the wings.

# CHUCKS

## Woodchuck, or American Marmot

*Marmota monax*

## Rockchuck, or Yellow-Bellied Marmot

*Marmota flaviventris*

## Hoary Marmot

*Marmota caligata*

The chucks as game animals are currently in a kind of limbo. They are a sporting challenge because of their wariness and inclination to dive into their burrows the instant danger is sighted. In settled country especially the woodchuck becomes so uneasy over human intrusion that shooters must make extremely long shots at it. The same occurs with the rockchucks in the high-country west. For many years woodchuck shooting has been so popular particularly over the eastern, northeastern, and midsouth mountain states that the animal actually sparked the development of most of the

Woodchuck

long-range, small-caliber, flat-shooting "varmint" rifles presently manufactured, and a number of calibers now obsolete but once famous.

Yet whether woodchuck hunting should be called varmint hunting or game hunting is arguable. The same applies to shooting rockchucks in the west. The hides of the chucks, excepting that of the hoary marmot of the Canadian northwest and Alaska, have never been utilized for fur, because the hair is too coarse and the underfur inconsequential. The far-north hoary marmot has a fine, soft, dense underfur. Since ancient times Eskimos and Indians have highly prized its hide for making parkas and clothing. But it is not an item of any consequence on the world fur market. In early days tough woodchuck hides were often tanned after the hair had been taken off and used for leather patching, for boot laces, and in general as a kind of rawhide for varied repairs.

Woodchucks, and the marmots, are good eating. Many Indians in the eastern United States eagerly sought the woodchuck for food. Eskimos and Indians throughout the range of the hoary marmot have always hunted it for food and considered it a delicacy. But American hunters, aside from those early-day hunters who ate it because they needed to eat practically anything they killed, have never been avid diners on the chucks. Lip service is paid to its edibility, especially in magazine articles. Here and there in the east groups of hunters proclaim the woodchuck a delicacy, but in the west fewer bother to prepare the rockchuck for the table, even though it is excellent fare.

Thus the standing of the chucks as game animals hinges today basically upon the sporting qualities of the stalk involved, and the usual long-range shots presented at a small target. Is this merely pest shooting? Many a farmer in the east and the Great Lakes region would certainly call the woodchuck a pest, or varmint. Where they are abundant they dig deep burrows and throw up large mounds of dirt, their dens scattered over meadows. This interferes with growing crops such as hay, and the harvest of them.

Some landowners worry about their livestock unwittingly stepping into a woodchuck burrow and breaking a leg. It is a kind of old wives' tale that farmers have repeated and passed down to progeny, and still do in some places. But finding a case of a broken horse or cow leg has always proved difficult. Certainly a running horse that stuck a foot into a burrow *could* break a leg. And somebody in every farm family always knew of a case — a man who knew a man who said that he had heard . . .

Rockchuck

# Range of the Woodchuck

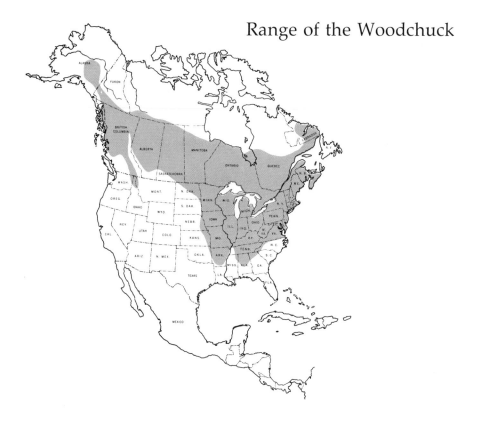

So we have the paradox of the chucks as game animals. In some states woodchucks receive protection. They are on the game list in Connecticut, Iowa, Illinois, Michigan, New Jersey, Pennsylvania, New York, and Tennessee, for example, with a stipulated season, and, it is predicted that more states will follow. Most dedicated woodchuck and rockchuck hunters strongly encourage others coming into the sport to treat these animals nowadays strictly as *game*, not as varmints, to try for clean kills that do not mangle the target, and to take only what they will actually dress and eat. So, sport animal or nuisance, challenging target or varmint, the chucks at least up to this time deserve to be named among the game animals. Many a chuck-shooting enthusiast would be ready to fight if it were suggested that the animals be considered pests, as for example, the jack rabbit and ground squirrel generally are.

The hoary marmot might be as game as the others, but it receives virtually no attention from sport hunters because of its far-north range. Within the lower-48 states there are a few in the high country of northern Idaho and central Washington. They are

# Range of the Rockchuck

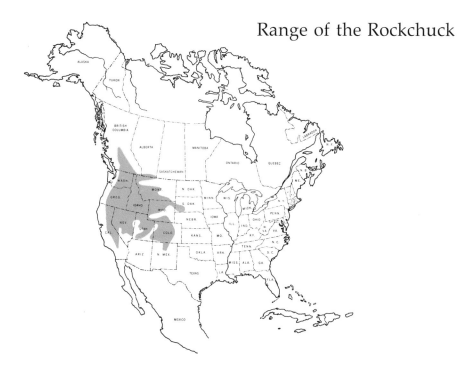

# Range of the Hoary Marmot

present over most of British Columbia and spill over along the southern half of its border with Alberta into the Rockies there. The range stretches on over the Yukon and much of Alaska, even into the far-north region. Some scientists believe there are several distinct species of marmots within this range, but there is no general agreement. Presumably one of those lives in the far fringes of the range in the north, and others on the Olympic Peninsula of Washington and on Vancouver Island. Probably these are simply races of the type species, *Marmota caligata.* The scientific species name, incidentally, refers to its black feet, the word meaning "boots"—it is "the booted" marmot. As noted, natives seldom hunt the hoary marmot for sport, but for food and fur.

The yellow-bellied marmot, which most outdoorsmen call a rockchuck, has been split into numerous races or subspecies that differ slightly as a result of specific ranges. All are mountain animals dwelling in the Rockies, from extreme northern New Mexico throughout the high country of Colorado, Nevada, and northeastern and central California on northward into central British Columbia. To the east they long ago found their way across northern Wyoming to the Black Hills of South Dakota.

The well-known woodchuck, which for not very logical reasons has since early times been whimsically dubbed a diminutive swine of sorts—groundhog, whistle pig—is the most wide-ranging of the chucks. In the south it reaches over much of Arkansas, northern Alabama, and Georgia, sweeps northward to Canada, and blankets all of the eastern, New England, and Great Lakes states. The Canadian range is even larger, from Labrador far west into portions of eastern Alaska, and south into the northern tip of Idaho.

A mark of the abundance and common popularity of any animal is the extent to which it has worked itself into the language and legends. Everyone knows the answerless riddle: How much wood would a woodchuck chuck if a woodchuck could chuck wood? Everyone also annually awaits the news of the appearance of the groundhog from its burrow on February 2. If it can't see its shadow, spring is about to arrive. Alas, if it does see its shadow, back it goes underground to snooze away the next six weeks, which are predicted as tough ones, continuing winter. Newspapers—and now television—always have made much of "Groundhog Day," which actually falls long before groundhogs come out of hibernation.

Children's stories since Daniel Boone's day have been populated with lovable little groundhogs. Many a country kid in years

## THE CHUCKS

COLOR: **Woodchuck,** brown, variable from reddish to nearly black, with guard hairs silvery-tipped and making general appearance grizzled; tail, feet, bridge of nose and forehead darker to black; all-black (melanistic) individuals not especially uncommon, albino specimens occasional. **Rockchuck,** upper parts grizzly brown, lighter as a rule than woodchuck, underparts variable, from yellowish to a distinct, bright red-orange; shoulders and sides of head below ears buffy, muzzle whitish, and more of the same near and between eyes; feet yellowish or matching belly; black specimens rather common, often with silvery-tipped guard hairs over shoulders and back, and with pale muzzle. **Hoary marmot,** body chiefly grizzled silvery gray to very pale whitish flecked with darker, sometimes with reddish rump; feet and tail darker to black; bridge of nose, top of head, and broad swath from each eye back across ear and down to shoulder dark to black; muzzle and forward of eyes pale to whitish, with band of dark crosswise midway across snout.

MEASUREMENTS AND WEIGHT: **Woodchuck,** overall length 1½ to 2-plus feet, with tail 5 or 6 inches of that; shoulder height 6 or 7 inches; weight 4 or 5 to a maximum of 10 pounds, very occasionally slightly more. **Rockchuck,** moderately larger to maximum of 2½ feet overall length, height 7 inches; average weight to 12 pounds, but some large males to 15–18 pounds. **Hoary marmot,** largest of the chucks, averaging 2½ feet overall length, height about 9 inches; weight 10 to as much as 20 pounds.

GENERAL ATTRIBUTES: Chunky, stocky body with, in comparison, short tail; short rounded ears and rather blunt rodent nose; short, strong legs; feet with sturdy claws for burrow digging; a habit of rearing up to sit on haunches to survey domain; utters shrill whistle when alarmed.

past raised a baby groundhog as a pet, and in general the animal is honored, although not always without some grumbling from land-owners.

### HABITAT

Over most of the eastern United States the woodchuck resides happily in farm fields in rolling country. But a more general view of woodchuck habitat encompasses all forest clearings and many forest areas that are open. In southern Michigan, for example, woodchucks inhabit the edges of crop fields and often burrow right out in the middle of alfalfa fields. In northern Michigan, a small clearing far out in the mixed forest of maple, poplar, oak, and various evergreens, a clearing perhaps where wild clover grows, may have a woodchuck den. In northern Manitoba, woodchucks have been observed living happily along roadsides where grass is abundant, even though the forest off the highway is thick, dark spruce.

Unquestionably woodchucks were able to increase their numbers and probably spread their range as settlement opened up the forests of the eastern United States. Typical of excellent woodchuck range are the green valleys and farm meadows of Kentucky and Tennessee, and sweeps of farm country in New York and New England. Much of the popularity of woodchuck hunting in the east resulted from the animal's ability to sustain itself on small farms, to the extent in fact that it is often considered a nuisance.

There are hazards for woodchucks in this kind of domain. Farm dogs harass them, and some learn to stalk and kill them efficiently. Much of the best woodchuck range is also inhabited by the red fox, an enemy that kills a good many younger woodchucks. A full-grown and crotchety old male woodchuck, however, is no slouch when it comes to a tangle with either a dog or a fox, and gives a good account of itself.

The rockchuck or yellow-bellied marmot of the high-country west carved a quite different home for itself out of the wilds. It lives on the slopes and among the rocks, in mountain country where views are long and summers short. Tourists going over high passes on western highways, passes that reach to above timberline in the Rockies, often spot rockchucks sunning on rocks in summer way up at 11,000 feet or more, feeding in the green mountain meadows, or even out pottering about in June over snowbanks.

Some scientists claim the rockchuck is a social colonial type, because it is usual, when one is spotted, to discover a number of them on the same slope. However, they do not seem especially gregarious. There is room for all without getting on each other's nerves or usurping territorial rights. Possibly the appearance of colonial living is the result only of dispersal of young over particularly suitable living and feeding territory. The animals utilize the talus and boulder-strewn slopes, the outcrops and cliff bases for homes, burrowing in among rocks or simply using holes in a rock pile for dens.

As many rockchuck hunters have discovered, old ghost towns in the western mountains are invariably taken over by marmots as favorite living places. They have been observed often living among the debris of mine tailings, and in old shafts. They also, like the woodchuck, love to set up a home under the floor of an old building or in some cranny within it.

In their mountain domain the rockchucks have a somewhat tougher life so far as native enemies are concerned. Hunters aren't much of a problem, except on rare occasions, because the region is vast and not heavily settled. Now and then a family of chucks gets down into a farming valley, mows its way through an alfalfa patch or a garden, and gets into trouble. But most of the time the dangers arise with predators—coyotes, bobcats, bears, eagles—all of which well know that a fat chuck is a delicacy.

The bailiwick of the hoary marmot is in general similar to that of its relative, except that it ranges over a region of more severe climate. It is a creature of the rock slides, the cliffs and crags fringed by alpine meadows. The grizzly bear digs it from its den, wolves harass the colonies. So does the coyote, and the lynx. Like the rockchuck, this marmot, largest of the tribe, is reasonably sociable, if living in colonies scattered over a slope can be considered that. Again, however, this habit is probably pursued only because of family dispersals and because forage happens to be ample in the region.

### FEEDING

The chucks are all vegetarians. All will occasionally eat a bit of meat, and woodchucks are known to fill up on grasshoppers and other insects now and then. But their main fare is vegetation in proximity to their den sites. Because of the vast range of the woodchuck, and the combined enormous expanse of the marmot tribe, various foods are available in various locations.

In the farm country of the eastern United States, crops such as clover, corn, field grains when green, fruits wild and domestic, browse from low shrubs, and garden vegetables all go into woodchuck diet. When a chuck discovers a home garden patch, with lettuce, beans, and sweet corn prime, it can eat its way through a ruinous amount in a day or so.

Throughout the woodland range, native grasses, clover, the alfalfa field of a forest-fringe settler, the leaves of wild strawberry, and various wild fruits are the mainstays. In the bailiwicks of the mountain chucks, the marmots, grasses and forbs of the slopes suffice. In spring, as any experienced high-country person knows, lush grasses and wildflowers seem literally to leap from the fringes of snowbanks when the first warm days arrive.

In the more rocky situations, marmots may forage in valleys and climb back to their homes. But that is seldom necessary, although when a group finds reachable farm crops the damage is as bad as the woodchuck manages. There are always browse shrubs on the slopes and along the mountain meadow edges to add roughage to the more succulent vegetation. The chucks, incidentally, worry little about water. Their intake of green foods is so large that enough liquid to suffice is in their diet. The forage of the big hoary marmot differs from that of its relatives only as it is limited to the plants that grow in its homeland.

All of the chucks are daytime foragers. They begin the day's work as soon as the sun is up, and like all animals follow more or less a routine of several active feeding periods during the day. During the in-between times they love to laze about, sunning at the burrow mouth or atop a rock, and then, when hunger nudges them, filling up again. Only on rare occasions do the chucks come out at night to eat.

The chucks and marmots belong to the large order of rodents, the Rodentia, which also contains the tree and ground squirrels, the prairie dog—actually a kind of ground squirrel—and the porcupine. One of the characteristics of all rodents is the two pairs— one upper, one lower—of incisor teeth. These teeth are in effect self-sharpening chisels that cut plant food.

The continuous sharpening of the cutting edges by perfect matching up of the two sets is a vital matter. The teeth continue growing as long as the animal lives, and the sharpening process by chewing keeps them tailored to a length that fits properly. Now and then individual rodents have mismatched incisors, a "malocclusion." For some reason not fully understood, the woodchuck seems to be especially prone to this dental problem.

Because the incisors continue growing, mismated pairs that do not strike and wear down each other soon become so long that they inhibit eating. Forage cannot be cut, and even if food can somehow be forced into the mouth, the grinding teeth at the back of the jaws cannot come together to chew the food. In some instances the upper incisors begin to turn backward into the mouth, keep on growing, and curve upward into and up through the roof of the mouth, and cause death. This affliction may be more common in other rodent species than is generally known, but it is believed to be a particular disability with woodchucks.

MOVEMENTS

Chucks and marmots are true homebodies. Many an individual at a ripe age, if it could tell stories to its great-great-grandchildren, would have nothing to relate except of happenings within 100 yards

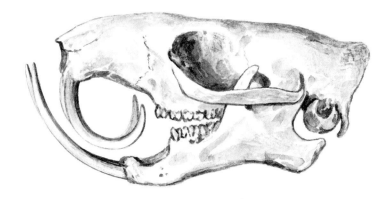

*A woodchuck skull, showing the long incisors that continue to grow during the animal's lifetime. The teeth may grow so long as to prevent the chuck from eating.*

of where it was born. How far a chuck travels depends only on the quality of the forage around its den, and this in turn depends on the quality of the growing year, or in some instances on how a landowner uses his fields.

A marmot on a green mountain slope starts out the day by eating whatever is nearest and most appealing. If after a few weeks it has pretty well cleared off the greens within a 50-yard circle, it keeps on nipping away until it has used up the resources over 100 yards, maybe 200, and perhaps as far as 300. These animals are hibernators, so they must eat for only part of the year. The next spring they start over again on the same turf with a fresh growing season.

The marmots, living among rocks on high slopes, may sometimes have to forage farther than the woodchuck. Some may even be settled in locations where they can slip several hundred yards down the slope, fill up in a rancher's alfalfa patch, then climb back up. But unlike the predators that must roam and make kills catch as catch can, these creatures have an ample larder in their yards, and that is where they live out their lives. To be sure, when grown young leave the family group, they must stake out a feeding patch of their own. But if conditions are suitable, a young adult may settle barely outside its mother's territory, and mow the vegetation almost up to her feeding circle.

The chucks are designed as perfect burrowing and mowing machines. Their claws are tough and their short legs sturdy. They walk, like miniature bears, flat on their feet. They cannot run very fast, and seldom need to. They walk along, feeding, and if danger threatens they do not lead an enemy a chase, in the manner of a rabbit, but hurry home in a bounding gait and dive down the burrow or the hole among the rocks. This is the simple plan on which their lives are based. The idea is to keep a sharp lookout for danger, never to be caught too far from the den site, and to take refuge in the burrow to thwart danger.

The forefeet are designed not only for digging but also to hold vegetation. Chucks are often observed snipping off a mouthful of grass, manipulating it in the forepaws with dexterous "fingers" while sitting upright on their haunches, then stuffing it into the mouth. Because the woodchuck does a lot of digging in loose loam, it is fitted with ears that it can close up to keep loose dirt out. This is important not just because it burrows and lives much of its life underground where cave-ins may occur. Chucks dig a pile of dirt with the forefeet, pushing it back under the belly as they progress. When the dirt needs to be moved, the scheme is to swap ends, put its head against the pile, and shove it outside the hole. This could get a Chuck's ears full of dirt if it didn't contrive to clap them shut.

When the burrow is finished, complete with side chamber for the winter sleep and another to serve as a toilet, a woodchuck has a big pile outside the main entrance. This is usually not the only entrance. Chuck burrows are often intricately designed. Woodchucks, which dig in soft dirt in most places, as opposed to the rocky dwelling places of the marmots, sink the main entrance down several feet deep — at least 2 feet and often twice that. Then they angle off with either a level tunnel or else one that rises slightly to a bedding chamber that may be a foot or more above the original shaft. This is a precaution against water running down the entrance. The sleeping and hibernating quarters aren't likely to be flooded. Some individuals carry dry grass or leaves into the chamber to line it.

At least one rear entrance — there may be several tangent shafts for a number of scattered "rear doors" — has no dirt mound around it. This hole, or in many instances several, are hidden in vegetation with no telltale sign. And they are some yards distant from the mound entrance. Thus, a foraging chuck caught out away from the mound can magically disappear right in the face of an enemy that suddenly appears.

Meanwhile, the entrance where all the dirt has been pushed out and compacted serves as the lookout station. Some elaborate dens

*A typical woodchuck burrow consists of a long tunnel with several chambers. One chamber may be used for hibernation, another as a nest for the young, another as a toilet.*

may have several entrances with mounds. This is where the woodchuck loves to lie sunning itself. The height of the mound gives it a chance to survey a substantial sweep of country. Among marmots, a rock or ledge above or beside the hole serves the same purpose. Here on its mound the chuck lazes. But every little while it rears up for a look around. It sits easily balanced on its haunches, back very straight, front legs dangling down against its belly. Its black, sharp eyes are set well out and a bit protruding, so it can sweep a large arc around it. All of the chucks have this sit-up-and-look habit, although the western and northern marmots, living on the slopes, are already situated for easy survey of a large expanse of country.

The upright position that allows chucks to look around for possible danger is accompanied by a vocal warning when something disturbing or frightening is seen. The woodchuck got its nickname "whistle pig" because of the sharp, shrill whistle of alarm it utters. Sometimes it also clicks and grinds its teeth together with a rattling sound. The sharp whistle may be followed by a series of trills at lower volume. The marmots of the west and northwest also whistle, with more volume than the woodchuck but not as shrill in pitch. The hoary marmot is the loudest whistler of all, with a rather melodious tone.

The cries of warning indicate that the animal uttering them has seen or heard something that disturbs it. When a number of marmots are on a slope within hearing of one that sends out an alarm, they all take it up. If danger seems imminent, into their holes they go. Some observers believe that a sentinel chuck feeds first and then watches to give alarm if danger appears. Most such sentinel tales about nature's creatures are born more of human imagination than scientific fact.

Although the woodchuck doesn't travel very fast, it makes surprisingly good time when it races in bounds for the safety of its burrow. And the rock-dwelling marmots scurry among them, or race up a steep slope and over sharp rocks and boulders with unusual agility for their blocky build. None of the chucks needs to swim often, but all can if they have to. One of the most curious habits of the woodchuck is its penchant for whimsically climbing trees. Rarely one will go up a handy tree if danger, as from a farm dog, threatens. However, many a woodchuck has been spotted in a tree, sometimes 20 feet or more above ground, simply sunning itself, or at least up there for no special reason that an observer can deduce. In farm country a chuck now and then shinnies up a big fencepost and lies down atop it.

During late summer and early fall the chucks stuff themselves with food, putting on an enormous amount of fat for the long period of hibernation. The woodchuck in most latitudes goes below ground about October, although in the far-northern parts of its range it retires earlier. The marmots must take to their dens about September to ride out the severe winters. On cold summer days marmots may not come out to feed, but this has nothing to do with hibernation. However, a curious phenomenon does occasionally occur among marmots when summer weather is unusually hot. One may retire to the coolness of its den and doze off into a semi-dormant state that is called aestivation. This is a kind of temporary hot-weather equivalent of hibernation.

*A marmot in hibernation curls itself into a ball and remains rigid and cold for four to five months.*

When the animals go into dens for the winter, however, authentic hibernation begins. The woodchuck and marmots are the only true hibernators among our game animals. Most of them close off their sleeping quarters—usually a side chamber—by pushing the dirt into the entrance to it. The hibernation process now begins with the animal curling not up but forward. The head is curled down under the body and the haunches also curled tightly down and under so that the chuck forms a ball.

Little by little now, as it drowses, all its bodily functions slow. This is like a racing motor that one adjusts slower and slower until it is idling at the slowest possible rate without stopping. True hibernation as exemplified in the chucks is an amazing natural device to help animals which exhibit it get through a winter during which they otherwise would not be able to survive. As sleep deepens, body temperature slowly drops, inching down, down until at its lower level it may be close to 60 degrees less than normal. With the drop in body temperature, the heart rate and breathing also slow. A chuck's heart may beat no more than five times every sixty seconds, and it may inhale and exhale only once every five minutes or so.

At full hibernation a chuck or marmot is actually cold to the touch—its body temperature is no more than 5 to 10 degrees above freezing! It looks and feels stiff and dead. During the four or five months of hibernation—the period for western and northern marmots is longer as a rule than that for the woodchuck, the hoary marmot seldom showing above ground until May—the stored body fat is slowly burned. When the animals come out of their dens they are thin, weigh about half what they did in fall, and must begin eating as soon as enough greenery can be found.

Often the chucks dwelling in the far north have to dig their way upward through deep snow to reach the surface, and the food situation is precarious for a week or so. Very occasionally during a midwinter thaw woodchucks appear above ground, leaving tracks in the snow and wandering seemingly bewildered. Curiously, the legend of the groundhog and February 2 rests on shaky factual ground. In few places is a woodchuck awake by that date. Most of them begin to appear toward the end of February or during early March.

### BREEDING

Life for several weeks after coming out of hibernation is a severe physical strain on the male. He must try to find food because his fat is dwindling fast. He may be able to find very little. But driving him more than hunger is the breeding urge. He immediately sets out to seek a mate. Other males are also out with the same urge pushing them. Each shuffles from burrow to burrow, sniffing, or follows the trails left by other chucks. Now and then a confrontation occurs between two males. Thin as they are, a severe battle may ensue. Growling, snapping, rattling their teeth, and uttering sharp, angry squeals, the males tumble and slash each other until one withdraws.

Scientists seem uncertain about several aspects of the sex life of the chucks. It is believed that some individuals mate with a single female and stay with her, while other males mate with more than one. Whichever way it may be with most individuals, it is the female that makes up her mind which swain she will accept, and she may be snappish with one suitor and drive him away, then finally succumb to another.

The chucks have anal glands that give off a musky odor. These undoubtedly are used as some form of communication, and conceivably a male traveling from den to den seeking a female can sniff at the den entrance and tell if a potential mate is below. When a willing mate is found, the male simply moves into her apartment for a short period. He may feel like continuing to hang around, or he may move out after breeding has been accomplished. Now and then a stubborn male doesn't want to leave. In that case, the female may move out and find some new housing for herself. Most of the time, whether or not a male is monogamous, chucks and marmots are solitary creatures, each staying within its staked-out den territory.

BIRTH AND DEVELOPMENT

About a month after mating, the female gives birth to a litter of young that number anywhere from two to eight or more. The average for woodchucks is four, but marmot litters are usually larger. They are helpless little creatures, eyes sealed, naked, pink in color, each weighing less than 2 ounces. After a few days a bit of fuzz begins to show and by the time the youngsters are twenty days old they are wriggling and crawling, and are covered with short, soft red-brown hair.

The mother carries out old grass or leaves from the nest as it becomes dirty and brings in a new supply. She may move the young much as a cat does, carrying each by the nape of the neck, so that she can clean up the nest chamber. When the young are a month old their eyes open. Now they are difficult for the mother to keep inside. They begin trying their legs and find their way to the entrance. At first they peer timidly around, but soon they venture out.

Like most young animals they like to play, tumbling and wrestling with each other, hiding in grass, diving down the den hole. They are still nursing. To accommodate them as they grow, the mother often sits upright on her haunches to let them nurse. During the first couple of weeks of experiment in the outside world, however, they begin to nibble at various greens near the den mound. The female occasionally carries fresh greens inside, to encourage them further to try more solid food. Soon they are weaned.

By the time the second month has passed, each young woodchuck is feeding mostly on vegetation and foraging on its own. The family stays together in the den for a short time after that. But now the young chucks, which each weigh a couple of pounds, begin to be a bit crowded in their home. The mother gets irritable with them. By the middle of the summer it is time to leave. She may hustle them along, literally driving some away, or in some instances lead them to nearby unoccupied burrows. Or one by one they may simply wander off, feeling the urge now to set up homes of their own. Most of them spend the remainder of the summer nearby in old dens that they clean out and renovate, or else they dig new ones.

By fall they are foraging farther, fattening like the adults. They also now begin a dispersal, each instinctively seeking a territory of its own. The move may not be to any great distance. In the case of the marmots, young may simply wander off along the same slope on which they were born, find a place that suits each on the fringes of the colony, and fix up a winter home for its first hibernation. Some, but by no means all, chucks start families of their own when they are a year old, even though they are not really fully grown until they are two.

## SENSES

Woodchucks and marmots depend on their eyes more than on their other senses. Even while busily feeding, one will sit up every few seconds to look around. Hunters have discovered to their exasperation that they must move very carefully even when several hundred yards away, or else the quarry will race for the den, sit up to look again, and then dive below ground. Curiosity about danger, however, is often their undoing. After a few minutes of hiding in the den, a chuck will crawl out to peek over the rim of the mound. If it sees nothing disturbing, it will sit up again. This habit often gets chucks into trouble.

Hearing also is sharp. Any unusual sound, even a distant one, will start marmots whistling on a hillside whether or not they see danger. Although all the species apparently have fairly well-developed scenting ability, it apparently plays no great part in alerting. Because of their constant visual appraisal of their surroundings, and no great need to use scent in finding food, these animals probably have never depended greatly on their noses.

## SIGN

Tracks of woodchuck and marmots are not too commonly seen because they don't register, of course, in vegetation. However, they are plainly printed now and then in snow or soft dirt. The hind foot, when the animal is walking, tends to overlap the forefoot print, but when a chuck runs, bounding along, the four prints show. The two hind-foot tracks are out ahead of those of the forefeet, the hind feet not quite side by side, the forefoot prints one behind the other but offset a bit.

The toes are quite long, and the feet are set flat down. A quick means of identification is that the "thumb" of the forefoot is very small. It does not show in the track. Thus the prints of the front feet show four toes, those of the hind feet five. Each track—fore and hind—when it shows the entire foot, measures on the average about 2 inches long.

Droppings are not too often seen around woodchuck dens. Some are buried, some are left in a special chamber below ground. Rockchuck scats, however, can be found around rocky areas where the animals live, and sometimes piles of them give an indication that marmots are residing in rock caves in the vicinity. Scat shapes are varied, and not particularly distinctive.

The plainest signs left by woodchucks, and sometimes by marmots where soil is soft enough, are den mounds. These dirt piles are several feet across and heaped high enough, even though packed by the animals sitting on them, so that they can be spotted from several hundred yards away. Chuck hunters glass a field or slope or find den mounds. Rockchuck dens can sometimes be discovered by walking along a cliff base or rocky slope and looking for well-worn paths leading from a hole among the rocks. Some dens may have heaps of dry grass or other vegetation outside them. The surest signs, of course, are the animals themselves. Hunters seeking woodchucks invariably look with a glass for the quarry sitting up in a field or on a mound. Marmot hunters glass a slope looking—and listening—for their targets.

## HUNTING

In some states a season has been set on woodchucks to make certain the young are of an age to care for themselves before hunting is legal. Whether or not there is such a regulation, hunters should not do any shooting until summer, when the young have been weaned. In moderate climates and latitudes most woodchucks are born in April. Rockchucks are born a bit later. Thus hunting should not begin, where unregulated to protect nursing females, before about the first week of July.

When a field with woodchuck dens has been located, or a western mountainside where vegetation is lush near rocky areas, patient glassing and watching are required to find a target. Eastern chuck hunters sometimes cruise around back roads looking over fields where they have permission to hunt. The western hunter has a slight advantage. He can take up a position from above where he can glass a vast amount of country. If no animals show, the best plan wherever feasible is to find den sites and then watch those. The owner will be nearby, and will be seen at least within an hour sitting up near either the mound or one of the blind entrances, or in the case of the marmots perhaps lying or sitting erect on a nearby rock ledge. In hills or mountains, hunters try to circle and climb to get above a colony or den. These animals habitually scan for danger from below, but not above.

Most hunters, east and west, use flat-shooting rifles such as the .222, the .22-250, and .243, the .223, and others, with powerful scopes. Many dedicated eastern chuck hunters rig all sorts of elaborate tripod rests or even shooting benches for the rifle, for shots may be extremely long, and the target is by comparison small. A 6-power scope is about the lowest power feasible. One of 10-power or 12-power is better. Of course, high-power scopes require an exceedingly steady rest. Western hunters usually can place a jacket on a rock and get a good rest that way. A good many eastern chuck hunters use rifles with heavy barrels, to get a finer, steadier hold.

No truly sporting chuck hunter is careless about shot placement. That is part of the challenge. Only the head is an acceptable target. This leaves the meat to eat, if desired, and avoids any possible chance of wounding an animal and having it duck down its burrow to die. The hunter either makes a clean hit or a clean miss.

Some specialists enjoy the greater challenge of using a pistol or a rimfire rifle, and a few make it still more difficult by using bow and arrow. All these weapons obviously require a close stalk. And that in turn requires the utmost in craft and patience. The hunter must get within a few yards. This is accomplished — occasionally! — by a slow, slow approach, and by waiting finally, aimed and ready, for the chuck to poke its head out of its den.

It is commendable that more and more states are giving the chucks at least some protection, with hunting regulations and even in a couple of instances a bag limit. Although in farm country the animals can be nuisances and are trapped and poisoned here and there, none of the species appears to be in any danger of drastically declining in numbers. The eastern woodchucks do very well living practically in the backyards of their human neighbors, and the majority of the marmots live and die without ever seeing a specimen of mankind. Since all the chucks live in burrows, never get far from the protection of those havens, and spend the intemperate part of the year snoozing in safety, their chances of thwarting the few enemies they have are good. Groundhog Day and groundhogs to sleep through it seem destined to help pace a good many centuries still to come.

# SQUIRRELS

# Fox Squirrel

*Sciurus niger and related species*

# Gray Squirrel

*Sciurus carolinensis and related species*

The tree squirrels, especially the forest-dwelling grays, began chiseling out a niche in American history during the earliest days of eastern-seaboard settlement. Squirrels in the virgin forests of mast-bearing trees were tremendously abundant. They quickly became a staple item of food for the colonists, as well as pests that swarmed over gardens and the edges of crop fields, causing severe damage.

As settlement pushed inland and fanned out north and south the same abundance was notable. And so was the depredation upon the basic crops such as corn and wheat. One of the earliest bounties established on the continent was aimed at controlling the awesome inroads of gray squirrels. In the mid-1770s, crop damage in Pennsylvania settlements was so severe that a three-pence bounty was instigated. To illustrate the abundance of the squirrels one needs only to consider that even though the human population

Gray Squirrel

Douglas Allen

## THE SQUIRRELS

COLOR: **Fox squirrel,** variable on different ranges, from rusty westward to grayish with rusty markings eastward, to melanistic (black) in south; individual variations in markings, some specimens for example gray-black with whitish nose and ears; underparts and portions of tail in rusty type bright orange-brown, in gray types pale. **Gray squirrel,** gray to silvery-gray above, finely grizzled, underparts white; some specimens with light-brownish markings on face and feet, others rich gray; tail with frosted guard hairs; black individuals common, albino ones moderately so.

MEASUREMENTS AND WEIGHT: **Fox squirrel,** overall length 18 to 28 inches, of which 12 or more inches is tail; shoulder height 3 to 5 inches; adult weight to 2 pounds, maximum of 3. **Gray squirrel,** overall length 16 to 22 inches, with tail 8 or 9 of that; adult weight an average of 1 pound, some specimens slightly heavier.

GENERAL ATTRIBUTES: Handsomely plumed tail, both varieties; alert, superbly agile tree-climbing rodents; intelligent, wary; a habit of sitting on haunches with tail often upright behind and curled outward at tip, while handling food in forepaws with pronounced dexterity; adept at hiding in the running through trees; moderately vocal, chattering to one another or when disturbed.

was small, some 8000 pounds sterling went to hunters who turned in over 600,000 squirrel scalps.

In the forests of Ohio, Kentucky, and Missouri squirrels were just as abundant. So serious were their depredations simply because of overwhelming numbers that in the early 1800s every white male in Ohio was bound by law either to pay a tax of $3—a substantial sum in those days—or turn in 100 squirrel scalps.

The marauding animals were mostly gray squirrels, because of the endless forests and their preference for this habitat. In numerous settlements throughout the east, and as the country was opened farther inland, meetings were held to plan ways of destroying the squirrels. Sometimes roundups were planned in which a concerted effort was made on a single day by all men with weapons. Some even carried clubs. Old records show that as many as several thousand squirrels were killed by these communal hunts in a single day. Occasionally contests were held, with groups competing to see which could kill the most squirrels in a stipulated period of a few days.

The swarms of squirrels were in part responsible for the development of new concepts in frontier firearms. The old military arms brought by the colonists from England and Europe were heavy, and not very accurate. As settlers pushed westward into the forbidding wilderness, they needed rifles that could kill any of a variety of animals, large and small, that would be easier to carry than the heavy-barreled old military guns, and that would reach out accurately past the range of Indian arrows. Accuracy, in fact, was one of the chief requirements. The famed Kentucky rifle, actually developed in the early 1700s on the very edge of the frontier at what was then Hickory Town (later Lancaster), Pennsylvania, was the first really accurate rifle the settlers had.

In some of its many following models it was dubbed the "Kentucky squirrel rifle." The name was a compliment of sorts to its accuracy. Squirrels offered small targets to the rather crude early guns, yet probably millions of them met their demise before these long-barreled, thin-stocked old rifles of the frontiersmen.

Many are the tales and legends of the early squirrel hunters. One of the best known concerns the techniques of "barking" a squirrel. Daniel Boone supposedly was one of the most adept at it. Undoubtedly there was some truth in the tales, at least for the very best shots. A direct hit with a ball from the long rifle would of course mangle a squirrel, ruining much of the meat. So a hunter aimed carefully to hit the bark of the tree branch where the squirrel lay or sat. Stunned, but with not an ounce of meat ruined, it fell to the ground.

Other legends moved over into the tall-tale category, but managed to find their way down the centuries to the present. Many a reminiscing grandfather told of aim so fine the bullet split a branch lengthwise on which a squirrel sat. Into the crack in the split limb the feet of the squirrel dropped, and the cleft snapped back together, trapping the animal. In some of these tales another shot snipped the branch off crosswise and the branch with its trapped squirrel fell to the ground, where a whack on the noggin dispatched it.

Of the two squirrels, gray and fox, the gray was always the more abundant, because of its forest-dwelling habit. The fox squirrel, chiefly an edge animal, was able to thrive more and more as the forests were cut, while the gray proportionately declined. Years ago the decline was so severe some believed the gray squirrel might become extinct. In some areas of the south today, where pine plantings have replaced the hardwoods, the gray squirrel has been seriously affected. However, there are still millions of acres of forest lands left where it thrives.

The gray has not only been the most abundant, but it has evidenced such astonishing cyclic population highs that endless incidents concerning its abundance and migrations to find forage have been passed down from the earliest settlement days. In addition, in certain places population eruptions may be seen still today. There are well-authenticated records of gray squirrels suddenly showing up by tens of thousands, all moving in the same direction. Wherever a crop field lay in the way, the crop was harvested by them then and there as the vast horde passed through it.

No very convincing explanations have ever been given as to why the squirrels should all have moved together, in the same direction. It is believed that over a period of several years probably the population built up and up, then some particular spring there was an unusual population explosion and at the same time a failure of the mast crops. The squirrels quickly cleaned up food available, then began seeking new foraging grounds. Conversely, some old records claim the forage was still plentiful and the squirrels plump when these movements occurred, that the animals got the urge to move at high population cycles. Why they did not—and do not—fan out from areas of overabundance, no one is certain. Or possibly they do, and the single-direction migrations are those seen only at particular spots by certain observers. It is at least certain that the gray squirrel's high-cycle abundance is not exaggerated, and that mass movements do occur.

The Current River in the Ozarks is a favorite float stream for canoeists and for smallmouth bass fishermen. For some weeks reports came in of squirrels by hundreds swimming the river, all going the same way. The following spring there were barely enough squirrels in the forest to furnish meager breeding stock.

In early times the squirrel hordes swam very large rivers, and even lakes. Some of the deadpan stories about squirrel migrations are wryly comic. One known far and wide, supposedly observed during days of early settlement, concerns hundreds of squirrels that, in migration to new feeding grounds, come to a river. Each squirrel scurries hither and yon looking for a piece of bark. It launches the bark, hops atop with its bushy tail curled high above its back to keep it dry, and sails down and across to a safe landing on the other side.

Even though gray squirrel movements do occur on occasion nowadays, they are trivial compared to some of those early ones.

Ernest Thompson Seton wrote of a month-long movement of squirrels in the mid-1800s in Wisconsin that he believed might have involved 500 million animals. Scientists have long studied squirrel population cycles, and many believe they are quite regularly timed. However, much is still to be learned about them and their causes, and about why at peak population the squirrels sometimes begin mass movements.

Distribution of the gray and fox squirrels blankets most of the eastern half of the lower-48 states. Gray squirrel range reaches a short distance into Canada, to southeastern Saskatchewan and southern Manitoba. There are modest populations in the eastern fringes of the Dakotas, and eastern Kansas. Greater numbers thrive in eastern Oklahoma and Texas. From these western regions the range of the gray squirrel covers the United States eastward to the Atlantic. It is most populous in the middle south, the Gulf states, and the forested areas of the east.

The western gray squirrel, which is given status as a full-fledged species, *Sciurus griseus,* lives in suitable forests of the Pacific-coast states. In Oregon, where it has long been called locally the silver gray squirrel, for many years it has been involved in serious depredations upon the English walnut crop, and in certain counties for that reason receives no protection. The western gray squirrel is larger than its eastern relative. Oregon has several colonies of eastern gray squirrels also, transplants from the east. Many intrigue visitors on the state capitol's grounds. A third species, the Arizona gray squirrel, *S. arizonensis,* has quite a restricted range, living in the oak and pine zone in southeastern and central Arizona.

There are a number of races or subspecies of gray squirrels scattered over the main range and the eastern half of the states. Most of these probably evolved from isolated groups, or because of influences of latitude. A curious sidelight on gray squirrel history is the fact that melanistic (black) phases of the gray have at one time or another been treated as a separate species of squirrel. Melanism is for some reason exceedingly common among gray squirrels. In certain areas the phase is so dominant that an entire local population of squirrels eventually is built up of black individuals.

For many years in Michigan there were hunting seasons on fox squirrels and gray squirrels, but "black squirrels," considered a third variety not as abundant as the others, were fully protected. These squirrels were for some reason especially abundant in portions of the northern part of the Lower Peninsula. The forest surrounding the city of Alpena on Lake Huron's Thunder Bay, for ex-

# Range of the Fox Squirrel

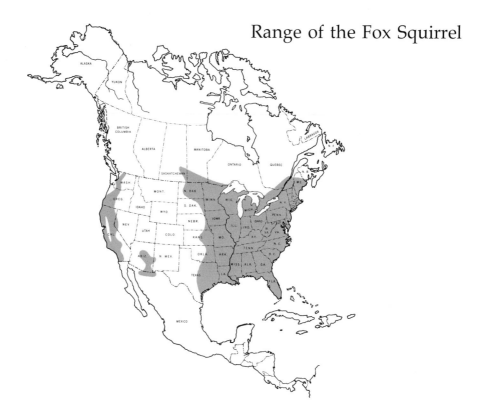

ample, contained abundant squirrels, almost every individual black. Melanistic gray squirrels show up here and there over the south, too, and they are almost everywhere occasional among populations of grays. However, the preponderance of black gray squirrels is found in the northern extremes of the range.

Some of the nation's most famous squirrels are white gray squirrels. These appear less often than black ones, but they are such handsome creatures, and squirrels (of both varieties) become gentle so readily when they live in parks or in towns, that these white squirrels have drawn national interest and found protection in several places. Probably most famous are the hundreds of white squirrels within the city of Olney, Illinois, a tourist attraction now for many years. This large population in which the white strain has stayed dominant are supposed to have started with a pair kept as pets back in the late 1800s.

The overall look of a gray squirrel is of an animal colored rich grizzled gray above, white beneath, and with the tail, beautifully

## Range of the Gray Squirrel

plumed, with frosted guard hairs. In parts of the south and the Ozarks, where gray squirrels are usually smaller than in their northern ranges, they appear much as described, without any, or many, distinctive markings. However, in some areas grays have very distinct yellow-brown or even in some instances reddish-brown washes on the outside of the legs, on the feet, the head, and along the back. Occasionally gray squirrels of unusually large size in the north, and so marked, are confused with the larger fox squirrel.

In the south the gray is commonly called a "cat" squirrel. Whether the name originated from its remarkable agility, its climbing and branch-running abilities, or its playfulness is uncertain. The generic name for the game squirrels, *Sciurus*, it is interesting to note, comes from combining two Greek words that mean "tail" and "shade" — thus, "the animal that shades itself with its tail" or "sits in the shade of its tail."

The larger fox squirrel is thought to have gained its common names from the reddish-brown or rusty red-fox-like color of many specimens, although by no means do all fox squirrels follow the rule. The scientific species name, *niger,* meaning "black," was given the fox squirrel back in the 1700s by the naturalist Linnaeus, who probably saw melanistic color phases of this squirrel and may not have known that rusty and grayish phases existed.

Black fox squirrels are found mostly in the south, the gray phase in the east and northeast and to some extent in the middle south, for example here and there in Tennessee. The rusty fox squirrel is especially abundant throughout the Mississippi and Ohio valleys, in the woodlands of the Great Lakes, throughout its westernmost range, in the Ozarks and in Texas. Among the color phases there are several races given full subspecies status, and the color differences and markings might cause confusion except that they are usually quite localized.

The gray phase of the fox squirrel has a pale belly, buff or even gray-white, an off-white to cream-colored nose and ears, with the head, cheeks below the eyes, and the nape black. Faint rusty washes also are usually present. The rusty phase has an almost orange belly and underparts, and the tail is fringed with the same. Black and rusty intermingle along the center. In some states the variety in fox squirrels is so pronounced that hunters think of them as different kinds entirely. Louisiana, for example, has three fox squirrel subspecies—Bachman's, the delta squirrel, and the big-headed fox squirrel. Each differs in coloration, size, and markings from the others. Some fox squirrel specimens are black on the back with orange or buff underparts. The fox squirrel, in fact, evidences the broadest color differences of all American squirrels.

The fox squirrel has lost range in the northeast over the past century or more, but it has spread westward to some extent. It is found along wooded stream courses and other suitable oases of woodlots in the Dakotas, Nebraska, Kansas, eastern Colorado, and Oklahoma, and over perhaps two-thirds of Texas. Eastward it blankets the country, spottily abundant, with the exception of New England, and the northern portions of the Great Lakes states. Pennsylvania is roughly the limit of the northeastern range. Subspecies are numerous. There is a separate, isolated species, the Apache fox squirrel, *S. apache,* that inhabits a small mountain area of southeastern Arizona and extends into Mexico. There are a few fox squirrels (and eastern gray squirrels also) in California. These are not native. The small colonies or in-city groups originated from escaped pets.

Few hunters will ever have to worry about it, but for one who visits in Mexico and observes squirrels, the species and subspecies of this southernmost part of North America are certain to bring confusion. Not only are racial variations numerous, but in some instances it is difficult to distinguish between squirrels of the fox and gray groups. For those of extra-inquisitive bent, an examination of the dentition of the upper jaw — and this is valid within the United States as well — sets the two groups apart. Gray squirrels have six premolar teeth, fox squirrels four.

There are at least ten species (some may be only races or subspecies) of gray squirrels and six of fox squirrels scattered throughout Mexico. There are gray squirrels with reddish bellies, gray bellies, and even black bellies. There are fox squirrels that are gray with a white belly, mostly black with some white in the tail, and others of both groups with distinct chestnut swaths on the back mingled with black — all of them well illustrating the variety found among the two chief groups of tree squirrels on the continent.

Considered the most handsome and unusual of North American tree squirrels, and least known or observed by both hunters and wildlife enthusiasts, are the tassel-eared squirrels. There are two, the Abert squirrel, which is hunted only in New Mexico and Arizona but is found also in Mexico and in Colorado and Utah, and the Kaibab squirrel, indigenous only to the Kaibab Plateau on the northern rim of the Grand Canyon in Arizona.

These squirrels at full adulthood and under optimum conditions are large, as big as maximum-sized fox squirrels. They have long, pointed ears, as opposed to the short, rounded ears of fox and gray squirrels. The length is furthermore much exaggerated by tufts of long hair thrusting up from the tips. These squirrels feed upon the cone nuts and the buds of huge yellow pine, as well as upon acorns and other available forage. But it is believed their range limits are tied up with that of mature yellow pine forests. It is common to see a tassel-eared squirrel race across the needle-matted ground of the high-country forest and up a 100-foot-tall pine, clear to the top.

The Abert squirrel is rich dark gray along the sides, with a swath of reddish chestnut down its back and over the top of its head. Its belly and insides of the legs are white, often with some dark to black at the edge separating gray from white. The ear tufts vary from black to reddish and gray intermingled. The tail, a stunning brush, is bright frosty white along the edges, with a grayish center swath beneath and a blackish one on top intermixed with frosted hairs. The Kaibab squirrel differs, with a gray-black to black

Fox Squirrel                    Kaibab Squirrel

belly and insides of legs, much of the same around the head, and with a long, broad, pure-white tail. Some specimens show a bit of grayish buried in the white hairs toward the tail tip.

Because the Kaibab squirrel is isolated on its plateau of forest, with the Grand Canyon on one side and the plateau falling away to desert on the others, some scientists suspect that far back in time, before the canyon was formed, there was only one variety. The Kaibab squirrels (fully protected) were cut off, the theory goes, and evolved their own characteristics. The Abert variety, on the south rim and with no barrier to ranging expansion, also developed individual characteristics. It is of curious interest that both squirrels have been able to protect their unique identities. Of similar interest, and perhaps helping to substantiate the theory of separation, now and then an Abert squirrel hunter on the south rim bags what appears to be a "throwback" specimen that has all the color characteristics of the Abert—except for a black belly.

Very occasionally the little red squirrel, called a pine squirrel or a chickaree in some places, is hunted. But it is so small—seldom more than 5 to 8 ounces—that few hunters bother it. There are several varieties. Prominent among them are the northern red squirrel, reddish above with pale-gray to white underparts and a light-reddish tail; the pine squirrel of the Rockies south from Wyoming, white beneath and with a whitish-fringed tail; and the Douglas squirrel that ranges west of the Rockies, a small squirrel as noisily talkative as the others, dark brown above, rusty beneath, with a yellowish fringe along the tail.

Although the fur of all the squirrels, especially in fall when they acquire heavy winter coats in the cooler ranges, is soft and beautiful, it has never been a useful item in the American fur market. To be sure, there are squirrel coats available, but the fur trade ever since it began has tacked names on various made-up furs that are strictly trade names. In years past when squirrel coats were fashionable they were made for the most part from imported pelts. One interesting use of squirrel in the United States today is the ready market for tails. Fishing-lure makers use the long, fairly stiff hair in fly tying and in the manufacture of spinners that have a treble-hook trailer swathed in squirrel-tail hair. One firm in Wisconsin has for some years advertised widely for hunters to ship properly prepared squirrel tails to them, for a modest payment per tail. This market, of course, must be carefully policed, to avoid traffic in tails from squirrels illegally killed just for their tails.

### HABITAT

Because they are tree-dwelling animals, the range of the squirrels and their habitats are limited to regions where trees grow. This has allowed them a broad variety of living conditions. However, habitat is moderately restricted according to what kinds of trees are present, for squirrels are dependent to a large extent upon taking forage—i.e., nuts and buds—from the trees so necessary to their way of life.

On the western fringes of the range of the eastern squirrels, as in the plains states of Texas, some of them have been able to push into otherwise open country by colonizing stream courses where trees grow. Pockets of meager abundance are thus found far from the forest areas.

Most of this range-stretching has been done by the fox squirrel. Although it is found in scores of locations living in the same habitat with the gray squirrel, the two follow quite different habitat preferences. The gray squirrel is fundamentally a forest animal. The fox squirrel is a creature of open woodlands, edges, and smaller woodlots. Throughout all of the midwestern and Great Lakes farm country, for example, it is the fox squirrel that lives happily in small pieces of woods, in scattered trees along a creek, or even in a shady farmyard.

Typical of fox squirrel habitat in a region of small farms is the 2-

to-5-acre woods, perhaps of elm, maple, oak, and a beech or two. There may be a corn field on one side, a wheat field on the other. Such a spot invariably has its quota of fox squirrels. Even a single large tree on a field edge, with a scattering of brush along a small nearby creek, may be home year after year to a family of fox squirrels.

Conversely, the gray squirrel cannot abide such situations. In many ways the gray squirrel is a much wilder personality. It is tuned to wilderness living. In some parts of the south, gray squirrels live in nearly impenetrable forest thickets where vines and Spanish moss, swamp growth, and dense forest all but shut out the sun. Invariably the largest populations of gray squirrels are found in the large expanses of forest.

Hardwood forests in which varied conifers intermingle are typical gray squirrel habitat across much of their range. In rolling forest country the grays live both in the dense stream bottoms and up on the ridges. West-coast grays are often found at several thousand feet altitude, and so are many in the eastern mountains. As long as there is ample forage and the forests are mixed, not entirely pine, the squirrels are at home.

Gray squirrels often move from treetop to treetop for long distances without coming to ground, a habit perhaps born of their forest preferences. Or it could be just the other way around—that they prefer the forests because they are so thoroughly arboreal. The fox squirrel isn't that particular, and in fact prefers forests or wooded plots that are much more open, or that have scattered openings.

One of the delights of the fox squirrel is to lie out on a branch or in a tree crotch soaking up the sun. The open-woodland habitat makes this possible. The gray squirrel sometimes suns itself, but it doesn't mind the dark forests, and some of its most prime habitat in the South is a veritable jungle. Over much of fox squirrel range this animal seems to prefer partially open, dry ridges where oaks and other forage trees grow. In some southern locations it inhabits pine woods, but invariably along the edges. It is also present around the thick cypress swamps, but again almost without fail along the edges, where the sun strikes through branches and open spaces are at hand.

In areas—and there are many—where both squirrel species range together, it is always interesting, and quite predictable for a hunter, to observe the different preferences of the two. For example, in the Ozarks both squirrels are plentiful. Even though the fox squirrel prefers rather dry places, in the Ozarks it is always most abundant along the streams, and around the fringes of the small farms that checkerboard the valleys. This is because the stream bottoms are openings of a sort. A mixed bag can be taken along any river or creek, but as soon as one moves back into the wholly forested hills, fox squirrels become rare and grays predominant.

### FEEDING

Whatever the particular habitat of either fox or gray squirrel, one may be certain that ample food is obtainable there. Squirrels and nuts are inseparable in the mind's-eye view of all wildlife observers, and in the habits of the squirrels, too. Acorns are one of the basic squirrel foods. Other nuts are just as important locally — beech, walnut, hickory, butternut, wild pecan — but because oaks are of such numerous variety and so widely distributed in our forests, the acorn has always been a staple of squirrel sustenance.

Acorns, and other nuts, are eaten when they are in the green or "milk" stage, become the main fare in numerous places in fall when soft foods are gone, and are cached or buried to furnish a substantial part of the winter livelihood. The habit of burying nuts is so ingrained in squirrel personality that they pursue it incessantly wherever nuts are available, but they do not always find every one they bury. Each squirrel goes about its nut caching in its own way. Some do a good job, some simply poke the acorn or other nut under a few leaves.

Routinely the forefeet are used to dig a small hollow, and then the nut is pushed with feet and nose down into the hole. In soft leaf mold most squirrels push the nuts just under the cover. This method in cold climes makes it easier to retrieve them if ground freezes. Most individual squirrels are exceedingly industrious in fall as soon as nuts ripen. They scurry around on the ground, pick up an acorn, toss it aside if it is not a good one. Their judgment seems to be keen about which ones are parasite-bitten, or shriveled inside.

Often an area — the yard of a home in the country, for example — will give no evidence of squirrels in the vicinity, but as soon as acorns begin to drop one or two will suddenly appear and begin industriously making winter caches. Not all oaks bear in any given year. The squirrels quickly find those with a heavy acorn crop. Squirrels that fail to work diligently at storing winter food often do not make it through the winter. The price of laziness may be the animal's life. Some individual squirrels, especially grays, make food caches in their dens as well as burying nuts.

Over the vast range of both squirrels the oak trees, as noted, furnish the most important food staple. However, a wide variety of forage goes into squirrel diet. In the spring when buds start, and indeed even in winter, squirrels nip them and gorge on them. As the buds begin to burst open in spring and the flowers of several varieties of trees and catkins of others appear, squirrels eagerly feast on them. Maples, birch, basswood, elm, oak, and similar varieties are favorites. So is maple sap. Squirrels cut into bark when the sap flows and also eat the inner soft layer, occasionally damaging maple trees.

Wild fruits are avidly sought. In June, for example, over much of the range of the several mulberry species, which coincides almost exactly with the ranges of both squirrel species, any fruit-laden mulberry will draw squirrels from a surprisingly large area. They simply gorge on the soft fruit, seizing the brief opportunity while it is available to satisfy a craving for sweets. Experienced squirrel hunters in states that offer spring seasons and mulberry trees habitually look first for fruit-laden trees rather than squirrels. It is not unusual to sit beneath a big mulberry and collect a limit of squirrels in a morning. Sometimes both gray and fox squirrels will be feeding simultaneously in a tree.

In locations where squirrels of either variety can get at a field of corn, they make severe inroads. They begin while the kernels are in the milk stage, Later they work on the hardened ears. Fox squirrels love to haul whole ears off to the edge of a nearby woods. Placing one husk and all atop a stump, the animal sits comfortably, expertly husks it, and snips the heart from each kernel, leaving the remainder.

Bulbs, roots, some insects, and mushrooms balance squirrel diets. These are mostly taken as incidentals. Fruit pits, as from wild plums, rose hips they happen to discover in winter, and apples in summer or fallen to ground in winter from volunteer trees or found in raids on orchards add tidbits. Squirrels are accused of robbing bird nests of eggs and young. Undoubtedly a few do, but as a rule they are not much interested in meat. Experiments with caged squirrels well illustrate that they will turn down meat offerings except for tentative nibbles. Seeds and nuts, chiefly acorns, are the mainstay of squirrel diet.

Before nuts begin to drop in fall, squirrels often diligently cut them and let them drop, then hunt for the harvest and bury individual nuts. Local food items in particular habitats furnish extra forage. In areas where the osage orange grows, squirrels gnaw the big fruits. Gourds are plucked from vines along woods edges while still not ripe. Fox squirrels have been observed in comic pose with a gourd, gnawed in half, held over the face with both forefeet while the squirrel cleans out the pulp and seeds.

## MOVEMENTS

Most of the movements of squirrels are concerned with the business of making a living. Aside from the striking migrations of gray squirrels, which certainly are not as common today as they once were, the average individual squirrel seldom gets more than a few hundred yards away from its den or nest tree. Even though it may change living sites from one tree to another, if food to sustain it is available many a squirrel probably never ranges over more than 2 or 3 acres. Even with the forage situation critical, 5 to 10 acres is the home range. Grays when hunted with dogs sometimes run surprising distances through the treetops, but as soon as danger passes they return home. Males may range out somewhat when the breeding urge is upon them. All is relative, however. The home range of the squirrel is small. In some instances of permanently plentiful forage a squirrel may never get over a 100 yards from its den site.

There is an interesting difference between gray and fox squirrels regarding their daily habits. Invariably the gray squirrel is up and working for a living at dawn. The fox squirrel, bigger and not as agile, extends its physical appearance to its work-ethic stance. It seems by comparison lazy. Fox squirrels seldom are out early. They get up when the sun bids them with its warmth. However, both species may continue to forage and to cache food or build nests in the day, right up until full dusk.

Of the two species, the gray squirrel is by far the more expert climber and branch runner. It seldom takes a spill branch to branch and rarely makes an error and falls. The bigger, more bumbling, fox squirrel noisily scrambles around, often slips and grabs for a new hold, and not uncommonly falls from astonishing heights to bounce up good as ever and run off. The gray simply seems to be more adept and agile and at home in a tree.

Much has been made of the fact, in popular nature writing, that the fox squirrel is a ground-loving creature and the gray an animal always of the treetops. This is one of those half-truths. All squirrels spend much time on the ground. It is necessary to do so in order to make a living. The big Abert and Kaibab squirrels of the yellow pine high country are spotted as often on the ground as up a tree. They will race across a long run of needled carpet to make for a tree that seems special to them. It is true that the fox squirrel is more inclined to run longer distances on the ground to flee danger, and to carry food farther on the ground, than is the gray.

When surprised, as by a hunter or dog, or any enemy, the two squirrels differ somewhat in reactions. Both will hide, edging quietly around a tree trunk to get it between them and danger, then eventually peeking around to see what's going on. However, a fox squirrel will run up a tree and lie flat on a branch, or on the side of a limb away from a searching hunter, and sometimes be all but impossible to move out of a tree. Conversely, a gray squirrel often does not wait to hide. It is a much wilder personality. It races off through the treetops to put distance between itself and possible danger. There are individual exceptions, of course.

Weather effects squirrel movements. On still days, whether cloudy or bright, they are active, although both varieties like bright weather. But when a sudden wind whips through the woods and a scud of clouds runs before it, squirrels get into leaf nests or dens and wait it out. In all latitudes, however, squirrels are active all winter. They are not hibernators. During the most severe weather a squirrel may stay denned up to keep warm, but it must forage, and many dig down through the snow after nut caches, or tunnel under it if necessary.

The fox squirrel, less nervous and less driven by the urge to keep busy than the gray squirrel, often strikes comic poses while resting or sunning. One may lie in a tree crotch or along a big limb, legs hanging limply down, chin resting on the limb, taking its ease in the grandest, laziest style imaginable. However, both squirrel species are diligent about homemaking.

Both utilize den trees, and leaf and stick nests. Most dens are in hardwoods. And most are in holes where a limb was broken off or decayed and a part of the wood rotted. If the tree has begun to form a bulge of new growth to heal the scar, the squirrel living in the cavity keeps snipping away at it to make certain the entrance remains. Cavities may be enlarged for greater comfort, with all the decayed wood cleaned out. Often a hollow tree is used, with an opening at the bottom, but the tenant then finds a hollow limb farther up in which to make a nest. Dry leaves, bits of shredded bark, and occasionally grass are carried into the cavity to make the bed.

Anyone familiar with squirrels has seen their leaf nests up in scattered trees. Hunters often examine a trunk where a leaf nest

*Gray squirrels often build their leaf nests in the crotch of a tree trunk.*

shows high up in branches, to check for fresh claw marks indicating the nest is in use. Fox squirrels build quickie, thrown-together leaf nests for use during mild weather. Some of these may be far out among small branches, or even in the top of a slender sapling. There may be a half dozen or more dotting treetops around a den tree, or at times near a good feeding location, as if the squirrel, or squirrels, had made spike camps off away from home base, so they might hunt food without tripping back and forth. These jerry-built leaf nests are put together in an hour or less if the squirrel keeps busy. They are used for resting places. A fox squirrel may simply lie atop such a nest, taking the sun, and of course when doing so it is well hidden from below. If one such nest begins to disintegrate, the squirrel swiftly throws together another.

The type of nest to be used for winter living is a much more professional building job. Squirrels in chilly climates commonly build these. First the animal weaves together snippets of twigs, using a spreading branch perhaps to help hold the structure. Then it builds up a layer of leaves, often wet ones, like plaster on a wall. The structure may be many-layered, to make it weather-snug against wind, rain, or snow. Completed, it is a rounded hut, with a roof, and a hollow or room inside. After it is well structured, the lining goes in, made up of shredded leaves and bark. The opening into the room barely admits the occupant, and enough extra material is placed inside to close the door when the squirrel is inside in cold weather.

Nest-building habits of the gray squirrel are similar to those of the fox squirrel. However, grays are not such avid nest builders. They prefer den trees, and usually make nests somewhat more sturdy than those of the fox squirrel and nearer the trunk or in a large crotch. They build both temporary and permanent nests, and both species, when they cannot find denning trees, make do with twig and leaf nests which they build as permanent dwellings.

On the ground, squirrels walk while foraging slowly, or bound when running or in a hurry. The bound may be a series of short hops, or a longer leap when escape from danger is the impetus. The hind feet strike ground ahead of the forefeet. Speed is not great, but when pushed either squirrel makes surprisingly good time, probably about 10 miles per hour or a bit more for some individuals. The gray squirrel is a master at quick and erratic dodging when pursued, either on the ground or aloft.

Both species use their tails deftly to assist in balance, as when walking a slender branch or making a quick, fast turn on the ground. Some naturalists believe the tail also is an assist as a kind of balance when the squirrel sits on its haunches, or as it undulates as a squirrel runs. It may also be helpful as a furry drag chute when a squirrel jumps through branches or happens to take a tumble. The tail is a most expressive appendage also. When a squirrel is agitated, either by presence of other squirrels or some disturbance, but not really frightened, the tail jerks incessantly as the squirrel chatters.

The jerking tail and a tense and agitated movement of the body are commonly an accompaniment to squirrel talk. Many written accounts of the sounds squirrels make are really not very accurate. Some describe the basic utterance as a *quack,* or repetitive *yak,* or a *kuaaa-aaa* cry. Some claim a gray squirrel has a soft voice, the fox squirrel a raucous, coarse one. Actually individual squirrels have slightly different voice timbre, just as people do. An old gray can be as coarse-cussing a tyrant as any fox squirrel.

There are slight differences in the sounds of the two varieties. However, a swiftly repeated coarse bark—*kuk-kuk-kuk-kuk-kuk*—perhaps with many more syllables, or fewer, is the sound most observers or hunters are likely to hear. Squirrels are able to fit this basic sound with varied inflections to a number of different moods. A gray squirrel may "chuckle" very softly, as if content. If another gray is heart from a distance, the sound may become more strident. A feisty old fox squirrel is often known to take true delight in pestering a dog in a farmyard. It clings upside down to a tree trunk almost within reach, and, tail jerking, swears at the dog with endless sharp barking. When the dog makes a run at it, the squirrel may leap over its back to the ground, race to another tree, and start over.

For hunters and wildlife photographers and observers, learning to use a squirrel call—several are marketed—to imitate basic squirrel sounds is an invaluable aid. Squirrels can be brought close, or at least located. Some won't reply but will come silently. The fox squirrel is more apt to do this than the gray.

Squirrels of both varieties may or may not make regular trips to water. Most scientists are of the opinion that squirrels need water and seldom live far from a water source large or small. However, it is known that they sometimes utilize sap to satisfy their need for liquids, and that they also get liquids from various foods. A most interesting recent experiment by a biologist working with squirrels in eastern Texas seemed to prove that with a suitable mixture of forage, squirrels can actually get along without water over extended periods. The researcher kept caged squirrels and gave them no water at all. On a mixed diet as would be available in their area in the wild, they showed no ill effects after several waterless months.

### BREEDING

Squirrel movements begin to accelerate as breeding season approaches in midwinter. Males, most of which are capable of breeding when a year old although many do not do so until fully adult at two, begin chasing females through the treetops and on the ground. During the year until now individual squirrels, even though living in proximity to others, have had little social life. They are not necessarily antagonistic. It is common to see several squirrels, even a mixture of gray and fox squirrels, feeding in the same large tree. Old males, however, are often crotchety and keep to themselves.

In late December or early January the chases begin. A female may not be in heat yet and may protest, irritably turning on the ardent male. Males get into noisy scrambling battles, biting and clawing. Now is the time when the *kuaa-aa* and the *kuwak* cries are heard more than ordinary squirrel conversation.

Latitude may influence breeding seasons. Ordinarily the first weeks of the year are the main time. However, numerous older squirrels go through a second mating season about May or June, and a second litter is born in summer. Females are ready to mate at a year old but seldom bear more than one litter the first year. Gray squirrels now and then mate at varying times, with young appearing in summer or even in fall. This is, however, exceptional.

Long ago, even in the days of the pioneers, the idea was bandied about that the males of the small red squirrel chase and emasculate every male gray or fox squirrel they see. They are presumed to be implacable enemies. The little reds are indeed ill-tempered creatures and often do chase after the larger neighboring squirrels. The castration theory, however, is false. It originated from the fact that the testicles of male squirrels are carried inside the body in a shrunken state until near to mating season. At this time, in December as a rule, they descend into the scrotum and become enlarged.

The impetus for this precise timing is not thoroughly explained. It is, of course, a bodily hormone change. But because big male squirrels taken by fall hunters seldom show evidence of testicles and because the smaller reds are noted for irritably or angrily chasing their large relatives, the emasculation idea came into folklore.

Once a female has accepted a mate, they stay together for several days, with frequent breeding. Then the male leaves. He may continue to seek other females, mating with as many as are willing and untaken. As the mating season winds down, the males go their own way, with no interest whatever in the families they have launched.

### BIRTH AND DEVELOPMENT

One and one-half months after mating, the litters are born in the den nests of the families. Baby fox squirrels are slightly larger than their gray relatives. Both varieties weigh much less than an ounce and are naked. The fox squirrels are pinkish puple in color, gray squirrels paler. Both the eyes and ears are shut at birth. The ears begin to open roughly thirty days from birth, and the eyes at least ten to fifteen days later. These periods differ slightly between species.

The number in a litter may be three to six, but on the average three youngsters is normal, or at least that is about the limit that live to leave the nest. They begin to show a sheen of fine fur at two weeks, and by the time their eyes open they are fully furred.

Now they begin to climb around inside the nest and soon are peeking out the den entrance and trying further exploration. They have grown to weigh possibly 4 ounces and are 8 or 9 inches long, including tail. Males sometimes attempt to raid dens and kill the young, their own or others. The mother is a fierce and devoted protector against all enemies. She may become disturbed by the presence of predators or attempts on the lives of her young, and will then move them to a new nest site. Unlike cats, which seize the young by the nape, a squirrel takes a grip with her teeth on the belly skin. The young squirrel wraps its legs around its mother's neck and head and hangs on as it is transported to a new home.

By the time the youngsters are able to climb around outside, they begin to pick at buds or other solid forage. At two months of age they are nursing less; the mother is leaving them for longer periods and starting to wean them. If the mother breeds again in the spring, she hurries the first brood along on their own, and they begin to disperse when they are weaned and able to shift for themselves. Now and then a group of young will stay with the mother, if she does not mate again, on through the summer and even into the first winter.

In general, however, after they're weaned and learning to fend for themselves, the young squirrels begin their instinctive dispersal. For some individuals, if the territory is uncrowded, this may mean a move of only a short distance. For others it may be a time of wandering, with dangers, unease, and perhaps some harassment from other squirrels, over several miles. Tagged young squirrels have been recovered in rare instances 10 to 30 or more miles from the den site where they were born.

As youngsters first climbing around in the home tree, and later during the dispersal period, squirrels must learn more and more about their enemies, and that danger for them lurks everywhere—on the ground, in the air, in a tree. Unfortunately, many don't learn because their first experience is fatal. Tree-climbing snakes are predators upon squirrels. So are climbing raccoons and bobcats. Hawks do in a surprisingly number of squirrels, catching them on tree branches, or lying atop a leaf nest, or while they forage on the ground. Foxes and coyotes always keep a lookout for an unwary squirrel intent upon feeding. Natural attrition, particularly upon baby and half-grown squirrels, is high.

## SENSES

Undoubtedly the most important senses of a squirrel are hearing and sight, and both apparently are about equal in acuteness. Probably each is used almost as an extension of the other. Squirrels are incessantly looking and listening. They do not need to have acute distance vision, and distant sounds are not important to them. But the slightest nearby footfall upon the forest floor instantly triggers alertness, and the most minor movement catches the eye. These are the senses a hunter must outwit if he hopes to be successful. It is never easy.

The sense of smell is keen for close-up use, as in locating a hidden acorn. At least naturalists assume this sense is utilized, for squirrels easily locate nuts they have buried under the snow, or under several inches of leaves and dirt. However, it is doubtful that a squirrel uses its nose to detect danger. Or, to put it another way, if a squirrel is aware of man scent, for example, it never seems to give any indication, or to connect the smell with danger.

## SIGN

It is interesting to be able to identify squirrel tracks, but tracks are seldom very important either to hunters or to observers of wildlife. The gray, fox, and tassel-eared squirrels all have four forefoot toes that leave imprints—a short "thumb" does not—and five rear toes that do. Tracks of the smaller red or pine squirrels should not be confused with the game squirrels, because though similar in pattern they are much smaller.

The general pattern of squirrel tracks is with the larger hind-foot prints ahead of the smaller forefoot prints. Of course tracks show only in snow, or in soft earth or mud. Obviously no prints are left on a leaf-covered or pine-needle-matted forest floor. The two forefoot prints are usually side by side, or nearly so, and the hind-foot prints also, but the latter spread wider because they are larger, and also because the hind feet are brought forward past the forefeet and must clear the forepart of the body. The whole pattern of four feet thus may be described as making four corners of a basic rectangle, as compared to the two widespread hind prints of a rabbit, with the two forefoot prints showing either as one, or one behind the other.

In snow or soft earth the squirrel is usually hopping or bounding. The distance between each set of four prints depends on how fast the animal is going. Short hops are only a few inches, but a running adult squirrel of the game varieties bounds 30 to 36 inches.

Leaf nests are an easily spotted sign. They are not likely to be confused with nests of large birds such as hawks, or crows, which show just a platform of sticks and twigs. Nor should those of the game squirrels be confused with the red squirrels' nests. Those are quite round as a rule, not more than a foot across, and formed of grass, small twigs, and bark. Most are built in the branches of conifers, rather than in the deciduous trees.

Squirrel scats are not an important sign because they are not often seen. An abundance of nut hulls cut by squirrels indicates presence of the animals, if fresh, or at least that they have been feeding in the vicinity. So do the scratchings and small holes dug among leaves and in dirt beneath nut-bearing trees. "Cuttings" of twigs below trees where squirrels have been budding, and snippets of the ends of yellow pine branches in tassel-eared squirrel range, are foraging signs to look for. So are claw scratches on the bark of trees. These show most plainly on bark of the smoother trees, such as beech and maple, where footholds slip some as compared to the easy hold on rough-barked trees. Hollows in trees, at bottom or up along the trunk, that are observable in detail, with binoculars perhaps, tell of occupancy when they show a smooth-worn entrance or evidence of gnawing around the perimeter.

## HUNTING

Hunters look for trunk scatches, leaf nests, den sites, and cuttings beneath a tree as tipoffs for productive stands. Taking a stand and waiting quietly for a squirrel to bark or rustle leaves, or drop cuttings, or just for one to move and give itself away is one of the most productive of all squirrel-hunting methods. It requires patience, a stealthy, silent approach, and a foreknowledge of the location of den trees and feeding places. Squirrels have always been exceedingly popular game animals. In fact, for many years they have been in second place among all game in popularity. Only the cottontail attracts more hunters and is harvested in greater numbers.

For the stand hunter, full camouflage is an excellent idea. This should include a headnet, or camo grease paint, camo net gloves, and camo suit. It is better to case a piece of squirrel woods and locate feeding areas than to make a stand beneath a den tree. The less the homesite is disturbed, the better. A beech grove, in the south a stream bottom where wild pecans grow, a fruit-bearing mulberry tree in spring, the edge of a woodlot next to a cornfield — these are examples of productive squirrel-hunting stands. The hunter should sit absolutely motionless. If a shot is presented, it's a good plan not to get up instantly to retrieve the animal. Squirrels are filled with curiosity. After a disturbance, a wait of fifteen minutes often will find one unable to resist peeking out to see if the coast is clear.

Stand hunting is best for fox squirrels from after sunup to mid-morning, and again from late afternoon until dusk. For gray squirrels one should be in place before dawn. Listening is as important as watching for slight movements. Squirrels may begin talking to each other, or chuckling contentedly. The swish of a branch as a squirrel leaps from one to another may be a giveaway.

There are several other techniques generally employed. One most interesting one is using a squirrel call. A call can be operated at a stand or while prowling from place to place. All squirrel calls have full instructions packed with them, telling you what series of sounds to make and how often. Don't overdo it, unless a squirrel talks back in high agitation. Some of these will hurry right to you, usually but not always while aloft. Some squirrels, however, come to a call in total silence. So you have to stay alert. With practice, a careful hunter can turn calling into an unbelievably successful technique. If you take a stand and call in one spot and get no results after twenty minutes, move to another. In selecting a stand, always sit rather than stand if at all possible, and get into surrounding low cover to break up your outline if any is available.

Still hunting, simply prowling silently and very slowly through a good piece of squirrel woods, is the method favored by many hunters. This should be truly a slow-motion endeavor. And, binoculars are an excellent assist. The experienced hunter doesn't ever try to find a whole squirrel, whether still hunting or standing. He looks for a piece of one — an ear, the end of a tail blowing in the breeze.

Squirrels are keenly adept at hiding. Even among leafless trees one can be most difficult to find. If a lone hunter circles a tree quietly, looking up to scan for movement or squirrel, the crafty animal simply keeps moving around to the other side. Numerous tricks are employed to subvert this common squirrel tactic. Sticks or stones tossed into leaves on the opposite side of a tree often cause a squirrel to zip around a limb or trunk into plain sight. Sometimes a hunter hangs his jacket on a bush on one side of a tree, then steals very quietly around toward the other. The squirrel, suddenly seeing a disturbing scene (the jacket) on the side it sneakily had left, either scurries up a limb or else back around, confused, and lays itself open to a shot.

A few hunters use a stick-tossing technique, particularly when leaves are on the trees, to get squirrels to move. The procedure is to hurl a stick up into the leaves to "shake 'em up a bit." Such ruses are more needed with fox squirrels than with grays. Most gray squirrels will run at the first disturbance.

Stand hunting, still hunting, and calling are the methods most will use. But a few fortunate hunters own trained squirrel dogs. Hunting with such a dog is perhaps the most dramatic of all squirrel-hunting procedures. All sorts of mongrels, and other dogs, small and large, from diminutive, noisy terriers to collies and dalmatians, can be trained on squirrels. Some years ago hundreds of sharp squirrel dogs were in use, but with the movement to urban areas of the past few decades, fewer and fewer hunters have time to train such a dog or a place to keep it.

Squirrel dogs are taught to work both by scent and by sight. They bark at a tree where a squirrel has gone up or where they can catch its scent. If it jumps, they race off, keeping an eye on it by looking up while running. A topnotch sight-scent squirrel dog turns out an amazing performance. It circles a tree to keep a squirrel in sight and thus push it around so a hunter can spot it.

There are different preferences in guns for squirrel hunting. Many a still or stand hunter prefers a .22 rifle, with a scope. The full-size scopes, just as for big-game hunting, are better than cheap small-diameter scopes. Other hunters like to use a shotgun. Certainly the shotgun is handy when squirrels run through the trees, and especially when leaves are thick. The hide of a squirrel is tough, and with leaves or branches often in the way, a substantial load is needed in a shotgun to bring a squirrel down and avoid wounding animals that may run off into dens and die. Many hunters use high-base shells with No. 4 shot, although No. 6 will do.

One of the most delightful methods of squirrel hunting that is related to the prowl or stalk or still-hunt is floating a stream. Be sure to check for legality. Some states allow no hunting from a boat. In numerous areas stream courses have abundant squirrels living in bordering trees. Floating can at times be combined with fishing, or, if the seasons integrate properly, even with duck hunting.

Whether you hurt squirrels or simply enjoy watching the partially tame ones that are residents of city and village parks all across the nation, these are intriguing and handsome creatures. Habitat loss over the past several decades has without question harmed squirrel populations in numerous regions. Yet they are still abundant and in no danger over vast expanses of forest and woodland wherever forage-bearing trees grow. As long as there is an acorn left to ripen and fall to the ground, there is certain to be a squirrel still around to find it and bury it.

# RABBITS

**Common, or Eastern, Cottontail** *(Sylvilagus floridanus)*
**New England Cottontail** *(Sylvilagus transitionalis)*
**Mountain, or Western, Cottontail** *(Sylvilagus nuttalli)*
**Desert, or Audubon, Cottontail** *(Sylvilagus auduboni)*
**Swamp Rabbit** *(Sylvilagus aquaticus)*
**Marsh Rabbit** *(Sylvilagus palustris)*
**Brush Rabbit** *(Sylvilagus bachmani)*
**Pygmy Rabbit** *(Sylvilagus,*
in some listings *Brachylagus, idahoensis)*

It is inconceivable that even in this day of overwhelming urbanization anyone would fail to recognize a cottontail, whether or not they had ever seen a live one. The Easter Bunny, Molly Cottontail, songs such as the one about "Peter Cottontail hopping down the bunny trail," and, much farther back but the basis for endless following bedtime stories, the dramatic incidents concerning Flopsy, Mopsy, Cottontail, and Peter and their trials and tribulations with Mr. McGregor—the ubiquitous cottontail rabbit has been an important character on the American scene, both in and out of the stew pot, even since the first blunderbuss uttered its stern warning to all Peters and their friends to stay shy of the first colonial garden or be dined upon in turn.

Dined upon the cottontail always has been, incessantly. No creature so bland and innocent was ever brought into a world so teeming with enemies. No matter how cuddly and lovable the human race may consider the soft-furred, wide-eyed little rabbit, the plain fact is that nature in effect tailored the rabbit to perfection as a benign forage animal, and as good as hung a sign on it saying

"Born to be eaten." Every conceivable predator that savors flesh and blood, from snakes to coyotes, ticks to raccoons, ants and internal parasites to hawks, owls, cats and dogs, domestic and wild, and man gobbles up rabbits as fast as parent rabbits can produce them.

And that is fast! In its veritable flood of reproduction swiftly and endlessly repeated lies the mighty weapon of the lowly cottontail. Timid the creature may be—or at least so people interpret its personality. It has no fangs with which to rend an enemy. It is trusting, not very fast afoot, and cannot climb trees to escape attack. It has only moderate intelligence. The only protest of which it is capable when seized by a predatory enemy is to wail out its anguish in a scream of pain.

Yet who is it the Bible tells us shall inherit the earth? Indeed, the meek! While other North American game animals have been able to carve out special ranges for themselves, some of them to be sure expansive, the prolific cottontail, by sheer overwhelming numbers and adaptability in one variety or another to every possible habitat from southern Canada throughout all the remainder of North America southward, has outdone all the others. It lives happily on the hottest deserts, on temperate grassy plains, in the rain forests of the Pacific Coast, in the swamps of the southeast and the south, in midwestern woodlots and farm fields, in mountains to above 10,000 feet altitude, and even in hedges and on lawns in the midst of cities. As colonists, and as adaptable mammals, the rabbits have no equals on this continent.

No one is certain how many cottontails hunters in the lower-48 states annually bag. But in state after state where rabbits are eagerly sought—nationally they are the number-one game animal—the harvest runs into several million each season. A rough estimate sets an average total U.S. cottontail bag every year at between 30 and 40 million, and there are a number of states particularly in the west where rabbits are extremely abundant yet draw little hunter interest.

Consider now that naturalists and game biologists believe no more than one in twenty rabbits born each year lives to become a full year old. Some are of the opinion that in an average litter, which will number from five to seven or eight, no more than two or three ever live to leave the nest. They may be drowned by rains, attacked by ants or other insects, or succumb to disease, perhaps pneumonia from damp bedding or having been born too early in the year in the northern ranges. The mother may be seized by some predator and

Cottontail Rabbit

Douglas Allen

## THE RABBITS

COLOR: **Cottontails,** brown, shade variable among varieties, with some buffy to rusty in cast or on portions of body; longer guard hairs generally tipped with darker to black; underparts white; underside of short, fluffy tail white, from which the name derives. **Swamp and marsh rabbits,** darker in general color; underparts and underside of tail paler but not white as in cottontails. **Brush rabbit,** dark brown to dark grayish; underparts and underside of tail paler but not white. **Pygmy rabbit,** gray-brown, summer, to pale gray in winter; tail buff with no white.

MEASUREMENTS AND WEIGHT: **Cottontails and marsh rabbit,** average, with species variation, 15 to 19 inches, 6 or 7 inches at shoulder, with weight from 2 to 3½ pounds. **Swamp rabbit,** larger, to 22 inches or more, and averaging 3 pounds with maximum of 5 or 6. **Brush rabbit,** smaller than cottontails. **Pygmy rabbit,** smallest North American rabbit, 9 to 12 inches long, one-half to slightly more than 1 pound in weight.

GENERAL CHARACTERISTICS: Sprightly, quick and nervous little animals; the telltale flash of white on underside of tail invariably shows as a bobbing signal as the cottontails run; fairly long ears; strong and moderately long hind legs which propel these animals in hops and long running bounds; a habit of twitching nose as if interested in some scent, and of occasionally rearing to hind legs, with ears erect, to survey surroundings.

the youngsters then starve. Those that do live to leave the nest and eat solid food stand a good chance of feeding some meat eater during their first several weeks of roaming.

It is obvious therefore that predation aside from that of man, plus varied other natural attrition, takes a prodigious toll of the potential annual crop. And yet there are in most years enough rabbits grown to adulthood to allow all those millions for hunters and still leave ample seed for the new crop. Perhaps mankind should be thankful that rabbits are born to be eaten. If population controls upon them were not so severe, we would be literally overwhelmed by them. The nation—perhaps the world—would be theirs.

Numerous researchers have run up projections to show what would happen. Just suppose, for example, that each rabbit litter numbered seven young, and that all survived to grow up and each was capable of living to the ripe age, say, of three years. Rabbits bear several litters each year. Take four litters as a good average. So at the end of the first year we have 28 young and the 2 parents—30 rabbits. But meanwhile many of the young have already started families. Both males and females are able to breed at six months of age, although not all do start then. Studies show that for the most part the sex ratio is about 50-50. So, we now have fifteen breeding pairs, some of which before one year have already produced off-spring.

Each of the 15 pairs produces another twenty-eight offspring. So now there are at least 420 plus the 30 older animals, or 450—or 225 pairs. Carry this on for ten years and there will be rabbits numbering in millions! The physical attraction every few weeks of one rabbit for another of opposite six is indeed a mighty weapon with which they battle the hordes of hungry predators. So far as man is concerned, the blessing is that the life expectancy of each rabbit is so brief.

Although cottontails are to some extent cyclic, having eruptions of population that subside and in due time spurt again, these occur for the most part only in the warmer climes. They are seldom as dramatic as the cycles of snowshoe hares. In fact, in most parts of the range rabbits hold a fairly steady population level, dropping down some seasons when weather perhaps may cause severe breeding losses, but rising only to nominal level when they do come back. Here and there, however, astonishing population highs do appear.

In the southwest, for example, in the years prior to 1957 there was an extended drought that just about put farmers and cattlemen out of business. On the ranges of Oklahoma and Texas, two of the states hardest hit, everything was shriveled and brown, even the prickly pear cactus. Then in 1957 rains came, one after another. The dry stretches of country exploded in greenery—and rabbits. That fall in many places the cottontails were so abundant one could not walk fifty paces without jumping one, or more. By late fall they had cut every stalk of vegetation that was edible. Bark on the vast sweeps of dense scrub mesquite was eaten off as high as the rabbits could reach. A hunter told of sitting on the tailgate of a pickup early one cool morning while a friend drove, and popping a dozen rabbits for a quail-camp stew pot while moving only a scant 200 yards along a ranch trail through brush!

Most hunters and others use the term "rabbit" to mean the cottontail, unless they prefix it with "jack." The matter of terminology can be confusing, but need not be if a few basics are learned. Rabbits and hares belong to two different animal groups and have quite different distinguishing attributes. The so-called jack "rabbits" and the snowshoe "rabbit" are actually hares. Young hares are born with eyes and ears open, bodies fully furred, and almost literally ready to run at the moment of birth. Rabbits are born "blind"—that is, with eyes sealed shut, and ears also. They are naked and nearly helpless. Another difference: rabbits spend much time underground in burrows dug by other animals, and hole up when chased. Hares do neither.

The word "hare," however is not often used in America. Hunters say they are going rabbit hunting when they are after cottontails or one of the other rabbits with which this chapter deals. Varying hare hunters—who never use that name—speak of their favorite quarry as the "snowshoe," although where only snowshoe hares are found "rabbit" hunting may apply to them. Jacks—always called "rabbits" by sportsmen and others in America—cannot truly qualify as game animals, but rather are hunted as pests, seldom for food.

Among the rabbit group, the cottontails are the most diverse. There are at least ten or a dozen different members of the tribe given full species status, and five or six dozen variations that qualify in the view of some taxonomists as subspecies. However, most of these look so much alike it would be impossible for the layman to distinguish among them or—in most cases—between any two. There are only four main cottontail species with substantial expanses of range, some of which overlap.

The common or eastern cottontail blankets almost all of the contiguous states east of the Rockies, spills over very slightly into a few places in southern Canada but is not found in northern New England. The New England variety is present in New England—not always abundantly, however—and ranges down the Appalachians to northern Georgia and Alabama. The mountain cottontail, occasionally dubbed the western cottontail, is an animal of the Rockies region from parts of northern New Mexico and Arizona to and a short distance into Canada in Alberta and Saskatchewan. The desert cottontail, properly the Audubon cottontail, is native to the western half of Texas, westward into the lower half of California, and on up into parts of Nevada, Utah, Colorado, Wyoming, Montana, and the western fringes of the plains states. It is slightly smaller than the others.

The habitat preferences of these cottontails differ notably, as discussed below. There is also a difference, species to species, in general coloration. Foot and leg measurements and some other physical characteristics also differ. However, to the average hunter or observer of wildlife they all are readily recognizable as cotton-tails, but would be difficult for the layman to distinguish readily, or even to identify positively. Telling them apart isn't necessary any-way, except to a scientist or an advanced student of wildlife.

The marsh and swamp rabbits really aren't, strictly speaking, "cottontails." They don't exhibit a cottony ball of fluff for a tail. The underside of the tail in these rabbits is brownish to grayish or dirty white, and the underparts match or are brownish. These rabbits, particularly the marsh rabbit, are darker than most cottontails, the marsh species definitely dark brown, the swamp variety grizzled gray. They are lowland varieties, as their names indicate, and don't mind swimming, in fact enter water without being forced to. The marsh variety, colloquially sometimes dubbed a "pontoon," is a southeastern rabbit of the Atlantic Coast area, all of Florida, and portions of southern Georgia and Alabama. It compares roughly in size to the larger cottontails.

The swamp rabbit takes over the range westward—parts of Georgia, most of Alabama, all of Louisiana and Arkansas, eastern Texas and Oklahoma, and northward into portions of Missouri and on up the Mississippi Valley into Illinois and its stream-bottom bordering fringes. This rabbit is a big one, from the size of the average large cottontail at maturity on up to a maximum of 4, 5, or 6 pounds. Few hunter enthusiasts in the dense lowland country where this rabbit dwells call it by its "rabbit" name. To them it's a "cane cutter," a name originating from its habitat preference for lowland cane brakes and its habit of feeding on, or cutting, cane.

The brush rabbit is an animal of the Pacific coast, its range extending from Mexico to the southern fringes of Washington, but only over the western portions of the states involved, California and Oregon. It is a small rabbit, and not a "cottontail." It is dark-colored, wears a stubby brown tail, and has legs that seem to fit its short body, for they are shorter than the legs of the true cottontails.

The miniature of the rabbit tribe, the pygmy rabbit, lives in eastern Oregon and a bit of eastern Washington, the southern half of Idaho, and much of Nevada and spills over into bits of western Utah, southwestern Montana, and northeastern California. These diminutive rabbits, many of them only 9 or 10 inches long, change coat seasonally, are gray-brown in summer and dusty gray in winter. The tail is a buff color. They match their surroundings per-fectly, are difficult to spot, and are often mistaken by casual ob-servers for young of other rabbits. The pygmy is the only North American rabbit that digs its own burrow.

# Range of the Cottontail Rabbit

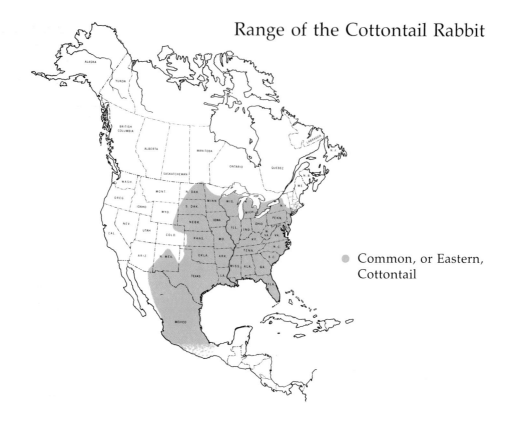

● Common, or Eastern, Cottontail

◍ New England Cottontail
● Mountain Cottontail

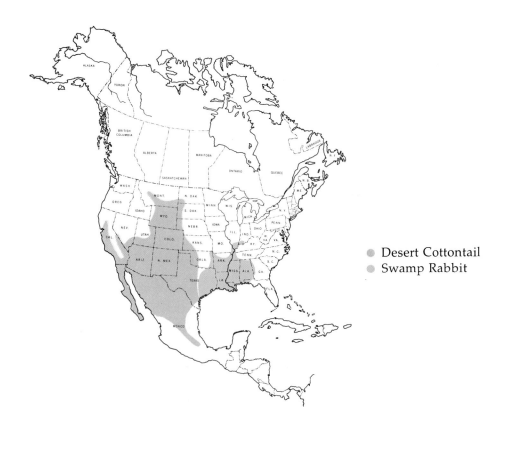

Desert Cottontail
Swamp Rabbit

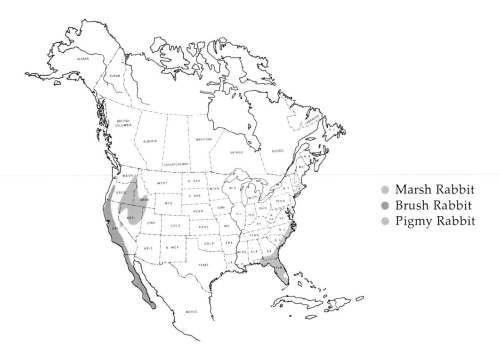

Marsh Rabbit
Brush Rabbit
Pigmy Rabbit

Several of the rabbits from the United States are also found in Mexico. Among these are the common, or eastern, cottontail, the Audubon cottontail, and the brush rabbit. For those who wish to study further, Mexico also has its own cottontail, *Sylvilagus cunicularius,* the Mexican cottontail, as large as the common cottontail. In addition, Mexico is home to the slightly smaller tropical forest rabbit, *S. brasiliensis,* a dweller in that country's humid southeastern tropical forests. There is also the tiny volcano rabbit, which belongs to another scientific group, and has the smallest range of any Mexican mammal. It is limited to the bunch-grass and pine uplands of the rim of the Valley of Mexico.

After the disease tularemia was diagnosed early in this century as a disease of rabbits that is easily passed on to man, many hunters became wary of handling rabbits, and here and there sportsmen even stopped hunting them. However, the disease seems rare today. It is a serious disease and has been fatal in a modest percentage of human cases, but modern medicines easily cure it. It is lethal among rabbits and some other animals. Any rabbit, of whatever variety, that appears not in top physical condition, that acts ill or lethargic, should be left alone. In addition, care should be taken in handling and skinning rabbits. It's a good idea to wear rubber or plastic gloves for the chore, and to sterilize them or throw them away. Humans can become infected with tularemia not only by handling rabbits infected with it, but by eating rabbit meat that is not thoroughly cooked. Although the incidence of the disease in humans is very low, caution is in order.

Hunters also often hesitate to pick up or use rabbits that have lumps under the skin, called warbles. These are caused by botfly "stings" during which the fly eggs are deposited. The larvae cut through the skin, grow under it, and hatch from there. Warbles do not ruin rabbit meat, but admittedly the discovery of warbles on an animal is distasteful. In cold climates the lumps usually disappear in fall. Either the larvae have hatched or the temperature kills them.

All the rabbits and hares are hosts to parasites, from ticks to fleas to internal parasites and microbes. Although rabbits are legal game during the spring and summer in a few states — that is, they receive no protection and may be taken at any time — the majority of hunters choose to wait until cool weather before hunting them. The theory is that cold and reduced food supply will kill off rabbits that are sick or unduly infested and weakened, leaving only healthy, lively animals. To some extent this is true.

A curious sidelight on the world of the rabbits is that, unlike squirrels, which evidence a rather high rate of melanism, that is, the incidence of black individuals, and a modest incidence of albinism, black or white phases among rabbits are very rare. Most white domestic rabbits are albinos, but these are animals from lines of imported varieties not closely allied to the cottontails and other North American rabbits.

Not many outdoorsmen and wildlife watchers have ever heard the wild squall of a rabbit caught by some predator. It is a hair-raising sound. It would seem that hunters in particular would often hear the scream. Yet oddly, a wounded rabbit seldom utters a sound. On occasion one may when actually picked up. But even this is rare. Yet in nature the sound must be heard often, for every predator from hawks to foxes and coyotes to raccoons, crows, bears, and bobcats apparently is well aware of its meaning.

This is the sound on which practically all predator calling is based. This sport, which has grown vastly over the past twenty years or so, depends almost entirely upon an imitation of the "dying rabbit scream." What is so interesting about this is that it works border to border and coast to coast, and that it brings in to the caller all of the chief enemies of the rabbit. Hawks come swooping at times, foxes and coyotes are eager, bobcats stalk the sound, even black bears and mountain lions are intrigued by it. No phenomenon could more succinctly illustrate the fact that the prolific clan of the rabbits is to the meat eaters an exceedingly important staple of diet.

### HABITAT

The cottontails and other North American rabbits are animals of the brush, the open woodlots and woodlands, the stream courses. They are not forest animals, in the sense of liking the deep forests. In many places in large expanses of forest, such as in the Great Lakes states or the south, where stretches of National Forest are present, cottontails may be found in modest populations far back in them, but invariably living on the edges of openings. In northern Michigan, for example, out in the Pigeon River State Forest hunters now and then bag some unusually large cottontails, but always from hidden openings where clover and wild strawberry grow, and where perhaps poplar saplings intermingle with evergreens to form the border.

Indeed, the rabbits — most varieties — are edge animals. In small-farm country a brushy fence row bordering a grass or crop field forms a home for cottontails. An Ozark valley where farms long ago were cut out of the forest offers perfect cottontail habitat. A small red-willow swale, a brushy creek course meandering across an open meadow, an open maple woodlot surrounded by crop fields — all such places have their rabbit quotas.

However, because rabbits have colonized such vast expanses of this continent, obviously habitats differ from place to place, even though the fundamentals may be the same in each instance. In southern Oklahoma, for example, along the Red River there is no great amount of authentic woodland, but there are scattered trees, endless dry gullies and brush, and in places fanning out from this region on both sides of the state's border there are stretches of low, thorny mesquite and dwarfed cactus clumps. This is a perfect habitat for the cottontails of the region.

In the so-called Brush Country of southern Texas, an undulating massive stretch of low thornbrush of numerous varieties interspersed with prickly pear flats, cottontails often literally teem. Some of these arid-country rabbits are the eastern cottontail, and some are the Audubon or desert cottontail. But when one moves into the best habitat of the Audubon variety, farther west and north, it will be found in low growing catclaw clumps, and out in the modest cover of prairie grass also. A prairie dog town is a favorite habitat for this rabbit, and in fact it has been called colloquially a "prairie dog rabbit."

The mountain cottontail, like the rest, needs cover, and is as thoroughly an edge animal as its eastern cousin. However, its edges are the brushy slopes and openings of the Rockies region and the eastern slopes of the Cascades and the Sierra. The Brush Rabbits of the west coast would not abide the open grass country that the Audubon cottontail sometimes inhabits. They are brush animals almost entirely, sticking to the dry thickets from Baja northward, and to the humid undergrowth up the Oregon coast.

The diminutive pygmy rabbit loves the dry sagebrush and rabbitbrush expanses of the arid flats and plateaus typical of the Great Basin to the west of the Rockies. In its way, too, it seeks edges, even though these may be difficult for an observer to discern. They are the borders of the denser patches, where the little rabbits move about to feed early and late, the edges of the eroded gullies and washes, and the tiny openings between rabbit brush clumps.

The most curious, and exaggerated, edges loved by rabbits are those inhabited by the marsh and swamp varieties. These are the cypress jungles bordering ponds, lakes, streams, and swamps in the southeast, and the brushy stream courses, boghole borders, and lake shores of the southern and midsouthern states. The marsh rabbit of Florida and the southeast, far from trying to avoid getting wet, as cottontails often do, purposely goes swimming. It crosses a swamp pond by swimming rather than hopping around the edge. It feeds on water plants, makes runways through the bordering jungle, suns on small hummocks in ponds, and when frightened flees by swimming, and sometimes hides by sinking below water so only its eyes and nose show.

It is interesting to note that the marsh and swamp rabbits are the only ones of the world's rabbits that have such aquatic habits. Some scientists believe they are closely related to the tropical woods or forest rabbits of Mexico and Central and South America. The marsh rabbit is even found in brackish swamps along the coast, but is chiefly an animal of the freshwater cypress swamps. One old account tells of a captured marsh rabbit kept by the naturalist Bachman (for whom the western brush rabbit is named) that would lie in its cage for long periods in a trough of water. The swamp rabbit is not quite so insistent on dabbling in water, but when hunted takes to the awesomely dense thickets of swampy areas within its favorite bailiwicks, and also does not hesitate to plunge into a stream and swim across to throw dogs off its trail. It swims when undisturbed, too.

## FEEDING

It would be pointless to attempt to list all the foods rabbits eat. In fact, it might be impossible. At the least such a list would look like the index to a fat botany book. Rabbits are vegetarians, but they are not finicky vegetarians. They will eat anything green, including poison ivy, and when the green is gone in wintry latitudes they start in on twigs and bark.

This limitless and nondiscriminatory intake of the rabbit tribe is one of the main reasons these animals have been able to spread over such a vast expanse of range, including altitudes from sea level or below to timberline. The only control on range expansion for the rabbits seems to be temperature. Although they manage in some rather cold places, such as the fringe of their ranges into southern Canada, they do not appear able to spread on northward.

Even so, this may be partially a matter of food supply as well as an inability to cope with sustained and extreme low temperatures. The basic foods of rabbits become less available northward. In much of Canada the spruce forests may be a kind of barrier. There are pulp woods such as birch and poplar but perhaps not in the proper places and quantities. The snowshoe hare, and farther north the arctic hare, do nicely in cold and with only stunted vegetation, but the rabbits are not equipped physically for a far-north life, and prefer a broader diet.

Not only do rabbits have within a few hops all they need to eat in almost any situation within the lower United States and Mexico, but the variety assures that they'll eat well regardless of what may happen to a favorite type of forage. If a group of cottontails is feeding heavily, for example, on a farmer's crop, and he harvests it, they simply shift to some nearby wild crop and continue eating. Clover is always, in rabbit stories, pictured as a favorite food. Rabbits do like clover. It usually is a lush crop, contains ample moisture, and probably tastes good to them. But so do dozens of varieties of legumes and forbs and grasses.

Several nature writers have said that it would be easier to list what rabbits won't eat than what they will eat. However, that too might prove to be a puzzle. In agricultural country, rabbits appear especially fond of soybean plants, alfalfa, winter wheat and oats, or the growing crops in summer. If they discover a garden, cabbage, lettuce, carrot tops—they do not dig for food and thus don't pull such foods—and sprouting corn all are eagerly eaten.

Fruits that they can reach add to the diet. Rabbits often stand on hind legs to reach low-growing fruits or to nibble at hanging vines or succulent twigs. These are specialties, however. The staples in almost any habitat are grasses and forbs. Following those in lesser quantities are leaves from a wide variety of shrubs.

In the more humid parts of the southern range there is much greenery to be found all winter. Rabbits can pick and choose, leaving dried grasses and weeds and seeking the still-green shoots beneath. But wherever vegetations dies down thoroughly, there is a rather abrupt change at the end of the growing season and the beginning of killing frosts. Rabbits must switch to twigs, buds, bark, and various woody forage. Fruit-tree orchards often have difficulties with cottontails that girdle the trees, eating the soft inner bark. They do the same to many domestic decorative shrubs. If an apple has fallen to the ground and shriveled, rabbits seek it, even digging down through snow, which is easy enough for them even though they are not—except the pygmy rabbit—burrowers.

In ranges outside agricultural pursuits, rabbits turn to cutting brambles in wild berry patches, snipping the sprouting young trees such as birch and poplar, and seeking shrubs—witch hazel, sumac, sassafras. In areas where pulp wood is cut, rabbits congregate to eat the bark from trimmings of poplar, for example, and they also dine on needles of varied conifers. In the west and southwest, where the several varieties live out their lives in arid country and in brushy covers, the cover that hides them in summer serves as forage in winter. Sagebrush, and even in some instances dry prairie grasses and weeds, must be eaten. However, rabbits find the switch to woody diet by no means intolerable, even though their preferences are always for greenery.

### MOVEMENTS

As with all wild animals, the major share of the movements and travel of rabbits is the search for food. But no rabbit, except in the extreme exigency of prolonged drought, has to move very far to keep its belly full. Nonetheless, the amount of home range needed per rabbit varies widely from one location to another, depending upon the quantity of forage and cover available.

Some rabbits probably are born and die without moving outside an area of 1 or 2 acres. Others may call a 5- or 10-acre patch of cover home, but some studies on the living room needed show that under certain conditions a rabbit may move about over 100 and more acres, even up to exploring here and there throughout a square mile of range. Adult males usually move about much farther than females, but probably an average home of 5 to 20 acres is normal for most individual rabbits. Hunters who observe tracks in snow in winter have a pretty fair idea how much territory individual cottontails cover, and it's never very extensive.

Rabbits are built for hopping and bounding, the long, sturdy hind legs propelling the animal and the forelegs functioning chiefly as a kind of landing gear. The feet have a dense covering of hair on the bottoms, which possibly assists in gripping for the hop or bound, and also softening the bouncy landing. When meandering around undisturbed, rabbits use several gaits. The standard hop may be only a few inches at a time, with the powerful hind feet not pushing much, and not moving up past the forefeet as in a bound. The animal simply reaches out with its forefeet and then brings the hind feet up behind.

All of the varieties also walk or creep at times, one forefoot, then the other, and the hind feet similarly following. This motion is common when they are feeding, or interested in others of their kind. Rabbits get along fairly well, incidentally, and don't seem to have strict territories that they defend, except when a female with young bristles at another that comes too near her nest, and of course during breeding seasons when there are fights between males. The walking or creeping gait of some of the smaller rabbits is interesting to observe. They sneak along close to the ground, almost like rats.

When disturbed, a rabbit bounds away. It is never as fast as it seems when it is pressed to full speed. But in fleeing dangers rabbits do not run straight away. They zigzag wildly, darting through cover or across an opening, and the flashing tail of the cottontail varieties gives the illusion of sizzling flight. Ten to 15 miles an hour is normal, although when severely pressed a rabbit may rev up to 20. The normal bound of a running cottontail varies from 1 to 2 yards, but longer leaps are possible, and common. A rabbit easily spans a ditch 15 feet wide when it decides to, but the usual flight pattern is a dodging going-away trail full of quick deft and unpredictable turns. Some observers believe that a sudden very high leap into the air, a common tactic of cottontails, is made so the animal can get a better look behind. Perhaps. Or perhaps it is just a matter of excited getaway technique.

Although rabbits are considered innocent little creatures without much craftiness, old cottontails that have had experience with dogs and hunters and lived to run again are often amazingly clever in their trickery and schemes. The downfall of many a rabbit has been its unyielding attachment to its home territory. A rabbit that is pushed hard by a fast dog may larrup off at full tilt, perhaps covering a half-mile or more across fields and woodlot. But it will invariably circle, and come right back to the point where it was jumped. If the dog is slow, the rabbit keeps hopping just fast enough to stay well ahead after its first burst of speed. Sure enough, back it comes. Rabbit hunters often climb atop a stump or brushpile or other handy object to get a view from above ground level. They simply listen to the dog, and when it is coming around and back their way, they watch close in for a sight of the circling rabbit.

Rabbits do most of their feeding and moving about during late afternoon and very early morning. Often they move out of cover just before dusk. They are said in scientific language to be crepuscular—active at twilight. This is really an exaggeration. A rabbit moves around anytime it feels like moving around. Sometimes cottontails feed in the middle of the day, sometimes at intervals during the night. On moonlit nights in winter they are often seen busily moving about. On cloudy days they may feel that twilight is simulated, and thus be active. Nonetheless, it is true that their most active periods as a rule are at sundown and dawn. Hunters without dogs often move along trails or ranch roads at these times and pot cottontails with a .22 rifle.

During most of the daylight hours, rabbits sit in what are called "forms." A form is a small depression, sometimes fashioned by the animal, sometimes simply a comfortable sitting place in grass that takes on the shape or form of the animal's hunched body, from being used several times. Some forms are used habitually, some are not. Usually there is nearby cover for protection, if the sitting spot is out in the open where the rabbit can doze in sunshine. A tall grass clump with one side more open, a clump of bushes, or a single bush may back the form. It may be against a stump or log under the edge of a brushpile. Particularly in winter in colder climates on bright, still days, rabbits often use forms right out in the middle of a field of dead grass. They get the warmth of the sun here.

The form—and the individual animal usually has several of them scattered about its domain—is a kind of bed. A rabbit has a strong attachment to each one. That is why when jumped and run by a dog it returns as a rule to the form it left. There may be another motive: by coming back to the starting point, it can tell if the dog, or other enemy, is still on its trail.

The immediate reaction of a rabbit when danger nears its sitting place is to hug the ground, ears flat to its head, utterly still. This "freeze" habit is a ruse to avoid detection. A dog or predator may catch the scent and flush the animal. But many enemies, man among them, do not scent the rabbit and may step within inches of it. A hunter without a dog who walks slowly, pausing every few steps, will flush rabbits, because they get uneasy if danger stays quiet and still too long. But one who walks along at constant pace won't flush a cottontail but will pass on by as it lies flattened in its form.

As noted earlier, rabbits do not dig burrows, with the single exception among North American varieties of the pygmy rabbit. They do utilize burrows of other animals—woodchuck, skunk, fox, badger—that they hopefully believe to be abandoned. They dart in these when hard pressed, and they also use these hides for protection from the cold. A wise old cottontail, however, will often run before a slow dog for a long time, around and around. Presumably it is hesitant to go to ground because it then gives away its secret hiding place. If pushed fast and hard, however, it uses any burrow available.

In addition to burrows of other animals, rabbits pop into holes

*A cottontail keeps its runway clear by snipping twigs that block the way.*

among rocks, into hollow logs, into the base of a hollow tree, under an old building, and under brush piles. They use these for forms of a sort in cold weather, and often also at any time as favorite resting places. Many a country boy learns early in his hunting career to climb atop and jump up and down on every brush pile in and around a woodlot. Invariably a rabbit, sometimes more than one, will be resting underneath.

Rabbits move about rather commonly on paths they have worn and used incessantly. This habit differs in emphasis species to species. For example, the marsh and swamp rabbits, and the small brush rabbits, and cottontails in dense cover, make a lacework of well-worn trails and in some instances snip away twigs or weeds that are in the way, to keep the runways open. Obviously, living in a small area a rabbit knows every bush and opening and trail.

However, too much has been made of this habit in some accounts. There are hundreds of places where rabbits move helter-skelter through the brush, never need to clean out pathways, and seldom use more than a few short stretches of runway over and over. It is true that the area under piles of brush or other debris that rabbits habitually use is laced with definite runways. These are simply the result of taking the easiest routes as they move around in their hiding places.

As mentioned previously, the little pygmy rabbit digs its own home. It is sometimes called a burrowing rabbit. Its burrow may have several well-screened entrances. The burrow is never very deep. This burrowing habit is common among European rabbits, but the pygmy is the only American digger. In fact, the forefeet and legs of the rabbits, though fitted with strong claws, are not sturdy enough to allow extensive digging. Nor can they be used as the squirrels and other rodents, and the raccoon, use their forefeet — to hold food. The physical design of rabbit feet precludes this use.

One interesting use of the hind feet occurs now and then when a rabbit is suspicious of danger, and it also is used occasionally as a signal of annoyance with a rabbit of like sex. The hind foot is raised and thumped smartly upon the ground. This is perhaps a warning to other rabbits, or may be just a sign of tenseness and concern. The sound can be heard over a modest distance.


BREEDING

About the first of the year, male rabbits begin to roam more, to look for mates, and to quarrel with other males they meet. During the fall and thus far into winter the testicles are held inside the body but now become enlarged and move down into the scrotum, which, curiously and unlike that of other American mammals, is situated ahead of the penis. The breeding season in most areas is launched early in the year, but it continues, with several litters born to most females, on through until late summer or even into fall.

The males are by no means timid creatures during breeding. The larger males in particular become bossy and quite literally throw their weight around. They pick fights with other males, biting out wads of fur catch as catch can. Battling males sometimes rear up and cuff each other in a comic display of fisticuffs. They also leap high and flail with their strong hind feet, trying to smack an opponent momentarily senseless. These battles seldom last very long or do any severe damage. One decides it has had enough and the dominant rival chases it briefly as it leaves the scene.

These battles are just the beginning of troubles for the male. Now as he approaches a female, she may slash with her teeth, ripping out balls of fur, and she too will dish out husky belts of her hind feet. Yet this is mostly sham. The suitor makes a flying leap into the air as she charges. Her rush carries her beneath and he whirls in the air to come down facing her and perhaps makes his own rush, striking her in turn, as if to demonstrate that he is boss and won't take no for an answer.

After a few such charades the female decides maybe he's not so bad after all. She acquiesces. Mating may occur several times in succession. The male then may wander off to try again, and the female, by no means monogamous, may accept other suitors. In fact, she often has several after her at one time, and is seldom very hard to convince. However, a dominant male may hang around for a couple of days. It doesn't take long for the sated female to get sick of him. Now he's in for still more temper tantrums on her part. If he hasn't had the good sense to leave, she'll fly at him angrily, ripping out more wads of fur until he gets the idea that he should leave her territory and find peace and comfort somewhere else.

## BIRTH AND DEVELOPMENT

As if hurrying to get on with another litter, the female bears her young after only twenty-eight days, give or take a couple of days. Several days before the birth, the mother prepares a nest. This is a shallow depression she digs in the dirt, sometimes hidden in brush or among tree roots, often simply scooped out in a grassy field. She lines the nest with dead grass, and covers this padding with fur that she pulls from her own belly. More fur, mixed in with bits of grass, is molded into a kind of cover that will keep the coming youngsters warm and also help to hide the nest location.

The number in a litter is variable, from three to seven. The babies weigh no more than an ounce each. They are naked, their eyes and ears are sealed, and their ears are short and flat against the head. The mother draws the furry blanket over the newborn youngsters and leaves them. She usually stays a short distance away, watching the nest, and she will try desperately to drive enemies away, sometimes losing her own life in the attempt.

If birth is imminent and the mother is feeding at a distance from the nest she has prepared, she simply pauses and gives birth, then carries the babies in her mouth, trip after trip, to place them in the nest. Very occasionally if something makes her nervous the mother may decide to move young from one nest site to another. She goes to the nest at dusk to nurse the young, and continues to let them nurse every couple of hours during the night. When she leaves to go to feed or keep watch in the daytime, she may not only cover the babies with the fur blanket, but also scratch grass or leaves atop the nest to hide it.

In seven or eight days the little rabbits have grown short fur, their eyes are open, and their ears are erect and open also. All individuals may not follow the same timing within the litter. But when all have their vital senses, they grow and develop even more swiftly. At two weeks of age they are beginning to creep out of the nest and hop about its vicinity.

Some females are bred again almost as soon as the young are born, in fact occasionally during the same day. The male to which she succumbs is then chased away. Males have been known to kill the young. It seems as if all the birth and development and breeding routines are geared to produce more rabbits as soon as possible. The young nurse their mother for only a couple of weeks, and before the first month of their lives has passed they have left the nest and their parent and are off on their own. They are nearly fully grown by the time they attain six months, and some of them may even at that time be capable of breeding and beginning the prolific cycle all over again—even as their mother is perhaps well along on her third litter of the year!

### SENSES

The nose twitching for which rabbits are well known probably has little to do with gathering in scent. Undoubtedly rabbits have a useful sense of smell, and may select certain foods by scent. However, they are so broad-spectrum in their feeding that choices are not important enough to necessitate a keen sense of smell. Scent plays little or no role in the appraisal of danger.

Hearing is an important sense. The long, upright ears turn this way and that to catch the slightest sound. Rabbits will run, or freeze flat to the ground, at the rustle of a footstep even though they may not have seen danger. But hearing is important only at close range. Distant loud noises do not disturb rabbits.

Sight also is sharp, but its high development is mainly useful over short distances, for rabbits are low to the ground in sighting plane, and usually in cover. The eyes are large, set well out from the sides of the head, and the range of vision for each eye covers almost the entire half-circle on that side of the head. Only vision straight forward is slightly limited. A rabbit watching motion in front turns its head to look more directly with one eye. It is interesting that the eyes of certain animals, among them the rabbits and hares—and also deer—do not close in death. A rabbit that happens to be hunching in a form as it dies has the eyes open and looks alive.

SIGN *(Tracks are illustrated on page 254.)*

Tracks are the common sign of rabbits, but they do not show very well in any medium except snow. Of course close scrutiny of dusty places in arid areas or of muddy borders where the marsh and swamp rabbits live will discover tracks. In winter, however, rabbits leave such a profusion of tracks in areas where they feed and move about that hunters and others quickly discover the abodes. Typically the tracks of rabbits form a kind of triangle, the two large hindfoot tracks not quite parallel out in front, a muddled single print where both forefeet strike a short distance behind. However, just as often all four feet make prints, the forefoot prints spaced one behind the other behind the widely spaced hind prints.

The span in length measured from the forefoot prints to the toes of the hind prints differs depending on whether the animal is hopping about feeding, or running. Each set averages anywhere from 6 inches to a foot, and the hop or leap in between may be less than a yard, or when going full out more than a yard and up to several. The toes show very little in rabbit tracks, or at least only indistinctly, except in tracks of the aquatic rabbits in soft mud. Cottontail tracks are not often confused with the larger tracks—in which the splayed-out toes commonly show—of the snowshoe hare, because the two species seldom are on the same ranges. Jack rabbit tracks are larger and also not likely to be confused with those of the smaller cottontails.

Well-used rabbit forms are a sign sometimes spotted. They are not as obvious as the forms of the jacks, however, and usually are hidden much better. A sign not often recognized is a dusting place. This, too, is more abundant on jack rabbit ranges, but in dry places cottontails now and then leave dust-bed signs. It is simply a place slightly hollowed out on a dusty spot where the rabbit has scratched and wriggled around, probably in attempts to get rid of pests such as fleas and ticks.

Wherever the rabbits are plentiful, droppings are certain to be much in evidence. On snow, where rabbits have been feeding, they are invariably numerous, and here and there also will be found urine stains on the snow. Rabbit droppings on most diets are round. Where jacks and cottontails range together, it is not difficult to identify the much larger droppings of the jacks. The round shape of both set them aside from oblong deer droppings, or those from sheep and goats on the same range.

Cuttings—the evidence of foraging left on the ends of shrub branches or vines from which twigs have been snipped off—also tell of the presence of rabbits. However, it is all too easy for the casual observer to confuse cuttings of rodents and of deer with those of rabbits. Tracks and or droppings nearby clinch identification either way. Bark stripped from shrubs or from pulpwood branches and other brush piles indicates the presence of rabbits. Invariably there will be copious droppings and numerous tracks to further substantiate it.

### HUNTING

Rabbit hunting is a homely and delightfully uncomplicated sport. The most enjoyable approach is with dogs. All sorts of dogs, from finely bred beagles to mixed-up mongrels, run rabbits. Hunting thus in snow country is considered typical. It is invigorating, and tracking is made easy for the dogs. In country where snow is uncommon, the dogs may have to work harder and the hunters look sharper for the bounding rabbit, because there is no brown-furred contrast on white snow.

There is really no special technique involved. The hunters simply move into an area known to have rabbits, release the dogs, and let nature take over. Obviously, early and late, when rabbits are moving about, means faster action because there are fresh tracks for the hounds to work out. Few hunters worry about that. They let the dogs nose about and jump rabbits from forms, or they themselves climb atop brush piles and jump up and down to flush rabbits for the dogs to run.

Experienced hunters usually fan out when a rabbit is put up, and remain in the vicinity of the flushing spot. The animal will circle and almost without fail come back around to or near its starting point. If there is a stump or rock or brush pile handy, a hunter who climbs up on it has a better view down into the nearby cover. Most hunters prefer dogs that work rather slowly. This keeps the quarry also hopping along slowly. A fast dog that pushes a cottontail hard will all too often frighten it into holing up, and that ends that particular chase.

Thousands of hunters, of course, do not own dogs. Among these the pleasant pastime of wandering around "walking 'em up" is the approach. There are two main schools of thought as to when is the best time. Many hunters like to get out on still, bright winter days, walk the fields, kick out the bramble patches and the brush piles, and flush rabbits from their forms where they are taking the sun. Some sharp-eyed hunters even prowl with great care, slow-motion, and try to spot rabbits hunched flat in their hiding places. This random method of hunting is effective in territory where rabbits are abundant. It pays to watch for sign and to hunt the locations with the most of it.

The other technique is the early-and-late approach. A hunter searches for trails—old roads, farm and ranch trails—or openings and field edges where he suspects cottontails may be present. Then he hunts at dawn or else late in the afternoon and toward dusk. All these edges are prime foraging grounds for rabbits. In the west the borders of alfalfa fields, the banks of washes or streams, a sweep of sagebrush with openings where grass grows all are worth checking. In some parts of the south and southwest, patches of winter oats, for example, draw scads of cottontails when the afternoon shadows grow long.

The hunter simply walks along and watches for rabbits flickering here and there, in and out of cover, or sitting to feed at the edge of a trail. Most hunters who use dogs or who walk up rabbits, flushing them from their forms, use a shotgun. This is because the running, zigzagging cottontail is by no means an easy target. A modified or improved-cylinder barrel is just the ticket. Fine shot should not be used. Field loads of No. 6 are about right. However, the early-and-late, dogless hunters often favor a .22 rifle, with a scope. When out and feeding, rabbits are alert and quick to dart to cover. The rifle will reach out to pick them off before they decide to leave, whereas getting in shotgun range is nearly impossible.

It is hardly conceivable that a rabbit-hunting enthusiast will ever need to worry about the decline of his favorite game animal. As long as the habits of rabbits remain as they have been for centuries, the production line is certain to keep humming.

# Varying Hare

*Lepus americanus*

The varying hare is so named because its coat varies in color-
with the seasons, except in its extreme southwestern range:
brown in summer, white in winter, a mixture in between. For all
the insistence by scientists upon clinging to this official name,
however, the layman—whether a hunter or a wildlife enthusiast—seldom uses the "hare" part of the name and never the "varying" portion. Its common name everywhere within its range
derives from its big, furry hind feet, which allow it to move easily
across drifts of snow; almost without fail "rabbit" is tacked on—
"snowshoe rabbit." A check of the game laws in states where this
animal is found shows only one or two listing it as a "hare," and
then as a "snowshoe hare." The correct—or at least book—name may
be used occasionally in Canada, but the average American hunter
wouldn't know what a varying hare was unless shown a picture of
what he calls a snowshoe rabbit.

Nonetheless, the animal is a true hare. Although the hares and
rabbits belong to the same scientific order, Lagomorpha, and are
even placed in the same family, Leporidae, the two groups have

## THE VARYING HARE

COLOR: Summer, brown or gray-brown above; underparts and underside of tail white or gray-white; center of back, rump, and top of tail darker than remainder of body; tips of ears dusky to black; eye, black; winter, white, except for dusky to black tips of ears and black eye; early and late in winter some individuals flecked with patternless rusty patches; the race of varying hares present on the west slope of the Cascades and Sierra Nevada, and in the coastal forests of the northwest do not "vary" but remain brown to grayish all year.

MEASUREMENTS AND WEIGHT: Overall length 16 to 21 inches; height at shoulder 8 to 9 inches; weight 2½ to 4 pounds.

GENERAL CHARACTERISTICS: Ears and hind legs much longer than those of the rabbits; hind feet extra-large, with toes long, tending to splay when hare walks or runs; feet heavily furred all year but especially so in winter; an animal of dense forests and conifer thickets that lives above ground and does not run into a hole when pursued.

distinctive physiological characteristics that plainly set them apart. The hares are larger animals than the rabbits, have ears and hind legs much longer, and are born fully furred with eyes and ears open and are able to move about almost immediately, whereas rabbits are born naked, nearly helpless, with eyes and ears sealed. Hares seldom if ever hide below ground, rabbits commonly do. There are other differences, some of them internal, but those mentioned easily separate the two animal groups.

Especially in winter coat the snowshoe is a strikingly handsome creature. Many husky adults weigh as much as 4 pounds, and when the coat is completely changed the animal is pure white with the exception of the round, black eye, which stands out surprisingly to a sharp observer even at 30 to 50 yards, and the tips of the ears. Most written descriptions describe the ear tips as black. In some specimens the ear tips are black, but in most the contrast is not that distinct. A better description perhaps is "dusky."

As the coat is changing from its summer brown to winter white, splotches and specks of each often intermingle. Among individual varying hares the change is not as neat and regular as many accounts describe it. In general the fall change starts on the feet, legs, and ears and more and more white appears progressively higher and rearward on the body. Actually the brown summer coat, if examined closely, shows gray underfur tipped with reddish hues.

The gray remains, and as the white hair comes in the rusty

# The Varying Hare

*Summer*

*Winter*

speckles may show here and there until the whole white coat is completed. Even then, if the soft fur is blown apart the pale gray is evident underneath. Thus this animal is often called, in some parts of its range, a "gray hare" or "gray rabbit." In fact, in some places the outer summer coat is more gray than brown. And some individuals, when presumably in full winter coat, still show rusty bits and tinges around the head and face and on the legs and feet.

When winter begins to wane and the change to summer coat is launched, the brown is first evident in reverse order, on the rump, back, and head and working its way down to legs and feet. Some naturalists believe these change routines may be a sequence of camouflage patterning—the fall change which is spread over about two months shows whitish first at the level where light snow and the browns of leaves and cover intermingle, and the spring change shows the brownish higher up where twigs and branches match and the white remains near ground level until the snow is gone.

Whether or not this is true, the triggering of the changes is intriguing. As days grow shorter in fall, exposure of the hares to light grows less and less, and presumably this sets off chemical body changes that result in hair-color changes. Then as days begin to lengthen, the opposite reaction occurs. Thus it can be said either that fall and the oncoming winter, and the going of winter as it changes to spring, cause the switches, or that lack of light with lowering temperature and increasing light with rising temperature are responsible.

Whether the chicken or the egg comes first is arguable. Scientists choose to believe that temperature has nothing to do with it—only light. Yet one is unalterably tied to the other. It is claimed that varying hares in experiments have been shut off from all light in summer and have changed to white coats. But how do we explain the hares on the Pacific coast that do not change? Some accounts say it is because there isn't enough snow in their domain. Yet their days grow shorter and then longer, too, just as do the days for their relatives on the eastern slope of their coastal mountains. Perhaps its best to leave it all to the scientists, and the hares!

"Sports" among hares and also among rabbits—albinos and black or melanistic individuals—are rare. But a few black specimens do occur among snowshoe hares, and most of these noted have been in the northeast. It is interesting to note that these black ones, so far as is known to date, do not change to a white winter coat. This is one more item to add to the color-change puzzle.

This big northern hare, with the bulk of its range throughout Canada and Alaska northward to the latitude where trees disappear, has for centuries been an important food source for native peoples, and source of light, soft, and warm fur cut in strips and woven into blankets. Although some sport hunting for it occurs across Canada and a small amount in Alaska, it is chiefly within the southern fringe of its range, in the northern contiguous states, that sport hunting is pursued. A limited but enthusiastic group of snow-country hunters takes to the forests after it every winter.

Further, the major share of snowshoe hare hunting has always occurred in the east and the Great Lakes region. The range here spreads across northern North Dakota, Minnesota, Wisconsin, and Michigan, much of New York, and throughout New England. It extends down the Appalachians over parts of Pennsylvania, the Virginias, and along the mountainous border of North Carolina and Tennessee. In the west the snowshoe is present in the Rockies, the

# Range of the Varying Hare

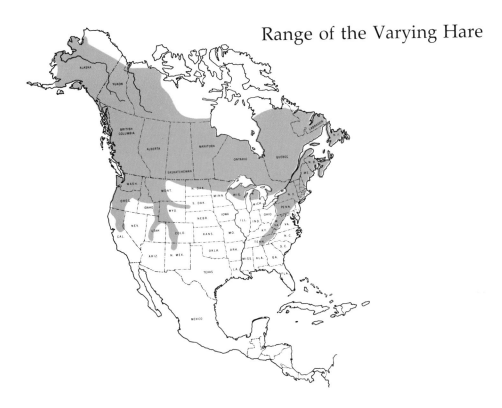

Cascades, and the coastal belt of Washington and Oregon. and on down the Sierras into the northern half of California. Thus these hares in the Rockies are found in high areas in northern Idaho, western Montana and Wyoming, central Utah, central Colorado, and across into northern New Mexico.

Their importance as a food source in the north has always been based on their abundance, and the comparative ease with which they can be snared, trapped, or shot. It is well known among natives of the far north, however, that a steady diet of either birds or rabbits during severe cold is in effect one of starvation, because of the lack of fat. The snowshoe, even though vastly important for food in the north, has often been an undependable source, because of the phenomenal cycles through which these animals pass.

Accounts of naturalists and others are legion regarding the unbelievable abundance on high population cycles. These cycles, according to carefully documented studies, occur about every decade, and used to peak in the even-numbered years, but early in this century somehow were switched to odd-numbered years. Whether or not this is too pat and precise is open to question. It is well known that both lows and highs do not always extend throughout the range, but are exceedingly spotty, with awesome numbers of hares in one area and practically none in suitable habitat in another sometimes only a few miles distant.

Claims have been made by observers of thousands of varying hares to the square mile at peak population highs. When such a peak has built up, there follows a swift decline of debacle proportions. Usually the die-off occurs during late winter and into the spring. Food becomes scarce, and disease sweeps through the hordes because of overcrowding and ready transmission. In addition many researchers have concluded that stress of crowding leads to a kind of shock that is in itself a fatal disease. Presumably there are internal effects that cause a lowering of blood sugars, which in turn produces listlessness, low food intake as a consequence, and eventual death from paralysis or convulsions.

These massive die-offs can be quite accurately predicted even by hunters. In northern Michigan, as an example, snowshoe rabbit hunting has long been a prime midwinter sport for a clique of enthusiasts who themselves wear snowshoes and take to the woods in deep snow. But when the hares are extremely abundant and the hunting is at its best, everyone knows that possibly the next season opportunity will be poor to nil. Spring may find hardly a hare anywhere in the forest, and from then on it's a long wait until the next cycle peak.

Not all declines, however, are that sudden. More usual is a definite but slower drop in numbers for several years, then possibly a rather sudden drop to bottom, and then a slow rebuilding of the population. Most of the more severe and sudden drops in population occur in the northern ranges. Because the hare is a staple diet for all predators of those regions—wolves, foxes, lynxes, bobcats, owls, and hawks—the populations of these, especially the less-mobile ground-dwelling predators, is drastically affected by the cycles. When hare hunting is at peak for them, their numbers also rise to peak levels. Then when the hares disappear, within a couple of seasons there is a matching debacle among their enemies. The fur catch in northern regions is always matched in highs and lows to the cycles of the big hares.

For some reason not easily explained, the dramatic fluctuation in snowshoe populations does not occur noticeably in the U.S. Rockies and along the Pacific coast. There the level remains fairly even season after season. There are never the extreme highs found in the east and north. Presumably there are other controls that work toward a stable population.

At about the northern limit of range of the snowshoe hare, that of a much larger Arctic relative begins. In a few areas the ranges overlap, but an observer would have little difficulty distinguishing between the varying and the arctic hare, of which there are two rather similar species, *Lepus articus* and *Lepus othus.* These hares weigh up to a maximum of 15 pounds and have enormous hind feet and thick fur, and large specimens stretch out almost a yard in overall length. In its snowy-white coat, the arctic hare is white in undercoat as well as outer fur. This also distinguishes it from the snowshoe.

The arctic hares live on the tundra, the rocky hillsides with sparse, low vegetation, and among dwarf willows above the tree line. Their range blankets the northern and western fringes of Alaska and the Alaska Peninsula and all of far-northern Canada and the Arctic islands, even to within only several hundred miles of the North Pole, where, curiously, the largest specimens of the tribe find a home in the bleakest and most inhospitable of terrains imaginable. The arctic hare can hardly be included among the game animals. It is seldom even seen by sport hunters, and it is in general a naive and trusting creature. It is, of course, an extremely important supplier of food and fur to arctic people.

The jack rabbits well known across the western United States also are hares and thus related to the snowshoe hare. The white-tailed jack is the largest of the several varieties, some weighing 8 to 10 pounds. In the northern part of its range it changes to a white winter coat, but southward it is a mixture of white and pale tan, or fails to change. The black-tailed jack is next in size, weighing at maximum about 7 pounds. This is the jack rabbit known to the greatest number of westerners and visitors to the west. There is also the white-sided jack, rare nowadays but known to inhabit parts of southern New Mexico.

All of the jacks have extra-long ears. The prize of the lot is the antelope jackrabbit, found in southern Arizona and on into Mexico. It has ears 7 to 9 inches long. It is one of the so-called white-sided group of jacks. The several white-sided jack varieties have the unique muscular ability when running to pull their white side swaths around in several directions. Much guessing among naturalists has centered on why these animals use this trick. Like the arctic hare, but for other reasons, the jack rabbits can hardly be classed as game animals, and are not so classed in this book. To be sure, many volumes about North American game animals do insist these hares should be included. They are indeed hunted, but invariably as pests, the endeavor a kind of live target shooting. Seldom is a jack rabbit eaten. The snowshoe hare is the only member of the hare group native to North America that is a true game species.

## HABITAT

This hare is strictly a forest animal. But within the true forests it also requires a dense understory. Rarely do snowshoe hares consort even in forest openings or meadows. When hunted with dogs, a hare may hop along in dense cover, but the moment it needs to cross even a small open place, such as an old logging trail, it zips at high speed to get into cover again.

Mixed forests of poplar, aspen, birch, maple, and other deciduous trees heavily sprinkled with conifers such as hemlock, cedar, and balsam are typical of varying hare habitat in New England and the Great Lakes area and on into southern Canada. Farther north, the hushed tangles of spruce where moss carpets the ground are home to these hares, and if there are willow and alder thickets along lakes and streams, they often hold a heavy hare population.

In winter in the northeast and the Great Lakes range they gang up in what natives often refer to as "greenswamps." These are not actually swamps, and are not wet as a rule, but are ribbons of dense cedar, balsam, tamarack, or hemlock that wind along low valleys between ridges on which poplar and other deciduous trees grow. The greenswamp cover is low and heavy, offering abundant hiding places, protection from weather, and forage.

In the west, a simulation of the same type of habitat is chosen. Such places are found either fairly high up in the mountains, or else in the crisscross of heavy growth so typical of the coastal slopes of the northwest, and the rain forests of this region. Burns, and areas where timber for lumber or pulp has been cut, leaving much slash and new growth sprouting, offer ideal varying hare habitat. Unquestionably the appeal of these is the welter of sprouted new growth that furnishes endless forage as well as cover.

Wherever clearing for agriculture has occurred within snowshoe range, the animals disappear or else are present only in surrounding fringes of forest. In parts of the eastern range human settlement and clearing have seriously depleted populations of this animal. In addition, in scattered locations overpopulation of whitetail deer is believed to have shattering consequences for the varying hare. The deer, game managers point out, eat the same foods in general, and are able not only to browse at the low level of the hare but to clean out forage higher than the hares can reach.

Whether there are other reasons besides competition with deer for decline of the snowshoe in certain locales is not well documented. There may be, for deer and snowshoe rabbits have lived together a long time. Of course, man's incursions have over many years assisted the whitetail by creating openings and edges, allowing a pronounced buildup of population, whereas the same influences of settlement remove prime hare habitat. In some places in the east, experiments have been tried, some successful, some not, in transplanting snowshoes in attempts to establish or reestablish them in suitable areas.

The whitetail deer, which we often envision as an animal of the wilderness, has been able to adapt to man's influences far better than the winter-white hare, which seems in many ways to be a far less wild forest personality. Fundamentally, it is a wilderness creature. For nature lovers who enjoy pondering such difficult questions, its inability to colonize wilderness forest regions that exist outside the north, and in its temperature simulations in the mountains both east and west, is thought-provoking. There is dense cover elsewhere in more temperate climates. It seems almost as if without seasonal snow to walk on with its snowshoelike feet this ghost of the greenswamps has difficulty feeling at home.

### FEEDING

In its forest habitat with ample undergrowth the snowshoe hare is not often hard put to make a living. During the growing season there are endless varieties of grasses and weeds. In some locations clover, dandelion, and wild strawberry are abundant. So is wintergreen. In the low, partly shaded places and along water courses grasses grow verdantly. All these softer green foods are the staples of the spring and summer seasons.

Added to them are snippets of green twigs, bulging buds, and tender new leaves. Later on, when first frosts come and even prior to that as growing slows or ceases, more and more woody material is eaten. Aspen, for example, and its closely related species, the varied poplars and birches, are staples. In some instances these are also abundant summer forage. Wherever pulpwood cuttings of poplar, for example, have occurred, a welter of new shoots soon springs up. These sweeps of woodland are bonanzas for hares, which commonly congregate to clean up the growth.

Willow, maple, alder twigs and bark, and aspen bark are eagerly sought. It is a unique scheme between nature and the hare that as it sweeps a small area clean of easily reached forage in early winter, in normal years more snow falls, and drifts. Now the hares can move atop the drifts and start in on a whole new crop of bark and twigs that was out of reach after the first snowfalls. If there are deep-woods bramble thickets—while blackberries, for example—drifts give the animals ready access to the slender ends of the branches, even though they have perhaps already girdled the larger bases a few weeks before.

Where snowshoes are plentiful, they do a substantial amount of tree damage in winter. Much of this, however, is upon saplings, and in numerous locations the small maples or poplars or birches need thinning anyway. Except when snow is deep, the hares are restricted to roughly the bottom 2 feet of the trunk. They peel off the bark from trees a couple of inches through, and of course this kills the saplings. In most instances if there are enough twigs and small branches available, the animals eat those or peel bark from them. If this source plays out, then they must go after the saplings.

Over much of the range, a diet of conifer needles, twigs, and bark is a mainstay of midwinter and late-winter diet. In some states the hunting season runs as late as the end of February. If there has been much snow and cold, the snowshoes have ganged up in the spruce, hemlock, cedar, and balsam, very much like deer yarding up during a severe winter. And, like the deer, which browse cedar and jack pine, the rabbits eagerly go after the pitch-strong food.

In both New England and the Great Lakes region, centers of snowshoe rabbit hunting, a good many hunters give up the sport late in season if they discover the hares reduced to eating conifer needles. Cedar and balsam, of which they appear fond and not entirely forced into eating, give the meat an unpleasant pitchy flavor when taken in large and steady quantities. This big hare, incidentally, is excellent table fare. The meat is never fat, the legs and saddles are heavy and thick. Baked, or parboiled until tender and then fried, it is a delicacy.

### MOVEMENTS

As mentioned earlier, hares never live in or flee into burrows of other animals, as rabbits do, and the snowshoe only occasionally will move into a hollow log or under a pile of slash. It sits in its form under a bush, or between roots of a tree, against a log, in a sedge grass clump, or just out among fallen leaves. It does not scoop out a form. The resting place is simply shaped by its body hunched there, invariably with feet well under it so it is ready to jump. Ordinarily while resting and unconcerned, and also when trying to avoid detection, it keeps its ears laid flat back onto its shoulders. Thus sitting immobile in either white or brown coat that matches its surroundings, it is not easy to spot. Still hunters who prowl slowly after snowshoes in winter snows learn to look for the small, round black spot that is the eye. Nothing else in the forest has that marblelike shape.

When mildly disturbed, the hare may hop slowly away, screened by cover. But when scared or chased, it can rev up to a startling speed, almost as fast as a running whitetail deer, at top pace probably at least 30 miles an hour. It makes flying leaps of 10 to 15 feet. In deep, even soft, snow, with toes splayed wide, it sails along over drifts that founder a pursuer. It is adept at dodging, and is capable of throwing its fore-end around at sharp angles even while airborne so that it lands running in another direction.

Like other hares, the snowshoe does not go into a hole when run by a dog or a predator—or at least rarely does except when wounded. It simply keeps running. If others of its kind are gathered in a conifer thicket of several acres, the one a dog is following may run a half-circle, then just hop slowly, listening to ascertain if the dog is on its trail or has jumped another meanwhile. Often a crafty old snowshoe will follow one of its well-packed trails, which are evident in winter in its coverts, then leap aside, circle, and run in the opposite direction.

The most common tactic is to circle in rather small rounds two or three times. Then when pushed hard it takes off over the ridges at full speed and in great bounds, leading a dog through more open timber, apparently hoping to lose it. Some such runs may last fifteen or twenty minutes, but in due time the hare comes back to home base, where the routine starts all over again. It is a tireless runner, if it can get brief rests by ruses intermittently. Many a wise old individual does elude pursuit, often because a dog jumps another and can't resist that hot scent—or else cannot resist pursuit of a deer that happens to be in the way of the run.

The home range is invariably small. In some circumstances it may cover a section of land, a square mile. But that is unusual. Many snowshoe rabbits in good cover and with plentiful forage never know any part of their forest more than 100 yards in any direction. On the average, 50 to 100 acres suffice for most individuals.

Feeding accounts for most of the animal's daily movements. Snowshoes are active on overcast days, and occasionally at any time even on bright days. But for the most part they are nocturnal, leaving their resting forms toward dusk and moving about off and on during the night and dawn. Each has several forms it uses, but ordinarily one is really home. Between forms, and throughout its intimate domain, it habitually follows paths it has laid out and worn by much travel. These are not so evident in summer, but in snow they show plainly. In a location where a number of hares are spending the winter, there may be hardly a place in old snow where a hunter could make a palm print without touching one or two tracks where feeding hares have wandered. But cutting a crisscross in this bailiwick there are invariably deep-packed trails. If a new snow falls, often the depression troughs of the old trails will quickly be packed again.

When moving casually, the snowshoe may simply walk. Or it may make short hops, bringing the hind feet up behind the forefeet. But the hind feet always appear spraddled somewhat out to the sides, and at a run the powerful hind legs shove the animal ahead, it lands on the forefeet, and the hind ones come past and commonly hit the snow or ground 2 or 3 feet ahead of where the forefeet have touched down.

Like the rabbits, and other hares, the snowshoe has a habit of thumping a hind foot, making a sound that can be heard at modest distance. Whether this is a sign of alarm, or of annoyance, is not clear. Also like others of this large family, when seized by a predator the snowshoe sometimes — but not always — utters a loud squall of anguish, repeated over and over as it weakens and dies, or becomes resigned apparently to its fate. Snowshoe hares do not often take to water except in a dire emergency. They are able to swim, however, with surprising skill, using their big hind feet like paddles. On rare occasions one has been observed swimming a stream or pond presumably without being pressed.

### BREEDING

Late in winter male varying hares a year or more old are ready for mating. They ordinarily get along reasonably well with neighbors, and are even mildly gregarious. After the first of the year, however, males easily become irritated by the presence of other males. There are battles — biting, tearing out wads of fur, vicious kicks with the stout hind feet. Seldom is much serious damage done, and the fights are not especially common.

As March arrives attention of the males turns to females. The males chase them around and around. The female tries to elude, or at least runs helter-skelter, making the pursuing swain wear himself frazzled. She dodges and leaps, whirls and runs toward him, perhaps passing under him as he leaps into the air. Both hares and rabbits follow these routines. These chases sometimes continue for days, but at last the female is convinced, and mating occurs. She may be bred several times by the same male, but she has no special attachment for him, nor does he for her. If another male happens along, he also is accepted by the female, or vice versa.

### BIRTH AND DEVELOPMENT

Roughly five weeks after mating, the young are born. Unlike the rabbits, which go to much bother building a nest, the snowshoe hare simply gives birth wherever she happens to be. Ordinarily this is in one of her forms. However, she may simply be feeding along and pause and have her young. The average litter is three to six, although sometimes there are more, or less.

If the young are born in the daytime, the mother, of course, nurses them right away. From then on she stays away, usually keeping watch from a short distance, and comes back at dusk or after to allow them to nurse. Because the youngsters are born with eyes open and fully furred, they quickly begin moving about. However, they continue nursing for two or three weeks, but are by then beginning to eat some grass, and at the age of a month are usually weaned and on their own.

They grow at a surprising rate. By the time they are $2\frac{1}{2}$ months old many young hares already weigh a couple of pounds. At the time their mother, by then long forgotten, may already have had a second litter, and she may continue with others for a total of as many as five litters in a season, although two or three is considered average. This high production is needed. Natural attrition is severe. In an average season, not one during which a sudden die-off occurs, it is estimated that roughly three out of ten young hares live to become mature adults a year old.

### SENSES

It is doubtful that scent plays a very important part in avoidance of enemies, although it undoubtedly is sharply attuned to finding and testing various forage. Possibly snowshoe hares catch scent of some predator coming down a breeze, but certainly the sense of smell of the enemy, which must live partly by it, is keener. Hunters commonly prowl within mere feet of snowshoe rabbits that simply sit immobile in their forms. Probably this freezing in place is a ruse to avoid detection. A better one, if scent were keenly developed, would be flight long before an enemy got close.

Sight is sharp for motion, but a snowshoe pursued by a hound will hop along within mere feet of a hunter motionless on a stand. Also, because it is a cover animal, the sight of a moving enemy at a distance doesn't unduly disturb it. Sounds of danger are what most disturb the snowshoe. A hunter or a dog, or other predator, moving through brush noisily will cause every one in the vicinity to move, except for the scattered individuals that apparently feel secure in a form and believe themselves hidden.

In general, probably hearing is the animal's most important defense. Its large ears, nervously turned this way and that when it is mildly disturbed, would indicate this conclusion. The same is true for all rabbits and hares. However, it seems almost as if in the grand plan all of these animals were meant to help sustain the meat eaters, for regardless of how sharp their senses may be, far more are caught and killed than live to run away.

**SIGN** *(Tracks are illustrated on page 251.)*

The track patterns left by snowshoe hares are similar in general arrangement to those of the rabbits, but they are larger, the hops and bounds are longer, and the long toes of the feet, especially of the hind feet, usually spread widely and print plainly in snow. Hare tracks are not likely to be confused with rabbit tracks because few cottontails or other rabbits are found as a rule in territory heavily used by the hares.

Tracks, and trails, are not often distinct in summer, although in moss in some forest snowshoe trails may be spotted. In winter they are easily seen. In a cedar or balsam swamp trails may be solidly packed down 6 inches or more in depth. Occasionally there are also tunnels under deep drifts or into debris. Droppings, round and rather similar to those of the smaller rabbits, are copiously in evidence in winter snow. They are larger than scats of the rabbits.

Branches and tree trunks stripped of bark tell of snowshoe presence, but in winter at least it is hardly necessary to search for these signs because the tracks and droppings will be so plainly and profusely in evidence. In instances where cuttings are observed on twigs or brush, it is easy to read whether a deer, or a rabbit, hare, or rodent has been there. Deer and other antlered animals pinch off or rip off twigs, the others slice them neatly on a slant.

The reason for this is that the antlered animals do not have teeth in the front of the upper jaw. The rabbits and hares have four upper incisors and two lower ones. The rodents, with which rabbits and hares were once classed, have only four, two upper and two lower that work against each other.

## HUNTING

There is no hunting experience more intriguing than waiting on a cold, bright day in a silent forest for a hound to open on a snowshoe rabbit track. The branches of conifers are bent with their loads of fluffy snow, there may be a couple of feet of it underfoot, and the hunter, his own snowshoes perhaps thrust heels down into the snow beside him to allow him to climb atop a stump or log, waits beside a well-worn hare trail. Or perhaps he has taken a stand on an old forest road so he can watch both ways. Or he awaits his quarry beside a small forest opening at the edge of a cedar swale, hoping a target may come larruping along the edge of the dense cover.

Presently his eye catches the slightest motion. It is never easy to spot, for a big hare in full winter dress is simply white on white. It runs silently, except for the faintest eerie whisper of its big, furry feet as it bounds across soft snow. Here it comes—and there it goes—all before he can swing his gun into position. It may be close to an hour as the chase goes, sometimes swiftly and off over the surrounding hills, sometimes slowly, the dog puzzling out a ruse-laced trail. Then suddenly there is the hare, this time tentatively hopping, warily twitching its ears. The gun booms, and the chase is ended.

But not for long. If there are numerous snowshoes in this winter greenswamp, the chase has caused all of them to move at least short distances. That means they've laid trails smoking with scent, and almost instantly, after nosing the dead hare, the hound is off pottering in the brush again and has started another.

Indeed, hunting the varying hare has a flavor and atmosphere all its own. Most enthusiasts use dogs of foxhound size. Smaller hounds such as beagles are willing enough, but not often burly enough to work in deep snow, nor long enough of leg. Hunters who use hounds for this sport try their best to break the dogs of chasing deer. Invariably there are whitetails in the same cover, and all too often a hound can't resist.

For weapons, the average hunter carries a shotgun, with a barrel at least partly snugged down in choke, and a load as a rule of No. 4 shot, or perhaps short-magnum No. 6. These big hares are fairly tough, and there's a lot of brush in the way. A few riflemen who are exceptional shots employ a .22 rifle, with or without scope, and pride themselves on taking the quarry as it runs — or once in a while collecting one. With the small rifle there are always more misses than hits.

Snowshoe rabbit hunting is in some ways a simpler affair than going after cottontails. The big hares are inclined to gang up in suitable stands of brush and conifers in winter, which makes locating a good place rather easy. It's a matter of checking several locations for abundant sign, then selecting good stands, and turning loose the dog or dogs. After a run is started many a hunter quickly ascertains the pattern the hare is running, and switches his stand quietly for a more productive placement.

He learns to stand very quietly. He also learns to listen attentively to the dog. If it is moving swiftly, undoubtedly the hare is, too. That usually means the target will be well out in front, so the hunter must be alert while the voice of the dog is a long way off. And it also means the snowshoe will go past in a hurry. If the dog is pottering — slow dogs often are the best for this work because they don't push the game hard — then he watches closer in to the dog sound, and for a slowly moving or pausing quarry.

An interesting method has long been practiced by a few hunters in the Great Lakes region. Two or three go out together without a dog. All use shotguns. They look for a small cedar swale or other likely spot that has ample sign. An ideal spot is such a dense thicket across which an old logging road runs, cutting it in half. In such a situation, two hunters stay on the old trail, midway of the swale, and standing back to back, watching in opposite directions along the trail. The third hunter plays dog.

He may feel a bit silly on his first hunt, but he soon learns that it works beautifully. He moves into one half of the swale, begins to circle around in it, and bays like a hound. He doesn't try to walk quietly. If he sees a snowshoe he is allowed to shoot at close range, because his partners are in no danger. He knows exactly where they are. Because he moves slowly, the hares will.

Soon one comes hopping out to cross the trail, intent on getting into the other half of the swale — for these animals know every foot of their home range. After one side has been well worked, somebody else plays dog and works the other side. The routine varies, of course, with the location. It is amazingly effective. Now and then practical jokers have been known to sneak off, after a partner has started baying, to hide and watch his foolish grin when he finally comes onto the trail to find he's been "giving tongue" with nobody listening.

Another method that many sportsmen enjoy is still hunting. This is often done with a .22 rifle. It is a matter of simply going into an area covered with sign, prowling slow motion, and watching for targets. A stealthy, quite hunter who is sharp-eyed can often bag a limit of hares this way, taking most of them at extremely close range sitting in forms. This is the approach where looking for the round, black eye among the whiteness below evergreen branches is an important part of the craft.

Occasionally in midwinter an interesting opportunity to seize some advantage over the game is offered during a heavy thaw. The so-called "January thaw" that residents of the Great Lakes and New England snowshoe range experience many seasons is often the time. If accumulated snowfall has been light, practically all of it may melt. The white hares stand out against the wet, drab-brown forest floor like winking lights. A scoped .22 rifle for this project is the ticket, for getting close is not easy. The hares seem to realize they are at a disadvantage, and are spooky.

In the western mountains the sport of snowshoe hunting has to date never been followed by many outdoorsmen. A few thousand snowshoes are bagged annually in Colorado. In Idaho and Wyoming they receive virtually no attention. The same is true in California and Oregon. Washington has a scattering of enthusiasts. Part of the reason for little focus on this animal is the steep terrain, some of it rather remote, and hard to get into in winter. Another reason is that the snowshoe is scattered here, and seldom as abundant anywhere in the west as it is on moderate to high cycles over its range elsewhere.

Much habitat of the varying hare has been destroyed both in the east and the Great Lakes states by timber clearing, by settlement, by the awesome tourist business, and by road building in the forested areas. However, the snowshoe rabbit, as most sportsmen insist on calling it, is a resilient creature well inured to a difficult existence. Because of this, because of its prolific replenishment of losses, its love for the remote corners of dense forests in the northern states and its vast wilderness holdings across Canada, it certainly is in no danger of disappearing from the list of authentic North American game animals.

# Javelina

or Collared Peccary

*Tayassu tajacu*

More pure hogwash has been written and related concerning this little desert pig of the southwest than about any other American game animal. Some of it originated with exaggeration of the tall-tale variety, and some perhaps because of the small and remote range within the United States, which discouraged accurate knowledge and observation. Yet it seems odd that in this supposedly enlightened age in the study of wildlife, even numerous standard scientific references as well as popular ones include "facts" about this unique and interesting creature that are either suppositions or plainly incorrect.

At one time the range of the javelina blanketed much of Texas, to the Red River in the north and the fringes of what is now Arkansas, and east to the region of the Brazos valley. It was also present across a rather narrow band of southern New Mexico, with the main centers in the southeast and southwest. In Arizona the range reached across much of the south, and up toward the Mogollon Rim, with the preponderance of the population in the southeastern quarter.

Today the range is decidedly cut down in Texas. The animals are plentiful across southern Texas in the so-called Brush Country and westward to and throughout the Big Bend Country and all of the Trans-Pecos. In New Mexico there may, or may not, be a remnant left in the southeastern desert country. Extreme southwestern New Mexico is the location of a modest population, beefed up by transplants, and in Arizona the range remains about as it was originally. The population there is substantial, although the greatest number are in Texas. Southward, javelina range covers most of Mexico, except Baja, and the species is joined far to the south, in tropical regions, by the larger white-lipped peccary.

Because the range in our southwest and in northern Mexico was the last of the true frontier, and some indeed still is rather authentic frontier, it is probable that authentic information about the javelina was slow to accumulate. In addition, the bands habitually cling to areas of dense desert thornbrush and cactus, and were not as easily observed or even seen by early travelers or by natives of the settlements as some other animals were. To top it off, the frontier and the tall tale, the deadpan ribbing of the visiting tenderfoot, have always gone together, and the javelina played its part.

The javelina—or as most books insist on calling it, the peccary— was, it was alleged, a vicious, cantankerous critter. A band would surround an unwary traveler and cut him to ribbons. A cowboy who took a spill from his horse was certain to be set upon, if any javelinas were present, and ripped to bits on the spot. In early western fiction the javelina was a valuable wildlife character to ring in to keep the action humming. The villain was treed up a dagger-thorned mesquite and kept there for hours by a band of fifty-odd slavering peccaries. Meanwhile the protagonist rescued the girl who'd been tied to a cactus clump, retrieved the ranch deed, and chuckled as he rode off with her into the sunset, enjoying the mental vision of the awful fate of the bad guy when he finally had to come down to earth.

So intertwined with fiction did fact finally become that rumors spread widely about these dangerous and ill-tempered boars of the border brush. Numerous respected authorities passed the rumors along. Even today it would be almost sacrilege to many an outdoorsman and wildlife enthusiast to hear such a personage as Teddy Roosevely discredited—but Teddy has been widely quoted to the effect that it was not at all uncommon in early days for a drove of javelinas to tree a man, attacking without provocation and keeping him treed for many hours.

The truth is that hundreds of thousands of peccaries were taken years ago for their hides, most of them killed with clubs. Hundreds of thousands more, at the rate of an estimated 30,000 to 40,000 a

Javelinas

year, have been bagged by hunters each season for many modern years now, and untold numbers killed as "varmints" by landowners. Yet there are no authenticated "treeing" incidents, no authenticated incidents of unprovoked attack, and none of attacks of any sort by these animals except a very few in situations where the javelina or javelinas were wounded or cornered, or simply cornered, or among animals kept as pets.

Make no mistake, the canine teeth of the javelina could seriously harm a person. A pet boar, full-grown, kept in the 1950s by the then sheriff of Tombstone, Arizona, an animal coddled by the whole family, somehow became annoyed with the eight-year-old daughter who often petted him, flung his head against her leg — this quick twitch of the head is the way the lower canine is used for slashing — and cut her so badly numerous stitches were required to close the wound.

Dogs have been used for many years to run javelinas. A few years ago a rancher from south Texas owned a brace of burly, marble-eyed cattle dogs that loved to chase them. There was not a spot on their hides as big as a human palm that was not scarred by slashes. Several other dogs this rancher owned had been killed by single bayed javelinas. On several occasions peccaries kept in pens and zoos have seriously slashed people who pestered them. But every known instance of harm has been from animals unable to escape, and in situations where obviously they felt they were cornered, or crippled.

Many of the "attack" tales have grown also from incidents in which the animals were simply trying to get away, or else were bluffing. Hunters commonly experience the "charge" of a band after one is shot at close range. What actually happens is that the sudden disturbance frightens the group. They simply explode in flight, scattering. The routine pattern of instant herd flight is for individuals to run in every direction. They have extremely poor eyesight. A "charged" hunter is simply one who happens to be in the way of fleeing, frightened javelina.

A hunter from the east, having his first experience with the javelina in Texas, relates: "We saw the band and made a careful stalk, my guide and me. We were separated by maybe seventy yards of thornbrush. He was motioning. I saw a pig. I shot. It fell, and suddenly there were I don't know how many running right at me. I was terrified. I didn't even think to use my gun. I just stood frozen. One big one brushed my pants leg as it raced past." Had he been attacked? Even as shaken as he was, he soon admitted he had not. The animals were simply trying to get away.

## THE JAVELINA

COLOR: Grizzled gray-black; those in Texas *(T. t angulatus)* very dark, nearly black, those in New Mexico and Arizona *(T. t. sonoriensis)* lighter; paler collar, variable in distinctiveness, extending from throat on a slant back and upward in front of shoulders and across withers.

MEASUREMENTS AND WEIGHT: Average height at shoulder, 17 to 20 inches; length 28 to 36 inches average, a few perhaps slightly larger; weight, adults, 30 to 45 pounds, unusual specimens to 50-plus.

GENERAL CHARACTERISTICS: Piglike; head and shoulders heavy in appearance, rear end higher but more slender; coarse, bristlelike hair; mane from crown of head to rump erected by skin muscles when animal is alarmed; musk gland high on rump; tail extremely short; quick, agile brush dwellers that run in small to large bands.

Because the javelina has had such a bad press—that is, such an inaccurate one—one needs to take time to sort out the facts about this unusually interesting animal. Its size, for example, has invariably been exaggerated, even in a surprising number of standard references. Mounted specimens, head and shoulders, are too often done with mouth agape and hackles up, making the animal appear as large as a European wild boar. Hunters often claim to have seen 200-pounders, and have used the name "wild boar" to describe them. Many references, which all too often copy each other, give the shoulder height at around 22 inches, and at least one has it at over 30 inches, which is about the height of a European so-called Russian boar of 300 to 350 pounds.

Many peccaries, when seen and aware of the observation, have their mane bristles raised. They do look amazingly large. A Texas study in which several hundred adults were weighed showed, however, an average adult at just 37 pounds. A check of javelinas taken by hunters in New Mexico over several seasons gave an average weight for field-dressed adults of slightly under 30 pounds. Some unusual specimens have been weighed before field dressing, and a few at live weight, that went above 40, a few to and above 50. A very few have been recorded in the 60-pound class. This, however, is highly unusual.

Shoulder height is from 17 to about 20 inches. Taxidermy shop forms, for example, used for whole-mounts of javelinas, and measured to include the extra height of the hoof, are 15 inches for small,

19 for large, 19½ for extra-large. An illusion of height and size is that the javelina has a stance with a hump in its back, so that with head straight on, not raised high, the rear part of the back just forward of the rump is the highest part of the animal.

Tusk length also is usually exaggerated by hunters and others. Some sportsmen say they want to hold out for a specimen with 4- or 5-inch tusks. The javelina does not have true tusks. It has upper and lower matching pairs of enlarged canine teeth. The so-called tusks of a European boar or of domestic swine usually grow curved out from the jaw so that when long—4 to 5 inches—they show plainly even when the mouth is closed. The canine teeth of the javelina may make a slight bulge in the cheek, but do not show outside the lips with the mouth closed, and hardly ever when it is partly open.

They are set so that the back of the lower is in front of the upper. With jaws shut, the lower is in front of the upper. As the jaws work, the paired canines constantly are self-honing. They are always extremely sharp, on the points and along the honed edges. They continue growing, but the constant sharpening never allows growth past perfect closing. Measured from the gum, all adult javelina canines are about 1½ inches long, with 2 inches occasional in large specimens.

The name "javelina," of Mexican origin, comes from the sharp "tusks." The Spanish word for wild boar is *jabali;* for wild sow, *jabalina.* The *j* is of course pronounced as *h,* and the *b*—at least by Anglos—as *v.* Mexicans often call the animal *jabalin,* which is pronounced "ha-va-leen" and means one, and use the plural *jabalinas.* Many border-dwelling Anglos say "havaleen" and "havaleens," but among hunters and game-management people the animal is invariably called "javelina"—pronounced "ha-va-lee-na." The name almost always used in reference books, "peccary," which comes from the Brazilian *pecari* ("animal that makes trails in the woods"), is seldom if ever used in speech, or in game laws, or written accounts anywhere in the southwest. "Musk hog," a reference to the musk gland on the back, is never used by anyone in javelina country.

The musk gland is an interesting physical attribute of the javelina, and one among several that sets them apart from the true swine. Domestic swine were brought to America by the early Spanish. The peccaries are North American natives, the only pig—or piglike relative—of this hemisphere. The animal family to which it belongs dates back millions of years. Some early forms on this continent, known from fossils, were huge animals.

The musk gland is located 7 to 8 inches from the extremely short tail, up atop the rump. It is a superficial gland, that is, not embed-

*The canine teeth, or "tusks," of the javelina are actually quite small, about 1½—2 inches long, and barely visible when the animal opens its mouth.*

ded deep in the muscle of the back, but simply lying under and attached to the skin. It is easily removed simply by slicing it out with a patch of hide around it. The appearance of the gland has been described as like an inverted navel. There is a small opening from which a whitish liquid is excreted at will.

A number of fallacies exist about the musk gland. Most common among hunters is the belief that unless it is immediately removed it will taint the meat. The pungent odor is admittedly unpleasant. Numerous references describe the odor, erroneously, as similar to the smell of a skunk. It is not remotely similar. But it is indeed distinctive. A group of javelinas in heavy cover can easily be scented from 50 yards or more even on a faint breeze. Once smelled, a hunter always remembers it.

The removal of the gland after a javelina is killed—if one does this—has nothing to do with tainted meat. There is no possible way the excretion from the gland can get into the flesh. It can, however, get onto the hands of the hunter who field-dresses one, or accidentally onto the meat at that time or during skinning. But cutting out a surrounding skin patch, that chance is eliminated, without getting any scent on the hands. It is difficult to remove even with several washings.

There are, incidentally, mixed opinions among hunters about the edibility of javelina. It is never fat, like pork. An old boar may be strong and not pleasant fare. However, when properly cooled out, and simply roasted, the meat of most individuals is excellent. When cooked it is pale in hue, slightly distinctive in taste, reminiscent of pork, but mildly.

The various purposes of the musk gland have been much discussed in scientific literature. Consensus among both naturalists and hunters favors the theory that the odor is—like that of numerous other animals—a means in general of communication. When a javelina is excessively startled and frightened at close range, it bounds away, the long bristles opening instantly all around the gland, which then shows plainly. The musk literally puffs out. When the animals are casually consorting, often two will stand facing oppositely, and the side of the head or chin of each will rub across the musk-gland area while the animals edge around in a circle.

Undoubtedly the scent helps the javelinas, which are gregarious, to keep together or to find each other, probably to locate trails where others have passed, and also has a role in mating. Both male and female are equipped with the gland. The sexes, incidentally, are not easy to distinguish at a glance. Old boars are sometimes loners, but only close inspection tells positively whether the animal in question is boar or sow.

Some surmise about the musk gland has considered that one use may be as a pest repellent. Most observers doubt it. An amusing bit of javelina publicity occurred a few years ago when an Arizona gentleman who claimed javelina knowledge stated unequivocally that these animals never are host to fleas. One south-Texas game warden who was forced to examine a number of freshly killed ones, and who was trying to get the abundant fleas off himself, was difficult to convince. Javelinas, as several careful studies have proved, are indeed host to fleas, ticks, and lice, though not always in large numbers. Whether or not there is a relationship between modest numbers of external parasites and the musk is not known.

Another unusual physical attribute concerns the feet. Unlike true swine, which have two prominent and useful dewclaws on each foot, toes by which they are partly supported, the javelina has only vestigial, useless dewclaws, and though there are two rather high up on each front leg, there is only one on each hind leg. Old ranch tales have it that cowboys often used to rope javelinas just for sport. The truth is, as tests have proved, it's all but impossible to keep a loop on a javelina, unless by some remote chance it is quickly snugged around the head behind the ears. Invariably the animal bounds through with forefeet, the tightening rope slips on the coarse bristles of the arched back as if on grease, may hold for a second or two on a hind leg, but the single inconsequential dew-claw won't catch a stiff rope for long.

There are other popular fallacies. The javelina is often described as having a "white" collar. The collar is paler than the rest of the hair, but is never pure white. The Texas subspecies is very dark, many specimens nearly black and with the collar, though present, indistinct. The Texas variety is also a little smaller than the Arizona javelina. The grizzled general body color of the javelina is produced by intermittent portions of black and white or off-white on each hair. This lends a salt-and-pepper look, with the dark predominant. The bristlelike hairs over much of the body are about 2 inches long, but the mane on the head crown, the neck, and along the back has numerous bristles from 4 to as much as 6 inches in length. These, when raised, are what give an exaggereated impression of size to a first-time observer.

According to many written accounts, javelinas are deadly enemies of snakes, chiefly in their domain the rattlesnake. There may be as much snake oil as dead rattlesnake involved. According to the oft-repeated tale, a group of javelinas surrounds a snake. They flare their manes and fill the air with musk. The herd leader—always in such tales an outsized boar—gathers all four feet under him and leaps upon the snake. Others join. Their little hooves cut the snake to bits. Of course the snake is never able to strike one of its tormentors. The curious sidelight on this habit, which is accepted as fact and repeated endlessly, is that no one, apparently, has ever *seen* it happen. Whether or not it does, the animals don't seem to have much effect on rattlesnake numbers, although some accounts claim snakes are relished by the javelina and that a band quickly clears an area of snakes. Some of the highest rattlesnake populations in the southwest occur on the ranges where the javelina is most abundant.

It is odd that with all the attention this unique animal has had, misleading and otherwise, in print and in legend, it has for so long had such a shoddy deal as a game species. Late in the last century and during the first several decades of this one, hundreds of thousands of javelinas were killed for their hides. The skins, small and difficult for tanners to work with, are thin, strong, beautifully bristle-pocked and endlessly durable when made into jackets, moccasins, gloves, and billfolds. After the larger droves were cleaned out of the United States, buyers went into Mexico and encouraged country people to hunt them for a few cents per hide. Several border ports of entry at times passed as many as 20,000 to 30,000 a month.

In the United States, hide hunting was stopped long ago, and the imports also. But landowners, who firmly believed—as many still do—that javelinas were killers of varied livestock, or at least in competition with livestock for the grass of this arid region, thought of them as vermin, slaughtered whole bands on sight, and left them to rot. In New Mexico, where the range was and is comparatively restricted, they had been all but wiped out by the 1930s, and the javelina did not gain protected status until 1937. That didn't stop the killing. Natives and big-game hunters used bands for target practice.

In Texas to this day many ranch hands routinely kill any they see, just to get rid of them. Amazing as it seems, Texas gave very little legal protection—some in name but virtually none in practice—until into the 1970s. Now Texas has a stipulated season and bag limit in most counties, but some without regulatory authority still offer the animal no protection. Some deer and varmint hunters still kill them as they shoot jack rabbits, as pest practice.

Slowly, however, the javelina has gained and is gaining full game-animal status. In Texas, where fee hunting is the system, the demand from nonresidents to collect a javelina as a trophy has been most helpful. Landowners finally became convinced that this was a money crop. At $100 to $150 per javelina as an extra bonus on a package-type deer hunt, the idea of protection and management suddenly struck home. Arizona long has done far better. For many years now the javelina has been well protected and hunted under special permit, and indiscriminate killing has never been winked at. Current New Mexico management is just as meticulous.

Presently the javelina within the United States is holding its own quite well, in limited numbers. Texas has the most, although no one can more than guess at the population, which is undoubtedly substantial. Helicopter surveys give the best results, and are used in all three javelina states nowadays. Arizona is next in population. Presently hunts there are by permit and drawing, with 20,000 to 30,000 permits for some years an annual average, and hunter success from 20 to 30 percent. Now Mexico has the smallest number of javelinas, with 200 to 300 hunting permits annually by drawing.

## HABITAT

The favored habitats of javelinas are to some extent excellent protection for them. They like the dense thornbrush and prickly pear flats of their arid southwestern domain. Low to the ground,

# Range of the Javelina

they are not easily spotted by hunters or those who would destroy them as pests. Further, their grouping habits make them all the more difficult to find. One might hunt a large expanse of brush and just happen to miss the entire local population, which is at any given time banded together either in a single large group or several small ones.

In western Texas, southwestern New Mexico, and Arizona, the foothills of the individual mountain ranges are home to the javelina. They move along the brushy draws, crawl into catclaw clumps to lie down, or secrete themselves up rimrock crevices. However, they are not always in heavy cover. In the Big Bend Country of western Texas, for example, bands are often seen on the open, rocky slopes, where scattered sotol, Spanish bayonet, cholla, and grass make up the ground cover and where the dark animals plainly stand out.

The desert floor such as that south of Tucson, Arizona, is typical of prime javelina habitat. Here, and elsewhere in comparable areas, scrub mesquite, varied cactus species, and a welter of thorny desert shrubs furnish cover and food. Along the Rio Grande River in

Texas, javelinas are found in the arid foothills, the all but impenetrable thornbrush and pear thickets of the rolling to flat Brush
Country, and also in some instances in the lower valley jungle,
often with wet places.

To the east in Texas they inhabit a quite different type of cover.
Here there are grasslands mixed with mottes of scrub live oaks. A
somewhat similar but much higher-altitude javelina habitat is
found in southeastern Arizona and southwestern New Mexico.
Here small Mexican gray oaks and scattered junipers stipple the
tall-grass zone at about 6000 feet, well below the pine zone and well
above the desert floor.

Open, plainlike valleys are usually avoided, except as they may
need to be crossed. Invariably, however, javelinas found in grassy
valleys between mountain ranges will be along or in the edges of
brushy washes large or small which meander across or down the
length of the lower country. On the whole, javelina bands, except in
the Brush Country of southern Texas where no low mountains are
available, seem to prefer the foothill regions throughout their range
in the United States and much of Mexico.

### FEEDING

Over all of that area prickly pear cactus is abundant almost everywhere. It is a favored food. The thick pads and the fruits are high
in water content, and nutritious. Bands rip pear clumps to pieces,
and chomp down the pads spines and all. They also feed on the
roots. Hunters in country where large expanses of lush pear crowd
out much other vegetation always search the cactus first for signs of
javelina presence.

However, the variety of forage taken includes almost every kind
of vegetation that grows on the desert and the low mountain slopes,
except grasses, of which they eat sparingly. Mesquite beans, catclaw beans, varied tubers they root out of the ground, including the
bases of sotol clumps, and the tender bases of the stiff sharp
lechuguilla leaves all are important forage. In some areas the grub
list includes bits of the tough-thorned ocotillo, and cholla.

Along stream courses and the higher country where varied oaks
grow, acorns are eagerly sought in fall. Juniper berries are also
eaten, and in the range of the piñon fallen nuts popped from the
cones draw droves until every nut has been devoured. It is said that
the javelina eats mice, birds' eggs, lizards, snakes, and whatever insects it comes upon. Whether these and perhaps items such as car-

rion, young rabbits, and pack rats are very important in their diet is doubtful. They are primarily vegetarians.

One of the reasons prickly pear is such a favorite food is that it is an excellent source of liquid. So are tubers rooted up. It is common in javelina range to find places where long roots of several different desert plants, with bulblike nodules scattered along them, have been uncovered. A small trench follows the root along for several feet, and each tuber has been eaten. When water is scarce during extremely dry periods, the javelina can get along quite well on the liquid intake it derives from pear and other arid-country vegetation that stores water. However, the animals cannot do entirely without free water. Every desert waterhole, no matter how small, shows evidence of visits from resident bands. Their small tracks are everywhere, and often well-beaten trails through the thornbrush lead to their watering places.

## MOVEMENTS

When feeding along undisturbed, javelina bands are never in any hurry. A group may potter about on a foothill slope, traveling rather aimlessly, for an hour at a time, Or, it may set a course along a wash, moving in and out but following at a walk the meandering course. The abundance of food, of course, influences the amount of territory any certain band ranges. There are cattle tanks in the south-Texas brush and cactus around which groups live and never get more than a half-mile away. In the mountain country, the home range is usually much larger. The walking gait is deceptive in the distances covered in a brief time when the animals are intent on getting over a ridge or combing a broad slope to pick at favored forage.

Probably no drove utilizes more than four or five sections of land at maximum. The daily routine is to feed early. If the day is to be hot, all morning feeding is finished by the time the sun is midway up the horizon. Even though they live in country that has high temperatures much of the year, javelinas dislike both temperature extremes. Ranchers have often observed that at about 70 to 80 degrees the little pigs will begin to bed down.

The resting place in rocky desert mountain areas is commonly a rimrock. The animals head up the slope as soon as the temperature reaches above their comfort level. They find innumerable shady places along the rim where a cool breeze reaches them. Or in flat to rolling country they head for the vicinity of a waterhole, around which vegetation is more dense than elsewhere, or they push into catclaw thickets, or those dense stretches along so-called creek bottom—the low washes that run only when it rains but along which heavy vegetation always is present.

Sometimes a group has a favorite wallow, a moist area with a moderate amount of soft soil or mud, hidden in brush. They are not, however, the mud wallowers that domestic swine are. When the sun is on a long slant in the afternoon, they emerge again and feed during the cool hours. They also feed at night, but cannot be considered nocturnal creatures. They simply like the cooler temperature.

On cold days a band may feed at any time, and take the sun in a bedding area at any time also. If a bitter wind blows, they invariably move into a protected canyon if one is available. On overcast, cool days movement may take place at any time. Their coats and hides are thin, however, and they dislike extreme cold.

When startled, a javelina may simply trot away, disappearing into the brush, or it may leave at a bounding gait that sometimes takes all four feet off the ground at once. It has been estimated that at a full run a javelina may reach a speed of 20 to 25 miles an hour. It cannot keep this up for long. Hunters using dogs discover that once an animal is jumped it is quickly bayed. In fact, a startled javelina that races away from danger will slow to a walk within a short distance if it can get into cover. It may even rush into cover and then stand still. Inexperienced hunters often are puzzled because a small group runs into a dense brush thicket and simply disappears. Persistent scrounging around in the cover will suddenly put one to flight, chuffing and grunting, within a few feet. Others may let danger pass and never be discovered.

Although enemies are not numerous, a good many javelinas are killed, both as young and as adults, by various predators. In some areas mountain lions, though seldom numerous nowadays in javelina territory except in some parts of Mexico, form a taste for them. The big cats—jaguars also—presumably find the javelina an easy stalk and kill. Coyotes and bobcats kill many young ones. A bobcat or lone coyote is not much danger to an adult javelina, and certainly not to a group of adults. Those who recall the Disney film about desert wildlife will remember seeing a small group of javelinas put a bobcat up a saguaro cactus. The cat obviously had less concern for the vicious cactus spines than for the canine teeth of the pigs. A golden eagle may occasionally grab a baby javelina, but on the whole their enemies, except for men and various diseases and some internal parasites, are not numerous.

**BREEDING**

There is still much to be learned about the details of breeding among javelinas. Young have been observed with bands almost every month of the year, so it is evident that there is no special breeding season. Females are capable of producing young when just over a year old. Many early-bred sows, it is known, lose their first litter. Most apparently are past 1½ years of age when they are first bred, although a yearling sow that loses a litter may breed again in slightly over a month.

The groups made up of members of both sexes intermingle constantly, so males are always on hand. And a male will breed whatever sows are ready. Possibly the older, stronger males may dominate the scene, keeping younger males away from an available sow. There appears to be no evidence, however, of special displays or battles.

**BIRTH AND DEVELOPMENT**

The javelina, despite early maturity and breeding around the year, is by no means a prolific creature. As a rule only a single piglet is born. Twins are not rare, but studies show an overall average among any given population of about 1.5 per litter, or even less. Biologists have discovered as many as half a dozen fetuses in a sow, but there are no records of that many young with a sow.

There may be a good reason for the singles and twins. The female javelina has four teats, but only two are definitely known to be functional. Thus if large litters were born the mother probably would be unable to raise them. Even with such small numbers to each birth, the javelina is still able to maintain itself. Game management people are certain, however, that if indiscriminate killing were allowed the population on most ranges would quickly be wiped out. Apparently they do stand quota hunting easily, and it is an indication of their toughness and lack of serious natural enemies that they continue within our range at a substantial level of population.

To illustrate lack of accurate detailed knowledge about the javelina after all these years, most references give the gestation period as anywhere from 3½ to four months, to almost five months. It is actually twenty to twenty-one weeks. The mother leaves the band to give birth, and bears the young in any convenient and secluded spot. It may be a dense thicket, a cave, a sheltered hole among rocks, under an overhanging bank, or any hollow that offers some protection.

Baby javelinas, like all wildlife young, are appealing little creatures. They are fully haired, but their color is grizzled yellowish-black to reddish, with a black stripe down the back. Each weighs about a pound. They are precocious youngsters. Soon after their first nursing they easily stand and wobble about, but within three or four hours are able to walk and run. When a day or two old they can dodge about in brush so that a person intent on taking one for a pet has a real chore trying to run it down. The youngsters squeal loudly, talking to their mother and following after her. If caught they bite ferociously, their tiny canines making blood spurt.

The mother rejoins the band, or another, when the piglets are only two or three days old. She takes good care of them and will bluff any enemy, drive off a coyote or a fox or bobcat. She will, however, abandon her young if pressed hard by man or a group of predators such as coyotes or dogs.

It is interesting to watch the youngsters follow their mother. If she trots, they trot close to her heels. If she stops, they stop instantly and stay put until she moves. If she runs, they are able to keep up even though she races swiftly away. They seem to know when she's running away from danger. When she bounds off with them at her heels, then suddenly pulls up, hackles raised, to appraise the situation, invariably the youngsters run under her belly and stand there as if hiding or at least feeling the protection of her above them. When sow and young join the band, there is no resentment of the young. They mingle with the others, may eventually trot along with another sow, joining her young, and are not bothered by others of the gang.

## SENSES

Because the javelina is built low to the ground, does not need to chase after food, lives much of the time in medium to heavy cover, and doesn't need to watch distantly for enemies, it has little need for acutely developed sight. Whether or not these reasons have had anything to do with evolvement of its seeing ability, its sight is one of the poorest known among the game animals. A hunter who is a careful stalker, and who moves quietly and with the breeze toward him, can move to within mere feet of javelinas at times without disturbing them. Or several may be aware that something is wrong, but they stare and do nothing about it except possibly to raise their hackles and pop their teeth.

The sense of hearing is sharp. But whether or not a particular individual or band is alarmed by what it hears is never predictable.

*A baby javelina is fully haired, weighs about a pound, and bites ferociously if caught.*

Some will flee at the snapping of a twig. Others will pay little attention to human voices nearby. Indeed, their reactions are erratic. One band, suddenly aware of a cowboy on horseback, may bound up a slope and into a thicket as if thoroughly frightened. Another may simply up-end bristles, grunt and mill about, or walk or trot with little concern into cover.

The sense of smell is the most acute of the three. A hunter or photographer with the breeze behind him or across, so that it drifts his scent to a band, has little chance of getting close. Again, however, reaction is unpredictable. The animals may run, even scattering in wild flight, some as likely to run toward as away from the danger. Or all may bound straight away downwind. Or they may simply run briefly into cover and stop.

Anyone who has hunted or observed these animals at length soon decides that in all probability they are not very intelligent creatures. Certainly they readily pick up scents and sounds that disturb them. But some individuals may seem as wild as deer, and others simply perplexed.

**SIGN** (*Tracks are illustrated on page 251.*)

Anyone seeking javelinas should make a point of first checking known waterholes. If they are present, tracks are certain to show here, except, of course, on rock. Javelina tracks are unmistakable. Now and then a tyro may confuse them with tracks of deer fawns. There is no need to. Fawn tracks show sharply pointed toes. The toes of the javelina are blunt and rounded, each half of a hoofprint a long oval. Each track is small and short, and as noted earlier, the dewclaws are vestigial and do not show.

In a few places—for example, southern Texas—there are feral swine living in javelina country. They are wilder and more secretive than the javelina. The tracks cannot easily be confused. The pig tracks are much larger, the dewclaws show prominently in most prints, and the two toes of the hoof have a wide, U-shaped cleft between them. Javelina prints are individually 1 to 1½ inches long, the front-foot prints slightly larger than the rear.

Around waterholes or in washes, tracks are usually such a welter that individual trails do not show. When one does, the walking gait shows prints of two feet near together every few inches, 5 or 6 to 10. A javelina can make surprisingly long jumps when startled into flight, bounding stifflegged and leaving the first few sets of tracks as much as 6 feet apart. They also dodge artfully and switch directions in midleap.

Javelina wallows are not seen very often. When one is located, tracks and bristles and the unforgettable musk smell easily tell what made the wallow. Where the animals have bedded, they often scratch out small hollows and turn to lie in comfort in the dust. Picking up and sifting a handful of loose dirt at these will invariably show dropped bristles that tell what made the sign. Javelina dung, though dropped in quantities where a band has been bedding or feeding, is not easily found or recognized. It dries quickly, and its form depends on the food eaten—soft when a diet of prickly pear is being taken, in bulky, unsymmetrical, elongate wads or pellets when on harder forage.

The signs experienced hunters most often seek are torn vegetation, and rootings. In a pear patch, a group will rip whole pear branches to shreds, tear pads off, and eat portions. When one comes upon this sign with juice still wet, it means the pigs are not far away. Deer, pack rats and other small desert animals, even rabbits, gnaw pear leaves also. The bites of small animals go around the perimeter of a pad in small scallops, and deer bite out perimeter chunks, leaving shredded fibers. Thus it is easy to identify the work of javelinas. Rootings are invariably shallow, each one small, therefore quite unlike the deeply plowed and ripped-up patches where domestic or feral swine have rooted.

### HUNTING

There are three basic methods of javelina hunting practiced within the U.S. range. A very few hunters, in Texas, use dogs. This is an interesting chase. But few ranchers own dogs they'll put on the javelina. If a dog is lucky enough to live through its first couple of runs, it may learn to bay a pig, or even put a small band with its back against a rock wall or into a cave. Many a dog isn't that smart, and either doesn't live to run twice, or else is crippled. Mexican cowboys in both Texas and Mexico occasionally use mongrel dogs to chase javelinas. But very little of this hunting occurs nowadays, and within a short time it may not be legal anywhere.

In the Brush Country of southern Texas a common method of hunting is to cruise around the grid of *senderos,* as border-country Texans call bulldozed oil-exploration trails, and keep watch for bands that cross. Or a hunter takes a stand early or late on such a trail, where he can watch from a ridge top where it crosses small valleys on either side. Bands moving about are sure to cross one or another. A stand watching a wash crossing in a dry creek bottom also is a good one. Cruising by vehicle, or taking a stand, or watching a waterhole early or late are the typical methods for hunting in flat to rolling dense brushlands. Trying to jump pigs during midday in such country, by walking the dry creek beds with dense thickets or working the prickly pear stands, may pay off, but it is hard, thorny work and most of the time not very productive.

The third and most enjoyable productive manner of hunting is that generally pursued in western Texas, and in New Mexico and Arizona. Most of this hunting is in terrain of low mountains and desert valleys. The slopes are more or less open. Javelinas, singly or in groups, show plainly as they move in and out of draws, or work the foothills, feeding. Hunters either cruise the valley trails by vehicle, or walk there or up on the slopes or the rims, and spend much of their time watching distantly. Binoculars are mandatory for this procedure.

When the quarry is spotted, what happens next depends on the weapon selected. In some of this terrain shots up to 300 yards are offered. These call for a rifle of deer caliber, one that shoots flat. The .243 is a good example of an excellent and adequate long-range arm. Some hunters like to specialize with a bow, or a black-powder rifle, or with a pistol, or even with small-caliber rifles such as the .22 magnum. All these require a stalk, the closeness depending on the weapon employed. One should check the state regulations to be sure what is and is not a legal arm for javelina.

Although an ordinary .22 Long Rifle will kill javelinas at close range, it is not recommended, and is likely to be illegal. The .22 magnum is adequate, at ranges to perhaps 60 yards, using a hollow-point bullet, and placing it carefully. Hunters should keep in mind the size and weight of the target, and the fact that for a specimen to mount, head shots obviously can't be used. To avoid spoiling a trophy and ruining meat, a rib shot carefully placed is best. Running shots are precarious, as well as difficult. It's best to let the animals run, then make another stalk.

In mountain country, as elsewhere, the cool dawn and late-afternoon hours see the most action. If one wishes to hunt during the middle of the day, in almost any mountain-slope location the rimrocks are the places. A bit of scouting often turns up definite trails. Some may be deer trails or stock trails, but javelinas also follow them. A good many trails are those made by javelinas themselves going from the slopes and draws and washes up to the rims to bed down. The hunting requires a check on the wind direction, quiet movement, and alert nose. Often bedded bands can be smelled.

Any hunter who becomes familiar with an expanse of javelina range quickly learns precisely where each band operates. A certain ridge top, a known watering place, a particular thicket—such places may be heavily used and it can be predicted that pigs will be found there at certain hours time after time. They will even continue to use these favorite haunts, given ample food, water and cover, for year after year.

It is unfortunate that so many decades have been required to bring the javelina to full game status. The interest all across the country in trophy hunting and in trying new hunting experiences, plus the ease of swift travel, have focused attention of numerous hunters everywhere in the nation on this interesting animal. From here on things should get better and better for it. All three states now have serious management programs. Population levels remain stable. Even in Mexico the situation slowly improves. As long as the brush and the cactus is not all cleared away and there are cattle ranges in it, as well as large expanses of federal lands left in a wild state, the javelina will make out fine.

# Index